During the reign of Queen Victoria, herself an ardent play-goer as well as Supreme Head of the Church of England, a remarkable *rapprochement* was effected between the Church and the theatre. At the beginning of her reign considerable antagonism existed between these two institutions, but by the end reconciliation was almost complete.

In a wide-ranging account of this multifaceted subject Dr Foulkes explores the implications for the theatre of the great religious movements of the period: Tractarianism, Christian Socialism and Latitudinarianism. This central relationship is seen in the context of other important themes in Victorian cultural history such as censorship, urbanisation, transport, leisure, education and women's emancipation.

The volume contains portraits of significant churchmen (Keble, Newman, Manning, Maurice, Kingsley, Stanley, Farrar and Headlam), dramatists (Bulwer Lytton, Charles Reade, Tennyson, H. A. Jones and Shaw), actors (Macready, Phelps, Wilson Barrett and Irving) and actresses (Fanny Kemble, Helen Faucit and Ellen Terry). These were influential figures who participated in the search for a common culture which preoccupied the nineteenth century.

To the Victorians the Church and the theatre were important parts of everyday life; in this study the two institutions are explored in relation not only to each other but also to the social, economic and intellectual movements of the period.

CHURCH AND STAGE IN
VICTORIAN ENGLAND

CHURCH AND STAGE
IN VICTORIAN ENGLAND

RICHARD FOULKES

CAMBRIDGE
UNIVERSITY PRESS

PUBLISHED BY THE PRESS SYNDICATE OF THE UNIVERSITY OF CAMBRIDGE
The Pitt Building, Trumpington Street, Cambridge CB2 1RP, United Kingdom

CAMBRIDGE UNIVERSITY PRESS
The Edinburgh Building, Cambridge CB2 2RU, United Kingdom
40 West 20th Street, New York, NY 10011-4211, USA
10 Stamford Road, Oakleigh, Melbourne 3166, Australia

First published 1997

Printed in the United Kingdom at the University Press, Cambridge

Typeset in 11/12.5 Monotype Baskerville by Servis Filmsetting Ltd, Manchester

A catalogue record for this book is available from the British Library

Library of Congress cataloguing in publication data

Foulkes, Richard.
Church and stage in Victorian England / Richard Foulkes.
p.   cm.
Includes bibliographical references and index.
ISBN 0 521 45320 8
1. Theatre – England – History – 19th century.   2. Theatre – Religious
aspects – Church of England.   3. Church of England – Doctrines –
History – 19th century.   4. Anglican Communion – England – Doctrines –
History – 19th century.   I. Title.
PN2594.F68   1997
792'.0941'09034–dc20   96–44874   CIP

ISBN 0 521 45320 8 hardback

To my wife, Christine, for her
faith in the book
and the author

Contents

List of illustrations		*page* x
Acknowledgements		xii
Introit		xiii
1	Heralds of change	1
2	Censure and censorship	18
3	Two professions	35
4	Clerical attitudes	50
5	Self-improvement	69
6	Shakespeare	92
7	From Passion Play to pantomime	108
8	The ancient universities	125
9	Actresses	144
10	Headlam, hell and Hole	166
11	Henry Arthur Jones and Wilson Barrett	186
12	Henry Irving	211
Epilogue		237
References		242
Index		257

Illustrations

1. Fanny Kemble as Juliet (from the collections of the Theatre Museum. By courtesy of the Board of Trustees of the Victoria and Albert Museum). *page* 12
2. Presentation to Charles Kean at St James's Hall (*Illustrated London News* 29 March 1862). 44
3. Charles Kingsley, John Henry Newman, Frederick Denison Maurice and Arthur Penrhyn Stanley (from Henry Morley, *Illustrations of English Religion*, 1890). 53
4. Bishops on the stage. Bishop Fraser of Manchester (*Punch* 3 March 1877). 65
5. Contrasted college gateways. A. W. N. Pugin (from A. W. N. Pugin, *Contrasts*, 1841). 72
6. W. S. Penley in preparation for his role as Revd Robert Spalding in *The Private Secretary* (from W. S. Penley, *Penley on Himself*, 1884). 85
7. Concert in the Royal Agricultural Hall (*Illustrated London News* 30 April 1864). 97
8. The Crucifixion in the Oberammergau Passion Play (from Mrs Alec Tweedie, *The Oberammergau Passion Play 1890*, 1890). 114
9. Tableau of the Adoration of the Shepherds at Christ Church Mission, Poplar (*Illustrated Church News* 6 March 1896). 116
10. Benjamin Jowett and the *Agamemnon* cast, Oxford (from Constance Benson, *Mainly Players*, 1926). 140
11. 'Ellen in Heaven', pastel study of Ellen Terry by W. Graham Robertson (from W. Graham Robertson, *Time Was*, 1931). 152
12. The Princess Hall, Cheltenham Ladies' College (The Cheltenham Ladies' College, with permission). 156
13. Wilson Barrett, *The Sign of the Cross* (author's collection). 208
14. Lyceum Theatre, *Faust* (from the collections of the Theatre Museum. By courtesy of the Board of Trustees of the Victoria and Albert Museum). 219

15. Henry Irving as Becket (from the collections of the Theatre Museum. By courtesy of the Board of Trustees of the Victoria and Albert Museum).   223
16. Admission card for Henry Irving's funeral (author's collection).   236

Acknowledgements

I have carried out my research in the following institutions, libraries and collections, to the staff of which I am greatly obliged: the Actors' Church Union; the British Library Reading Room and Manuscript Collection; Canterbury Cathedral Archives; Cheltenham Ladies' College; Chetham's Library, Manchester; the Folger Shakespeare Library, Washington D.C.; Harvard University; the Garrick Club; King's College, University of London; Manchester Central Library; Marlborough College, Wiltshire; the Public Record Office, London; Queen's College, London; the Shakespeare Centre, Stratford-upon-Avon; the University Centre, Northampton – the Henry Arthur Jones Theatre Collection; the University of Leicester; and the University of Manchester – John Rylands Library.

I have been the grateful recipient of information and advice from Dr Russell Jackson, who scrutinised my typescript, Mrs Vivian Allen, Dr Robert Chapman, David Cheshire, T. F. Evans, Derek Forbes, Professor Joel H. Kaplan, Julia Matheson, Dr Philip McEvansoneya, Professor David Mayer, Christopher Murray, Canon Albert Radcliffe, George Rowell, Dr John Russell Stephens, Dr Shearer West and Professor Glynne Wickham.

I acknowledge the assistance of a research award and sabbatical leave from the University of Leicester and a British Academy award.

I express my sincere appreciation to my editor Dr Victoria Cooper for her commitment to this book and to Miss Pat Perkins for triumphing over my handwriting and the foibles of the word processor.

My family has responded to my preoccupation with Church and stage in a spirit of toleration befitting the subject. My wife, to whom this book is lovingly dedicated, has been a ready source of encouragement and wise counsel throughout.

Introit

Enter boldly, for here, too, there are gods.

Henry Morley

The relationship between the Church and stage in Victorian England is a vast and many-faceted subject. I have ventured outside Queen Victoria's reign by a decade or so at the beginning and by four years at the end, but I have rarely strayed beyond England into the other lands over which she held dominion. By 'Church' I mean the Church of England. I make some allusions to other denominations, but do not attempt to deal with them substantively.

From its earliest manifestations the theatre attracted opposition and in Plato it was challenged by a critic whose objections were known to and reiterated by the better-educated members of the nineteenth-century anti-theatrical persuasion. By then the arguments of antiquity had been reinforced by those of early Christianity (Tertullian, St Augustine), Puritanism and the controversies of the English Restoration stage.

At one level the Victorians were engaging in the timeless debate about the nature of mimesis and mankind's disposition towards imitation or catharsis, but they were doing so in the context of a society which was confronted by hitherto undreamt-of social, technological and intellectual challenges. Both the Church and the theatre were profoundly affected by developments as diverse as urbanisation, the expansion of the railways, the education of women and revisionary concepts of hell. The Victorian experience crystallised issues which continue to preoccupy advanced and emerging nations – for instance: the expansion of an élite culture to the masses; the balance between education and recreation; centralised direction and individual choice; and the creation of national institutions and a sense of nationhood. It has been my endeavour to weave these and other threads together to produce a picture of Victorian England in which church spires and theatre fly-towers occupy the foreground. From certain perspectives this may not always seem to be the case and educational edifices of one sort and another do undeniably figure prominently.

I have approached the subject of Church and stage in Victorian England from my own discipline of theatre history. In that of church history I have served an all too brief, but totally absorbing, novitiate, which has been revealing not only in terms of material for this book, but also as an insight into another branch of scholarship. As a subject, theatre history suffers from the same lack of status as bedevilled the theatre itself for much of the nineteenth century. Entertainment in general and the theatre in particular occupied as vital a place as religion in the lives of many Victorians, but this is not reflected in late twentieth-century academia. If this volume has a mission, beyond attempting to do justice to its subject, it is to contribute to the process whereby the study of the theatre is no longer disparaged as mere anecdotage, but is recognised as part of the mainstream of social, economic, intellectual and – in this case – religious history.

As the tide of history flowed through the nineteenth century it shaped the lives of generations of men and women, who in their turn collectively and – exceptionally – individually influenced its course. The pages of history can be written in terms of the unfolding of God's purpose, the deeds of Carlylean heroes or Marxist masses. This account of Church and stage in Victorian England is peopled with prelates and prima donnas, perpetual incumbents and attendant lords, and the faceless members of countless congregations and audiences. Even with historical hindsight the task of discerning a pattern is difficult enough, to prophesy and influence one is an altogether rarer faculty. Amongst the contenders for this distinction (Bentham, Keble, Newman, F. D. Maurice, Carlyle, Arnold and Ruskin) in the nineteenth century, Samuel Taylor Coleridge emerges in terms of this study as pre-eminent. Visionary, poet, sage, dramatist, literary and dramatic critic, Coleridge wrote: 'It is the privilege of the few to possess an idea: of the generality of men, it might be more truly affirmed that they are possessed by it' (Colmer, 1976, p. 13).

This work essays the task of establishing connections between the religious ideas of the few (the leaders of the Oxford Movement, Christian Socialism, Latitudinarianism and the Broad Church) and 'the generality of men', to show that those ideas, sometimes intentionally but more often unintentionally, were instrumental in the transformation which the theatre underwent in Victorian England.

Enter boldly, for here, too, there are gods. (Morley, 1891, p. 25)

CHAPTER I

Heralds of change

ALFRED EVELYN: greatest happiness of the greatest number –
greatest number, number one!

Bulwer Lytton *Money*

As the nineteenth century was drawing to its close the drama critic
Clement Scott proclaimed: 'Unquestionably the theatre in this country
and all connected with it, be they actors, actresses, managers or dramatists, were never in such a flourishing and healthy condition as they are
today, within a few hours of the close of an eventful century' (1899, vol.
II, p. 430). Scott advanced two reasons for the theatre's healthy condition: '1. The first is the strong advocacy for it, and the complete success
after winning it, of Free Trade in the Drama. 2. The second is the
Independence of journalistic and other criticism' (p. 432).

The second explanation was obviously coloured by Scott's desire to
promote the importance of the profession to which he himself belonged
as drama critic of the *Daily Telegraph* and other journals, but his first
explanation requires further consideration. Scott's claim for the benefits
of free trade in the theatre did not rest simply upon the expansion which
it facilitated, but also, more significantly, on the elevation which he
thought it had brought about: 'In addition to elevating the artistic tone of
the drama in this country, in addition to popularising it as it never was
before, free trade with its countless advantages has purified the lighter
amusements of the hour in every direction' (p. 433). By linking the profusion, prestige and propriety of late nineteenth-century theatre to the
principle of free trade Scott was making a direct connection with the
reforms of the 1830s and 1840s and the political thinkers whose ideas
had provided the intellectual driving force for those reforms.

Jeremy Bentham died in 1832, the year in which the theatre, like other
parts of the nation's life, came under the scrutiny of parliament – in its
case in the form of The Select Committee appointed to Inquire into the
Laws affecting Dramatic Literature. Bentham had applied his principle

I

of 'utility', or the greatest happiness for the greatest number, to recreations of all kind. In 'Reward Applied to Art and Science' he wrote:

It is not, however, proper to regard the former [the arts and sciences of amusement] as destitute of utility: on the contrary there is nothing, the utility of which is more incontestable. To what shall the character of utility be ascribed, if not to that which is a source of pleasure? All that can be alleged in the diminution of their utility is, that it is limited to the excitement of pleasure: they cannot disperse the clouds of grief or of misfortune. They are useless to those who are not pleased with them: they are useful only to those who take pleasure in them, and only in proportion as they are pleased. (Bowring 1962, vol. ii, p. 253)

In Bentham's view 'the value' of amusements lay 'exactly in proportion to the pleasures they yield . . . Prejudice apart, the game of push-pin is of equal value with the arts and sciences of music and poetry. If the game of push-pin furnish more pleasure it is more valuable than either. Everybody can play push-pin: poetry and music are relished only by a few' (p. 253). Bentham's only concession to poetry and music was that if they 'deserve to be preferred before a game of push-pin, it must be because they are calculated to gratify those individuals who are most difficult to be pleased' (p. 253). What all amusements had in common was that: 'They compete with, and occupy the place of, those mischievous and dangerous passions and employments, to which want of occupation and ennui give birth. They are excellent substitutes for drunkenness, slander and the love of gaming' (p. 254).

Bentham was dismissive of 'those critics, more ingenious than useful, who under the pretence of purifying the public taste, endeavour successively to deprive mankind of a larger or smaller part of the sources of their amusement . . . There is no taste which deserves the epithet *good*' (p. 254). To Bentham the state's role was to facilitate amusements, not to provide them: 'Among rich and prosperous nations, it is not necessary that the public should be at the expense of cultivating the arts and sciences of amusement and curiosity. Individuals will always bestow upon these that portion of reward which is proportioned to the pleasure they bestow' (p. 255). In this respect Bentham was following Adam Smith, who, in *The Wealth of Nations* (1776), advocated

the frequency and gaiety of public diversions. The State, by encouraging, that is, by giving entire liberty to all those who, for their own interest, would attempt, without scandal or indecency, to amuse and divert the people by painting, poetry, music, dancing, – by all sorts of dramatic representations and exhibitions, – would easily dissipate, in the greater part of them, that melancholy and gloomy humour which is almost always the nurse of popular superstition and enthusiasm. (1838, p. 357)

Adam Smith and Jeremy Bentham endorsed the value of amusements for individuals and acknowledged their social use. Bentham rejected the notion of some amusements possessing in themselves a higher or lower value. By the mid nineteenth century Bentham's disciple J. S. Mill had modified this view in his essay on 'Utilitarianism. Its Meaning' (1859): 'It would be absurd that while, in estimating all other things, quality is considered as well as quantity: the estimation of pleasures should be supposed to depend on quantity alone' (Warnock 1972, p. 259). His mind closed to such accommodations Bentham concluded his chapter: 'That which governments ought to do for the arts and sciences of immediate and remote utility may be comprised in three things – 1. To remove the discouragements under which they labour; 2. To favour their advancement; 3. To contribute to their diffusion' (p. 256).

Parliament directed its attention to these issues through The Select Committee appointed to Inquire into the Laws affecting Dramatic Literature, which was constituted on 31 May 1832, just days before the passage of the Reform Bill, extending the franchise and redistributing Parliamentary seats, on 7 June. Of the twenty-four members of the committee Edward Bulwer Lytton (listed as Edward Lytton Bulwer) was the key figure. Already a published novelist and a playwright in the making, he had been returned as the Liberal MP for St Ives in 1831 and was a strong supporter of reform. It was Bulwer Lytton who carried the report of the Select Committee forward as legislative proposals. The views of forty-seven witnesses were heard by the Select Committee before it produced its report in July 1832, but although Bulwer Lytton was undoubtedly influential in framing that report he did not, of course, give evidence. A valuable source of Bulwer Lytton's own opinions is therefore *England and the English*, published in 1833.

Like Adam Smith and Bentham, Bulwer Lytton subscribed to the need for amusements for all, decrying 'the noticeable want of amusements for the poorer classes' (1833, vol. 1, p. 32) and also finding pragmatic social advantages in such provision:

Amusement keeps men cheerful and contented – it engenders a spirit of urbanity – it reconciles the poor to the pleasures of their superiors which are of the same sort, though in another sphere; it removes the sense of hardship – it brings men together in those genial moments when the heart opens and care is forgotten. Deprived of more gentle relaxations the poor are driven to the alehouse. (pp. 34–5)

For Bulwer Lytton, however, amusements were more than a diversion and a safety-valve: 'The physical condition of the Working Classes in Manufacturing Towns is more wretched than we can bear to consider' (pp. 174–5), and he diagnosed 'the moral cure is Education' (p. 190) for which he saw 'The Christian clergy', as historically 'great advancers and apostles of education' (p. 281), having a responsibility. Compared with continental nations England made 'the Sabbath dull' and therefore 'dangerous'; 'idleness must have amusement or it falls at once into vice; and the absence of entertainments produces the necessity of excess' (p. 326). In contrast to Bentham (the subject of an appendix) Bulwer Lytton did see a qualitative scale to pleasures:

In short, with the lower orders, as education advances, it will be as with the higher, – the more intellectual of whom do not indulge generally in frivolous amusements, solely because *it amuses them less* than intellectual pursuits.
'Why do you never amuse yourself?' said the rope-dancer to the philosopher. – 'That is exactly the question', answered the philosopher, astonished, 'that I was going to ask you!' (p. 327)

The sentiments attributed to 'a mathematician' at the beginning of Bulwer Lytton's chapter on 'The drama': 'One may always leave the amusements to the care of the public; they are sure to pay for those well' (1833, vol. ii, p. 133) are a paraphrase of Bentham, reinforced by the mathematician's subsequent advocacy of 'free trade'. In reply Bulwer Lytton cites France, as Matthew Arnold was to do four decades later, where 'amusement is a necessary, while here it is scarcely even a luxury' (p. 134). Acknowledging the adverse effects of the monopoly of 'legitimate' drama enjoyed by Covent Garden and Drury Lane, Bulwer Lytton judges the audiences at the minor theatres 'not sufficiently guided in their tastes by persons of literary refinement' (p. 138), those very arbiters of quality whom Bentham had dismissed as 'those critics, more ingenious than useful, who . . . deprive mankind of a larger or smaller part of the sources of their amusement'.

Reformer as he undoubtedly was, Bulwer Lytton was not content simply to 'remove discouragements' to amusement, but went further to argue that there were higher and lower forms of amusements and that the state had a role in promoting the former:

No! Individual patronage is not advantageous to art, but there is a patronage which is – the patronage of the State . . .
You must diffuse throughout a people the cultivation of Truth and the love of Beauty. (pp. 176–7)

The patronage of the State is advantageous in producing a general taste and a public respect for cultivation [of art and science] . . . to enlarge and still the assembly, and to conduct, as it were, through an invisible ether, the sound of divine voices amidst a listening and reverent audience. (p. 183)

Bulwer Lytton's contempt for unrestrained Utilitarianism is reflected in Alfred Evelyn's retort to the political economist Stout in his play *Money* (1840): 'O, Stout, Stout! greatest happiness of the greatest number – greatest number, number one!' (Rowell, 1960, p. 92).

The report of the 1832 Select Committee certainly reflected the principles of free trade in its proposal for the abolition of the monopoly of the patent theatres (Covent Garden and Drury Lane), but its advocacy of 'fair competition' and its reinforcement of the Lord Chamberlain's controlling authority were informed by the commitment to preserve and encourage qualitative standards in the theatre in the context of a freer market:

Your Committee believe that the interests of the Drama will be considerably advanced by the natural consequence of a fair competition in its Representation, they recommend that the Lord Chamberlain should continue a Licence to all the Theatres licensed at present, whether by himself or by the Magistrates. Your Committee are also of opinion partly from the difficulty of defining, by clear and legal distinctions, 'the Legitimate Drama', and principally from the propriety of giving a full opening to the higher as to the more humble order of Dramatic Talent, that the Proprietors and Managers of the said [hitherto minor] Theatres should be allowed to exhibit, at their option, the Legitimate Drama, and all such Plays as have received or shall receive the sanction of the Censor. (*British Parliamentary Papers, Stage and Theatre 1*, 1968, pp. 3–4)

In other words the abolition of the monopoly was perceived as a means of extending 'the higher . . . order of Dramatic Talent' with the Lord Chamberlain exercising his authority as licenser (and censor) of plays. This was hardly unfettered free trade in the Benthamite mould. The report concluded: 'While, as regards the Public, equally benefited by these advantages, it is probable that the ordinary consequences of competition, freed from the possibility of licentiousness by the confirmed control and authority of the Chamberlain, will afford convenience in the number and situation of Theatres, and cheap and good entertainment in the performances usually exhibited' (pp. 5–6). Of the two bills presented to parliament by Bulwer Lytton consequent upon the Select Committee's report, that establishing copyright for dramatic authors was passed, but that proposing the abolition of the patent theatres' monopoly, though approved by the House of Commons, was defeated in the House of Lords and did not succeed until 1843.

Of the witnesses to the Select Committee a particularly doughty defender of the monopoly was Charles Kemble, younger brother of John Philip and Sarah (Siddons), although his own experience at Covent Garden had been deeply troubled. J. P. Kemble had transferred his one-sixth share in Covent Garden to his brother in November 1820, and Charles Kemble became manager of the theatre in March 1822 (Williamson, 1970, pp. 143 and 144), but by 1829 he was reduced to bank-ruptcy, from which he was rescued by his daughter Fanny's stage debut as Juliet. Nevertheless Kemble presented himself as the successor and defender of the patent granted to Sir William Davenant by King Charles II. When asked 'Is it supposed this patent is perpetual?', he replied: 'I have always so understood it' (*British Parliamentary Papers, Stage and Theatre 1* 1968, p. 43). Kemble further justified his case by claiming that certain forms of entertainment (by implication the higher, including Shakespeare) could only be done in larger theatres and that the pool of acting talent was insufficient to sustain an increased number of theatres. Kemble attempted to scale the moral high ground by arguing that minor theatres provided 'stronger excitement and a coarser species of entertainment at a much cheaper rate' (p. 46) and that 'you will have the rabble of London going to those theatres in preference to others, where they can be instructed and improved' (p. 51). Economic considerations were clearly central to this view and Kemble grasped at the straw of 'indemnification': 'Yes; suppose the Government would step forward and say, you have expended so much money on this theatre, we will sell the theatre and advance you so much money', to which the response was: 'You cannot expect the Government to be responsible for an improvi-dent bargain you may have made' (p. 48). Kemble was, of course, sug-gesting that the government should buy him out of a venture which would be rendered – even more – uneconomic by greater competition, but in his proposal it is possible to detect the embryo of the idea that higher forms of theatre should be supported by state subventions. Kemble, who had earlier cited 'the increase of religious feeling' as one of the causes of the theatre's decline, concluded his evidence, defiantly or desperately, by asserting: 'The qualifications of a true actor are a gift that God gives, and they are not to be multiplied as theatres may be' (p. 55).

Such a viewpoint was not one to be found on the bench of bishops when the Dramatic Performances Bill was debated in the House of Lords on 2 August 1833. The Bishop of London felt compelled to offer 'a few observations on a subject which in my opinion deeply affects the morals of this great city with which I have so important a connexion' (*Mirror of Parliament*, 1833, vol. IV, p. 3490). He objected to the prospect of new theatres which would not 'contribute to the moral improvement of the public', a view not dissimilar to Kemble's, but went on to say 'indeed, I doubt whether it be possible to conduct theatres so as to effect that

object' (p. 3493). With the zeal of Bulwer Lytton's mathematician he calculated that 'Under this Bill there may be erected within a circuit of two
miles from the General Post Office, 250 theatres' (p. 3493) and went on to
express his fundamental opposition to the theatre. He exampled the
Garrick Theatre, in Lemon Street, Goodman's Fields, where a 'young
woman being enabled to obtain admission . . . for 6d, contracted an
invincible taste for theatrical amusements and the dissipations connected with them. She remained out late at night, and at last all night,
and the result was the poor woman [the girl's mother] lost her daughter,
and the daughter lost her character' (p. 3493). In the bishop's opinion the
reduction in admission charges resulting from greater provision and
competition would bring the theatre within the means of the humbler
members of society who were poorly equipped to resist its potential for
ill effect. He spoke of apprentices who had acquired habits which led
them to rob their masters and have their indentures cancelled and concluded by warning his fellow peers that 'by consenting to this Bill, you
break asunder the bands of society, and throw this great Christian community into confusion' (p. 3494). Suitably chastened, the House of Lords
rejected the bill by nineteen votes to fifteen.

The Bishop of London in question was Charles Blomfield who had
been appointed to the see in 1828. A Whig early in life, he voted against
Roman Catholic emancipation in 1829, but for the Reform Bill in 1832.
During his episcopate, which ended with his resignation in 1856, nearly
150 churches were built in his diocese – rather fewer than the number
of theatres of which he was fearful. Although unsympathetic to the
contemporary theatre Blomfield was a 'Greek play bishop', having
produced translations of Aeschylus (Blomfield, 1863, vol. i, pp. 23–4).
Blomfield had been educated at Bury St Edmunds Grammar School and
at Trinity College, Cambridge. Coincidentally these were the educational establishments to which Charles Kemble had sent his son John
Mitchell, with the expectation that he would make his career in the
Church.

For an actor, even a member of the distinguished Kemble dynasty, to
aspire to a university education and clerical career for his son was
unusual in the early nineteenth century. Charles Kemble's own education had included three years (from the age of thirteen to sixteen) at the
Roman Catholic College at Douai in France, which his brother John
Philip had also attended. Charles Kemble left Douai with 'a gentleman's
education' (Williamson, 1970, p. 13) in the classics, but did not pursue a
clerical vocation. Indeed he transferred his allegiance to the Church of

England, as his daughter Fanny's account of the family's religious routine indicates:

Our habits were those of average English Protestants of decent responsibility. My mother read the Bible to us in the morning before breakfast . . . We learnt our catechism and collects, and went to church on Sunday, duly and decorously, as a matter of course. Grace was always said before and after meals by the youngest member of the family present and I remember a quaint old-fashioned benediction which, when my father happened to be at home at our bedtime, we used to kneel down by the chair to receive, and with which he used to dismiss us for the night: 'God bless you! Make you good, happy, healthy and wise!' These, with our daily morning and evening prayers, were our devotional habits and pious practices. (1878, vol. I, pp. 199–200)

The impression conveyed by Fanny is of a conventional Christian routine and determined respectability rather than deep religious zeal. The Kembles numbered several clergymen in their circle of friends and clearly derived considerable satisfaction from these social connections, in particular that with Henry Hart Milman.

Born in 1791, a younger son of Francis Milman, baronet and eminent physician, Milman was educated at Eton. There in the Long Chamber the boys clandestinely staged plays: 'We acted *Tom Thumb* the other day, and a most ludicrous piece of work it was. I (a future Dean of St Paul's), being of an elegant height and shape, represented the Queen of the Giants, and with wooden-soled shoes of about four inches, a kind of cap about one yard high, managed to cut a pretty Brobdingnagian appearance' (Arthur Milman, 1900, p. 18). At Oxford (Brasenose College), Milman won the Newdigate Prize in 1812 with a poem on 'The Apollo Belvedere'; he was Professor of Poetry at Oxford from 1821 to 1831. Milman was ordained in 1816 and his career was marked by outstanding ecclesiastical and scholarly distinction, the former culminating in his appointment as Dean of St Paul's in 1849. Milman's *A History of the Jews* (1829) caused controversy at the time by treating its subject along the lines of secular history; but it became a standard work, as did his *History of Latin Christianity to the Death of Nicholas V* (1855). These achievements placed Milman in the forefront of his profession, but he was also the author of a successful play 'the tragedy *Fazio*, produced in 1818 at Covent Garden, with a star part beloved of leading ladies for the next forty years' (Smyth, 1949, p. 12), including Fanny Kemble at Covent Garden in 1831.

In his advertisement to the published text of *Fazio* (1815) Milman wrote: 'The following attempt at reviving our old national drama with greater simplicity of plot, was written with some view to the stage. Circumstances and an opinion of considerable weight induced me to prefer the less perilous ordeal of the press.' Milman had been deterred by the size of the two metropolitan theatres legally entitled to stage his play, but had then been the victim of the lack of copyright when he discovered that it was being staged at the Surrey Theatre under the title of *The Italian Wife* 'and it had been acted some time before I was aware that the piece of that name was my work. That theatre was then, I believe, only licensed for operatic performances, but the company contrived to elude this restriction by performing all kinds of dramas with what they called musical accompaniment' (Arthur Milman, 1900, pp. 33–4). Milman therefore had first-hand experience of the two obstacles to theatrical progress which the 1832 Select Committee set out to address.

Milman's *Procida, or the Sicilian Vespers* was staged by Charles Kemble at Covent Garden in 1822, but, other considerations apart, the subject matter of his three religious dramas *Fall of Jerusalem* (1820), *Martyr of Antioch* and *Belshassar* (both 1822) ensured that they remained unperformed, as did his historical tragedy *Anne Boleyn*. Milman maintained his interest in the theatre, partly of course because of the continuing success of *Fazio*. He contributed several articles to the *Quarterly Review* including a lengthy review of J. Payne Collier's *The History of English Dramatic Poetry, to the time of Shakespeare and Annals of the Stage to the Restoration* in which he wrote 'Religion was the parent of the modern, as of ancient drama' (vol. 46, no. 92, January 1832, p. 479), dealing at some length with the development of medieval drama, as he was to do in his *History of Latin Christianity* (1855, vol. VI, pp. 492–9).

A more personal testimony of Milman's commitment to the theatre, as embodied by the Kemble family, was his review of Fanny Kemble's play *Francis the First*, which she had begun in 1827, when she was eighteen years of age. Milman's review in the *Quarterly Review* (vol. 47, no. 93) in March 1832 was of the printed text; the play was staged at Covent Garden the following month. In keeping with her father's belief that the patent theatres were temples of the higher drama Fanny Kemble's play 'was very much in line with current thinking in literary circles' (Marshall, 1977, p. 27). Milman wrote of 'reuniting the poet and the actor in their former close alliance' and continued: 'The most remarkable characteristic, however, of the tragedy before us, is its total and disdainful want of conformity to the present state of the stage. Far from accommodating itself with servile docility to the taste of the day . . . Francis the First is conceived in the spirit and conducted on the plan of a far different period' (*Quarterly Review*, p. 244). This period was Shakespeare's; the play used a 'double current of interest' (p. 245) and in one incident betrayed 'too close a resemblance to "Measure for Measure"' (p. 254), but in its departure from historical sources *Francis the First* 'is of a holier and purer nature' (p. 255). Milman acclaimed Fanny Kemble's first play as 'the most extraordinary work which has ever been produced by a female at her age' (p. 261).

Such fulsome encomiums from a family friend seem inseparable from personal regard for the youthful authoress. If such was Fanny Kemble's effect on a middle-aged, married scholar and cleric, her impact on her brother's contemporaries at Cambridge can be guessed at. Fanny Kemble described John Mitchell's circle as 'among the jewels of their time, and some of their names will be famous and blessed for genera-tions to come' (1878, vol. I, p. 299). The undergraduates amongst whom J. M. Kemble found himself during his time at Cambridge, from 1826, included F. D. Maurice, John Sterling, William Donne, Arthur Hallam, W. M. Thackeray, Alfred Tennyson and Richard Monckton Milnes. Most were at Trinity College or Trinity Hall and belonged to the Cambridge *Conversazione* Society, founded in 1820, generally known as the Cambridge Apostles. John Mitchell Kemble's personality introduced a dramatic element into university life: 'giddy and flamboyant . . . hand-some, talented extrovert with a compelling personality, some unfortu-nate mannerisms and traits and a flair for all sorts of things . . . his ability to sing, dance, shoot, row, fence, debate and drink. But Kemble did most things to excess and might fairly be called intemperate, both in character and personal habits' (Peter Allen, 1978, p. 97). If in hindsight ordination seems an improbable prospect for John Mitchell Kemble, Tennyson's sonnet 'To J. M. K.' provides a contemporary testimony:

> My hope and heart is with thee – thou wilt be
> A latter Luther, and a soldier-priest
> To scare church-harpies from the master's feast;
> Our dusted velvets have much need of thee:
> Thou art no sabbath-drawler of old saws,
> Distill'd from some worm-canker'd homily;
> But spurr'd at heart with fieriest energy
> To embattail and to wall about thy cause
> With iron-worded proof, hating to hark
> The humming of the drowsy pulpit-drone
> Half God's good sabbath, while the worn-out clerk
> Brow-beats his desk below. Thou from a throne
> Mounted in heaven wilt shoot into the dark
> Arrows of lightnings. I will stand and mark.   (1905, p. 25)

Kemble's most obvious effect upon his contemporaries was to raise their interest in the theatre. This reached its summation on Friday 19 March 1830 when *Much Ado About Nothing* was staged at the Hoop Hotel with Kemble as Dogberry, Arthur Hallam as Verges and R. M. Milnes (later Lord Houghton) as Beatrice (Burnand, 1880, pp. vii–viii). Other contemporaries turned to playwriting. Harrovian Richard Chenevix Trench, subsequently Dean of Westminster, Archbishop of Dublin and originator of the *Oxford English Dictionary*, aspired 'to compose a tragedy that might be produced upon the stage – an ambition which had stirred another future Dean (Milman) . . . *Bernardo del Carpio* was to be the title, and the manuscript was handed around for the private criticism of friends. There ensued a correspondence with Macready' (Bromley, 1959, p. 22). The correspondence between Trench, his father, Kemble, Donne and others (Lowder, 1888) charts the play's progress, but although Macready replied: 'It [the play] ought to be acted and I think it will' (Bromley, 1959, p. 22), Trench's ambition was not realised. John Sterling took longer to try his hand at playwriting, beginning his tragedy *Strafford* at Clifton in October 1839; it never reached the stage, but was published in 1843.

Then there was Fanny Kemble, under whose spell all her brother's friends fell. She herself doubted F. D. Maurice's fealty: 'She [Fanny Kemble] is reported to have said to him [F. D. Maurice], "Oh, you are so proud that you would not be seen with me in public!" To which he retorted, "If you go down Regent Street on an elephant, I will ride beside you on a donkey!"' (Frederick Maurice, 1884, vol. 1, p. 77). Of John Sterling, Thomas Carlyle wrote: 'He much admired her genius, nay was thought at one time to be vaguely on the edge of more chivalrous feelings' and proceeded to quote a letter from Sterling dated 10 November 1829:

I have the happiness also to be acquainted with his [J. M. Kemble's] sister, the divine Fanny; and I have seen her twice on the stage, and three or four times in private since my return from Cornwall . . . She is not handsome, rather short, and by no means deliberately formed; but her face is marked, and the eyes are brilliant, dark and full of character. She has more ability than she can ever display on the stage, but I have no doubt that by practice and self-culture, she will be a finer actress than anyone since Mrs. Siddons. (Carlyle, 1857, pp. 228–9)

On his visits to the Kembles' house Sterling read Fanny's verses and admired Sir Thomas Lawrence's portrait of her, but 'divine' though he found her, his reservations about the theatre persisted: 'I hate the stage; and but for her should very likely never have gone to the theatre again' (p. 229).

Sterling is identified by Carlyle as the author of the essay 'Fanny

1. Fanny Kemble as Juliet

Kemble', which appeared in the *Athenaeum* on 16 December 1829. The *Athenaeum*, which had been launched in January 1828 by James Silk Buckingham, subsequently a Whig MP, was under the editorship of F. D. Maurice from July 1828 until May 1829 (Marchand, 1971, p. 14). At the outset the *Athenaeum* had stated its position regarding the theatre: 'We are not among those who affect to despise the stage . . . to hold the drama in contempt is a mistaken affectation' (2 January 1828). In October 1829 the *Athenaeum* carried a review of Fanny Kemble's Juliet (illustration 1) at Covent Garden, which it hailed as 'a true Juliet, tender, graceful, dignified, energetic and occasionally sublime'. Fanny Kemble's assumption of the role of Juliet had been motivated by the desire to support her father's endeavours in what the *Athenaeum* described as 'a sinking cause', but the reviewer expressed hopes for 'a triumphant season' to 're-establish the affairs of the theatre' (7 October 1829). A further review on 21 October discoursed on Fanny Kemble's Juliet in more detail and on 16 December Sterling's appreciation of her appeared:

let her be faithful to her own mission of embodying before the eyes of myriads, who will be in some degree influenced for good or evil by her efforts, the conception of genius which no-one can better appreciate . . . let her be true to this purpose and to herself, let her despise popularity that she may be secure of fame; and she will be certain of giving to all men a kind and degree of pleasure, which is good for us to experience, and still better for her to communicate.

Sterling's words prompt a number of comments: 'faithful' and 'mission' suggest a religious quality; 'influenced for good or evil' indicates the theatre's potential to achieve either; 'the conception of genius' places Shakespeare on that elevated plane; 'let her despise popularity' asserts that art should not compromise; but 'all men' implies that art should not be an exclusive preserve of the few; above all 'a kind and degree of pleasure' refutes Bentham's solely quantitative criterion. Lacking though he was in enthusiasm for the theatre as such, Sterling's response to Fanny Kemble's Juliet suggests an experience on an altogether different plane from the pleasures of push-pin.

Sterling's Cambridge generation was engaged in a fierce battle of ideas. Both Sterling and John Mitchell Kemble entered the university as staunch Benthamites. In January 1828 Fanny Kemble described her brother as 'neither a tory or a whig; but a radical, a utilitarian, an adorer of Bentham, a worshipper of Mill, an advocate of vote by ballot, an opponent of hereditary aristocracy, the church establishment, the army and navy, which he deems unnecessary national expense' (1878, vol. I, p. 199). Bentham and Mill were the Kembles' 'near neighbours here, and whose houses we never pass without John being inclined to salute them, I think, as shrines of some beneficent powers of renovation' (p. 293). John Mitchell's desertion of Benthamism was swift: 'Under the direct influence of F. D. Maurice, Kemble abandoned his earlier Benthamite views and adopted the mystic's course as his own. The change, which occurred in late 1828, was greeted by his friends with delight. "Give my warmest regards to Kemble", Sterling wrote to Trench; "he is a brand plucked from the burning"' (Peter Allen, 1978, p. 99). Sterling's tutor Julius Hare had written of the achievement 'in getting [Sterling] out of the slough of Benthamism' (1848, vol. I, p. xxix).

In Bulwer Lytton's *Money* Alfred Evelyn, for whom the degrading experience of having been a sizar at Cambridge still rankles, contemplates turning opium-eater. Kemble did more than merely contemplate this during the year which he took off from Cambridge to study philology in Germany. To Evelyn and Kemble, in their shared disillusionment with Benthamism, opium would have been inseparably associated with the man who advanced arguably the most credible alternative to Utilitarianism – Samuel Taylor Coleridge. Julius Hare actively promoted Coleridge's ideas (though not his addiction) and even took some favoured undergraduates to visit the sage of Highgate. Peter Allen has identified Coleridge as the chief among the Apostles' idols (1978, p. 81) and Basil Willey has listed Thomas Arnold, J. H. Newman, James Martineau and Charles Kingsley amongst those who acknowledged their debt to Coleridge, before pronouncing F. D. Maurice 'Coleridge's most eminent theological disciple' (1964, p. 3).

Although F. D. Maurice's early series of 'Sketches of Contemporary Authors' for the *Athenaeum* included no essay on Coleridge they are as A. J. Hartley has observed 'Coleridgean in tone and spirit . . . [saturated] with Coleridge's Christian (social) philosophy' (1970, 'Preface'). In *The Kingdom of Christ* Maurice referred to his own work as 'a very poor expansion of a single page, which is found in the fragment, at the end of Mr Coleridge's book upon the Church and State' (1838, vol. III, p. xviii).

Coleridge's *On the Constitution of the Church and the State* (1830) was prompted by the passage of the Catholic Emancipation Act in 1829. In chapter 7 Coleridge addressed himself directly 'to the parliamentary leaders of the Liberals and Utilitarians' advancing the idea of 'a permanent, nationalized, learned order, a national clerisy or church' (Colmer, 1976, p. 69). He proposed 'That in every parish throughout the kingdom there is planted a germ of civilization' (p. 75). By 'civilization' Coleridge meant material progress which in itself was 'but a mixed good, if not far more a corrupting influence . . . where this civilization is not grounded in cultivation, the harmonious development of those faculties that characterise our humanity. We must be men in order to be citizens' (pp. 42–3).

The idea that the progress of society depended not merely on 'civilization' (material conditions) but also on 'cultivation' (the spiritual, intellectual and aesthetic) was fundamental to the nineteenth century. In *Culture and Society Coleridge to Orwell* Raymond Williams identifies 'Five words' as 'the key points from which this map can be drawn. They are *industry, democracy, class, art* and *culture*' (1987, p. xiii). Of these five words

Williams deems 'culture' as 'the most striking' (p. xvi), tracing it to 'culti-vation' as used by Coleridge (p. 61). Williams recounts the different meanings of 'culture' in the nineteenth century:

It came to mean, first, 'a general state or habit of the mind', having close rela-tions with the idea of human perfection. Second, it came to mean 'the general state of intellectual development, in a society as a whole'. Third, it came to mean 'the general body of the arts'. Fourth, later in the century, it came to mean 'a whole way of life, material, intellectual and spiritual'. (p. xvi)

The crucial points about Coleridge's 'cultivation' (culture) are that it was rooted in religion and that it was something for which the state, as embodied by the Established Church, had a responsibility. The arts were elevated into a virtuous trinity with the Church and the state; Ben Knights writes 'literature is taking on the social and moral functions of religion' (1978, p. 15), borrowing Leszek Kolakowski's term 'from jester into priest'.

There is no reason to suppose that drama and the theatre, at least in their higher achievements, would be excluded by Coleridge from this alliance. He wrote *Remorse* in 1797, 'expressly for the stage, at the instiga-tion, and with the encouragement of Mr. Sheridan, by whom, however, it was not deemed to be suitable for that purpose. Ultimately it was brought out at Drury Lane in the year 1813 ... when it ran twenty nights' (Derwent Coleridge, 1852, p. v). *Zapolya*, published in 1817, was pro-nounced impracticable for the stage; Coleridge also translated Schiller's *Wallenstein*. In *Table Talk* Coleridge records: 'I always had a great liking – I may say, a sort of nondescript reverence – for John Kemble' and writes of 'Dear Charles Mathews – a true genius in my judgment' (Ashe, 1888, p. 16). Of Garrick and Shakespeare, despite 'weights so unequal' in respect of the transience of the former's art and the durability of the latter's, he avers that 'this transcendent power sprung from the same source in both, – from an insight into human nature at its fountain-head, which exists in those creations of Genius alone ... We may then hope for a second Garrick or an approach to a Shakespeare' (p. 337). Endowed with 'his creative and almost Protean genius' Garrick was worthy of a place in the pantheon of great artists.

Edmund Kean, of whom Coleridge memorably wrote 'To see him act, is like reading Shakespeare by flashes of lightning' (Ashe, 1888, p. 14), was another contender for the pantheon. In 1816 he appeared in *Bertram, or the Castle of Aldobrand*, by Revd Charles Maturin, which was staged at Drury Lane on the recommendations of Scott and Byron. Coleridge's 'Critique on Bertram' in *Biographia Literaria* places the play in the context of the proprietary subscribers' avowed object, 'the redemption of the British stage' and restoration of Drury Lane to 'its former classical renown' with the plays of Shakespeare, Jonson and Otway 'with the expurgated muses of Vanbrugh, Congreve, and Wycherley' (1917, p. 303). For the purposes of comparison Coleridge took 'the old Spanish play, entitled *Atheista Fulminato*, formerly, and perhaps still, acted in the churches and monasteries of Spain, and which, under various names (*Don Juan*, *The Libertine* etc.) has had its day of favour in every country throughout Europe' (p. 307). Identifying 'the doctrine of a godless nature' in Don Juan, Coleridge nevertheless observed the character's 'intellectual superiority, and the accumulation of his gifts and desirable qualities, as co-existent with entire wickedness in one and the same person . . . which gives to this strange play its charm and universal interest' (p. 308). The possibility that the depiction of such an engaging and wicked individual might encourage imitation was discounted by Coleridge: 'There is no danger (thinks the spectator or reader) of *my* becoming such a monster of iniquity as Don Juan! *I* never shall be an atheist! *I* shall never disallow all distinction between right and wrong! *I* have not the least inclination to be so outrageous a drawcansir in my love affairs' (p. 309). The purpose of *Atheista Fulminato* was to display the hollowness of such qualities 'in order to put us on our guard by demonstrating their utter indifference to vice and virtue, whenever these and the like accomplishments are contemplated for themselves alone' (p. 313).

Coleridge had been put in mind of *Atheista Fulminato* because the substance of *Bertram* was derived from act 3 scene 1 of Shadwell's *The Libertine*, itself a reworking of the Spanish play. He found Maturin's play 'an insult to common decency', in particular the fifth act: 'Of the fifth act, the only thing noticeable (for rant and nonsense, though abundant as ever, have long before the last act become things of course) is the profane representation of the high altar in a chapel, with all the vessels and other preparations for the holy sacrament. A hymn is actually sung on the stage by chorister boys!' (p. 323). The play ended with Bertram stabbing himself and in 'a superfetation of blasphemy upon nonsense . . . this loathsome and leprous confluence of robbery, adultery, murder, and cowardly assassination . . . first recommends the charitable Monks and holy Prior to pray for his soul and then has the folly and impudence to exclaim – "I die no felon's death, A warrior's weapon freed a warrior's soul!"' (p. 324). Coleridge had demonstrated that the morality of a play is not dependent upon its subject matter. *Atheista Fulminato*, acted in the churches and monasteries of Spain, despite its unpromising subject matter, possessed moral integrity, whereas Revd Maturin's *Bertram* was a farrago of stage tricks with an unconvincing and contrived, though ostensibly moral, conclusion.

The debate about the theatre that took place in the 1830s and 1840s revolved around the maintenance of quality in the wake of expansion. The increased population in London and the force of free trade arguments rendered the maintenance of the patent theatres' monopoly untenable. Bulwer Lytton, a reforming liberal but not a Utilitarian, saw the need not only for regulation – principally through the Lord Chamberlain – but also for the state to assume a responsibility for patronage. Coleridge's idea of a clerisy which embraced the Church, the state and culture provided a framework by which liberalism could be moderated in an increasingly democratic, urban and mechanised society. As Ben Knights observes 'Liberalism offers guarantees neither of the preservation of culture nor of control over the mass' (1978, p. 200). Dean Milman's concern was principally with the preservation, indeed regeneration, of culture, through plays of literary distinction; Bishop Blomfield's concern was principally with the 'control of the masses'. These two concerns were crucial to the aspirations of the theatre in the nineteenth century and to the Church's attitude towards it.

CHAPTER 2

Censure and censorship

You may say '*Him*' and point upwards, but you may not say '*God*'.
G. H. Lewes *The Noble Heart*

In book 2, chapter 1 of W. H. Mallock's *The New Republic or Culture, Faith and Philosophy in an English Country House* (1877), Dr Jenkinson, a thinly disguised portrait of Benjamin Jowett, incongruously delivers his sermon from the stage of a miniature theatre. Amongst Jowett's many claims to scholarly distinction was his translation of Plato (1871), but few early nineteenth-century clerics would have admitted to the need for a translation, having received an education steeped in the literature of Ancient – pre-Christian – Greece and Rome. For a clergyman bent on attacking the theatre Plato's *The Republic* (*c.* 380 BC) provided an armoury of ammunition which had been effectively deployed through successive ages.

In 'Civilized Society' (part 2, book 1) Plato is concerned with the change from a simple society, which he preferred, to the second stage when 'a variety of dainties, and incense, and courtesans and cakes' will be demanded and 'a multitude of callings which are not required by any natural want' will come into being:

The whole tribe of hunters and actors, of whom one large class will have to do with forms and colours; another will be the votaries of music – poets and their attendant train of rhapsodists, players, dancers, contractors; also makers of divers kinds of articles, including women's dresses. We shall want more servants. Will not tutors be also in request, and nurses wet and dry, tirewomen and barbers, as well as confectioners and cooks; and swineherds, too, who were not needed and therefore had no place in the former edition of our State, but are needed now? They must not be forgotten: and there will be animals of many other kinds, if people eat them. (Jowett, 1888, p. 54)

The society thus described had many similarities with that which emerged in nineteenth-century England. Self-sufficiency gave way to the development of professional skills and the buying and selling of those skills. Such a society needed the basics for living – on an increasing scale – and an underclass ('swineherds') expanded to provide them; but those who now prospered by virtue of their skills enjoyed greater leisure and could pay others to help them pass it in an agreeable manner.

Plato viewed the very nature of theatre (representation/imitation) with hostility: 'human nature [is] . . . incapable of imitating many things well, as of performing well the actions of which the imitations are copies' (p. 80). Manifestations of imitation on the stage reinforced this attitude:

> And surely not bad men, whether cowards or any others, who do the reverse of what we have been prescribing, who scold or mock or revile one another in drink or out of drink, or who in any other manner sin against themselves and their neighbours in word or deed, as the manner of such is. Neither should they be trained to imitate the action or speech of men or women who are mad or bad; for madness, like vice, is to be known but not to be practised or imitated. (p. 80)

In his 'Theory of Art' (part 10) Plato advanced his case against imitation with reference to the concept of Forms: 'Whenever a number of individuals have a common name we assume them to have also a corresponding idea of form' (p. 308). The artist's representation 'is thrice removed from the king and from the truth' (p. 310) as demonstrated in the example of a bed: 'Well then, here are three beds: one existing in nature, which is made by God . . . There is another which is the work of the carpenter . . . And the work of the painter is third' (p. 309). Thus 'Of the many excellences which I perceive in the order of our State, there is none which upon reflection pleases me better than the rule about poetry . . . the rejection of imitative poetry, which certainly ought not to be received' (p. 307). Despite his comprehensive condemnation of the theatre (the pursuit of popularity will result in vulgarity), Plato rather surprisingly concedes: 'Notwithstanding this, let us assure our sweet friend and the sister arts of imitation, that if she will only prove her title to exist in a well-ordered State we shall be delighted to receive her – we are very conscious of her charms; but we may not on that account betray the truth' (p. 322). Plato's burden of proof was carried forward to the Victorian theatre, which had to refute his assertions that theatre (imitation of life) was intrinsically wrong and that the depiction of 'men or women who are mad or bad' was necessarily corrupting.

Jonas Barish, after acknowledging Aristotle's rehabilitation of mimesis and theory of catharsis in the *Poetics* (*c.* 330 BC) concludes:

> The actual theater, the theater as known to Plato and practised by his contemporaries, can in the last analysis be allowed no virtue. It has corrupted society,

and it continues to symbolize the evils which have led to Athens' downfall. And Plato's hostility toward it is destined to become the cornerstone of an anti-theatrical edifice that is only now, after two and a half millennia, finally crumbling. (1981, p. 28)

The advent of Christianity provided no respite for the theatre. Joseph Wood Krutch has argued that the ancient philosopher's asceticism and contempt for pleasure was reinforced by the Christian tenet of self-denial, which was linked with the prospect of 'incalculable blisses in the future . . . Thus many a man unable to follow the inextricably Stoic in the contempt of pleasure was appealed to on prudential grounds and resolved to take some thought of the future. In this manner asceticism became a religion not only for the philosopher but also for the rabble' (1949, pp. 89–90). The rejection of the theatre became a matter of individual self-denial and – in the long term – self-interest:

Fundamentally the objection was not to bad plays – to indecency and profaneness – though of course these aggravated the evil; but to plays as such, and indeed, to all art; for the beautiful is pleasant and pleasant is damnable. This life is, *a priori*, a vale of tears, and any attempt to make it otherwise is sinful. Moreover any interest in the affairs of the world is dangerous. The more man can withdraw from life the safer he is. (p. 90)

Early Christian writers to attack the theatre were Tatian (*c.* 160 AD) and Tertullian half a century later, both of whom denounced the process of imitation and the indulgence in pleasure. Tertullian had been a theatre-goer in his youth when he had experienced the frenzy and excitement induced amongst crowds at theatres. The, generally debased, forms of entertainment current in Rome and elsewhere at the time were a powerful counter-attraction for potential converts and even those nominally in the fold. Actors were a particular target for opprobrium and during the fourth and fifth centuries the Church introduced the penalty of excommunication and denied them the sacraments. By then the writings of St Augustine had added weight to the Church's opposition to the theatre. In the *Confessions* St Augustine recalls his youthful fascination with the theatre in Carthage:

The drama enthralled me, full of representations of my own miseries and fuel for my own fire . . . I am not now past compassion, but in those days, in the theatre, I rejoiced with lovers wickedly enjoying one another, imaginary though the situation was on stage . . . But in those days, wretch, liked to be made sorrowful and looked for something to be sorry about when, in someone else's woes, though they were mere dramatic fiction, that actor most pleased me and strongly attracted me who drove me to tears. What wonder then, that, an unhappy sheep straying from your flock and irked by your shepherding, I should become infected with a foul image? (Blaiklock, 1983, pp. 59–60)

St Augustine recognised – 'that actor most pleased me . . . who drove me to tears' – that the more faithful (truer) an actor was to the character he was portraying the falser he was to his own personality. Augustine defined two types of falsehood – the 'fallacious' and the 'fabulous':

the first being born of the wish to deceive, the second the wish to tell a story. Deceivers all hope to deceive, but the same cannot be said of those who tell tales, 'for farces and comedies are full of fables whose purpose is to give pleasure rather than to deceive, and almost everyone who tells a joke, tells a fable'. Augustine thus removed the onus from fabulation by differentiating the impulse behind it (the desire to please) from that behind falsehood (the desire to deceive) . . . He makes the application not only to jokes and fables alone, but to plays and not to plays alone, but to those who act in them. (Barish, 1981, p. 55)

Despite making this crucial distinction Augustine ultimately condemned imitation, advocating instead truth to our own nature, arriving 'By a somewhat awkward and illogical route . . . at roughly the same final view as Plato's: a condemnation of both painters and players for seeking a truth which is "self-congratulatory and two-faced", rather than one which conforms to the single, indivisible, eternal truth promulgated by God' (p. 57).

In the Middle Ages the Church and the drama converged with little dissent from the former, but with the rise of Puritanism the battle lines were drawn up again. Ironically anti-Papist Puritans occupied positions previously manned by the early Catholic church. In England the offensive was led by John Northcote, Philip Stubbes and William Prynne, and has been fully chronicled by Elbert N. S. Thompson (1903), M. M. Knappen (1939) and others. The closure of the theatres during the Commonwealth was a victory, albeit only temporary, for Puritanism, but the more permissive climate of the Restoration, when Charles II established the patent theatres' monopoly, provoked a backlash, culminating in Jeremy Collier's *A Short View of the Immorality and Profaneness of the English Stage With the Sense of Antiquity upon this Argument*. As the title indicates Collier was conversant with the historic arguments against the theatre, but, though he recites them at the end of the book, he does not clamour for the suppression of the theatre, but advances a moralistic notion of what it should be: 'The business of Plays is to recommend Vertue, and discountenance Vice. To shew the Uncertainty of Human Greatness, the suddain Turns of Fate, and the unhappy Conclusions of Violence and Injustice. 'Tis to expose the Singularities of Pride and Fancy, to make Folly and Falsehood contemptible, and to bring every Thing that is Ill under Infamy, and Neglect' (1698, p. 1).

The plays (by Wycherley, Etheridge and Congreve amongst others) which formed the contemporary context for Collier had long since disappeared from the repertoire by the beginning of the nineteenth century. The extent to which the eighteenth-century Church's generally more quiescent attitude towards the stage can be explained in terms of it being itself in a state of torpor is open to dispute (see Hempton, 1996), but in any case the theatre was less exceptionable than it had been for centuries. By 1832, however, Charles Kemble noted the increase of religious feeling against the theatre (particularly by Methodists). The reasons for this were threefold: the Established Church's resolve to reassert its authority, heightened by the threat from other denominations including Roman Catholicism after the 1829 Emancipation Act; the prospect of more theatres, following the 1832 Select Committee recommendations; and the gathering pace of urbanisation.

Of the numerous clerics who mounted their pulpit to denounce the theatre two provide good examples: Revd Thomas Best in Sheffield (see Dann, 1994) and Revd John East in Bath. Revd Thomas Best, 'a graduate of Worcester College, Oxford' (Mackerness, 1979, p. iii), delivered his first sermon against the theatre in 1817 and thereafter '[f]or forty-seven successive years, with but one single exception, arising from a sudden attack of illness, Mr Best delivered his annual protest against the amusements of the stage from the pulpit of St James's' (Roberts, 1865, 'Preface'). Best always took a biblical text as the starting point of his sermons. Since an outright denunciation of the theatre is not to be found in the Bible, Best's practice was to select a text which could, in his view anyway, be applied to the theatre – for instance in 1832, Ephesians 5. 11: 'And have no fellowship with the unfruitful works of darkness, but rather reprove them.' This necessarily required the presupposition that the theatre was amongst 'the unfruitful works of darkness'. In 1832 Best preached his sermon on 18 November, so the proposals of the Select Committee would have been fresh in his mind and he referred to 'a renewal of those amusements which have ever proved a fruitful source of those gross and open sins, which so greatly provoke the Lord' (p. 2). He contrasted the end of the recent cholera epidemic – 'God . . . in His good providence has Himself, as it were, mercifully closed the doors of our cholera hospital and shut up the gates of our cholera burial ground' – with the reopening of the theatre, 'from whence will issue a moral infection, more pestilent and pernicious than any forms of plague and sickness which followed in her fatal train, when sin entered into the world and introduced all our woes' (p. 6). Of the two evils the theatre was the greater – victims of cholera could still enter heaven, whereas attenders of the theatre were doomed to hell: 'for anyone to have and to hold present fellowship with the theatre is without repentance and pardon, to have and to hold for ever and ever future fellowship with hell' (p. 13).

To Best the progression was as simple as it was inevitable: 'In youth a reckless pleasure-taker, in advanced life a confirmed worldling; in eternity a lost soul' (3 November 1833; Roberts, 1865, p. 32). The depiction of immorality, the derision of pious people and the clergy, oaths invoking God's name were at least overt manifestations of irreligion, but more insidious was 'much that is brilliant, and beautiful, and sublime, and touching, in the language of the stage. An occasional lesson of moral virtue may be uttered, as correct and Christian in its sentiment as it is eloquent in its expression . . . these things just serve to give force to the temptation . . . They serve as baits' (31 October 1841, pp. 183–4). The devil was ever-resourceful and even these apparent virtues 'may be the instruments of Satan; they may be aiding the author of evil in spreading a net for the temporal and clerical ruin of such as shall be entered into the snare' (22 October 1850, p. 268).

Best's attack on the theatre was founded on the conviction that it led inexorably to hell. After all the name for the least salubrious part of the theatre – the pit – conveyed strong associations with hell. The belief, upon which Best's case rested, that the theatre was indeed one of 'the unfruitful works of darkness', was increasingly challenged; but, more importantly, the force of Best's admonitions depended upon the doctrine of the reality of Satan, hell and eternal perdition. During the mid nineteenth century these concepts were questioned (notably by F. D. Maurice) with far-reaching consequences for morality in general and the theatre in particular (Geoffrey Rowell, 1974).

Sheffield was one of the rapidly growing new urban conurbations, in which, as Kathleen Barker (1985) has shown, a wide range of entertainments developed to serve the expanding population. Even Best acknowledged that 'Amusements and recreations of one kind or other occupy more or less of the time and attention of most persons . . . The subject of amusements, therefore, is one which comes within the compass of ministerial instruction' (16 November 1851, Roberts, 1865, pp. 278–9). Bath, with its long history as a resort and its established theatre tradition, was principally the preserve of the well-to-do. However Arnold Hare has noted that, through a combination of national and local (the Bristol

Riots of 1831) factors: 'the moral climate in parts of Bath society was turning strongly against the theatre' (1986, p. 264). In the 1830s and early 1840s a succession of managers had failed and, when Revd John East delivered his sermon on 7 January 1844 (the year after Bulwer Lytton's bill was approved by parliament), a proposal 'to support the theatre, either by a grant of money, or by taking the theatre under the patronage of the Association' was under consideration (East, 1844a, p. 6).

For his sermon, delivered in St Michael's Church at the evening service, East took as his text Titus 2. 11–15 'denying ungodliness and worldly lusts, we should live soberly, righteously, and godly, in this present world'. East asked: 'Is, then, pleasure itself an evil?', answering: 'The good or evil of pleasure is not settled by a general question and a corresponding answer. That must be determined by an examination of particulars. The individual character of each pleasure, and the manner and extent of its being pursued must be taken into consideration' (1844b, p. 6). In locating the good (or evil) in the particular amusement, rather than in the amount of pleasure derived from it by individuals, Best's position was fundamentally un-Benthamite. Best, who cited Bacchus, Tertullian, St Augustine, Miracle plays – an aberration of the Papacy – and Shakespeare to whom he allowed – despite Hamlet's 'most horrid and blasphemous imprecations' – 'almost divine inspiration' (p. 16), was adamant: 'Now the pleasures of the Theatre are at irreconcilable variance with the joy and peace of that man to whom God [has] . . . brought salvation' (p. 7). The playhouse was:

adverse to individual, domestic and social happiness, exciting as it does, the worst of passions, loosening the bonds of relationship, honour and love, and producing a feverish expectation of enjoyment, never to be realised. But our chief and last objection to the profession and its peculiar literature is, that both are hostile – directly hostile to man's attainment of eternal blessedness. (p. 25)

As with Best, East's ultimate deterrent against the theatre was the forfeit of 'eternal blessedness'.

At this time the defence of the theatre from the pulpit was unthinkable, but its supporters weighed in with lectures and pamphlets. Best's sermons provoked responses from F. B. Calvert in 1822 and from T. H. Lacy, then manager of the Sheffield Theatre, in letters to the *Sheffield Iris* (reprinted as a pamphlet, 1840). F. B. Calvert is an interesting figure in several respects – he attended the Roman Catholic College at Old Hall Green, Hertfordshire, with a view to ordination, but instead took to the stage alternating leading roles with Edmund Kean, Macready and Vandenhoff the Elder. In 1829 he became lecturer in elocution at King's

College, Aberdeen, and subsequently wrote *The Art of Reading and Preaching Distinctly: A Letter to The Rev. Dean Ramsay* (1869) and revised T. Ewing's *Principles of Elocution* (1852) in both of which he surveyed the common ground between preaching and acting. In *A Defence of the Acted Drama In a Letter Addressed to the Rev. Thomas Best MA of Sheffield* Calvert upheld the stage for its example of fine elocution, and went further: 'Drama on the contrary invokes some excellent moral delight by the elegance of its language and the splendours of its imagery, and powerfully excites our sympathies by the charm of its sentiments and the interests of its situations' (1822, p. 8). Expatiating on the moral force of drama he instanced *Hamlet, Macbeth, King Lear* and *Othello*: 'No where is virtue arranged in more imposing and attractive attributes, no where are the ravages of unlicensed passion depicted in more appalling colours' (p. 10). He issued a challenge to Best:

But, Sir, I confidently assert, and I call upon you to falsify the assertion if you can, that in no portion of the Sacred Writings can there be found a prohibition of Theatricals, either direct or implied; from no portion of the Sacred Writings have you yourself been able to extract a single text, nay a solitary expression, which with all your expository skill can be brought to bear upon the question or wear the semblance of an argument in your favour. On the contrary, that excellent volume abounds in language of a directly opposite tendency – 'to serve the Lord with cheerfulness of heart', 'there is a time to play'. (p. 5)

From St John's College, Cambridge, came John Denman's testimony in favour of the theatre, citing Acts 17. 28, 1 Corinthians 15. 33 and Titus 1. 12. He proclaimed that in his estimation 'the stage though debased at present by the character admitted and tolerated upon it, inculcates notwithstanding good morality, on the main and is therefore conditionally entitled to renewed patronage and support, in the sanguine hope of shortly disentangling itself from that obloquy by which alone it is sullied' (1835, p. 53). Fanny Kemble, 'a young lady so amply calculated to adorn and elevate the profession selected' (p. 46), still cast her spell in Cambridge and thanks to the Kembles 'the seeds of virtue may gradually take root, and the most sanguine expectations may reasonably be entertained that they will finally eradicate vice' (p. 47).

A dramatist closely allied with the Kembles' cause was James Sheridan Knowles, whose verse dramas received their first performances at one or other of the patent theatres. Charles Kemble appeared as Icilius in *Virginius* at Covent Garden in 1820 and as Sir Thomas Clifford in *The Hunchback* at the same theatre in 1832, with Fanny as Julia. For many of his contemporaries the best hope for the regeneration and elevation of the drama rested with Knowles. R. H. Horne, whose *Gregory VII* (1840), followed the same neo-Elizabethan model as Knowles, wrote in *A New Spirit of the Age*: 'The visible Drama is most eminently portrayed in the works of Sheridan Knowles' (1844, vol. I, p. 86), and Hazlitt considered '*Virginius* inferior only to Shakespeare' (Murray, 1986, p. 164). Leslie Meeks traces Knowles's dramatic style to Coleridge, who 'it is said, once gave Knowles, *more suo*, an extemporaneous lecture on poetry . . . Clearly the spell held fast, for Knowles later practised some of Coleridge's ideas on play-writing', with stultifying effect (1933, p. 26).

J. W. Calcraft (1839, p. 139) and Westland Marston, a fellow dramatist in the same vein, testified to Knowles's deep religious convictions, tending to Calvinism: 'That there was a pious and reverent tone in Knowles's mind may be seen in nearly all his serious dramas' (1890, p. 274). Between 1820 and 1850 Knowles delivered 'Lectures on Dramatic Literature' in which he recurrently asserted the religious nature of the theatre:

Because of partial error, the stage is indiscriminately repudiated, and dramatic poetry shares its disgrace; yet it is the proper fruit of that faculty which the creator has vouchsafed for the constitution of the dramatic poet – a teacher in his way, a teacher in a pleasant way. Inferior in office to him who handles things exclusively divine, but still a teacher and a useful one. (1873, p. 85)

The assertion that talents displayed in the theatre were as much God's gift as those professed in other walks of life gained increasing currency as the century wore on. In an exchange of letters with four Devon clergymen (*Devonport Independent* 30 July 1836) Knowles went on the offensive: 'The Almighty has employed the drama as a vehicle of Revelation. This fact which I presume they will not attempt to disprove, I follow up with the position – That the dramatist may plead Sanction of Revelation.'

Knowles drew an analogy with the art of painting, asking: 'Do they [reverend gentlemen] condemn an artist when he paints a storm?', behind which lay the objection to imitating God's thunder and lightning on the stage. The artist in Knowles's mind was John Martin, whose depictions of biblical scenes gained the approval of clergy, who would have been appalled by theatrical representations of the same subject matter, as Martin Meisel observes: 'His vast physical spectacles were . . . made instruments of edification, they found their way into that unwitting nursery of the Romantic imagination, Haworth Parsonage, and pious and respectable households by the thousand' (1983, pp. 168–9).

Byron adopted the dramatic form for his literary treatment of historical and biblical subjects, infusing his closet dramas – 'Byron thought that a single glance should assure critics that his plays were not for acting' (Howell, 1982, p. 4) – with apocalyptic romanticism in the vein of Martin. Closest in subject matter was Byron's *Sardanapalus* (1821), which actually pre-dated Martin's *The Fall of Nineveh* (1828) and was staged by Macready (1834), Charles Kean (1853) and Charles Calvert (1877), whose scenic artists deployed their imagination and all the resources of stage technology to realise the great set pieces on stage. Indeed most of Byron's allegedly closet dramas found their way on to the stage in some form, save for *Cain* of which Margaret J. Howell writes: 'Byron's lyrical "Mystery", *Cain*, based on the Genesis story, might have been amplified into a spectacular musical drama, like Bunn's *Manfred*, had the subject been uncontroversial. But no producer would have dared stage *Cain* in the nineteenth century' (p. 181). It was Stanislavsky who first tackled *Cain* at the Moscow Arts Theatre on 4 April 1920.

Byron's *Cain* was published in 1821, but back in 1798 Coleridge had embarked on a prose composition, *Cain,* in collaboration with Wordsworth when the two poets were staying at Nether Stowey in Somerset:

The title and subject were suggested by myself, who likewise drew out the scheme and contents for each of the three books or cantos, of which the work was to consist, and which, the reader is to be informed, was to have been finished in one night! My partner undertook the first canto; I the second: and which ever had done first, was to set about the third. (Derwent Coleridge and Coleridge 1852, p. 146)

Coleridge despatched 'my portion of the task at full finger-speed' and hastened to show it to Wordsworth, who was still confronting 'his almost blank sheet of paper'. The two poets were overcome by 'the exceeding ridiculousness of the whole scheme – which broke up in a laugh: the Ancient Mariner was written instead' (p. 146). Thirty years later Coleridge was encouraged to rework the piece, which is important, above all, for its reinterpretation of the fate of the first biblical murderer in the after-life:

The Shape that was like Abel raised himself up. But Cain said, 'Didst thou not find favour in the sight of the Lord thy God?' The Shape answered, 'The Lord is the God of the living only, the dead have another God.' Then the child Enos lifted up his eyes and prayed; but Cain rejoiced secretly in his heart. 'Wretched shall they be all the days of their mortal life', exclaimed the Shape, 'who sacrifice worthy and acceptable sacrifices to the God of the dead; but after death their toil ceases.' (pp. 152–3)

Of this passage Murray Roston writes:

The heresy is further elaborated into a rejection of the after-life as recompense or punishment for earthly acts. The effect of the heresy is to cut from Cain's neck the albatross of guilt . . . Coleridge's Cain is, at the conclusion, eager to set out upon a quest for the new God of whom he has just learned. The interpretation of Cain as the symbol of intellectual curiosity had begun. (1968, p. 203)

Coleridge's stage play *Remorse* is suffused, as its title suggests, with ideas about the nature of temporal and eternal punishment for a murderer. Don Ordino avows a conventional view of hell:

> And you killed him?
> Oh blood hounds! May eternal wrath flame round you!
>
> (Derwent Coleridge, 1852, p. 24)

and

> Let the eternal justice
> Prepare my punishment in the obscure world   (p. 70);

whereas his elder brother Don Alvar locates punishment within the sinner in this world:

> The Past lives o'er again
> In its effects, and to the guilty spirit
> The ever frowning Present is its image   (p. 17);

> That worst bad man shall find
> A picture, which will wake the hell within him,
> And rouse a fiery whirlwind in his conscience   (p. 34)

and – in the closing speech of the play – :

> DON ALVAR: In these strange dread events
> Just Heaven instructs us with an awful voice,
> That Conscience rules us e'en against our choice.
> Our inward monitress to guide or warn,
> If listened to; but if repelled with scorn,
> At length as dire Remorse, she reappears,
> Works in our guilty hopes, and selfish fears!
> Still bids, Remember! and still cries, Too late!
> And while she scares us, goads us to our fate.   (p. 73)

In *Remorse*, set in the reign of Philip II towards the end of the civil wars against the Moors, Coleridge was exploring ideas about retribution and punishment. The Inquisition looms large. Act 3 scene 1 is set in a 'Hall of Armoury' with an altar at the back of the stage and act 3 scene 2 is located in the 'Interior of the Chapel with painted windows'. Other scenes represent popular dramatic locations of the time: act 2 scene 1 'A wild and mountainous country'; act 4 scene 2 'The Interior Court of a Saracenic or Gothic Castle' and act 5 'A Dungeon'. As Martin Meisel (1983, pp. 170–1) has shown, the theatre was attracted to biblical and kindred subjects more for their visual potential than for their religious content. He points to W. T. Moncrieff's *Zoroaster; or, The Spirit of the Star* (Drury Lane, 19 April 1824) in which Clarkson Stanfield's sets for 'The City of Babylon in All Its Splendour' giving way to 'The Destruction of Babylon' were much indebted to John Martin's *Fall of Babylon* (1819). At Covent Garden in February 1833 the Grieves's sets for *The Israelites in Egypt; or, The Passage of the Dead Sea* were similarly beholden to Francis Danby's *Delivery of Israel out of Egypt* (1825).

The manager of Drury Lane, Alfred Bunn, had engaged in a correspondence about the morality of the theatre with Revd J. A. James in 1824 (Bunn, 1824). For *The Israelites in Egypt* Bunn had obtained the sanction not only of the Lord Chamberlain, but also, more surprisingly, of the Bishop of London, who later that year was to voice his objections to the theatre in the House of Lords' debate. The reason for this indulgence was the inclusion of 'An Oratorio, Consisting of Sacred Music . . . The music composed by Handel and Rossini'. The next season Bunn embarked on a staging of another sacred subject, *Jephtha's Vow*: 'its announcement continued before the public, until the day preceding its proposed performance, when it was suddenly withdrawn' (Bunn, 1840, vol. 1, p. 177). Bunn had bowed to pressure from above and even 'a repetition of the *Israelites in Egypt* . . . was interdicted' (p. 177). Faced with such glaring inconsistency from the Lord Chamberlain's office Bunn speculated:

I can perfectly understand, that the Lord Chamberlain of the day had a very difficult game to play – for by refusing a licence for the present, he would exhibit the impropriety of having granted one for the past; and by granting a licence at all, he would be committing an offence against the religious feelings of a great portion of the community. The error in my humble judgment, was blowing hot and cold with the same breath – he should either have peremptorily prohibited, or unhesitatingly granted, both. (pp. 177–8)

The holder of the office of Examiner of Plays in the Lord Chamberlain's office at this time was George Colman the Younger. Colman's personal life (a secret marriage), his comic poems and some of his plays hardly placed him beyond reproach, but as Examiner of Plays (1824–36) he showed an unexpected prudery and strictness. In his evidence to the 1832 Select Committee he affirmed: 'I conceive all

Scripture is much too sacred for the stage, except in very solemn scenes indeed, and that to bring things so sacred upon the stage becomes profane' (*British Parliamentary Papers, Stage and Theatre 1*, 1968, p. 60). He confessed to having been 'a careless immoral author, I am now the Examiner of Plays. I did my business as an author at the time, and I do my business as an examiner now' (p. 60).

Charles H. Shattuck has described Colman as 'a stupid man without principle, who behaved in a reactionary manner because he thought he was supposed to and because nobody told him otherwise' (1948, pp. 65–6). On his death in 1836 Colman was succeeded by Charles Kemble whose four years as Examiner of Plays J. R. Stephens describes as 'among the most obscure and least documented of all nineteenth-century terms of office ... [he] took very little interest in the work and ... the major portion was delegated to his son John Mitchell Kemble' (1980, p. 26). An indication of Charles Kemble's lack of interest was the licensing of Bulwer Lytton's *The Duchess de la Vallière* (Covent Garden, 4 January 1837) 'without a word of protest' (Shattuck, 1948, p. 67), but this did not make the play immune to attacks from the press and public. Bulwer Lytton had 'smeared piety' over the story of Louis XIV and Louise de la Vallière 'where little existed' (p. 67), including two scenes in a nunnery. *The Times* (5 January 1837) wrote: 'We have all but an enforcement under the crucifix, and in a temple consecrated to religious worship.' Mere 'enforcement' might have been tolerated, but not under a crucifix. Bulwer Lytton's language, though it had escaped the censor's blue pencil, was condemned by the press: 'This extract contains not only the expression and application to heaven in this play, which is shockingly irreverent' (*Monthly Review* February 1837). *The Duchess de la Vallière* survived for only eight performances (Bulwer Lytton subsequently toned it down) and its reception demonstrates that public taste could be a greater constraint than the censor upon the treatment of religion on the stage.

John Mitchell Kemble's appointment to succeed his father as Examiner of Plays in 1840 obviously owed much to family influence. Though his rakish, not to say dissolute, personality made John Mitchell Kemble an unlikely guardian of public morality, intellectually he was aware of the difficulty in maintaining venerable traditions and established creeds amongst a mass population largely motivated by self-interest. During the 1840s Kemble was preoccupied with his historical study *The Saxons in England* (1849) and the dissolution of his 1836 marriage to the daughter of a Göttingen professor. Although he remained nominally in office until his death in 1857, from 1849 his Cambridge contemporary

W. B. Donne deputised for him, becoming Examiner of Plays in his own right in 1857 (to 1874).

Peter Allen writes describing Donne's 'warm, charming, gentle personality . . . A stabilizing factor . . . for his fellow Apostles, above all his unswerving loyalty to the giddy and flamboyant Kemble, who might have tried the patience of the most devoted friend' (1978, p. 97). Like all their Cambridge circle Donne had fallen under the spell of Fanny Kemble, attending her debut as Juliet; he was also captivated by the Swedish singer Jenny Lind, as Bernard Barton's letter (20 June 1847) indicates: 'Thou wouldst be of no religion which interdicted thee from hearing Jenny Lind' (J. O. Johnson, 1905, p. 131).

A keen play-goer, Donne contributed articles on the theatre to *Fraser's Magazine*, the *Quarterly Review* and the *Westminster Review*, which were collected by John W. Parker. In *Fraser's Magazine* (December 1854) Donne articulated a judicial attitude to the theatre:

> Nor must we omit the increased religiosity of the times. Whether abstract scruples against the stage be well-founded or not, this is neither the time nor the place to inquire. But it is certain that the passions of the theatre are frequently such as a moralist would discourage; and although the actor may at times be a useful auxiliary to the preacher, yet his text and his doctrine are not necessarily in accordance with those of the pulpit . . . If it is good to be amused, it is better to be instructed. (Parker, 1858, pp. 165–6)

Donne's lengthy period of office as Examiner of Plays has been analysed by J. F. Stottler (1970) and John Russell Stephens (1970). Both Donne and his superior the Hon. S. C. B. Ponsonby gave evidence to the 1866 Select Committee appointed to Inquire into the Workings of the Acts of Parliament for Licensing and Regulating Theatres and Places of Public Entertainment. When asked 'On what special grounds has the Lord Chamberlain refused a licence for a play at any time?' Ponsonby replied: 'The object has been principally to exclude any scriptural subject, or plays in which highwaymen or immorality are exalted; and any personal or personally political questions' (*British Parliamentary Papers, Stage and Theatre 2*, 1970, p. 30). Ponsonby cited Appendix K listing the nineteen plays (out of 2,816) refused a licence between 1852 and 1865. Of these nineteen cases two were religious: *Hebrew Son* (1852) and '*Triumph of Jewish Queen* taken from Esther at first refused, afterwards altered and licensed' (1855).

In a letter to the Lord Chamberlain (30 August 1855) regarding the latter work, Donne wrote: 'I feel no doubt of the unsuitableness of its subject for theatrical representation. The story is that of Esther: several names in the Bible are retained ... with the treatment of the subject I have no fault to find; my objection lies against the employing a portion of the Bible which moreover is occasionally read in the Church service, as a dramatic theme' (British Library Add. MSS 53.703). A licence was withheld until an amended version, from which all traces of the play's biblical origins had been expunged, was submitted.

Donne was equally rigorous about oaths. G. H. Lewes in his preface, addressed to Arthur Helps, in *The Noble Heart* (1850) voiced his resentment:

The prudery of theatrical aesthetics is astonishing, and hurtful as all false pretences must be. What think you, my dear Helps, of the established conviction among 'experienced' men, that English audiences will not tolerate the name of the Deity pronounced on the stage! You may say '*Him*' and point upwards, but you may not say '*God*'. I am dull enough not to see the merits of this distinction; and moreover, I am curious to know where this prudery will stop. I write
'The heart hath but one resting place – in God.'
But I am not allowed the expression: it is 'softened' into 'Heaven'. Very well: but how long may I say 'Heaven'? – will they not force me to *soften* that into 'sky', and then again 'sky' into 'that place'?

Clearly the rules were so well known that dramatists regulated themselves, but the fact that oaths in Shakespeare's plays – which did not of course require a licence – were consistently softened or omitted suggests that the public's susceptibilities were a powerful factor as well. Formal constraints on biblical subjects continued to operate under Donne's successor E. F. S. Piggott, who in 1892 dealt summarily with Oscar Wilde's 'miracle of impudence' *Salomé* (J. R. Stephens, 1980, p. 112).

By then another source of aggravation to the theatre, the restrictions on performances during Lent, had come to an end, except for on Good Friday. In March 1837 Alfred Bunn, still smarting from officialdom's inconsistency over *The Israelites in Egypt* and *Jephtha's Vow*, wrote to the Lord Chamberlain pointing out that the convention that theatres closed on Wednesdays and Fridays during Lent, though still enforced at Covent Garden and Drury Lane, was being flouted with impunity by minor theatres (Bunn, 1840, vol. II, p. 200). The Lord Chamberlain refused any dispensation for the patent theatres and indicated that penalties would be exacted if they disregarded his ruling. On 18 February 1839, in the House of Commons, T. Duncombe presented the case for opening. He objected to these 'restrictions on the amusements of the people ... on Wednesdays and Fridays during Lent' (*Mirror of Parliament* 1839, vol. I, p. 343), but to no avail, his 70 'Ayes' being swamped by 160 'Noes'.

Duncombe returned to the attack on 28 February 1839 with the proposal: 'That it is the opinion of this House that during Lent no greater Restrictions should be passed upon theatrical entertainments within the city of Westminster than are placed upon the like amusements at the same period in every other part of the metropolis' (Nicholson, 1906, pp. 398–9). Duncombe appealed to 'the plainest principles of equal justice and common sense', pointing out that those employed in theatres in Westminster had 'one third of their income . . . stopped by these absurd and unjust regulations' (*Mirror of Parliament* 1839, vol. I, pp. 620–1). Strongest opposition came from Lord John Russell who recounted the views expressed to him by the Bishop of London – namely that 'he [the bishop] considered that out of respect to the established religion of the country, these theatrical performances should not be allowed in the city of Westminster on Wednesdays and Fridays in Lent' (p. 623). Mr J. T. Leader emphasised the point that the closure was not merely a matter of denying amusements to the public, but also 'the livelihood and subsistence of several hundreds of industrious and deserving people' (p. 626). Benjamin Disraeli, supporting the proposal, recalled: 'those mysteries and moralities which were acted by the monks. This is the only mode in which humanity has tolerated the religious observance of Lent' (p. 630). He pointed out that 'the birth of Protestantism and the drama, in England, was almost simultaneous' and that 'Lent had never been observed rigidly or completely in Protestant times' (p. 631). This time Duncombe's proposal gained approval by fifty-two votes to seventy-two, but its status was only that of a resolution, and, at Lord John Russell's instigation, the Lord Chamberlain continued to enforce the ban, which was eventually overtaken by the 1843 Theatres Act.

The complete ban on performances during Passion Week continued until the Lord Chamberlain relented in 1862. It was not without its compensations for better-paid and socially well-connected actors, such as Fanny Kemble – who recalled with evident pride 'a delightful talk with Lord John Russell' (1878, vol. I, p. 34) – looking forward to spending 'Passion Week at Sutton Park, with the Arkwrights, who have written to beg me to do so' (1882, vol. III, p. 168). For humbler members of the profession the prospect of a whole week without pay was dire. In support of a petition which resulted in the Lord Chamberlain's change of heart in 1862 Frederick Wilton submitted a list of every member of his Britannia Theatre – a total of 132 individuals – who, together with their dependants, had been denied their livelihood for a whole week by this religious observance (J. Davis, 1992, pp. 24–5). In fact, as Wilton's diaries reveal, the rescission of the Passion Week ban proved to be a mixed blessing as he recurrently records 'very bad house' for performances during that period. Evidently the public, whether from religious conviction or mere habit, were disinclined to avail themselves of their new freedom.

By the first anniversary of the opening (in 1869) of the Gaiety Theatre, John Hollingshead could boast: 'with the exception of Christmas Day, Ash Wednesday and Good Friday, this house . . . has been open every day of the year' (1895, vol. II, p. 25). The Ash Wednesday closure still rankled as Hollingshead's letter to the *Daily Telegraph* (2 March 1870) indicated: 'Tonight the refined and intellectual entertainment which I am in the habit of placing before the public is suspended by order of the Lord Chamberlain . . . I pay two hundred pounds a year in Church and Rectors' rates, and have never had a prayer offered up for the success of my entertainment.' In 1875 Hollingshead collected 491 signatories to a letter of protest to *The Times* (30 January 1875), but it was not until 1885 that officialdom relented: 'I am sorry that I have to thank a Conservative Minister for this act of common sense and justice' (1895, vol. II, p. 92).

The redoubts of religious opposition to the theatre were diverse and formidable ranging from provincial pulpits to the bishops' bench in the House of Lords. Legal sanctions on managers were reinforced by the prospect of hell-fire for individual souls: but the climate of opinion was changing, both in terms of the temporal life and the eternal: instanced in the former case by the concern for the loss of livelihood caused by Lenten restrictions, and in the latter by the rebuttal of the two-pronged assertion that the theatre was innately evil and that the after-life to which its practitioners and audiences were consigned was one of hell-fire.

CHAPTER 3

Two professions

I am the son of a clergyman . . . and I see nothing before me save
the stage or enlistment.

Cambridge graduate

On 3 March 1803 the ten-year-old William Charles Macready entered
Rugby School. For actors, provincial ones at that, to aspire to a public
school education for their son singled the Macreadys out from the generality of their profession. Macready's father, 'an ambitious, ill-tempered,
modestly talented Irishman . . . The son of a prosperous Dublin uphol-
sterer' (Downer, 1966, p. 5), was zealous in advocating the status of his
profession, though he personally achieved little to enhance it;
Macready's mother came from more genteel stock, her 'family background was composed of clergymen and surgeons and was untainted by
trade' (p. 6). Her grandfather, Revd Jonathan Birch, had been Vicar of
Bakewell in Derbyshire; two of her paternal uncles were clergymen; her
father was a surgeon (W. Archer, 1890, p. 3); and her cousin, Revd
William Birch, was a master at Rugby School. Despite the protection
afforded by Birch, Macready's first term was marked by bullying.
Though devastated by his mother's death on 3 December 1803, thereafter Macready gradually acclimatised to his school, then under the
headship of Revd Dr Inglis, whom he described as 'a pale, ascetic-
looking man, whose deportment was grave, dignified and awe-inspiring'
(Pollock, 1876, p. 9).

When asked by Dr Inglis if he had considered the theatre as a profession the young Macready replied 'I very much dislike it' and expressed
his preference for the law (p. 12). Nevertheless he and Birch's son Tom
absented themselves from Rugby to see the 'Infant Roscius' Master Betty
as Richard III in Leicester and Macready helped the 'bigger boys' in
Bucknell's House with their play-acting with 'the loan of books, and
afterwards . . . dresses' from his father (p. 11). In 1807 Inglis was suc-

ceeded by Revd John Wooll DD from Midhurst Grammar School, who, to the surprise of many, was preferred to Samuel Butler, an old-Rugbeian and headmaster of Shrewsbury School. Macready described Wooll as 'a very good-natured, amiable, pompous little man. I think of him with great regard and he was very kind to me' (p. 17); 'with Wooll's benign influence the young tragedian's light comes forth from beneath its bushel' (Rouse, 1898, p. 210). Wooll's innovations in the curriculum were such as to bring out any dramatic tendencies amongst his pupils:

Dr Wooll varied the exercises of the older boys by introducing composition of English verses; and in addition to the prizes for these and Latin verses, gave prizes for speaking as a test of the elocutionary powers of the fifth and sixth formers. Young Macready had clearly struck him as a declaimer above the average. He assigned the boy the closet scene in 'Hamlet' for public declamation. (Martin, 1889, p. 120)

Macready also took part in full-scale productions of plays. On 15 October 1807 he doubled Reginald and Motley in M. G. Lewis's *The Castle Spectre* with costumes and scenery provided by his father (Lobb, 1955, pp. 65–7). The cast also included a future Prebendary of Wells, a British Chaplain in Ceylon, a Master of the Temple and a Judge of the Supreme Court, Madras (Rouse, 1898, p. 211). Acting was useful experience for careers in the Church and the law, and as William Birch stated in the report which he sent to Macready's father in 1808, the qualities which the boy possessed would serve him well in any of these professions:

Your eldest son improves in everything and I think will make a very fine man, to whatever he turns his abilities. I cannot omit (though I don't know whether you will thank me) expressing my admiration for his wonderful talent for acting and speaking. Such a combination of fine figure, expression, countenance and propriety of action, modulation of voice and most complete power of representation I have formed an idea of, perhaps, but have never before met with; and that is the sense of everyone who has heard him. I know this rare talent may be turned to good account in the Church or at the Bar; it is valuable everywhere. Whatever is your intention I will second it, and if you determine to send him to Oxford next summer I will endeavour to prepare the way. (Toynbee, 1912, vol. II, pp. 292–3)

Ten years later Macready was still harking back to this path not taken:

My wish was to make a trial of my talents in some other profession, and the Church offered me apparently facilities for the attempt. There was little or no doubt among my old school-fellows that I could with ease take my degree at Oxford (a much more arduous ordeal then than now), and a friendly proposal to advance me the amount requisite for my residence there seemed to open the path directly for me. (Pollock, 1876, p. 117)

Circumstances had overtaken Macready's ambitions to enter Oxford and the Church. He was withdrawn from Rugby at Christmas 1808 because his father could no longer meet the fees and on 7 June 1810, in an effort to improve the family fortunes, he made his stage debut as Romeo in Birmingham. When, shortly afterwards, he appeared as Hamlet, Dr Wooll travelled to Birmingham to see him (Evers, 1939, p. 33). Whatever satisfaction Wooll may have felt in seeing his former pupil's performance, Macready himself was at best merely resigned to his calling. As J. C. Trewin observed: 'It might be very fine to act at school . . . but to devote his life to mumming . . . that was sharp physic' (1955, p. 24). Denied the opportunity to devote the qualities enumerated by Birch to a career in the Church or the law, Macready set himself the challenge of making his enforced profession worthy of him:

My experience has taught me that whilst the law, the church, the army and the navy give a man the rank of a gentleman, on the stage that designation must be obtained in society (though the law and the Court decline to recognise it) by individual bearing. In other callings the profession confers dignity on the initiated, on the stage the player must contribute respect by the exercise of his art. (Pollock, 1876, p. 20)

Frustrated though Macready was in pursuit of a profession, Rugby School imbued him with social and educational advantages which were to serve him well in his campaign to elevate the status of the theatre. Macready's diaries abound in accounts of meeting the *literati* of the day (Dickens, Thackeray, Browning, Tennyson, Bulwer Lytton, Forster, amongst others) and leading churchmen – the Archbishop of Canterbury (William Howley), Bishop Stanley of Norwich, Dean Milman whose *History of the Jews* he read, Revd J. C. M. Bellew and Revd James White, whom he encouraged to write plays. In February 1838 Macready was elected to that bastion of the establishment the Athenaeum Club. As William Archer noted: 'Latin he seems to have read fluently, and he knew enough Greek to astonish a dinner-party with a quotation from Homer' (1890, p. 11). Nevertheless Macready could not completely throw off the stigma of his profession as this vignette by Jane Welsh Carlyle indicates:

To see a man, who is exhibiting himself every night on a stage, blushing like a young girl in a private room is a beautiful phenomenon for me. His [Macready's] wife whispered into my ear, as we sat on the sofa together, 'Do you know poor William is in a perfect agony at having been brought here in that great coat? It is a stage great-coat, but was only worn by him twice, the piece it was made for did not succeed, but it was such an expensive coat, I would not let him give it away; and doesn't he look well in it?' I wish Jeannie had seen him in the coat – magnificent for neck and sleeves, and such frogs on the front. He did look well, but so heartily ashamed of himself. (Froude, 1883, vol. i, p. 189)

If Thomas Carlyle witnessed this sight it would not have been lost on the author of *Sartor Resartus*.

Within the privacy of his own home Macready was the model of a Victorian *paterfamilias*. He presided over family prayers, even wrote them in Latin: 'Heard my dear babes their prayers and hymns' (Pollock, 1876, p. 415). He maintained 'a well-stocked library containing Chambers's *Vestiges of the Natural History of Creation* and Mantell's *Wonders of Geology*; his guest book recorded Lyall, Farraday and Darwin' (Downer, 1966, p. 354). Conversant therefore with current scientific thought Macready wrestled to affirm his belief in providence, not least during recurrent bereavements. Macready concluded his diary for 1835 as follows: 'Let me offer up prayer to God Almighty, Who thus far has protected me and mine, to continue His gracious blessings on the dear heads of my beloved family and to grant me health and energy to make them worthy disciples of Jesus Christ, and happy denizens of this our mortal state' (Pollock, 1876, p. 362).

Macready was an early member of the Garrick Club 'founded in 1831 by a dilettante writer and art collector named Francis Mills, with the Duke of Sussex as Patron' (Lejeune, 1984, p. 121). Initially the Garrick occupied former hotel premises at 35 King Street, Covent Garden, moving into its own Italianate edifice (designed by Frederick Marrable) in 1864. Mills had established the Garrick Club 'with the design of constituting a society in which actors and men of education and refinement might meet on equal and independent terms' (Revd D. H. Barham, 1880, p. 138). Not surprisingly the likes of Charles Kemble and Sheridan Knowles were members, though Alfred Bunn dismissed the Garrick as 'a sort of Junior Law Club' (1840, vol. i, p. 94). In his diary entry for 20 May 1834 Macready recorded: 'Called at Garrick Club, where I looked at newspapers and dined . . . Got into conversation with Mr. Barham, who came out with me and walked to Drury Lane' (Pollock, 1876, p. 318).

Barham was Revd R. H. Barham, a minor canon of St Paul's and the author of *The Ingoldsby Legends*. Though a founder-member, Barham, according to Guy Boas, 'expressed the wish that as he was in Holy Orders his name should not be inscribed on the Club's printed lists' (1948, p. 15). In fact the Roll of Members (Garrick Club library) records a dozen clergymen joining in the 1830s, and a further half-dozen in the 1840s. Barham apart, none of these members was of note, but they constituted a peak in clerical membership, which suggests that there was a conscious effort to recruit churchmen in these early days. Despite his initial reticence about his membership of the Garrick, Barham was indiscreet in his *The Garrick Club: Notices of One Hundred and Thirty-Five of its Former Members*, not published until 1896, describing John Forster as 'A low scribbler, without an atom of talent and totally unused to the society of gentlemen.'

An actor whose talents were frequently questioned, but who was used to the society of gentlemen, was Charles Kean who attended Eton between 1824 and 1827. There his contemporaries included William Gladstone, Arthur Hallam and William Bouverie Pusey. Two masters 'Benjamin Heath Drury and Henry Hartopp Knapp', both 'enthusiastic admirers of the drama, would take favoured boys to the theatre in London' (Lyte, 1911, p. 400). In his *Reminiscences of Eton* Revd C. Allix Wilkinson, sometime chaplain to the King of Hanover, devoted a whole chapter to acting, recalling rehearsals in college and performances of 'a regular theatre with permanent scenery at Barney Levi's large room about half-way up town, conducted by a joint "troupe" of collegers and oppidans' (1888, p. 196).

In his diaries William Gladstone chronicled not only his voracious reading of plays (the Greek dramatists, Shakespeare, Jonson, Massinger and Otway), but also 'the rehearsal of a play at my Dame's, all the fellows, save self and three above me, actors. They have provided themselves with swords and shields – have tin helmets and some Breastplates – dresses principally made by themselves – scenes of paper, which have been made and painted' (3 February 1826; Foot, 1968, p. 32). On 8 February Gladstone recorded 'long Church in the morning . . . Present at the representation of Lodoiska by eight of my Dame's fellows – first night of acting' (p. 33). The reason for the 'long Church' was that 8 February was Ash Wednesday though the fact that public theatre performances were prohibited on that day obviously did not constrain the Eton thespians.

Gladstone had confined his role in Eton dramatics to that of observer. In vacations he occasionally attended London theatres, seeing Charles Kemble as Hamlet on 28 August 1827 and as Falstaff on 3 December that year; but on 29 December 1832 Gladstone confided in his diary:

Yet I still do think that mirth may be encouraged, provided it have a purpose higher than itself: it may be a humble minister to recruit that strength which is necessary to sustain exertion at all, but which cannot sustain it without remission. Nor do I now think myself warranted in withdrawing from the practices of my fellow men. Except when they really *involve* the encouragement of sin: in which class I do certainly rank races and theatre. But I have incurred danger by too lax a creed. (p. 595)

Though Gladstone rejected the theatre, he had already, as a great orator in the making, absorbed many precepts and practices founded on the common ground between acting, preaching and public speaking. Maxwell Lyte describes Revd John Keate DD, headmaster of Eton 1809–34, as 'a great master of oratory' (1911, p. 398); and M. R. D. Foot affirms that Gladstone learnt the art of oratory from Keate and the prescribed textbooks of the day. Of textbooks on rhetoric and oratory there was no shortage in the early nineteenth century: Hugh Blair's *Lectures on Rhetoric* (1783); James Walker's *The Melody of Speaking Delineated* (1787), *The Academic Speaker* (1801) and *A Rhetorical Grammar* (1816); Richard Whateley's *Elements of Rhetoric* (1828); and Revd Edward Irving's *For the Oracles of God, Four Orations* (1823) which, together with Cardinal Maury's *Essai sur l'Eloquence de la Chaire*, received a lengthy review by Milman in the *Quarterly Review* (29 July 1823, pp. 283–313).

Educated at Oriel College, Oxford, Richard Whateley was a close friend of John Keble and, until their estrangement over Roman Catholic emancipation, of J. H. Newman, who assisted him with *Elements of Logic* (1826). A liberal churchman, interesting himself in political economy and education, Whateley served a lengthy, if generally undistinguished, archiepiscopate as Archbishop of Dublin (1831–63). In *Elements of Rhetoric* Whateley ranged across Sheridan's *Lectures on the Art of Reading*, Molière and Shakespeare, advocating natural delivery distinctly articulated: 'yet a natural voice and delivery, provided it be clear, though it be less laboured, and may even seem low, will be distinctly heard at a much greater distance' (Golden and Corbett, 1968, p. 369).

Whateley advocated different techniques for preaching, leading public prayers and reading from the Bible. Sermons were personal expressions of the preacher's most earnest thoughts and should therefore come straight from the heart; 'prayer, thanksgiving and the like, even when avowedly not of our own composition, should be delivered as (what in truth they ought to be) the genuine sentiments of our own minds at the moment of utterance' (p. 387); but

It is not, indeed, desirable, that in reading the Bible for example, or anything which is not intended to appear as his composition, he should deliver what are, avowedly, another's sentiments, in the same style, as if they were such as arose in his own mind; but it is desirable that he should deliver them as if he were *report-*

ing another's sentiments, which were both fully understood, and felt in all their force by the reporter; and the only way to do this effectually – with such modulations of voice, etc. as are suitable to each word and passage – is to fix his mind earnestly on the meaning, and leave nature and habit to suggest the utterance. (p. 384)

Thus with readings from the Bible the crucial distinction between the preacher (who remained himself) and the reader/actor (who assumed another identity) was made.

In *The Melody of Speaking Delineated* James Walker placed passages from Shakespeare, such as John of Gaunt's 'sceptred isle' speech in *Richard II* (1787, pp. 52–3), on facing pages, that on the left hand being marked for pauses and emphasis, with additional directions for tone (simple, solemn, plaintive, etc.). In *The Academic Speaker* thirty-eight out of eighty-four examples of oratory were from Shakespeare's plays. Walker conceded that 'to waive every objection from prudence to morality, it may be confidently affirmed, that the acting of a play is not so conducive to improvement in elocution as the speaking of single speeches . . . In short it is speaking rather than acting that schoolboys should be taught' (1801, pp. xi–xii). Nevertheless at Eton, as at Rugby, the official teaching of oratory was supplemented by play-acting, which combined to give pupils destined for a variety of professions an appreciation of, and aptitude for, the dramatic.

The benefits to the acting profession of Macready's and Kean's attendance at leading public schools were immense. When Queen Victoria, at Prince Albert's instigation, established the Windsor Theatricals 'in an attempt', as she wrote to the King of Prussia on 6 January 1849, 'to revive and elevate the English drama which has greatly deteriorated through lack of support by Society' (Rowell, 1978, p. 47), there was an old Etonian at hand to take charge – Charles Kean. Over eleven seasons fifty performances were given, those in 1858 being part of the celebrations of the Princess Royal's marriage to Frederick William of Prussia. The most apt performance was that of *Richard II* in St George's Hall on 5 February 1857. A huge success at the Princess's Theatre in Oxford Street, Kean's painstakingly accurate costumes, heraldry and scenery accorded with the prevailing fascination with the Middle Ages. Kean modelled his appearance as Richard II on the so-called 'Jerusalem Chamber' portrait of the king which had not been publicly displayed since 1775 until Dean Buckland and the chapter of Westminster Abbey consented to its inclusion in the Art Treasures of the United Kingdom Exhibition in Manchester in 1857. There the picture 'partly it may be from its size, partly the subject, and most of all, from its Gothic quaintness, attracted universal attention' (Scharf, 1867, p. xxxiv; see also Foulkes, 1986b, pp. 44–5). Even this level of identification between a church treasure and the stage must have afforded some reassurance to the clerical members of the Court, including the Dean of Windsor, who joined the Supreme Head of the Established Church to witness the Windsor Theatricals. Less privileged clergymen attended the Princess's Theatre, one at least – Revd James Cardew – soliciting free admission (Folger Shakespeare Library y. c. 460 (1)) .

Encouraged by royal patronage actors sought other symbols of professional status. Dulwich College ('God's gift'), founded and sustained by the rich legacy of actor Edward Alleyn combined a prestigious educational establishment with alms-houses for the elderly. The college's extensive archives had been explored by John Payne Collier – *The Memoirs of Edward Alleyn – Founder of Dulwich College* (1841) and *The Alleyn Papers* (1843) (Ganzel, 1982) – but it was the college's material assets of which actors wished to avail themselves. Charles Dickens lent his support to a public meeting on 13 March 1856 (Fielding, 1960, pp. 215–20). The theatre's case was that Alleyn's endowment had been for the benefit of districts in which significant numbers of actors then resided. The theatres had migrated, but it was argued that in keeping with the spirit of Alleyn's bequest 'one fourth of the benefits may be extended to poor players of both sexes, and also to the children of poor players' (*Era* 16 March 1856). The 'Act of 1857 created a revolution at Dulwich educationally' (*Era Almanack*, 1880, p. 68), but no provision was made for actors and their children.

The campaign to enfranchise members of Alleyn's profession at Dulwich having foundered, attention was turned to the founding of the Royal Dramatic College, initially to provide alms-houses to which a school for actors' children was to be added later. At a packed meeting at the Princess's Theatre on 21 July 1858 Charles Kean announced the munificent gift of a five-acre site in Buckinghamshire by 'A kind and benevolent gentleman, Mr. HENRY DODD' (*Era* 25 July 1858), the original for Dickens's 'Golden Dustman', Nicodemus Boffin, in *Our Mutual Friend*. Negotiations with Dodd faltered and an alternative location at Maybury, near Woking, was secured from the London Necropolis Company. The profession's attention had already been attracted by the more obvious facilities provided by the London Necropolis Company and in June 1858 *Era* reported the inauguration of the burial ground of the Dramatic, Equestrian and Musical Sick Fund:

The origination and completion of this beautiful place of rest belongs in entirety to the indefatigability of the Secretary of the Association, Mr. J. W. Anson. Before this was obtained a parish funeral or, cast among strangers, too frequently in from 6–16 inches of water was the fate of many . . . Having made a survey of all the cemeteries around London the many advantages of the 'Necropolis' at once presented themselves – but how to obtain such a boon? He published after much labour and research an almanac, the profits of which laid the foundations of the present 'arts' repose. It has been planted at a cost of £50 . . . [and is] large enough to receive 2,000 bodies allowing a space of 9 ft by 4 ft never to be opened again. It is beautifully situated in an amphitheatre of hills. (13 June 1858)

The ceremony was attended by Revd Horace Roberts, Revd R. Churchill, minister of the Necropolis, and leading actors including Benjamin Webster.

Having secured for its deceased the dignity which they had so often been denied, the profession raised funds to build the College. On 9 June 1860 Prince Albert journeyed to Woking to lay the foundation stone of the central hall. The prince's speech articulated and endorsed the highest aspirations of the profession:

And the importance cannot be overrated by endeavouring to combine with such amusement that instruction and mental improvement which every well-regulated mind must derive from following the actor in his attempt to give life and reality to the noble conceptions of the dramatist and poet, or to inculcate some high moral lesson, in interesting our best feelings and sympathies in the love of virtue and detestation of vice. *(Era* 7 June 1860)

The chaplain (Revd Mr Sumner, son of the Bishop of Winchester) read the prayers after which the stone was lowered into place. The Prince of Wales succeeded his late father as patron of the Royal Dramatic College and opened the central hall on 5 June 1865 (Foulkes, 1985, p. 79).

With the death of Prince Albert the Windsor Theatricals were discontinued. Mrs Kean imprudently solicited a knighthood for her husband – to no avail, though his election as FSA was recognition of his scholarly credentials and reassured fellow antiquarians and others that a visit to the theatre was educational. An indication of the changing attitude towards the theatre and the value of influential social connections was the testimonial given to Charles Kean at St James's Hall in March 1862. Kean's Eton school-fellows had collected £2,000 for a set of nine pieces of oxidised silver, which were displayed like communion plate on an altar (illustration 2). The centre-piece was a vase depicting Charles and Ellen Kean in several of their most successful Shakespearean roles, inscribed 'as a tribute to a Great Actor, and in recognition of his un-

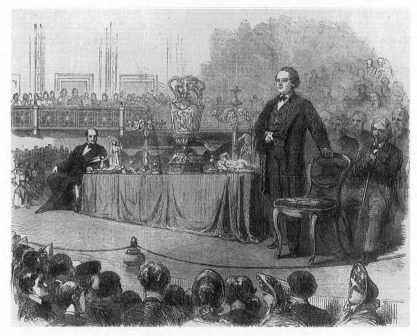

2. Presentation to Charles Kean at St James's Hall

remitting efforts to improve the tone and elevate the character of the British stage'. William Gladstone presided and spoke of the theatre in terms which reversed his hostile judgement of thirty years earlier:

Mr. Gladstone considered it was no trifling matter to labour in the elevation both in the intellectual and moral tone of the drama, which, he said, could not be fairly treated as among the light amusements of the world. The drama, he continued, had been characteristic of the whole history of man, and we could not assign a secondary place to it in this country, which had given birth to by far the greatest dramatist in the world. The drama belongs to no particular age, to no particular country, to no particular race, to no particular form of religion. Religion herself has not always disdained to find in it a direct handmaid for the attainment of her purpose. (*Illustrated London News* 29 March 1862)

Queen Victoria, Prince Albert and William Gladstone constituted a formidable trinity of support for the theatre. The warmth of the letter which Charles Kean received from his former school-fellow C. J. Abraham, then Bishop of Wellington, during his visit to New Zealand in 1863, further reflects the breaking-down of anti-theatrical prejudice:

My dear Kean,

I do not like to think of you being in our Hemisphere without writing a line to say how pleased I should be to see you and Mrs Kean, if you thought of running down before your return to England.

You will find an Eton bishop wherever you go through New Zealand. You probably remember Edmund Hobhouse one of Chapman's pupils. He is at Nelson. Then I need not tell you that George Selwyn is in Auckland. Harper, the Conduct is at Christchurch. Old Judge Pattison's son is Bishop of Melanesia but lives during the summer in Auckland. (Hardwick, 1954, p. 90)

On the voyage to the Antipodes aboard the *Champion of the Seas* Kean acted as the ship's Protestant chaplain (p. 74). Of the 597 pupils listed in the Eton College Election of 1826 (Staplyton, 1863, pp. 122–33), 127 took holy orders, but by the 1850s the sons of the rectory were considering the theatre as an alternative profession as this letter to Charles Kean reveals:

I am the son of a clergyman, and lately a member of the University of Cambridge. My father has left me to work my own way in the world; – in fact to live by my wits, and I see nothing before me save the stage or enlistment, as my education fits me for nothing else. I need not say I should prefer the former, and could you give me any employment, however small the emolument, and in the humblest capacity, I should be much obliged. In short, if there is any post in your establishment in which a gentleman, and, if I may so call myself, a scholar, may be of use to you, I shall rejoice to fill it, and do my best to merit your approval. (J. W. Cole, 1859, vol. II, p. 20)

Kean's biographer J. W. Cole commented that: 'In every scientific or intellectual profession, the stage excepted, some rudimentary acquirement is deemed necessary. There must be instruction, preparatory discipline, examination, a qualifying certificate, a degree or a diploma' (p. 21). By 1870 competitive entry, usually by examination, had become the rule for the law, the Church, medicine, engineering, the Civil and military services. Recruits, having satisfied standard entry requirements, became members of a recognised professional body. The problem for the theatre, shared by other arts, was that entry could not be formally regulated and within its ranks were individuals of varying degrees of talent, competence and status. As W. J. Reader puts it: 'The "artistic" group gave social commentators grave trouble. It was evident that some actors, some artists, some authors were educated, cultured men and women, even well-known and sought after in the best society. It was equally well-known that the majority were not' (1966, p. 148).

This state of affairs inevitably placed far greater responsibility upon the leaders of the stage than upon their counterparts in other profes-

Table 3.1

	Numbers of		Percentage increase	
	actors	Church of England clergy	actors	clergy
1841	1,463	14,613		
1851	2,041	17,463	39.51	21
1861	2,202	19,336	7.89	9
1871	3,588	20,824	62.94	8
1881	4,565	21,786	27.23	5
1891	7,321	24,374	60.37	12
1901	12,487	25,363	70.56	4
1911	18,247	24,968	46.13	−1
Notes:	(T. C. Davis, 1991, p. 10),	(Haigh, 1984, p. 3),	(T. C. Davis, 1991, p. 10),	(Reader, 1966, p. 208, and Black, 1973, pp. 46–69)

sions. Anyone who became a lawyer or a doctor had achieved defined standards and all were accorded a basic level of professional status; in the theatre each actor had to prove his own worth. The theatre sought to compensate for its lack of credentials by invoking what Michael Baker has described as 'a cultural judgement, a view that art somehow embodied certain life-enhancing human values which were felt to be threatened by the advance of modern industrial society' (1979, p. 22). This perception of the theatre, together with its undoubted increasing commercial strength, helped to achieve professional status for its members in the 1861 census.

The census returns for England and Wales between 1841 and 1911 show a massive expansion in the number of actors, a percentage increase greatly in excess of that of the population (15,914,000 in 1841 to 36,070,000 in 1911) as a whole and that of Church of England clergymen during the period (see Table 3.1).

Two comments immediately need to be made: the returns for actors include men *and* women; such a great increase in the number of actors reflects more recruits from families outside the profession (see Baker, 1979, pp. 200–20). Alan Haigh has analysed the educational and family backgrounds of ordinands: 'in 1827–8 the proportion [of ordinands from universities] was 91 per cent' (1984, p. 31). Between 1834 and 1843 ordinands accounted for 76.2% of Oxford graduates and 70.2% of Cambridge graduates, these figures falling to 50.7% and 51.5% respectively in 1864–73 (p. 30). The percentage of ordinands with clerical fathers held steady between 1841 and 1843 (21%) and 1871 and 1873 (23.8%) (p. 36). In the first half of the nineteenth century the Church was in the privileged position of having the two ancient universities devoted primarily to the preparation of its initiates. The Royal Commission, (started in 1850), the Oxford University Act (1854), the Cambridge University Act (1856), the introduction of new triposes at Cambridge (1851) and the science and history schools at Oxford (1853), and the Universities Test Act (which swept away religious tests save for degrees in divinity) all combined to loosen the ties between the Church and the universities.

These developments took place at a time when the Church was adjusting to huge population shifts to urban centres, the proportion of the population in towns increasing from 48.3% in 1841 to 70.2% in 1881 (Best, 1989, p. 24). In 1827 there were 10,553 benefices, by 1893 there were 14,018 (Brown, 1953, pp. 15 and 188). A vast programme of church building was undertaken, principally in urban areas, 667 between 1831 and 1841, and 1,197 between 1841 and 1851, most of them so-called 'Commissioners' churches' erected with the help of government money (Brown, 1953, p. 237). In Manchester, the population increased from 70,000 at the beginning of the century to 300,000 by the middle (Messenger, 1986, pp. 8–9 and 115, and Briggs, 1968, p. 89). The diocese of Manchester, created in 1847, was even larger (population 1,123,548 in 1847); the first bishop, Henry Prince Lee (1847–69), consecrated 130 churches at a cost of £542,000 and by 1876 his successor, James Fraser, had consecrated a further 59 at a cost of £480,000 (Bishop J. Fraser, 1876, p. 9). In eleven years Fraser confirmed 117,804 people (44,050 men and 73,754 women) (Fraser, 1880, p. 7).

By 1880 Bishop Fraser had decided on a change of emphasis to employing 'one hundred additional clergymen, with stipends of £200 a year each' (p. 25). Fraser's own annual stipend was £4,200 of which he said: 'I spend a third, save a third, give a third' (Diggle, 1889, p. 506). Such philanthropy and prudence did not mitigate the disparity between the bishop's income and that of most of his clergymen. Fraser left over £70,000. The Ecclesiastical Revenues Commission of 1832 and the Ecclesiastical Commission of 1835 had attacked the most flagrant abuses of pluralities, sinecures and episcopal revenues, but in 1893 only 289 benefices (out of 14,018) carried incomes of over £700 (Brown, 1953, p. 188). Actors' incomes had always been widely divergent. When his son was at Cambridge, Charles Kemble's income was 'barely eight hundred a year' of which nearly £300 was needed for John Mitchell's university expenses (Kemble, 1878, vol. I, p. 200); Alfred Bunn complained of Macready receiving 'the outrageous sum of £25 per night' (Bunn, 1840, vol. I, p. 66); and when Ellen Terry joined Irving at the Lyceum in 1878 'Terms were then settled at forty guineas a week and a half clear benefit' (Manvell, 1968, p. 108). In the 1870s Adelaide Neilson, who married a clergyman's son, was said to earn £400 a week at Drury Lane and £700 in America (Scott, 1899, vol. II, p. 229). Lesser members of the profession received only a fraction of such sums but, as the century advanced, levels of remuneration and security (with long runs and touring) improved significantly.

Material gain was not of course a proper motive for a man considering holy orders, but the uncertain prospects of preferment no doubt weighed in his decision. Whether a clergyman was to achieve the bench of bishops or remain the perpetual incumbent of a country living, his calling required certain qualifications. The increasing difficulty of securing ordinands of sufficient calibre was on Bishop Fraser's mind when he addressed his Diocesan Conference in October 1883:

A clergyman who is in urgent want of a curate hears of a likely young man, takes him up and sends him to the bishop, who finds he has only been considering the subject of Christianity from a teacher's point of view for three months perhaps, and is lamentably ignorant of his Bible; he has read very little theology, but he passes the low standards with which we are obliged to content ourselves because of the very urgency and pressure of the clergy, and he goes to the parish and begins to preach. (Diggle, 1889, p. 223)

Twenty years earlier Dr Manning, who had been received into the Roman Catholic fold in 1851, reported a letter from Revd Arthur Stanley to Archibald Tait, then Bishop of London:

The intelligent, thoughtful, highly-educated young men, who twenty or thirty years ago were to be found in every ordination are gradually withheld from the service of the Church, and from the profession to which their tastes, their characters and gifts best fit them. For this great calamity, the greatest that threatens the permanence and usefulness of the Church of England, there are, no doubt, many causes at work. (Manning, 1865, vol. I, p. 42)

Stanley cited 'nineteen young men, within the acquaintance of a single individual, who were within the last few years known to have gone to Cambridge with the intention of becoming clergymen, every one has since relinquished this intention' (p. 43).

The rigour with which Frederick Temple, as Archbishop of Canterbury and in his previous episcopates, interviewed candidates for ordination was such as to deter any waverers. One such candidate was required to read 1 Corinthians 15. 35 first in English, then in Greek, being 'reduced to a proper state of humility' as Temple demonstrated that the Greek text gave a clear indication of the correct pronunciation – 'the emphasis on the personal pronoun'. The candidate, a Cambridge graduate though not in theology, was required to pass the Preliminary examination – 'IF YOU CAN' (Sandford, 1906, pp. 419–21).

Alongside such exigent standards for biblical knowledge was the absence of theological rigour which disillusioned F. C. Burnand when he embarked on ordination in the Church of England. After Eton, where his tutor Revd Gifford Cookesley was a theatre enthusiast and took his pupils to performances in Windsor, Burnand attended Cambridge University where in 1855 he was instrumental in founding the Cambridge Amateur Dramatic Club (ADC). He proceeded to the Anglican seminary at Cuddesdon, where he was received by the vice-principal Canon Liddon. He found Cuddesdon engulfed by 'trimming' on theological matters and 'a kind of Ritualistic epidemic' (1904, vol. 1, p. 308). Disenchanted with Cuddesdon, Burnand wrote to Manning who 'without any waste of words, simply answered my questions', on matters about which his former tutors had prevaricated. Burnand visited the cloaked Manning – 'his face hidden by a broad-rimmed, low-crowned hat' (p. 327) in his Gothic chamber, illuminated by a single gas-light. Although Manning placed Burnand at his ease and resolved many of his doubts and difficulties, the young man eventually decided that his future lay, not in the Church, but in the theatre: '"My dear boy", he interrupted, with a somewhat impatient sniff, "you forget what a 'voca-tion' means. When *we* speak of 'a vocation,' we mean a vocation for the priesthood."' (vol. 1, p. 347).

The fact that well-to-do young men, some from clerical families, some even considering ordination, were increasingly turning to the stage as a profession, a calling, a vocation even, reflected the theatre's success in elevating its status during the mid nineteenth century. The leadership of Macready and Kean was crucial, as T. H. S. Escott recognised:

From the personal life, character and wide social acceptance both of Macready first and of Charles Kean afterwards, the English drama directly as well as indi-rectly was a gainer. In those days, the social fusion was not nearly so complete as it has since become; but Macready and the younger Kean had both been popular in their school-days. In after life Rugby and Eton respectively rallied round them. (Escott, 1897, p. 211)

CHAPTER 4

Clerical attitudes

a Ballet of Bishops with their aprons properly licensed by the
LORD CHAMBERLAIN

Punch

Performed dramatists Milman and Maturin; aspiring dramatists Trench
and Sterling; headmasters Wooll at Rugby and Keate at Eton; Barham
and other clerical members of the Garrick Club; the admiration of F. D.
Maurice *et alia* for Fanny Kemble; 'Greek play bishops' such as
Blomfield; scholars of the theatre such as Revd John Genest (*Some Account
of the English Stage*, 1832) – the first three decades of the nineteenth
century provided numerous and diverse examples of links between the
Church and the stage. What was lacking, however, was any strand of
religious thought which was conducive to a more favourable attitude
towards the theatre. In their different ways, not always consciously, the
main movements of the Victorian Church – the Oxford Tractarians, the
Christian Socialists, the Broad Church and Latitudinarians – remedied
this deficiency.

When Revd John Keble delivered his influential sermon on 'National
Apostacy' before the Judges of Assize in St Mary's Church, Oxford, on
14 July 1833, he was also Professor of Poetry, a post in which he succeeded Milman in 1831 and which he held until 1841, by which time all
ninety of the *Tracts for the Times* had been published and sent shock waves
not only through the Established Church, but through the nation as a
whole. Keble's lectures as Professor of Poetry were heavily influenced by
Romanticism and as Geoffrey Rowell has said 'in Keble's hands . . . the
theological doctrine [of analogy] became closely linked with a poetic
theory' (1983, p. 26). Keble saw poetry lending religion her wealth of
symbols and similes as means of expressing the mystery of God:

Those who, from their very heart, either burst into poetry, or seek the Deity in
prayer, must needs ever cherish with their whole spirit the vision of something

more beautiful, greater and more lovable, than all that mortal eye can see. Thus the very practice and cultivation of Poetry will be found to possess, in some sort, the power of guiding and composing the mind to worship and prayer. (Francis, 1912, vol. II, pp. 482–3)

In place of the rationalist theology of William Paley, whose *A View of the Evidences of Christianity* still held its place on the Cambridge syllabus much to the indignation of John Mitchell Kemble and his contemporaries, Keble proclaimed that faith drew upon humility, acceptance and imagination. Far from his creations being dismissed as 'thrice removed . . . from the truth' as in the Platonic concept of Forms, the artist, the poet in particular, could through the power of his imagination enhance and deepen his fellow man's awareness of his spiritual and temporal existence. In Hilary Fraser's words, John Keble's signal achievement was to establish 'the analogues between religious experience and cultural imagination' (1986, p. 24).

In 'Sacred poetry' (1825), a review of *The Star in the East with other Poems* by Josiah Conder, Keble wrote of the two alternatives facing those wishing 'to do good by the poetical talent, which they may happen to possess' – either 'they must veil, as it were, the sacredness of the subject . . . or else, directly avowing that their subject as well as purpose is devotion, they must be content with a smaller number of readers; a disadvantage, however, compensated for by the fairer chance of doing good to each' (E. D. Jones, 1956, pp. 178–9).

Keble's *The Christian Year*, a series of meditative poems drawn from the lessons for each Sunday and Holy-day in the Anglican calendar, was published anonymously in 1827. There could be no doubt that its subject and purpose were devotion: '*The Christian Year* is packed full of thought, some of it obscure but all of it interesting. A mass of knowledge lies behind the book, and the reader would have to be extremely well-read in the Greek dramatists, especially Aeschylus, the Early Fathers, the Caroline Divines, to say nothing of knowing the Bible practically by heart' (Battiscombe, 1963, p. 105). Theologically *The Christian Year* is suffused with 'the doctrine of the Atonement . . . dear to the writer' (Lock, 1893, p. 69).

Though Keble was resigned to 'a smaller number of readers' for such an avowedly devotional work, *The Christian Year* enjoyed considerable popularity, running to 108,000 copies in 43 editions over 26 years (H. Morley, 1890, p. 406). Such widespread dissemination was in keeping with Keble's belief in the all-pervasiveness of devotion: 'How can the topics of devotion be few, when we are taught to make every part of life, every scene in nature, an occasion – in other words, a topic – of devotion?' (Jones, 1956, p. 173) In his poem for Palm Sunday Keble draws poetry and other kindred arts into celebratory worship:

Ye whose hearts are beating high
With the pulse of Poesy,
Heirs of more than royal race,
Framed by Heaven's peculiar grace,
God's own work to do on earth
(If the word be not too bold,)
Giving virtue a new birth
And a life that ne'er grows old –

Sovereign masters of all hearts!
Know ye, who hath set your parts?
He who gave you breath to sing,
By whose strength ye sweep the string,
He had chosen you, to lead
His Hosannas here below; –
Mount and claim your glorious meed;
Linger not with sin and woe . . .

Lord, by every minstrel tongue
Be thy praise so duly sung,
That thine angels' harps may ne'er
Fail to find fit echoing here:
We the while, of meaner births
Who in that divinest spell
Dare not hope to join on earth,
Give us grace to listen well.

But should thankless silence seal
Lips, that might half Heaven reveal;
Should bards in idol-hymns profane
The sacred soul-enthralling strain
(As in this bad world below
Noblest things find vilest using,)
Then, thy power and mercy show,
In vile things noble breath infusing

Then waken into sound divine
The very pavement of thy shrine,
Till we, like Heaven's star-sprinkled floor,
Faintly give back what we adore:
Childlike though the voices be,
And untunable the parts,
Thou wilt own the minstrelsy,
If it flow from childlike hearts.   (Morley, 1890, p. 407)

3. Charles Kingsley, John Henry Newman, Frederick Denison Maurice
and Arthur Penrhyn Stanley

Poets, minstrels, bards – all had their part to play in the joyous worship of
their Creator and 'noble breath' could be found 'infusing' even 'vile
things'. Two years after the publication of *The Christian Year* Keble's disciple John Henry Newman discoursed on 'Poetry with reference to
Aristotle's Poetics' in a review of a recent volume on *The Theatre of the
Greeks; or the History, Literature, and Criticism of the Grecian Drama. With an original Treatise on the Principal Tragic and Comic Metres*. He began by analysing
Aristotle's *Poetics*, which accord primacy to the plot, though 'it is not in
the plot, but in the characters, sentiments, and diction, that the actual
merit and poetry of the composition is placed' (E. D. Jones, 1956, p. 193).

Newman stated that 'Fidelity is the primary merit of biography and history, the essence of poetry is fiction.' Far from decrying fiction as a form of deceit Newman saw it as a means of shuffling off 'the confused luxuriance of real nature' by delineating 'that perfection which the imagination suggests' (p. 199):

Hence, while it [poetry] recreates the imagination by the superhuman loveliness of its views, it provides a solace for the mind broken by the disappointments and sufferings of actual life; and becomes, moreover, the utterance of the inward emotions of a right moral feeling, seeking a purity and truth which this world will not give . . .

It follows that the poetical mind is one full of the eternal forms of beauty and perfection . . . it feels a natural sympathy with everything great and splendid in the physical and moral world. (pp. 199–200)

Having made such elevated claims for poetry, Newman proceeded to 'show the applicability of the doctrine to the various departments of poetical composition' and adopted an inclusive policy: 'writers forfeit the name of poet who fail at times to answer to our requisitions, but . . . they are poets only so far forth and inasmuch as they do answer to them'. Thus the vulgarities of the grave-diggers in *Hamlet* though 'in themselves unworthy . . . the wantonness of exuberant genius . . . contain much *incidental* poetry' (pp. 200–1). Newman did not consider that the moral force of poetry was confined to the display of 'virtuous and religious feeling' (p. 211); 'Nor does it exclude the introduction of imperfect or odious characters. The original conception of a weak or guilty mind may have its intrinsic beauty' (p. 205), citing Richard III, Iago and Lady Macbeth as examples. Like Coleridge in his review of Maturin's *Bertram* Newman rejected simplistic moralising in favour of a more oblique and comprehensive approach:

With Christians a poetical view of things is a duty – we are bid to colour all things with lives of faith, to see a divine meaning in every event, and a superhuman tendency. Even our friends around are invested with unearthly brightness – no longer imperfect men, but beings taken in to divine favour stamped with His seal, and in training for future happiness. (pp. 212–13)

To those 'imperfect men' who passed their working lives in the theatre there was encouragement to be found in the notion of a 'divine meaning in every event'.

Not that the prospect held out by Newman and his fellow Tractarians in *Tracts for the Times* (6 vols., 1834–41) was an easy one. The Oxford Movement advanced a 'new Toryism . . . as well as a new Sacerdotalism' (Tulloch, 1885, p. 88) to counteract the advance of liberalism in Church and state. Tract 1, issued together with tracts 2 and 3 on 9 September 1833, 'Respectfully Addressed to the Clergy', called upon the Church to restore its historic offices, rather than curry popularity:

Is it not our office to oppose the world, can we then allow ourselves to court it, to preach smooth things and prophesy deceits, to make the way of life easy to the rich and indolent, and to bribe the humbler classes by excitements and strong and intoxicating doctrines? Surely it must not be so; and the question recurs, on what are we to rest our authority, when the State deserts us? (1834, p. 2)

The answer was the Apostolic Succession: 'that warrant which makes us *exclusively*, for God's AMBASSADORS'. Presbyterians, Roman Catholics and 'persons from other countries' were not excluded from salvation, but membership of the Church carried with it obligations: baptism (Pusey's tracts 67, 68 and 69), confirmation, 'three communions a year' (no. 26) and of the Church's burial rites: 'But it will be said, that, at least we ought not to read the service over the flagrantly wicked; over those, who are a scandal to religion . . . I agree with it entirely' (no. 3). The practice of excommunication was to be revived (no. 3), 'not as a punishment only, but as a remedy' (no. 37). Actors, of course, were no strangers to the threat of excommunication, but in the Tractarian scheme they were not imperilled *de facto* as a profession, but on the same basis as other individuals who were in default of their Christian duty.

The tracts addressing ritual and liturgy invoked practices with a strong theatrical element in them. Tract 63 dealt with 'The antiquity of existing liturgies' and tract 88, 'The Greek devotions of Bishop Andrews', provided a virtual manual of gesture to accompany particular prayers: 'sinking the head in shame', 'smiting the breast' and 'raising the eyes and head', etc. Tract 87, 'On eloquent preaching and delivery' challenged 'the modern system . . . attaching so great a value to preaching to disparage prayer and sacraments in comparison'. The Lord's was the House of Prayer, not of Preaching: 'It is in the present day, taken for granted that eloquence is the most powerful means of promoting religion in the world. But if this is the case . . . there is no intimation in Scripture . . . Many parts of it consist of poetry, none of oratory.' The pitfall with preaching was that 'men's opinions invest sacred appellations with new meanings according to the changes of their own views' – a hazard of which the theatrical profession had reason to be aware from the admonitions of Revd Best and others.

Newman's own – afternoon – sermons at St Mary's Oxford, of which he was incumbent from 1828 to 1843, served as a model and Colin Wilson has evoked his style as a preacher:

But Newman proved to be an extraordinary preacher. He did not shout or threaten fire and brimstone; he talked quietly and hesitantly, and with penetrating psychological insight. He had some sort of hypnotic power as a preacher . . . He had a light, silvery voice, and a habit of talking slowly, with long pauses, until his own words seemed to carry him away, and his conviction was transmitted like a warm current into his audience. (1957, pp. 219–20)

Newman took the decisive step over to Rome on 9 October 1845. In 1865 he completed *The Dream of Gerontius* with its choruses of angels and devils, though it was not until 1900 that Elgar composed the setting with which it is almost universally associated. *The Dream of Gerontius* contains the hymn 'Praise to the Holiest in the height', a notable contribution to a form of worship which the Victorians made peculiarly their own. As Michael Wheeler has observed, hymns with 'the dominance of the present tense' and 'the use of the first person singular' (1990, pp. 136–7) share two important characteristics with drama.

Another influential convert, Manning, was received into the Roman Catholic church on 6 April 1851 by Cardinal Wiseman. The two men's attitudes to the theatre were divergent. In 1864 Wiseman, a great admirer of Shakespeare (Darbyshire, 1907, p. 4), wrote *The Witch of Rosenberg* for the children of St Leo's Convent, Carlow, and David Mayer has identified Wiseman's novel *Fabiola, or The Church of the Catacombs* (1854), itself the subject of several stage adaptations, lurking behind the whole toga-drama genre (Mayer, 1992, p. 90). Both before and after (as F. C. Burnand's encounter with him showed) Manning was hostile to the theatre. In July 1847, then Archdeacon of Chichester, Manning and his companion Revd John Moultrie found themselves in the company of actress Helen Faucit on a journey up the Rhine (Martin, 1900, p. 185). Manning had already voiced his antipathy to the theatre in his sermon (xiv) 'On mixing in the world. And its safeguards':

Some things, indeed, are in their tone and effects, in the system by which they are supported, and in the consequence they produce so plainly and undisguisedly dangerous, that there can be no hesitation in naming them. For instance, the whole system of theatres is such, that I do not see how any one can go to them with safety. No special pleading about their great moral lessons, and elevated heroic or national character, and the like, will avail to save them from the most subtle, complex, and wide-spreading snares of the world. (1842, vol. ii, pp. 271–2)

Manning and Miss Faucit must have summoned up all the reserves of tact at their disposal to tide them through their journey. Old Etonian Revd John Moultrie, a poet of some renown (D. Coleridge, 1876) and since 1828 Vicar of Rugby, formed a lasting friendship with Miss Faucit. At the conclusion of her visit to Rugby in 1847 Moultrie presented his guest with 'Stanzas for Helen Faucit'. Although he addressed the actress as 'Noble, pure, high-hearted Helen', Moultrie showed little regard for her profession:

> He, who best the purpose knoweth
> Of the pure clad truthful will,
> E'en on bootless aims bestoweth
> Store of heavenly blessings still.
>
> (Martin, 1900, p. 189)

As her husband recounted Miss Faucit was indignant:

She who with a humble heart, and nature devout as his own, had felt it to be a duty that had been laid upon her, along with the power with which she had been endowed, to use that power for aims, which her own experience up to this time had proved, and still more thereafter was destined to prove, not to be 'bootless'.

Miss Faucit gave readings of Shakespeare to the Moultrie family and sent copies of newspaper reviews commending her acting and its influence for good to her clerical friend, but Moultrie 'had not the courage to place himself under her spell' (pp. 189–90) and resolutely refused to attend a theatre to see her perform.

Of her brother's Cambridge contemporaries who did fall under her spell, Fanny Kemble had doubts about F. D. Maurice. Maurice's son observed that it was 'somewhat curious that a man of his [father's] strongly dramatic tastes only occasionally visited a London theatre or opera' even when, as editor of the *Athenaeum*, he was in receipt of press tickets. Frederick Maurice advanced two reasons for this: 'one, that he never could be content with the amount of work he had done, and was therefore always unwilling to take a holiday; the other, that, as newspaper editor, he always thought someone else would do the criticism rather than himself'. In addition to diligence and modesty, however, there was also 'A certain unwillingness to traverse the feelings of his mother and sisters, even in matters in which he did not think them reasonable'. Nevertheless 'He retained a lively impression of the few occasions on which he did see a play, and used to be rather fond of talking in later life of various points in acting' (Frederick Maurice, 1884, vol. 1, p. 77).

In fact as a young man F. D. Maurice had created 'a lively impression' of an actor in the character of Mr Marples, 'manager of the T— Theatre', in his three-volume novel *Eustace Conway or The Brother and Sister*.

'Mr. Marples made a gallant remark to each of the ladies, and three bows, which could not have been surpassed on that memorable night when he enacted Sir Harry Wildair, and forced even the theatrical critics of the T—newspaper to confess "We never saw the perfect gentleman so brought out, as in Mr. Marples' performance"' (1834, vol. I, p. 7). Like most Restoration comedies, George Farquhar's *The Constant Couple* had disappeared from the repertoire by this time, though Maurice may still have invested Mr Marples with some of the characteristics he had observed in members of the Kemble family. Marples's treatment of a young Spanish girl who enlists in his company and refuses to play the highwayman Macheath in Gay's *The Beggar's Opera* – 'He assigned her a male character; she objected; he insisted, and she fled' (vol. I, p. 12) – is handled for humorous effect without any sense of moral judgement.

F. D. Maurice had an opportunity to express his views on drama when he agreed – somewhat reluctantly – to write the 'Preface' to Charles Kingsley's *The Saint's Tragedy* (1848). He endorsed Kingsley's view that 'A Drama . . . should not aim at the inculcation of a definite maxim, the characters should not be the author's spokesmen' (Kingsley, 1889, p. xiii). Maurice wrote of the dramatist 'divest[ing] himself of his own individuality that he may enter into the working of other spirits', but, unlike Plato, he regarded this as a strength: 'If a man confines himself to the utterance of his own experience, those experiences are likely to become every day more narrow and less real' (p. xv). A clergyman needed to relate to his fellow man, a process of understanding akin to that of the dramatist and of course the actor. That Maurice should have some qualms about the play's subject matter, however, and Kingsley's treatment of it, is not surprising.

Maurice's reputation in his own day and since rests principally upon his re-evaluation of the nature of hell. He had been developing his thoughts on the subject of hell for many years, but the publication of *Theological Essays* (1853) marked a watershed. The biblical text upon which Maurice based his ideas of hell was John 17.1–3:

These words spake Jesus, and lifted up his eyes to heaven, and said, Father, the hour is come; glorify thy Son, that thy Son also may glorify thee: as thou hast given him power over all flesh, that he should give eternal life to as many as thou has given him. And this is life eternal, that they might know thee the only true God, and Jesus Christ, whom thou hast sent.

In his preface, addressed to Alfred Tennyson, to one of whose sons he was godfather, Maurice wrote:

I admire unspeakably those who can believe in the Love of God and can love their brethren, in spite of the opinion which they seem to cherish, that He has doomed them to destruction. I am sure that their faith is as much purer and stronger than mine, as it is than their own system. But if that system does prevent me from believing that which God's word, the Gospel of Christ, the witness of my own conscience, the miseries and necessities of the Universe, compel me to believe, I must throw it off. I do not call upon them to deny anything they have been wont to hold; but I call upon them to join us in acknowledging God's love and redemption first of all, and then to consider what is or is not compatible with that acknowledgement. (1853, p. xxvii)

The publication of *Theological Essays* caused a furore and led to Maurice's dismissal as Professor of Theology at King's College, London, the Anglican counterpoint to the dissenters' University College. The council consisted largely of senior Anglican divines including Bishop Blomfield of London, who had been instrumental in founding King's. At a special meeting on 27 October 1853 Blomfield led the attack on Maurice from the chair with the resolution:

That in their judgement the opinion set forth and doubts expressed in the said essay and re-stated in the said answer as to certain points of belief regarding the future punishment of the wicked and the final issues of the day of judgement are of a dangerous tendency, and calculated to unsettle the minds of theological students of King's College. (Frederick Maurice, 1884, vol. II, p. 191)

Gladstone proposed a more tolerant amendment which was defeated; Dean Milman, taking it for granted that the council could not proceed with such haste, did not attend. In January 1854 Tennyson offered his support to the beleaguered theologian in poetic form ('F. D. Maurice'), suggesting a visit to the Isle of Wight:

> Come, when no graver cares employ,
> Godfather, come and see your boy:
> Your presence will be sun in winter,
> Making the little one leap for joy.
>
> For, being of that honest few,
> Who give the Fiend himself his due,
> Should eighty-thousand College-councils
> Thunder 'Anathema', friend at you;
>
> Should all our churchmen foam in spite
> At you so careful of the right,
> Yet one lay-hearth would give you welcome
> (Take it and come) to the Isle of Wight. (1905, p. 234)

Actors had a vested interest in Maurice's views on the nature of eternity, hell-fire having been the fate traditionally held out for them and their audiences from early Christian times to the sermons of Revds Best and East. In 1847 Fanny Kemble's correspondence was preoccupied with 'this same subject, of life after death' (1882, vol. III, p. 176). In December she wrote 'I would rather disbelieve in the immortality of my own soul, than suppose the boon given to me was withheld from any of my fellow creatures.' She rejected the idea of 'partial immortality', i.e. only the deserving achieving it, and avowed 'I can do neither – believe in hell hereafter, or a preparation for it here' (p. 390). Fanny Kemble admitted to a sense of incongruity between her inner thoughts and the practice of her profession: 'But there is something to me almost irreverent in thus catching up these everlasting themes, as it were between my theatrical rehearsals and performances' (p. 273).

Charles Kingsley never had any intention that *The Saint's Tragedy* would be embodied on stage. Indeed Kingsley, who had begun the play in 1842, had difficulty even in getting it published, though when it was the Prince Consort was amongst those who admired it (Cheity, 1974, p. 104). Kingsley wrote his play, set in Hungary between 1220 and 1235, as a means of exploring contemporary events, which in 1848 were in a state of turbulence across Europe. On 10 April 1848, the day of the great Chartist gathering on Kennington Common, F. D. Maurice was confined to his home with a severe cold, but nevertheless took the opportunity to effect a meeting between Kingsley and J. M. Ludlow. Thus were the founders of Christian Socialism constituted. In his preface to *The Saint's Tragedy* Maurice wrote: 'It suggests questions which are deeply interesting at the present time . . . he [Kingsley] has meditated upon the past in its connection with the present' (Kingsley, 1889, pp. xviii–xiv). In a letter to J. Conington, Kingsley averred 'throughout my play I have followed the Shakespearian method of bringing the past up to my readers, and not the modern one of bringing my readers down to the past' (Kingsley, 1877, vol. I, p. 153).

Thus Kingsley's depiction of the Middle Ages as 'a coarse, barbarous and profligate age' differed from the romanticised version promulgated by Pugin and others: 'time has been lost in ignorant abuse of that period, and time enough also, lately, in blind adoration of it' (1889, pp. 6–7). Kingsley intentionally ignored recent works on Elizabeth of Hungary (by Count Montalembert) preferring to 'draw my facts and opinions, entire and unbiassed, from the original Biography of Elizabeth, by Dietrich of Appold' (p. 3). Kingsley's treatment of the story of Elizabeth, daughter of the King of Hungary – her marriage to Lewis, Landgrave of Thuringia, his death on the crusades, her persecution for heresy and eventual canonisation – amounted to a Protestant revision of the life of a Catholic saint. He played down the many miraculous stories about Elizabeth, omitted all 'Mariolatry', and asserted 'the purity and dignity of the office of husband, wife and parent . . . that household purity which constitutes the distinctive superiority of Protestant over Popish nations' (p. 8). Elizabeth's concern with the physical welfare of the poor reflected that of Christian Socialism and drew a contrast with not only Roman, but also Anglican Catholicism:

> 2ND WOMAN: Why, yesterday,
> Within the church, before a mighty crowd,
> She mocked at all the lovely images,
> And said 'the money had been better spent
> On food and clothes, instead of paint and gilding'. (p. 129)

Kingsley had no inhibitions about 'mixing in the world' and sought no safeguards.

The most controversial scene in *The Saint's Tragedy* is act 4 scene 1 set in 'The Church of the Convent', in which Elizabeth, before the altar, says:

> Lo, here I strip me of all earthly helps [*Tearing off her clothes*]
> Naked and barefoot through the world to follow
> My naked Lord. (p. 116)

Since Elizabeth later remarks 'I have stripped of all, but modesty' (4.4) Kingsley does not seem to have intended full nudity, though that was how Philip Hermogones Calderon depicted her in *The Renunciation of St Elizabeth of Hungary* (Royal Academy 1891, Tate Gallery). As Philip McEvansoneya has shown, Calderon's painting provoked controversy, especially in the Roman Catholic press, and was parodied in *Punch* (9 May 1891) and *Fun* (13 May 1891) in connection with the 'alleged impropriety on the part of two officials of the London County Council, who were said to have demanded to inspect the bare back of Miss Zaeo, a famous aerial act at the Royal Aquarium Summer and Winter Garden'.

Kingsley would have been appalled by such sensationalism. In his most sustained commentary on drama, *Plays and Puritans*, he found much justification in the Puritan case: 'Now we cannot but agree with the Puritans, that adultery is not a subject for comedy at all. It may be for tragedy; but for comedy never. It is a sin; not merely theologically, but socially' (1873, p. 16). Though he had taken Shakespeare as his model Kingsley could not excuse Shakespeare's 'low art, the foul and horrible elements which he had in common with his brother play-writers' (p. 44), but he offset these with 'the higher elements in him . . . the deep spiritual knowledge which makes, and will make, Shakespeare's plays (and them alone of all the seventeenth-century plays) a heritage for all men and all ages' (p. 45). On balance Kingsley vindicated the Puritans' opposition to the theatre:

On the matter of the stage, the world has certainly come over to their way of thinking. Few highly educated men now think it worth while to go to see any play, and that exactly for the same reasons as the Puritans put forward; and still fewer highly educated men think it worth while to write plays finding since the grosser excitements of the imagination have become forbidden themes, there is very little to write about. (pp. 73–4)

Certainly the Victoria Theatre as described by Kingsley in *Alton Locke* (1850) is a den of iniquity into which 'the beggary and rascality of London were pouring . . . to their low amusement'. Indeed the theatre is explicitly likened to hell: 'These licensed pits of darkness, traps of temptation, profligacy and ruin, triumphantly yawning night after night – and then tell me that the people who see their children thus kidnapped into hell are represented by a government who licenses such things' (1879, p. 117). At this time the hoped-for benefits of the 1843 Theatre Regulations Act had not been realised in Waterloo Road, but in *Plays and Puritans* Kingsley acknowledged Macready's contribution to 'our comparatively purified stage' (1873, p. 27). Kingsley's objections were not directed to the theatre as such, but to its debased manifestations. In 1858 he approached Macready's former leading lady Helen Faucit, who in 1851 had married the Edinburgh lawyer Theodore Martin (in later life the Prince Consort's biographer), 'to ascertain if she would undertake the heroine's part in a play he wished to write for her' (Martin, 1900, p. 257). Kingsley met Miss Faucit and settled the subject for the play, but he abandoned the project when friends suggested that 'to write a play might injure his influence as a clergyman' (p. 257). Nevertheless Miss Faucit's encounter with Kingsley blossomed into friendship, as did those with Revd Moultrie, Dean Stanley and James Fraser, Bishop of Manchester.

In 1877 Bishop Fraser recalled that, thirty-five years earlier, prior to ordination, he had seen Macready and Helen Faucit in *Othello* and 'Last year I had the pleasure of meeting Mrs Theodore Martin (Miss Helen Faucit) at Lord Egerton's at Tatton, and a more accomplished lady I think you cannot find' (Diggle, 1889, p. 81). In 1858 Fraser had visited Macready's ragged school in Sherborne; in 1865 he had met Mr and Mrs Charles Kean aboard a steamer on the St Lawrence in Canada; on 12

October 1878, Henry Irving, 'a very striking and polished man' (p. 464), visited him in Manchester. Irving was a friend of Charles Calvert, manager of the Prince's Theatre, Manchester (1864–75, see Foulkes, 1992a), whose own upright character and high standards of management did much to elevate the theatre.

Fraser had been introduced to the theatre whilst at Shrewsbury School, where, under the liberal headmaster Dr Butler, the boys had attended performances by the Staunton Company, which he regarded as 'one of the formative influences which had not been for harm but for good in him' (*Era* 12 October 1879). An undergraduate at Lincoln College, Oxford, Fraser became a fellow of Oriel in 1840, but, though he never wavered in his veneration of Newman, Fraser did not subscribe to the Oxford Movement. At Oxford, Fraser met the Rugby triumvirate of Matthew Arnold, Arthur Clough and Tom Hughes. Hughes, who wrote a biography of Fraser (1887), described him as 'Tom Brown in lawn sleeves' (Diggle, 1889, p. 9). Between 1860 and 1870 Fraser was Rector of Ufton Nervet, but he made his reputation as a member of two Commissions on Education – Newcastle in 1859 and Taunton in 1865 (see Davies, 1990). Fraser declined the bishopric of Calcutta, but accepted Gladstone's offer of Manchester in 1870, the year of Forster's Education Act, which consolidated the Church's dominant role in elementary education, despite Nonconformist pressure for public control (Bebbington, 1982, pp. 127–52). Though he had strong links with the Oxford Movement and Christian Socialism, Fraser was the quintessence of the Victorian Broad Church. In contrast to his rather remote predecessor, Henry Prince Lee, Fraser engaged with the community at large: 'He was the head and front of every movement intended for the advancement of progress and culture' (Diggle, 1889, p. 521).

Fraser believed that the Church should go out into the world and, rather than wait for the people to come to church, he visited them. He ran missions to medical students, railway employees, cab drivers, slaughterhouse men and, on 2 February 1877, he addressed assemblies of the theatre profession at the Theatre Royal and the Prince's Theatre. Fraser had in fact been invited by the profession to address them and in his opening remarks, after a hymn and prayers, from a Gothic chamber on the stage of the Theatre Royal, he referred to 'feelings very mingled, in which anxiety very largely predominated . . . he must be the first bishop of the Church of England, if he was not the first bishop of the Church of Christ, who had ever addressed a congregation in a theatre'. Fraser ranged widely over the early Church's denunciation of the theatre

– then 'utterly corrupted and degraded'; Aristotle's – 'a great heathen teacher and philosopher' – theory of catharsis; the Oberammergau Passion Play which, he was told, 'had a most directly Christianising influence upon those who witness it'; and the elevating and strengthening experience of seeing *Othello* or *Hamlet* well performed. Fraser acknowledged that 'God had given men the faculty of laughter and amusement' and 'He [Fraser] did not want to abolish the theatre; he wanted to purify it.' He exhorted members of the profession 'to refuse to take part in any drama which would compromise his proper dignity as a man or her proper modesty as a woman'. The 'great cause' was 'purifying the public taste' and the profession had to co-operate and take the lead in bringing this about: 'If we ever get in the way of throwing the blame upon society it was all up with us if we did not recognise our personal responsibility.' Great cities were expanding, their citizens would demand amusement; it was up to the providers to ensure a high standard (*Manchester Evening News* 2 February 1877). The tone established by Fraser was more in keeping with a church than a theatre: 'The address was received in the most solemn silence and many of the audience were visibly affected during its delivery. There was a tendency to raise a cheer at some of the more popular passages, but this was quickly checked. The audience having sung "Rock of Ages", the Bishop pronounced the benediction and the company quietly separated' (*Manchester Weekly Times* 3 February 1877).

When he addressed the assembly at the Prince's Theatre, Fraser drew a theatrical parallel – they should not 'expect him on the second night to introduce variations upon the performance of the first night'. He did, however, introduce some new points, including the suggestion that the skirts of the ballet dancers should be a little longer, thereby avoiding men – 'very often old men' – 'gazing upon them with gloating and wanton eyes'. Again the onus was on the profession to make the theatre 'a place honest and Christian women, and modest women could come and take their part and not be ashamed' (*Manchester Evening News* 2 February 1877).

Fraser's sermons were widely reported in the local theatrical and national press. *Punch* seized on the bishop's remarks about 'the brevity of the Ballet Girls' skirts "which", had he wanted an illustration he might have said "were no longer than a bishop's apron"' (illustration 4) and fantasised about 'a Ballet of Bishops with their aprons properly licensed by the LORD CHAMBERLAIN' (3 March 1877). Dean Stanley expressed his admiration, as did Baroness Burdett-Coutts, who wrote of society's duty 'to guide and direct public taste, and keep it pure and healthy'. The Baroness excused herself for not 'naming the subject to

4. Bishops on the stage. Bishop Fraser of Manchester (*Punch* 3 March 1877)

him [Irving] as I think you perhaps thought I would' because the actor was 'so engrossed with Richard [III]' (Diggle, 1889, p. 84). The occasional clerical voice was still raised in protest (Close, 1877) and the events arising from the funeral of Charles Calvert in June 1879 showed how strong prejudice against the theatre was in some religious circles.

When the mortal remains of Charles Calvert were returned to Manchester for his interment at Brooklands Cemetery an estimated 50,000 people lined the route of the cortège. The funeral oration was given by Revd Paxton Hood, a prolific author and minister of the Cavendish Street Chapel who proclaimed: 'All genius is from God. The power to interpret great ideas, the power to impersonate noble emotions, no less than the power which expresses them, we are to conceive is derived from God, who is the giver of every great and good gift' (Mrs Calvert, 1911, p. 180). Paxton Hood's congregation took exception to him conducting an actor's funeral and he was forced to resign his living.

In a sense the theatre had its revenge as Paxton Hood's son became an actor: Sydney Paxton. In his autobiography Paxton refers to the effects of his father's troubles (1917, p. 28) and, in a letter (27 December 1897) to Alfred Darbyshire, he recalled his father's 'systematic persecution from the too professing, so called Christians' (Archives Department, Manchester Central Library).

After Fraser's sermons the theatre featured on the agendas of meetings of the Church Congress and the Social Science Congress. Fraser contributed to the debate on 'The Attitude of the Church towards Popular Literature and Reservations' at the meeting of the Church Congress in Sheffield in October 1878. He recalled a conversation with a Manchester theatre manager, whose defence for putting on *Pink Dominoes* was that 'The people will have it', an argument which, though he recognised the financial realities of the theatre, the bishop did not accept. He exhorted audiences to stay away from such fare and from pantomimes into which 'objectionable ballet' was introduced (*The Times* 4 October 1878).

The Social Science Congress was held in Manchester in October 1879 and a local cleric, Revd F. G. Woodhouse of St Mary's, Hulme, opened the debate with the suggestion that 'The Drama was a mighty power for good . . . It satisfied certain deep longings of the human soul.' Revd R. H. Haweis, who in the previous year had preached a sermon (1878) on 'Shakespeare and the Stage' from his pulpit at St James's, Marylebone, lent his support. The theatrical profession was represented by actor Hermann Vezin who said: 'One sermon by the Rev. Mr. Haweis was not a defence of the Stage – the Stage needs no defence – but a scathing indictment against those of his brethren who would thank God that they had never been inside a Theatre, and then vilify both without a scruple.' In a concluding address Bishop Fraser judged Vezin's remarks to be too sweeping. He expressed more concern about the taste of the upper classes, which he considered was often inferior to that of the lower and middle classes; but 'The theatre . . . must not preach, and it was from the fact that they did not preach that Shakespeare's plays derived their moral power' (*Era* 12 October 1879). The Social Science Congress became something of a platform for advocates of the theatre. Madge Kendal addressed the meeting in Birmingham on 23 September 1884 – 'an unprecedented thing for a woman to do in those days' (1933, p. 182).

Clergymen were now ascending their pulpits not to denounce the theatre, but to commend it. In Margate, Revd William Benham, 'the chief confidant' (Tomalin, 1991, p. 228) of Nelly Ternan, actress, intimate of Charles Dickens and, from 1877, wife of Revd George Wharton Robinson, invited sympathetic clergymen to preach on the subject of the theatre in 1879. One of the preachers was Revd G. J. Everest, who 'believed the drama to be a great power for good, and disapproved of the isolated position which actors and actresses were forced into by many professedly religious people' (*Thanet Guardian* 1 November 1879).

Benham was a disciple of F. D. Maurice and biographer – together with the future Archbishop of Canterbury, Randall Davidson – of Archibald Tait, successively headmaster of Rugby School, Dean of Carlisle, Bishop of London and Archbishop of Canterbury (Marsh, 1969). One of the controversies which had confronted Tait as Bishop of London was the use of seven London theatres for Sunday evening services. At a Conference of Christians of all Evangelical denominations held on 22 November 1859 Mr Arthur Kincaid stated that 'the Bishop of London was in cordial harmony with them, and cared not whether Churchmen or Nonconformists conducted the services' (Davidson and Benham, 1891, vol. 1, p. 263); But in reply to a correspondent the bishop explained 'that his attitude must for the time being be one of watchful neutrality'. The matter was debated in the House of Lords on 24 February 1860, when Lord Shaftesbury commended the services which were attended by immense multitudes of the poorer classes for whom church places were in short supply. The bishop's speech elevated neutrality into a fine art. The movement had not been officially sanctioned, but episcopal disapproval had been withheld – 'He was not prepared to say that he went entirely with the movement' (vol. 1, p. 264).

Neutrality, equivocation even, was not a strategy without its attractions for leaders of the Victorian Church. Today's heresy had a way of becoming tomorrow's orthodoxy as was proven by the controversies from Darwinism to *The Pentateuch and Book of Joshua Critically Examined* by Bishop Colenso (of Natal). Frederick Temple, who, like Tait, became headmaster of Rugby School, Bishop of London and Archbishop of Canterbury, was denounced by the Church establishment along with the other six contributors to *Essays and Reviews* (1860), which was essentially aligned with Latitudinarianism. In his essay 'The education of the world', Temple wrote of 'pure inspiration' in the great works of classical literature, but 'Greece can show few poets equal, none superior to Shakespeare' (1860, p. 27). Benjamin Jowett ('On the interpretation of Scripture') advanced the precept 'Interpret the Scripture like any other book' to ascertain its meaning 'in the same careful and impartial way that we ascertain the meaning of Sophocles or of Plato' (p. 377): 'It is to be interpreted like other books, with attention to the character of its authors, and the prevailing state of civilization and knowledge, with allowance for peculiarities of style and language, modes of thought and figures of speech' (p. 404). Biblical scholars increasingly interpreted the Bible not literally, but as literature, and explained accounts of supernatural occurrences in terms of myth and fable. In *The God of Miracles* (1875), Matthew Arnold invoked *Cinderella* in discussing 'those unsaveable things, the Bible miracles' (Super, 1970, p. 170). The vilification of drama on the grounds that it was mere story-telling could not be sustained as the Bible itself was being interpreted 'like any other book'.

From biblical scholarship to the Tractarian revival of liturgical rituals, to Maurice's revision of hell, to Kingsley's ventures into playwriting and to Bishop Fraser's mission to Manchester theatres, the tide was turning in favour of the theatre. The main strands of the Victorian Church – the Oxford Movement, Christian Socialism, the Broad Church and the Latitudinarians – were bringing about, sometimes unintentionally, attitudes which made the acceptance of the theatre possible, not merely by isolated individuals, but amongst the clergy and laity generally.

CHAPTER 5

Self-improvement

MRS WILLOUGHBY: And this is what he calls attending elocution
of a night, and improvin' of his mind
Tom Taylor *The Ticket-of-Leave Man*

In his preface to *Self-help* (1859), Samuel Smiles wrote 'the object of this
book briefly, is to re-inculcate those old-fashioned, but wholesome
lessons . . . that youth must work in order to enjoy – that nothing cred-
itable can be accomplished without application and diligence' (1905,
p. vii). Smiles recalled that the origin of his book had been some evening
classes in a northern town attended by 100 young men, who 'proceeded
to teach themselves and each other, reading and writing, arithmetic and
geography; and even mathematics, chemistry and some of the modern
languages' (p. x). Valuable though such learning was, the greater benefit
lay in the realisation 'that their happiness and well-being as inviduals in
after-life must necessarily depend mainly upon themselves – upon their
own diligent self-culture, self-discipline, and self-control – and, above all,
on that honest and upright performance of individual duty which is the
glory of manly character' (pp. x–xi).

Smiles upheld 'biographies of great, but especially of good men . . .
[as] most instructive and useful, as helps, guides, and incentives to
others. Some of the best are almost equivalent to gospels – teaching
high living, high thinking, and energetic action for their own and the
world's good' (p. 7). Amongst such he cites 'the indefatigable industry of
Lord Brougham' (p. 25) – lawyer (attorney-general for Queen Caroline),
ardent advocate of the abolition of slavery, and Lord Chancellor
during the passing of the 1832 Reform Act. Brougham was a prime
mover in the Society for the Diffusion of Useful Knowledge (founded
1826) (Stewart, 1985, p. 188) and, together with George Birkbeck (Kelly,
1957), the founding of mechanics' institutes of which 'By 1841 there
were over 300' (Kelly, 1962, p. 125). Both the Society and the mechanics'

institutes were preoccupied with practical, particularly scientific, education, but the reality was that, after a twelve-hour day, the average working man had little appetite for lectures on chemistry, mechanics, hydrostatics and the like. Fiction was excluded from the institute libraries, newspapers from their reading-rooms; politics, economics and literature were almost universally barred from the curriculum. No wonder therefore that 'the average working man returned to his public house, or his club, or his mutual improvement society' (p. 124). The mechanics' institutes only revived when, in the 1840s and 1850s, newsrooms, popular lectures, cheap concerts and coffee parties were added to their attractions.

The tension between improvement and amusement ran through the popular education movements of the nineteenth century, many of which were founded on the Nonconformist/Puritan ethic which, as Walter E. Houghton says 'laid great stress on hard work and moral discipline . . . and neglected, or viewed with suspicion the worldly distractions of philosophy and art' (1973, p. 126). Someone who, from a different perspective, was suspicious of worldly distractions was J. H. Newman. After his conversion to Roman Catholicism, Newman developed his ideas on education as rector of the new Catholic University in Dublin (1854–8) and in lectures and essays which formed *The Idea of a University Defined and Illustrated* (1873), but as an Anglican he expressed his views most fully in a series of letters to *The Times* in February 1841, in response to Sir Robert Peel's speech at the opening of the Tamworth Reading Room. Newman traced the views expressed by the Tory Prime Minister directly to Lord Brougham: 'It is, indeed, most melancholy to see so sober and experienced a man practising the antics of one of the wildest performers of this wild age, and taking off the tone, manner and gestures of the versatile ex-chancellor, with a versatility almost equal to his own' (Newman, 1891, p. 260). Newman acknowledged that 'The problem for statesmen of this age is how to educate the masses, and literature and science cannot give the solution' (p. 292). Newman's diagnosis of the challenge to the state was shared by Thomas Carlyle in his essay on 'Chartism' (1839): 'Let us now observe that education is not merely an eternal duty, but has at length become even a temporary and ephemeral one, which the necessities of the hour will oblige us to look after' (1915, p. 229).

Though Newman absolved Brougham and Peel of 'Benthamising', he detected the flaws of liberalism and Utilitarianism in their views and rejected both: 'An uneducated man is ever mistaking his own interests, and standing in the way of his own true enjoyment' (1891, p. 262) and

that the mind is changed by discovery, or saved by diversion, and can thus be amused into immortality, – that grief, anger, cowardice, self-conceit, pride, or passion, can be subdued by an examination of shells or grasses, or inhaling of gases, or chipping of rocks, or calculating the longitude, is the veriest of pretences which sophist or mountebank ever professed to a gaping auditory. If virtue be a mastery over the mind, if its end be action, if its perfection be inward order, harmony, and peace, we must seek it in graver and holier places than in Libraries and Reading-rooms. (p. 268)

Newman identified as 'a chief error of the day' the belief that 'our true excellence comes not from within, but from without' (p. 266) and asserted that 'Christianity and nothing short of it must be the element and principle of all education' (p. 274). Newman's belief that the individual's inner self was the core of his existence and that education should be founded in Christianity was fundamental, but he also had practical advice for those who proffered worldly distractions as a means to this end: 'they will find themselves outbid in the market by gratifications much closer at hand, and on a level with the meanest capacity' (p. 267). Victorian workers in the field of self-improvement were well advised to note Newman's warning.

Newman associated the 'Knowledge Society' and the Tamworth Reading Room with the 'Gower Street College' – University College, London – in the foundation of which – in 1826 – Brougham had taken a lead (as had Bentham) and which was dubbed by its detractors 'that Godless Institution'. King's College, founded in 1828, was the Established Church's response to the Nonconformist, free-thinking University College, though both became constituent colleges of the University of London in 1836. The site in the Strand chosen for King's College prompted disapproval from a correspondent to the *Mechanics' Magazine* (14 November 1829): 'In a moral point of view, the proposed site of the new college is notably the very worst that could have been selected in the whole metropolis or its vicinity. It is within about a five minutes' walk of five theatres, and of all the . . . other sinks of iniquity which derive their support from those celebrated schools of morality.'

Of Robert Smirke's design, A. W. N. Pugin – formerly a scenic artist – from the opposite end of the religious spectrum to the *Mechanics' Magazine*, was equally censorious contrasting its gateway with that of Christ Church, Oxford (illustration 5), in *Contrasts* (1836). Pugin's drawing includes a figure carrying a placard advertising 'Cheap

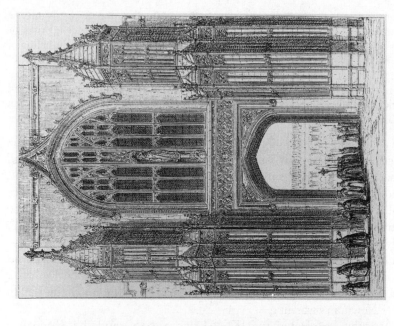

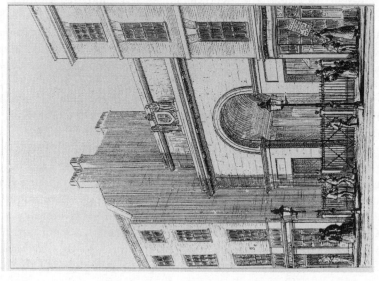

5. Contrasted college gateways. A. W. N. Pugin, King's College, Strand, Christ's College, Oxford

Knowledge Lectures' by 'Mr Gab'. Initially King's College did not award degrees, but catered for pupils aged sixteen to eighteen, some of them (notably John Ruskin, Charles Kingsley and F. W. Farrar) preparing for entry to the ancient universities. Evening classes were provided from January 1849.

In both the new colleges the traditional domination of the classics was challenged by the introduction of English Studies, but with different approaches which reflected the two institutions, as David Palmer indicates:

> The distinctions which divided University College and King's College so deeply were reflected in their respective approach to English Studies. At University College, as one would expect, the emphasis was upon the more practical aspects, upon composition and more 'scientific' and factual study of language; while at King's College there was at first nothing so utilitarian as a class in composition, and the reading of literature was encouraged on moral principles. (1965, p. 18)

The first occupant of the chair of English at University College was, rather surprisingly for 'that Godless Institution', Revd Thomas Dale, an Evangelical Anglican clergyman. The syllabus instituted by Dale was predominantly language-orientated, but, as his inaugural lecture revealed, Dale had strong views about the moral and religious dimension of literary studies and his views on drama would not have been out of place in Revd Best's Sheffield pulpit:

> In the history of our literature, more particularly the drama, it will be my painful duty to point out . . . too many, whose wreath of imperishable laurel is interwoven with bitter and deadly herbs, which, like the envenomed diadem that encircled the brow of the Christian virgin in the days of fiery persecution, insinuate a subtle poison into the veins and even to the heart! . . . I shall esteem it my duty . . . to inculcate lessons of virtue, through the medium of the masters of our language . . . never, in tracking the course of those brilliant luminaries that sparkle the firmament of our literature – never will I suffer the eye of inexperienced youth to be dazzled by the brilliancy of genius, when its broad lustre obscures the deformity of vice; never will I affect to stifle the expression of just indignation, when wit, taste and talent, have been designedly prostituted by their unworthy possessors to the excitement of unholy passions, the palliation of guilty indulgences, the ridicule of virtue, or the disparagement of religion. (Dale, 1828, p. 30)

Dale remained at University College for only two years (amongst his successors – in 1845 – was dramatist Tom Taylor) and in 1835 he became the first Professor of English Literature and History at King's College, being succeeded in 1840 by F. D. Maurice whose 'Sketches of Contemporary

Authors' in the *Athenaeum* vouched for his eligibility for the post. Maurice planned to give his first lectures on the 'Prologue' to *The Canterbury Tales* and, in a letter to Julius Hare, debated the propriety of lecturing on *King John*: 'But I was afraid that I should scandalise good people by choosing for my first subject a play, the first act of which would involve awkward skipping, or what would seem to them very unfit reading for boys' (Frederick Maurice, 1884, vol. I, p. 290). Inevitably Shakespeare did feature in Maurice's teaching as the recollections of F. W. Farrar indicate: 'Interesting and valuable to those who could appreciate them as were his lectures on History, those on English Literature were even more so. Here Professor Maurice showed a wonderful versatility in guiding and stimulating us. Sometimes he would make us read a scene from Shakespeare and comment on it' (p. 316).

In Farrar, subsequently a master at Harrow and Marlborough, head-master of Marlborough and editor of *Essays on A Liberal Education* (1867), Maurice had an attentive pupil, but, as Farrar's own remarks imply, others found Maurice's lectures far less riveting. Discipline problems ensued: 'Chaos supervened, and Maurice, who had as little ability to inflict temporal punishment as he had to imagine eternal punishment, was helpless' (Hearnshaw, 1929, p. 157). From 1846 Maurice combined the chair of English and History with that of Theology; his Cambridge contemporary Richard Chenevix Trench was appointed Professor of Divinity, but when, in 1848, Maurice attempted to secure Charles Kingsley's appointment as his assistant in English, the College, fearful of Kingsley's radicalism, objected.

Trench and Kingsley, together with Tom Taylor, constituted the core for the two educational initiatives which Maurice pioneered: Queen's College, founded in 1848 initially for the training of governesses, and the Working Men's Colleges from 1854. J. F. C. Harrison traces the origins of the Working Men's Colleges to the night-school established for the residents of Little Ormond Yard in September 1848 and the formation of Working Men's Associations, beginning with that of Working Taylors in January 1850 (1954, pp. 10–11). The Working Men's Colleges were launched with a series of public lectures by Maurice in Willis's Rooms in June and July 1854. Maurice advanced his ideas on education for working men in *Learning and Working* (1855), which Harrison describes as 'a classic in the literature of adult education; and, in this field . . . comparable with that contemporary classic of university education, J. H. Newman's *Idea of a University*' (p. 24). Common ground between the two men (Christian Socialist and Catholic) was the centrality of religion to education.

In Ford Madox Brown's *Work* (1852–65 – in Manchester City Art Gallery), F. D. Maurice stands alongside Thomas Carlyle as representatives of workers of the intellect. The force of the work ethic in Maurice is indicated by his son's observation (already quoted with reference to theatre-going) that 'he never could be content with the amount of work he had done, and was therefore always unwilling to take a holiday' (Frederick Maurice, 1884, vol. I, p. 77). Maurice's attitude to leisure was stringent; it had to be used purposefully: 'In other words constructive leisure means choosing on one's own account some activity which has to be worked at if it is to be successfully pursued' (Styler, 1968, p. 12).

Coleridge's idea of a clerisy was inherent in Maurice's thinking on education: how much it was the duty of every man, but above all, of every clergyman, to strive that the principle and power of Christian civilization, which is not based upon selfishness, which does not make the accumulation of material treasures or the increase of material enjoyments its main object, might be recognised in the past of Europe, and especially of our own country, – might influence and determine its future condition. (p. 27)

Maurice added Christian Socialism's concern with the social condition of men: 'We could not talk to suffering men of intellectual and moral improvement, without first taking an interest in their physical condition and their ordinary occupations', though this would be invalid unless linked to spiritual development – 'we felt that any interest of this kind would be utterly wasted, that it would do harm and not good, if it were not the means of leading them to regard themselves as human beings made in the image of God' (p. 28).

When it came to formulating courses of study for the Working Men's Colleges, Maurice signalled a fundamental difference from the scientific (utilitarian) subjects favoured by Brougham for the mechanics' institutes. History and literature which 'exhibit God's education of mankind' (p. 33) were central. Shakespeare's 'intercourse with the coarsest persons and occupations' was turned into a virtue:

And, therefore, instead of setting him up as a mere marvellous phenomenon and an excuse for our self-worship, it might surely be better to ask whether he does not give us the hint of cultivation at once popular and profound, humane and national, which might be available for thousands, who are not separated from their fellows by any accidents of class or condition. (p. 78)

'Cultivation'/culture (one of Raymond Williams's key words) that was both 'popular and profound' – this was the holy grail for Maurice and other Victorian educationalists of his persuasion. The ideal of bringing together the different classes of society in a common culture underlay

Maurice's somewhat guarded observations on the theatre. He considered that on careful examination 'we shall perceive that no good has come to the amusements of the higher class, except when they have sought to strengthen and refresh themselves by intercourse with the lower, to repair a jaded conventionalism by drawing new life from that which is essentially human' and that 'no good has come to the entertainments of the lower classes, except from the same course differently working, from their perceiving that they were interested in whatever has an interest for human beings' (p. 150). In fact the trend of Victorian theatre was the reverse – more theatres catering for different social groupings. On balance Maurice could not summon up much genuine conviction about the educational benefits of theatre:

> My own opinion would certainly be, that while no nation has more of a dramatic faculty than the English, or is more capable of contemplating history as a great providential drama, there is less of what is histrionic in us than in the people of the continent; less that it is likely to receive impressions from the acted play. On that ground I should hope more from exhibitions like those which the Crystal Palace offers, than from any attempts to purify and restore entertainments which many of our countrymen look upon with utter aversion, because they connect with a number of evil accidents, certainly not belonging to their essence. I am not, however, in the least sure that I am right; some facts would lead to quite a different inference. (pp. 151–2)

Maurice had much greater faith in music, for its mystical quality and ability to satisfy men's cravings for freedom and order. The great popularity and success of John Pyke Hullah's classes for working men showed what could be done with music; though Hullah had only turned pedagogue after the failure of his last attempt at dramatic music – *The Outpost* for Macready at Covent Garden in May 1838. Whatever the activity it had to be earnestly pursued; cricket and rowing might be permitted, but 'when they are pursued earnestly, – and every true boy must be earnest in all he does, – [they] become very hard work indeed' (p. 67). Maurice shared none of Bentham's indulgence towards the players of 'push-pin' and was contemptuous of 'the worshippers of Leisure' (p. 105).

As the early history of the mechanics' institutes demonstrated, the capacity of working men to subscribe to such a rigorous regime in their few free hours was limited. In June 1862 the Working Men's Club and Institute Union was formed on the initiative of Henry Solly, who became its paid secretary. Solly, who had been one of the first students at University College, London, was a Chartist and a Unitarian minister

(Bailey, 1978, p. 108). In his dedicatory letter to F. D. Maurice prefacing *Working Men's Social Clubs and Educational Institutes* (1867) Solly wrote of the difficulty in getting 'the Lancashire working men to accept the name of "College"' (p. 6). 'Club', and even 'Institute', had a less forbidding ring and the movement spread rapidly, but problems followed when the disposition towards amusement threatened to swamp more serious-minded activities.

Solly cited the specific issue of 'Dramatic Entertainments' which arose in the spring of 1864 (around the time of the Shakespeare tercentenary). The teaching of oratory, which had long been part of the curriculum in the public schools, found its counterpart in elocution for the working classes. 'The worst part, however, was that the Elocution Class became a Dramatic Class, and then regular Dramatic entertainments, with scenery and dresses, were introduced, not at good long intervals – which would have done no harm – but once a week' (1867, p. 84). Matters degenerated: 'the whole life of the Club seemed swallowed up in these entertainments . . . [which] after a time . . . became disreputable, little better than a "Penny Gaff"' (p. 84). Solly concluded that though occasional performances were 'simply beneficial', 'incessant dramatic entertainments . . . are a palpable perversion of the objects for which the Club was founded' (p. 85), namely to provide an alternative to such debased forms of entertainment as the 'Penny Gaff'.

Solly devoted a chapter (12) to 'Ought dramatic entertainments and dancing to be allowed at Working Men's Clubs and Institutes?' He passed no judgement on the propriety of such activities elsewhere, but concluded that when taken to excess they had a deleterious effect upon Working Men's Clubs – they displaced other activities, alienated members who were not attracted to them, and proved to be unreliable as a source of income. Nevertheless the shift in emphasis from Maurice's ideals for the Working Men's Colleges was fundamental:

While it is quite certain that amusement (including in that term social intercourse) is the first thing to be provided for by these Clubs, and that improvement of various kinds (mental, moral and pecuniary) is the second, it is a point of paramount importance for working men and their friends to see how they can make the second result follow out of the first. (p. 255)

Newman's disbelief in the idea that 'the mind . . . can thus be amused into immortality' was not shared here; 'the Worshippers of Leisure' were in the ascendancy.

Even self-improving elocution classes, far from diverting a young man from more dubious pleasures, might actually whet his appetite for them. In Tom Taylor's *The Ticket-of-Leave Man* (1863) Sam Willoughby is apprehended, by his mother, playing truant from his elocution class at the Bridgewater Arms pleasure garden, the delights of which include a rendition of the sensational ballad, 'The Maniac's Tear':

MRS WILLOUGHBY: And this is what he calls attending elocution class of a night, and improvin' of his mind – and me a-toilin' and a-moilin' for him
(George Rowell, 1960, p. 332)

Tom Taylor was an archetypal Victorian polymath – a graduate and fellow of Trinity College, Cambridge; barrister; art critic; Secretary to the Board of Health; editor of *Punch;* and, as already noted, Professor of English at University College, where he showed 'His excellence as a reader and speaker' to the benefit of his students (Tolles, 1940, p. 33). The author of over seventy plays (see Banham, 1985, pp. 227–9), Taylor subscribed to the theatre's potential as a means of social improvement, though he found much that was unworthy of this goal:

Besides, culture apart, the morals of the English public proper, the public of the pit and gallery, is still sound . . . It is not that part of your public that needs uplifting half so much as your half-educated young debauchees, whether of the upper strata of fast life, who have supplied the chief support to contemporary burlesque, at least to the coarseness, indecencies, and pruriences which have gradually eaten out all its salt. (1871, p. 8)

An active member of 'The Old Stagers', a group of amateurs who performed at Canterbury for a week annually, unflaggingly energetic in work and play, Taylor also lectured at Queen's College and the Working Men's Colleges. In his 'In memoriam' article on Taylor, Tom Hughes wrote that 'Few men were more interested in politics and social questions . . . he was a strong and steady Liberal, and in social matters a Radical reformer' (*Macmillan's Magazine*, August 1880, p. 301). Taylor uniquely spanned education, public administration and the theatre.

In the mid 1850s, as part of his duties as Secretary to the Working Men's Club and Institute Union, Henry Solly visited Cheltenham where he attended the Literary and Scientific Institution and met Major Macready, 'brother to the great tragedian' (1893, vol. II, p. 43). At that time W. C. Macready was spending the early years of his lengthy retirement in Sherborne where he established a night-school, which was visited by Revd James Fraser in his capacity as an Assistant Commissioner of the 'Newcastle' Commission appointed by the government to Inquire into the State of Popular Education in England. During the winter of 1858–9 Fraser visited night-schools in Dorset, Somerset, Herefordshire and Worcestershire and reported:

I saw several very *interesting* night schools, at Powerstock, at Beaminster, at Lyme, at Upton-on-Severn; but the only really efficient one that I witnessed at work, the only one full of life and progress and tone of the best kind, was one at Sherborne, which owes its origins and its prosperity to the philanthropic zeal and large sacrifices of money, time and personal comfort of Mr. Macready. If night schools of that class were at work generally in our towns, their influence upon the education of the people would be incalculable. (*British Parliamentary Papers*, *Education in England. Education General 4*, 1969, p. 52)

Fraser observed one particular pupil 'a little fellow, 12 years old, who worked 12 hours a day at a coachmaker's, who literally shortened his dinner time by a half an hour to get his work forward, and be able to leave the shop at half-past seven, in time for his evening school' (p. 53). Thus the best example of popular education, very much in keeping with Coleridge's idea of a clerisy, witnessed by the future Bishop of Manchester was conducted by a former actor, who appears to have made no concessions to easy popularity by diluting instruction with amusement. Fraser's subsequent attitude towards the theatre owed something to the favourable impression created by the former actor's night-school.

Solly himself had aspirations to playwriting in the more elevated vein favoured by Macready and Charles Kemble. In 1856 he published *Gonzago di Capponi A Dramatic Romance*, which he dedicated to Charles Dickens. In the 'Preface' Solly revealed that the piece 'written in the Author's youth, without any definite moral purpose . . . has been carefully rewritten in maturer years, and is now published, because he believes he has found the answer to those questions which he believes it alone can be discovered in the Christian Religion' (1856, p. vii). Solly sent a copy of the play, together with a sermon, to Charles Kingsley, who, having read the sermon first, assured him: 'And I shall read your poem with strong interest, now I know what manner of man you are' (29 June 1857; Solly, 1893, vol. II, p. 126). In due course (*c.* 1875) Solly's play was performed by an elocution class at St George's Hall, enjoying the patronage of the Duke and Duchess of Westminster and 'various other distinguished persons' (p. 477). A drama of such lofty ideals evidently escaped the strictures meted out to less worthy offerings. The experience encouraged Solly further and he wrote *The Shepherd's Dream*, which was sympathetically received by authoress Miss Anna Swanwick and Professor Henry Morley, and *Herod the Great* (1896) which was endorsed by Revd W. H. Freemantle, Dean of Ripon, Sir Walter Besant and Arthur Waugh.

Despite these ventures into playwriting Solly considered that readings were more appropriate for Working Men's Institutes and Clubs: 'Recitation in dialogue and parts are not only free from all the objections that can be urged against theatrical representations, but are both pleasing and useful in every point of view' (1867, p. 232). The precedent for readings was set at the highest level. The three-volume collection of Charles Kemble's readings from Shakespeare is dedicated to: 'Her Majesty the Queen Under Whose Generous Patronage Mr Charles Kemble Entered on His Course of Readings of Shakespeare, This Book is, With Her Majesty's Gracious Permission, Inscribed By Her Grateful Servant The Editor [R. J. Lane]' (Lane, 1870). Kemble had turned to readings after his retirement from the stage, giving his first before the Queen at Buckingham Palace on 24 April 1844, when *Cymbeline* was selected by the Prince Consort. A further reading of *Cymbeline* before Queen Adelaide followed, after which Kemble gave public readings at venues such as Willis's Rooms. The appeal of readings to those admirers of Shakespeare who would never enter a theatre is indicated by a dissenting minister's comments to Kemble in the north of England: 'Mr. Kemble, though I abominate the stage, and think the playhouse a school of vice, yet I am a patron of Shakespeare in my social hours, and I am glad to have an opportunity of paying my peppercorn of respect to a gentleman who like yourself has maintained his respectability in an immoral profession' (Dixon, 1879, p. 4). Kemble responded to this double-edged remark by pointing out that 'no actor has yet been sentenced to death or suspended on the gallows' (p. 4).

Fanny Kemble confessed to Lady Dacre that, should she fail to obtain a theatrical engagement, 'I shall fall back upon my original plan, to me so far preferable, of giving readings' (1882, vol. III, p. 215). She gladly accepted Dr Hawtrey's invitation to give a reading at Eton College, where 'The Eton young gentlemen addressed me with a kind and flattering compliment through their captain' (p. 280). After her marriage to Theodore Martin, Helen Faucit virtually confined herself to readings which she considered to be more in keeping with her new status. In January 1877 she was planning a variant on solo performances by involving other professionals and amateurs in a reading of *The Merchant of Venice*. She wrote to Henry Irving: 'My male assistants in the little reading, which I have been *talked into* giving, will be mostly clergymen. The Reverend Mr. Ainger of the Temple Church has a fine voice and

reads Shakespeare extremely well. He is to be Shylock. I am much
wanting a good Bassanio. I asked Canon Duckworth, but he is fully
engaged on 27th' (L. Irving, 1951, p. 288). The actor therefore found
himself not only reading Shakespeare with clergymen, but substituting
for one of their number.

Miss Faucit's enlistment of other readers was in marked contrast to
what must be regarded as the most curious reading ever given – that of
Hamlet by Revd J. C. M. Bellew. Leaving Oxford without taking his
degree, Bellew entered holy orders, having failed in his attempt to make
his way in the theatre under Macready. By the mid 1850s Bellew was
accounted the most popular preacher in London, with his *voix d'or*, fine –
allegedly bleached – white hair and impeccable ecclesiastical millinery.
Bellew took a proprietary chapel, where the pew rents exceeded his
rental by an estimated £1,000 annually. The very existence of pews
('dozing pens termed pews' as Pugin called them – 1841, p. 31) was contentious and the Cambridge Camden Society (Chadwick, 1966 , vol. I,
p. 213) had led the assault on them in its journal the *Ecclesiologist*, citing
and indicting the church of Langley Mark, Bucks., for its 'most remarkable pen [pew] . . . fitted with a comfortable sofa running the whole
length' (vol. II, 1842–3, p. 139). The principle that most, if not all, pews
should be free of charge was strenuously upheld by Bishop Fraser (1872,
p. 58) in the new churches erected in his diocese. In Bellew's case his
adherence to a quasi-theatrical form of seating and feeing was in
keeping with the generally dramatic tone of his services and preaching.
As a young man, actor J. H. Barnes attended Bellew's Bloomsbury
Chapel. He judged Bellew 'the very best reader and elocutionist that I
have ever heard down to to-day'. Barnes found Bellew's theatrical style
conducive to a greater appreciation of the Anglican service: 'I am the
last man to advocate theatricalism in devotion, but I am bound to say
that J. C. M. Bellew first opened my eyes and ears to the beauties and
strength of the Church service' (1914, p. 5). Bellew coached the French
actor Charles Fechter in the part of Hamlet. Bellew's own rendition of
Hamlet, in which the stage was peopled with living actors whose 'duty was
simply to suit the action to the word while Bellew recited the play', was
described by John Hollingshead as 'the real union of Church and Stage'
(1895, vol. I, pp. 195–6). Philip Collins provides a persuasive explanation
for the appeal of this literally unique performance:

Many respectable people, particularly those of Evangelical or Nonconformist
religious persuasions, would never enter a theatre, but attending a reading was
permissible – a reading by a clergyman was even more evidently unobjection-

able – and a reading with actors in costume, scenery and effects provided the happiest of accommodations with one's puritan conscience. (*Listener* 25 November 1971)

The spirit of Ben Jonson's Puritans, Tribulation – a Pastor of Amsterdam – and Ananias – a deacon there – (*The Alchemist*), was still alive in Victorian England. Bellew's personal life might have been the subject for a play: divorced from his first wife; remarrying to a divorcee; imprisoned – in Canterbury gaol – for bankruptcy; and eventually converting to Roman Catholicism. His son Kyrle Bellew became a successful actor.

Dickens's readings from his own works increased the public's appetite for this form of entertainment. He wrote of his experience visiting a mechanics' institute: 'I fancied I detected a shyness in admitting that human nature when at leisure has any desire whatever to be relieved and diverted.' Thus it was first necessary for members

to be knocked on the head with Gas, Air, Water, Food, the Solar System, the Geological periods, Criticism on Milton, the Steam-engine, John Bunyan, and the Arrow-Headed Inscriptions, before they might be tickled by those unaccountable choristers, the negro singers in the court costume of the reign of George the Second . . . the masking of entertainment and pretending it was something else . . . was manifest even in the pretense of dreariness that the unfortunate entertainers themselves felt obliged in decency to put forth when they came here. (*All The Year Round* 30 June 1860)

This was clearly getting the worst of both education and entertainment. Readings, however, developed an immense following. A journal, *Penny Readings*, was published in monthly issues containing pieces of suitable literary quality 'For the use of literary and scientific institutions, recreation societies, mutual improvement associations, mechanics' institutes, young men's societies, working men's clubs and all kindred societies' (in H. P. Smith, 1960, p. 35).

Up and down the land, clergymen organised readings as an inducement to attract and retain the interest of their parishioners (Meller, 1976, p. 135). The quality of the experience was distinctly variable. The parishioners of Ilmington, near Stratford-upon-Avon, were fortunate that their rector, Revd Julian Charles Young, had inherited the dramatic gifts of his father, the celebrated actor Charles Mayne Young. Julian Young was not born under a lucky star; within ten days of his birth on 7 July 1806 his mother died. The boy attended Dr Charles Richardson's school in Clapham where a fellow pupil was John Mitchell Kemble. At the age of fifteen Julian Young was admitted to the University of St Andrew's through the good offices of Walter Scott: 'When he was nineteen his heart was set on taking Holy Orders, and as it was necessary for him to go through a preliminary course of three years at one of the universities, his father was at a loss to know at what college to enter him' (Stoddard, 1874, p. xxii). Fortunately Charles Mayne Young was not without influential connections. The Duke of York advised Christ Church, Oxford, but a place was not available; however Robert Peel secured one at Worcester College, which Julian Young entered in 1825. He was ordained in 1830 and later that year was appointed Chaplain of the Palace, Hampton Court; Lord Brougham offered him the living of Barton in Lincolnshire, which he accepted, subsequently taking that at Ilmington. As with the Kembles, acting families of distinction met with no barriers to social advancement. J. M. Kemble rejected the Church, not it him. Though in Julian Young's case there was no doubt on either side about the genuineness of his religious calling – to which he devoted forty-three years' service – the aura of the theatre abided with him. To Fanny Kemble, a friend from childhood, 'he always seemed . . . rather the wrong man in the wrong place, being essentially and by nature an actor, which I do not think an advantage to a clergyman, though there is no doubt that the two professions have some elements and some temptations in common' (1890, vol. 1, p. 157).

F. C. Burnand's description of Revd Julian Young's reading from the Bible suggests little resistance, on the cleric's part, to such temptations:

Our attention was riveted on him. He took in the whole congregation at a glance; he directed his eyes so that each particular person feeling himself, or herself, addressed, thenceforth became intensely interested. The lesson was about the rebellion of Korah, Dathan, and Abiram (I trust I have the names correct . . .) and he made his 'great hit' with the climax to which he led up most artistically, without further reference to the book, which would have detracted from the effect –
  'The earth opened' –
  We were all thunderstruck . . .
He paused again the earth had opened; we saw the scene; we dared hardly anticipate the *dénouement*. He continued, as very slowly he lifted up the side of the book with his right hand, 'And (pause) the earth (pause – then very slowly) swallowed them up!' and here he perceptibly shuddered, closed his eyes as if to hide from his vision the dreadful spectacle, and then closed the book with a sharp snap (as if bottling up Korah and Co for ever), and then the congregation breathed again as Mr Young, having quite recovered from the effect of his own dramatic rendering, proceeded with the following portion of the morning service. (1904, vol. 1, pp. 77–8)

Readings were exempt from the reproofs which such histrionics in a church might provoke from some quarters. Julian Young's arena was more than merely geographically far removed from the scenes of his father's triumphs in the leading metropolitan theatres – 'our school-room, sixty feet long . . . crowded every night I read, not only with our own parishioners, but with many from neighbouring villages. Rain, snow, the darkness of Erebus, never prevented our people from atten-dance' (1871, p. 471). Inhospitable though the conditions might be, read-ings in rural communities did not have to contend with competition from other entertainments, save the public house. Young could actually cite an example of the redemptive power of his readings: a villager who in his wife's words 'were once r-a-ther given to drink; but, since he've heard your lecs [lectures], he seems an altered man, and never takes nothing but tea' (p. 471). The man himself averred that 'I've never liked church; and I never could abear sermons', but, after attending Young's readings 'I thought I'd go and hear you preach' and thereafter never missed church, morning or evening (p. 472). Revd Julian Young gave his fellow clergymen the benefit of his advice in 'On the proper mode of conduct-ing the Church service', 'a paper read at a clerical meeting in a rural dis-trict' (1875, p. 221).

The Suffolk parishioners of W. S. Penley's uncle were less fortunate. The actor visited his uncle by way of preparation for the role of Revd Robert Spalding in *The Private Secretary*, the farcical comedy by Charles Hawtrey, son of Eton master Revd Dr J. W. Hawtrey. At a croquet party, wearing full clerical dress, Penley (illustration 6) 'was naturally mistaken by the good folks for a genuine budding curate', until he emitted 'one short, sharp, hasty word', which aroused suspicions amongst the other guests (Penley, 1884, p. 64). Penley attended Penny Readings at which his uncle read

two or three chapters out of the *Pickwick Papers*. The good man could not read for nuts, but as he was the Vicar they seemed to be afraid to 'goose' him. Quite late in the evening, when a succession of maddening recitations and excruciat-ing songs had worked the audience into a delirium of enjoyment, I was asked if I could do a little something. (pp. 76–7)

Penley's choice, a poem entitled 'What could a poor girl do?', proved too much for the susceptibilities of the rural audience, one of whom lapsed into hysterics. The entertainment was curtailed; Penley left the next day.

A fundamental shift in the balance of power between the theatre and the Church had taken place. The Church was appropriating theatrical

6. W. S. Penley in preparation for his role as Revd Robert Spalding in
The Private Secretary

forms of entertainment to enhance its own attractiveness and, often, to
raise money in the process. As early as December 1857 'the
Churchwardens, overseers and other inhabitants of the parish of All
Saints, Poplar in Middlesex' applied to the Lord Chamberlain 'to grant
the Licence required by Law' for an amateur entertainment for the
benefit of their 'Literary Institution' (LC 1 58 Public Record Office). Not
that those promoting such activities necessarily approved of, let alone
indulged in, theatre-going. Moral scruples apart, in some cases they were
in competition with the professional theatre. Henry Solly confessed
'Twice I yielded in those days to the temptation of going to the theatre

(which would have been very great if I had not sternly fought it . . .)'
(1893, vol. ii, p. 264). The plays he saw were *Our American Cousin,* and
Byron's *Manfred* at Drury Lane with Samuel Phelps.

Born in Devonport on 13 February 1804 to a well-to-do merchant
family, Samuel Phelps received a good classical education, but,
orphaned at the age of sixteen, he moved to London and soon embarked
on a stage career, first in the provinces, then, uneasily, under Macready's
management. In 1844 Phelps took over the management of Sadler's
Wells Theatre in Islington, which had once been owned by a clergyman,
Revd William Baker (Arundell, 1965, p. 37). As Phelps pointed out in his
address to the residents of Islington, his venture at Sadler's Wells was a
direct consequence of the 1843 Theatres Act: 'the law has placed all theatres upon an equal footing of security and respectability, leaving no
difference except in the object and conduct of management. These circumstances justify the notion that each separate division of our immense
metropolis, with its 2,000,000 of inhabitants, may have its own well-con-
ducted theatre within a reasonable distance of the homes of its patrons'
(Phelps and Forbes-Robertson, 1886, p. 64).

The principle of neighbourhood theatres, which Phelps was advocating and himself implementing in Islington, was comparable to the
programme of church-building which Bishop Blomfield, the opponent
of the spread of theatres, had undertaken in the London diocese. In his
A Charge to the Clergy of the Diocese of London at his Primary Visitation in
1858, Archibald Tait, who had succeeded Blomfield in 1856, listed the
new churches consecrated by his predecessor. Of these 155 churches,
10 were in Islington, 9 of them (no figures were given for St Jude's)
served a combined population of 92,000, with a total 'Largest average
Adult Congregation[s]' of 8,550 and 4,098 'Children in Day Schools'
(Tait, 1858, appendix A). The capacity of Sadler's Wells at that time
was 2,600 (S. Allen, 1971, p. 79); crowded houses were reported from
the beginning of Phelps's management and could have amounted to
over 15,000 at six performances a week. There were, of course, places
of worship other than Blomfield's churches and the variable patterns
of church- and theatre-going make direct comparison impossible, but
Sadler's Wells's weekly attendances were in all probability almost
double those of the 'Largest average Adult Congregation[s]' listed by
Tait. In contrast to his predecessor, Tait endorsed the theatre as a force
for good. When the bishop met Samuel Phelps, who generally declined
social invitations, at Lord Campbell's house, the prelate 'took the
opportunity of thanking him [Phelps] for all the good he was doing,
especially among the masses, more good, in his opinion, he said, than

all the clergymen in the North of London put together' (Phelps and Forbes-Robertson, 1886, p. 14).

This was, of course, a reflection of Phelps's management. During his 18 seasons (1844–62) at Sadler's Wells, Phelps mounted 31 of Shakespeare's plays for a total of 1,632 performances (S. Allen, 1971, appendix 1). His productions were marked by good ensemble acting, tasteful and restrained settings and costumes, and – though indelicacy and impropriety fell victim to the blue pencil – texts which by the standards of the day were relatively full. In addition he revived Milman's *Fazio* (20 performances over 6 seasons), 6 of Sheridan Knowles's dramas and 3 new plays by Macready's protégé, Revd James White. White's plays were not outstandingly successful and during the run of *John Saville of Hampstead* Charles Dickens invited Phelps to join the dramatist 'For whose consolation a Lobster and glass of wine will be awaiting our return' from the play (Phelps and Forbes-Robertson, 1886, p. 390). Dickens was a strong supporter of Phelps's work as he showed in his speech at the Royal General Theatrical Fund's twelfth anniversary festival at the Freemasons' Tavern on 6 April 1857, when Phelps took the chair: 'I have as accurate a knowledge of that theatre [Sadler's Wells] as any man in the kingdom' (p. 251) proclaimed Dickens, who described the audience as 'most intelligent and attentive . . . a body of students' (p. 251).

The constitution of Phelps's audience is a matter of some dispute. Islington was a relatively poor district, populated by artisans and clerks. Phelps kept seat prices low (boxes 2s, pit 1s, gallery 6d), less than half those at Covent Garden and Drury Lane, but whether he changed the taste and behaviour of existing, hitherto unruly, theatre-goers or attracted a new more respectable following is beyond resolution. The sense that Phelps's regime would present competition for other cultural activities in Islington is discernible in Edward Smith's paper *The Theatre, A History and Moral Tendency* read to the Islington Literary and Scientific Institute on 2 February 1844:

The prevailing attachment to literary and scientific pursuits which happily exists in our country at the present day, has occasioned the interesting abodes of science and literature (in one of which in this locality we have now the high social gratification of assembling) to be preferred, and in some considerable degree to supersede, a resort by our intelligent and moral youth to assemblies and recreations, the gaiety and splendours of which are felt but feebly to compensate for the more sober and substantial benefits which institutions like our own are designed and found to yield. May we ever, therefore, cultivate and cherish these superior rational advantages, and not only give them our preference and our praise, but may we personally feel too that we are essentially profited by them. (E. Smith, 1844, p. 36)

As the reputation of Phelps's work spread, visitors came from further afield. Westland Marston described Sadler's Wells as 'a sort of pilgrim's shrine to the literary men of London' (Marston, 1890, p. 211). R. H. Horne, Tom Taylor, E. L. Blanchard and – from Germany – Theodor Fontane wended their way to Sadler's Wells. One of the most regular and enthusiastic visitors was Henry Morley, the drama critic of the *Examiner*. Born in 1822 Morley was brought up on a diet of 'A Heaven of glory and hell of groans' (Solly, 1898, p. 15), nevertheless at the age of nine he 'set up a theatre, with scenery and characters' (p. 12). Later at Dr Worthington's school in Bedford 'we had weekly recitations of poetry, and also got up the whole of "Julius Caesar"', in which Morley played Antony (p. 19); at sixteen he attended King's College where he 'continued about two years in the department of general literature' (p. 36) of which F. D. Maurice was then professor. Morley returned to King's in 1857 to give evening lectures, but as a Unitarian he was ineligible for a tenured appointment, though this did not bar him from one at University College, where he became Professor of English in 1865. Fired with missionary zeal, Morley continued to travel the country giving extension lectures and prepared the multiple volumes in the Morley's Universal Library series. Morley had no reservations about the theatre's moral benefits:

The mind that does not shut itself out from the world, or hold itself the universal arbiter, will find in all that breathes a spark of the Divine God, who gave to the moth his dainty wings, and to the violet a scent whose use is but the creation of pleasure, gave to man the delights of speech, faculties that weave them by the subtlest of his arts into a flower-world of intellect and feeling. At the playhouse door, then, we may say to the doubting, Enter boldly, for here, too, there are gods. (1891, p. 25)

Within the portals of Sadler's Wells, Morley's message seemed to have been received and understood:

There sit our working-classes in a happy crowd, as orderly and reverent as if they were in church, and yet as unrestrained in their enjoyment as if listening to stories told them by their own firesides. It is hard to say how much such men who have few advantages of education must in their minds and characters be strengthened and refined when they are made accustomed to this kind of entertainment. (p. 138)

Unlike Charles Kemble, Macready and Charles Kean, Phelps did not solicit the company and approval of high society, but the calibre of his work and the integrity of his personal life brought recognition without him seeking it. In keeping with his life Phelps's funeral at Highgate cemetery in November 1878 was 'a quiet one, without parade or ostentation' (*Era* 17 November 1878). Nearly 1,000 people were present, led by the deceased's brother, Revd Robert Phelps, a mathematician and Master of Sidney Sussex College, Cambridge. Present too was actor Johnston Forbes-Robertson, who, in the 'Preface' to the biography of Phelps which he co-authored with the actor's nephew, wrote:

When the two great institutions, then, – the Church and the Stage, – whose united function it is to lift us into the higher and cheerier life, are at one, and the ministry of the priest is as earnest as that of the player, and the latter, as well as the former, receives from the State, his due meed of countenance and honour, – then, and only then, may we hope to see light in dark places, and a worthy crowning of national education, whether the studies of our youth have been necessarily confined to the Board-School, or have been pursued under the fostering care of an *Alma Mater*. (Phelps and Forbes-Robertson, 1886, p. x)

Phelps's achievement in advancing the *rapprochement* between the theatre, the Church and education shone forth as an example for the rest of the nineteenth century. 'Enter boldly, for here, too, there are gods,' exhorted Henry Morley, but one theatre which offered a very different prospect was the Victoria in Waterloo Road depicted in such Stygian terms by Kingsley in *Alton Locke* (1851). In 1850 Charles Mayhew described the threepenny gallery, which allegedly held between 1,500 and 2,000 people, as 'peculiar and awful' (Quennell, 1969, p. 51); there thronged costermongers and young women – some with babies – in a disorderly rabble, vociferously expressing their pleasure or disapproval, lubricated by alcohol: 'Whilst the pieces are going on, brown, flat bottles are frequently raised to the mouth' (p. 54). Temperance had in fact been common ground between the theatre and religious organisations since Douglas Jerrold inaugurated the genre of temperance melodrama with *Fifteen Years in a Drunkard's Life* (1828) (Booth, 1965, p. 132).

As Brian Harrison writes: 'Religion and recreation had once been closely integrated, but by the nineteenth century they were beginning to compete, not only for time but also in values' (1967, pp. 98–9). Amongst the initiatives which sought to bring religion and recreation together was that at the Victoria Theatre. In 1879 John Hollingshead attended a meeting of the Coffee Palace Association 'with a proposition to turn the Victoria Theatre in the New Cut, Lambeth . . . into a Coffee-Music-Hall Palace' (1895, vol. II, p. 150). Responsibility for bringing this scheme to fruition passed principally to Emma Cons, who had become involved in the management of a block of 'model' dwellings in Lambeth at the request of Octavia Hill. Octavia Hill had grown up in her mother's

circle, which included John Ruskin, Tom Hughes, Charles Kingsley and
F. D. Maurice, whose 'part-time secretary at ten shillings a week Octavia
Hill became' (D. Richards, 1958, p. 29). At a meeting, under the chair-
manship of Dean Stanley, in the Jerusalem Chamber of Westminster
Abbey in February 1880, sufficient support was forthcoming for the
Coffee Music Hall Association to take an eighteen-year lease on the
Victoria Theatre. The leaflet announcing the opening of the Victoria
Coffee Rooms read: 'It is not proposed to provide for a higher class of
audience than that which at present frequents music-halls, but only to
offer that class an entertainment which shall amuse without degrading
them, and to which men may take their wives and children without
shaming or harming them' (C. Hamilton and Baylis, 1926, p. 179). After
expenditure of some £3,000 on alterations and decorations, the Royal
Victoria Coffee Hall opened on Boxing Day 1880 with a variety of acts
of suitable propriety and with alcohol banished from the premises.
Beginning with amusement Emma Cons gradually introduced improvement, with lantern lectures and the Royal Victoria Choir. In October
1881 William Poel took over as manager and remained in the post for two
years, during which the Prince and Princess of Wales attended an Irish
ballad concert on 9 February 1882. Poel had reservations about the
Victoria putting too much emphasis on education rather than entertainment, but progressively more educational activity developed with the
encouragement and support of Nonconformist politician and philan-
thropist Samuel Morley. The history of the parallel development of
Morley College and the Royal Victoria Coffee Hall (popularly known as
the Old Vic) is fully chronicled (D. Richards, 1958, and George Rowell,
1993, respectively) and stands as an example of the shared goals of the
theatre and education. In his influential study of Lambeth during
1870–1930 Jeffrey Cox places the Old Vic in the context of other similar
initiatives in the neighbourhood:

After the Bible Christians began Sunday services, the Old Vic, with its temperance lectures, improving concerts, temperance cafe, adult vocational class, gym-
nasium and library, was distinguishable only in its scale from any number of
church- and chapel-related institutions which had grown out of settlement and
parochial and mission hall activity – prompted by precisely the same improving
motives which had led Miss Cons to Lambeth in the first place. (1982, p. 88)

As adult education developed through the university extension work
(J. F. C. Harrison, 1961; Kelly, 1962) emanating from Oxford, Cambridge
and London, drama no longer had to justify its place on the syllabus.
William Poel staged *The Alchemist* for the Cambridge summer meeting

of 1902 and in 1903 he staged *Edward II* at the Oxford summer school (Foulkes, 1979, p. 35).

Education and self-improvement proved to be fruitful ground for the *rapprochement* between Church and stage. There was self-interest on both sides. It was in the theatre's interest to assert its educational value, and the Church saw the potential of entertainments to enhance its own attractiveness. As Newman foresaw, placing themselves in the market for such gratifications was hazardous for the Church and for education, as their integrity was all too easily compromised in the search for popularity. Newman and Maurice set high ideals, but in practice the latter's were diluted in the Working Men's Colleges. Ironically it was the work of retired actor W. C. Macready, actor's son Revd Julian Young and actor Samuel Phelps which most effectively maintained steadfastness of purpose in pursuit of the elusive goal of being 'popular and profound', qualities which F. D. Maurice identified in the plays of William Shakespeare.

CHAPTER 6

Shakespeare

We actually got two Bishops to preach the canonization sermons of Sunday last.

Saturday Review

On 18 February 1839 Queen Victoria attended Macready's performance of *King Lear* at Covent Garden. The next day the young monarch exchanged impressions of the play with her prime minister, Lord Melbourne, as she recorded in her journal: 'Talked to Lord Melbourne of my having seen *King Lear* and its being a fine play; talked of it for some time, of the way it was acted at Covent Garden. "I have always thought him [Lear] a foolish old fellow", said Lord Melbourne. "It's a rough, coarse play . . . written for those times, with exaggerated characters"' (Esher, 1912, vol. II, pp. 121–2). The charge of coarseness was one frequently levelled at Shakespeare during the early nineteenth century, by Revd Thomas Best, J. H. Newman, Charles Kingsley and F. D. Maurice amongst others. Thomas Middleton Raysor identifies Coleridge's defence of Shakespeare 'against the charges of coarseness and immorality' as one of the main achievements of his Shakespearean criticism (1960, vol. I, p. xxix): 'He [Coleridge] pointed out that Shakespeare's gusts of laughter drove away the poisonous mist of impurity; and he made the indispensable distinction between morals and manners of speech' (p. xxx). Coleridge's assertion of Shakespeare's morality was recorded by the nameless reporter of the first of his six Shakespearean lectures in Bristol (1813–14): 'The next character belonging to Shakespeare as Shakespeare was the *keeping at all times the high road of life*. With him there were no innocent adulteries; he never rendered that amicable which religion and reason taught us to detest; he never clothed vice in the garb of virtue, like Beaumont and Fletcher, the Kotzebues of his day' (Raysor, 1960, vol. II, p. 216). In addition to his assertion of Shakespeare's moral rectitude, Coleridge rendered other valuable services to the bard. He rebutted the neo-classical critics, who censured Shakespeare for disregarding the three unities, arguing that a genius such as Shakespeare cannot be lawless, but originates his own forms: 'No work of genius dare want its appropriate form; neither indeed is there any danger of this. As it must not, so neither can it, be lawless. For it is even this that constitutes its genius – the power of acting creatively under laws of its own origination' (vol. 1, pp. 197–8).

Shakespeare's dramatic form did not serve its nineteenth-century imitators well, but his treatment of characterisation provided a more valid model. Coleridge pioneered the psychological analysis of Shakespeare's characters, recognising that their strength lay in their many facets and apparent contradictions, in contrast to the two-dimensional, clear-cut characterisation of plays such as *Bertram* – 'all Hamlet's character' encompassed 'his meditative excess . . . his yielding to passion . . . his tendency to generalise . . . his true gentlemanly manners . . . his . . . fondness for presentiments' (vol. 1, pp. 33–4). Coleridge proclaimed Shakespeare's women as examples of the ideal in the real and, with reference to *Venus and Adonis*, defined imagination as 'the power by which one image or feeling is made to modify many others and by a fusion to force many into one' (vol. 1, p. 188).

The originality and range of Coleridge's writings on Shakespeare make them a landmark in Shakespearean criticism. S. Schoenbaum writes that Coleridge 'formulated an ideal of transcendent genius' (1991, p. 183) and Raysor declares: 'In the history of English literary criticism there is no work which surpasses in interest Coleridge's lectures on Shakespeare . . . Few English critics before Coleridge had praised Shakespeare ungrudgingly and sympathetically, and none of these with a critical genius worthy of his subject' (1960, vol. 1, p. xv).

Aron Y. Stavisky has outlined the trends in Shakespearean criticism, advances in scholarship and the foundation of the Shakespeare Society (1840–53) by John Payne Collier (see Ganzel, 1982) and the New Shakespeare Society (1873–94) by F. J. Furnivall (see Benzie, 1983) during the Victorian period, when 'Since God was dead, men transferred His attributes to great figures living and dead' (Stavisky, 1969, p. vii). Thomas Carlyle included Shakespeare in *On Heroes, Hero-Worship and the Heroic in History* (1841), hailing him as 'the Prophet of God': 'But call it worship, call it what you will, is it not a right glorious thing, and set of things that Shakespeare has brought us? For myself, I feel that there is actually a kind of sacredness in the fact of such a man being sent into this Earth. Is he not an eye to us all, a blessed heaven-sent Bringer of Light?' (1967, p. 343).

On the terrestrial plane Carlyle recognised Shakespeare as a national asset: 'He is the grandest thing we have yet done. For our honour among foreign nations, as an ornament to our English household, what item is there that we would not surrender rather than him?' (pp. 344–5). Peter Brooker and Peter Widdowson instance cases in which Shakespeare was appropriated for patriotic and imperialist ends (1987, pp. 118–19), a prerequisite for which was his enshrinement in English homes from the monarch's to those of her humblest subjects.

A key figure in the popularising of Shakespeare was Charles Knight, born in 1791 and brought up in Windsor, where he was active in the building of a new theatre, which opened in August 1815 to the protests of 'sectaries who regarded our proceedings as highly criminal. The time was far distant when Shakespeare would be quoted in the Dissenter's pulpit' (Knight, 1864–5, vol. I, p. 218). Knight himself saw no contradiction in supporting both Church and stage, being 'secretary to our Church Building Committee' (p. 219). He wrote a play, *Arminius,* which he submitted to Drury Lane in 1813, but he supported the abolition of the monopoly. Knight bewailed the lack of leisure facilities for the 'blithe-looking father in his Sunday coat, and happy mother in her smartest bonnet' and their children, with the British Museum closed on Sundays, 'no national gallery, no museum in South Kensington . . . no Zoological Gardens . . . The doors of St Paul's and Westminster Abbey were never open without a fee, except during the hours of divine service . . . When night came, the pit and gallery of the few theatres were crowded after such a fight at their entrances as the caricaturist depicted' (vol. II, pp. 26–7).

In the interests of the masses Knight cultivated many influential sympathisers. The Bishop of Winchester and Lord Lansdowne supported his membership of the Athenaeum, though Knight decided not to risk rejection, but he was elected to the Garrick and Reform Clubs. In June 1847 he joined Revd H. H. Milman and Viscount Morpeth (later the seventh Earl of Carlisle) to support a proposal to erect a statue to Caxton in Westminster Abbey. The next year Knight was involved in a series of amateur performances with Charles Dickens, Mark Lemon, John Forster, G. H. Lewes, Augustus Egg and Mrs Cowden Clarke, with the support of Lord Morpeth, to raise funds to endow a 'Perpetual Curatorship' of Shakespeare's house. Through Dickens, Knight became friendly with Revd James White who, 'as President of the Ventnor Literary Institute . . . gave a stimulus, as only such a man can give, to the intellectual pursuits of a mixed population' (vol. III, p. 114). The Amateur

Company of the Guild of Literature and Art (including Dickens, Knight, Douglas Jerrold, Forster, Westland Marston, R. H. Horne, Wilkie Collins, John Tenniel, Augustus Egg, Clarkson Stanfield) shared the same objective, performing not only at Bulwer Lytton's country seat, Knebworth, and at the Duke of Devonshire's Piccadilly mansion (before the Queen), but also to 'the sturdier critics and the more youthful and sympathising fair of the North' (vol. III, p. 118) in Liverpool, Manchester, Sunderland and Newcastle.

As publisher to the Society for the Diffusion of Useful Knowledge, Knight produced the *Penny Magazine* and the *Penny Chronicle*; he was the author of biographies of Caxton and Shakespeare. Knight began to prepare his pictorial edition of Shakespeare in 1837, his interest in the bard having been ignited in 1811 when he read *Remarks on Some Characters of Shakespeare* by Revd Thomas Whateley, father of Richard Whateley, Archbishop of Dublin of whom Knight wrote: 'I think I may venture to say that this eminent man had not fully imbibed the spirit of his father's book' (vol. II, p. 280). Knight's first concern in preparing his edition was to secure suitable illustrations; he rejected the contributions to Boydell's Shakespeare Gallery as 'little more than vehicles for the display of false costume' (vol. II, p. 284) and instead commissioned Messrs Poynter and Harvey. Knight also rejected any expurgation of the text along the lines of Dr Thomas and Henrietta Bowdler's notorious *Family Shakespeare* (1807 and 1818) and immersed himself in scholarly editions, disputed readings, emendations, copies of the quartos and folio in the British Museum and the chronology of the plays. Thus, although he was aiming at a popular readership, there was nothing condescending about Knight's editions. In his introduction to *Two Gentlemen of Verona*, Knight advanced his views on the nature of Shakespeare's genius, rejecting, like Coleridge, the idea of 'a sort of inspired barbarian, who worked without method, and wholly without learning', arguing instead that:

before Shakespeare can be properly understood, the popular mind must be led in an opposite direction, and we must learn to regard him as he really was, as the most consummate of artists, who had a complete and absolute control over all the material and instruments of his art, without any subordination to mere impulses and caprices, – with entire self-possession and perfect knowledge. (vol. II, p. 287)

In his goal of engaging 'the popular mind' with the works of 'the most consummate of artists' Knight was advancing the cause of the popularisation of culture, for which Shakespeare's own modest social background made him an apt subject. In *Self-help* (1859) Samuel Smiles wrote 'it is unquestionable that he [Shakespeare] sprang from a humble rank. His father was a butcher and grazier' (1905, p. 9). Smiles applied a Maurice-like rigour to 'Relaxation': 'Amusement of any kind is not wasting time, but economizing life' (1903, p. 370) and was at pains to stress that Shakespeare 'must have been a close student and a hard worker' (1905, p. 9). Smiles was, probably unconsciously, confronting the irony that those who provide for the leisure of others are often exemplars of hard work and industry in their own calling.

The right to perform Shakespeare's plays had been one of the most contentious issues before the 1832 Select Committee – the patent theatres seeking to maintain their monopoly over the minor theatres who thereto had to resort to various ruses to stage his plays. Annabel Patterson's contention that, in the early nineteenth century, populist Shakespeare became politically unpalatable (1989, pp. 5–7) has been countered by Jane Moody's 'more eclectic description of Shakespeare's cultural capital in nineteenth-century London': 'Managers employed their house dramatists to adapt or "melodramatize" Shakespeare for a particular playhouse. My argument is that this process of adaptation began primarily as a legal safeguard but also provided an opportunity to translate Shakespeare for popular consumption' (1994, pp. 62–3).

That Shakespeare did have a direct appeal to radicals and Chartists has been demonstrated by Jeremy Crump's findings in Leicester (1986, pp. 271–82), where the journalist and ex-shoemaker Thomas Cooper took the lead. In his autobiography Cooper recalled his youthful encounter with Shakespeare's work under the tutelage of Joseph Clark, a keen theatre-goer: 'All this directed me to a more intelligent reading of Shakespeare, for myself, though I did not yet feel the due impression of his greatness' (1872, p. 42). Cooper founded a breakaway branch of the Leicester Chartist Association which was known as the Shakespeare Chartist Association (1841) and also produced the Shakespeare Chartist Hymn-book. In December 1842 the Shakespeare Chartist Association staged *Hamlet* with Cooper in the title role.

The Shakespeare tercentenary of 1864 provided the opportunity for all sections of society to pay tribute to Shakespeare in their distinctive ways. In the capital, journalist W. Hepworth Dixon recruited dukes (two), earls (nine), lords (nine) and baronets (six) to the National Shakespeare Committee on which the Church was represented by: 'the Archbishops of Canterbury, York and Dublin, by the Bishops of London, Worcester, and St. David's, by the Deans of Canterbury, Westminster, St. Paul's and Chichester, and by many distinguished

7. Concert in the Royal Agricultural Hall

clergymen' (report read at a meeting on 4 January 1864). The National Shakespeare Committee was dogged by rivalries and disputes (see Foulkes, 1984, pp. 8–10) and although some London Shakespeare productions were included in its programme, the initiative was taken over by the Working Men's Shakespeare Committee, which promoted a concert in the Royal Agricultural Hall and a tree-planting on Primrose Hill.

The Royal Agricultural Hall concert on 21 April included a recitation by Samuel Phelps of act 1 of *The Tempest* and 'England's Minstrel King' with words specially composed by G. Linnaeus Banks, a keen supporter of mechanics' institutes. Seats were modestly priced, some at 10s. 6d. but most in the range 1s – 5s, all affording a view of the platform with 'THE COLOSSAL TERCENTENARY BUST' of Shakespeare modelled by Charles Bacon (illustration 7) . If the tone of the concert was egalitarian, that of the tree-planting on 23 April was radical, even though the sapling had been donated by the Queen. The occasion coincided with the unexpected departure that morning of the Italian soldier and politician General Garibaldi aboard the Duke of Sutherland's yacht *Undine*, his visit having aroused government fears of social unrest. There was considerable overlap between the membership of the Working Men's Shakespeare Committee and their Garibaldi Committee and the authorities were alert to the prospect of the ceremony turning into a political protest. After Samuel Phelps had planted 'the People's oak': 'In the name of the workmen of England' (*The Times* 28 April 1864), a splinter group of 60 to 70 people attracted a crowd of 4,000, which was addressed by the radical Etonian lawyer Edmund Beales, who alleged a government conspiracy behind Garibaldi's departure. The police moved in, but the crowd dispersed peacefully, though the Home Secretary, Sir G. Gray, was subjected to questions on the incident in the House of Commons two days later.

The metropolitan Shakespeare tercentenary celebrations had effectively been wrested from the great and good by the working classes, in whose 'English household[s]' the popular Staffordshire pottery figures of Shakespeare and General Garibaldi (Pugh, 1970) provided 'an ornament'. In Stratford-upon-Avon the principal tercentenary souvenir was a tripartite silk ribbon depicting a rather bloated Shakespeare, his birthplace and Holy Trinity Church in which his mortal remains were interred. The inclusion of Holy Trinity was apt since the Church played a prominent part in the Stratford celebrations. The originator of Shakespeare celebrations in Stratford was David Garrick, whose Shakespeare jubilee in 1769 belatedly commemorated the bicentenary of the poet's birth. Christian Deelman concludes the opening chapter, 'The birth of a god', of his *The Great Shakespeare Jubilee* as follows: 'The greatest truth that Garrick wished to diffuse was the pre-eminence of Shakespeare. For over twenty years he spread the gospel through his acting, until in 1769, he moved out of the limiting confines of Drury Lane to Stratford there to stage the greatest ritual he could devise to the God of his idolatry' (Deelman, 1964, p. 35). Although Garrick made the pilgrimage to Stratford his jubilee relied heavily on the metropolitan participation, both for performers and patrons, with the locals confined to – and resenting – a subservient, servicing role (see Deelman, 1964, and Stockholm, 1964). By 1864 Stratford was fortunate in possessing a leading citizen able and willing to orchestrate a fitting tribute – Edward Fordham Flower. By then Flower, an increasingly successful brewer, had lived in Stratford for over thirty years, but he brought wider horizons to the small Warwickshire town.

Born in 1805, Flower belonged to a notable liberal and Unitarian family. His father, Richard, and uncle, Benjamin, had founded the *Cambridge Intelligencer* to oppose the (Napoleonic) war with France and the persecution of dissenters. Benjamin Flower's two daughters were remarkable women: the elder, Eliza was a composer of hymns and political songs; the younger, Sarah, was a poet who wrote pieces for the Anti-Corn-Law League. After her father's death in 1829 Sarah, who had married fellow radical and inventor William Bridges Adams, lived with W. J. Fox, politician (Liberal MP), preacher and journalist. Both Sarah Adams Flower, as she was then known, and Fox's daughter 'Tottie' evinced an inclination to go on the stage from which Fox's friend W. C. Macready did his best to deter them, prevailing with 'Tottie', but not with Sarah until she had tried her skills unsuccessfully in Richmond (as Lady Macbeth) and Bath. Instead Sarah Adams Flower turned to play-writing, producing *Vivia Perpetua. A Dramatic Poem* (1841). As drama critic of the *Morning Chronicle*, Fox applied his earnest reforming zeal to the theatre, attacking the patent theatres' monopoly, eulogising Macready's Covent Garden management, and – in advance of Matthew Arnold – advocating a National Theatre: 'The great agencies of civilization are rarely called into existence commercially' (Garnett and Garnett, 1910, p. 250). Fox seized on the poetic dramas of Lytton, Sheridan Knowles, R. H. Horne, Westland Marston and Thomas Noon Talfourd as harbingers of regeneration, writing of Talfourd's *Ion*: 'It enshrines the purest spirit of Christianity in the gracefullest forms of ancient Greece' (p. 245). Fox's own sermons at the Unitarian South Place Chapel in Finsbury were virtually political discourses and John Hollingshead observed that 'Bentham's much quoted maxim – the "greatest happiness of the greatest number" – the essence of Free Trade – might have been emblazoned over the pulpit' (Hollingshead, 1895, vol. I, p. 45). Nevertheless Fox's advocacy of a state-subsidised National Theatre showed that he was no slavish Benthamite.

In 1823 Fox visited Robert Owen's practical experiment in paternalistic socialism at New Lanark and observed that 'The children of the factory have every provision for amusement and instruction that could be coveted by the wealthy' (p. 48). The following year Edward Flower accompanied his father to New Lanark on a visit from the 20,000-acre settlement in Wabash, Illinois, which Richard Flower had bought in 1817 to escape high taxation and political illiberalism in England. Edward Flower did not return to America, but 'remained for six months at his studies in New Lanark' (Smiles, 1880, p. 399), no doubt absorbing some of the social and educational ideas which Owen practised and preached, notably in *A New View of Society* (1813): 'It has been and ever will be found far more easy to lead mankind to virtue, or to rational conduct by providing them with well-regulated innocent amusements than to submit to useless restraints' (G. D. H. Cole, 1927, p. 46). Accordingly the upper storey of the New Institution building was 'arranged to serve for a School, Lecture Room and Church. And these are intended to have a direct influence in forming the character of the villagers' (p. 47).

As his business prospered, helped by the remission of beer tax in 1832, Edward Flower took a keen interest in civic matters, serving as mayor twice in the 1850s and again in 1864. His approach to the forthcoming Shakespeare tercentenary was energetic and efficient. He set up committees, engaged Ulster lawyer Robert Hunter as secretary, and secured the Earl of Carlisle, then in his second term of office as Lord Lieutenant of Ireland, as president. Carlisle was an apt choice – having won prizes for Latin and English verse as an Oxford undergraduate, he had tried his hand at drama (*The Last of the Greeks or the Fall of Constantinople*, 1828). In 1847 he was supportive of the purchase of Shakespeare's birthplace by public subscription and was wont to entertain fellow Etonian Charles Kean at Dublin Castle. Flower showed poorer judgement in placing responsibility for negotiating with London actors in the hands of Revd J. C. M. Bellew, who had advanced some suggestions for the tercentenary in *Shakespeare's House at New Place, Stratford-upon-Avon* (1863). Samuel Phelps, Helen Faucit and Charles Fechter all fell foul of Bellew and his services were dispensed with.

Although himself a Nonconformist, Flower recognised that the celebration of the national poet required the offices of the Established Church and in Revd G. Granville, Rector of Holy Trinity, he found a willing and effective ally, as he did in Revd Julian Young, Vicar of Ilmington, who also served on the committee. Granville and Young were amongst the clerics present at the banquet held in the specially constructed and versatile pavilion on 23 April: 'As for the clergy on the Shakespeare Committee, with blue and silver scarves over their black coats, they resembled a group of disorderly undertakers, who had plundered a milliner's shop on their way home from a funeral' (*Saturday Review* 30 April 1864). Fifteen toasts were proposed and twelve responded to: the Earl of Carlisle was quivering with nervousness; Richard Chenevix Trench, recently installed as Archbishop of Dublin, returned thanks for the clergy; his Cambridge contemporary Richard Monckton Milnes, now Lord Houghton, spoke eloquently; Professor Leitner from Germany brought an international dimension; Edward Flower resembled the doge of Venice; and William Creswick represented the theatre. Creswick was hardly one of his profession's brightest luminaries, though at the Surrey Theatre he had sought to emulate Samuel Phelps's Sadler's Wells management, but this did not diminish the significance of an actor taking his place alongside an archbishop.

'ST WILLIAM OF STRATFORD' ran the headline of the account of the 'Tercentenary Nativity' in the *Saturday Review*: 'We actually got two Bishops to preach the canonization sermons of Sunday last' (30 April 1864). In Holy Trinity, dramatist and journalist Andrew Halliday took his seat 'in the chancel exactly opposite the Bard's monument' in which he discerned 'strong vitality, freshness of spirit and liveliness of disposition . . . the face of a man who was full of natural genius and did not know it' (*All the Year Round* 21 May 1864). Unfortunately Archbishop Trench's preaching lacked such 'strong vitality'. Sarah Flower, wife of Edward's eldest son Charles, complained: 'The Shakespeare sermon preached by Archbishop Trench, but he had so bad a delivery that those a little way off could only catch the word Shakespeare – which rather shocked them' (in Foulkes, 1984, p. 28). Trench had evidently failed to heed the lessons on oratory of his archiepiscopal predecessor Richard Whateley.

Trench's text, 'Every good gift and every perfect gift is from above, and cometh down from the Father of lights' (James 1. 17), was in marked contrast to Revd Best's 'the unfruitful works of darkness'. Thanks and praise were due first to God 'that such a man has been among us' (Hunter, 1864, p. 201). The 'literature of a nation' was not 'merely an amusement of the cultivated few', but the means whereby 'the mighty heart of a people may be animated and quickened to heroic enterprise and worthiest endeavour' (p. 201). A source of national pride and a means of regeneration, Shakespeare was also upheld as a model for social stability: 'men . . . cheerfully working in their own appointed sphere the work which has been assigned to them, accepting God's world because it is His' (pp. 201–2), a view at variance with the previous day's events on Primrose Hill. The influence of Coleridge, the idol of Trench's Cambridge generation, was discernible in the archbishop's toleration of occasional coarseness, ascribable to the age in which Shakespeare wrote. The bard's works displayed 'healthiness, a moral soundness', which never challenged 'the everlasting ordinances' (p. 202), and consistently illustrated 'that men reap as they have sown' (p. 204), though leaving the readers to draw that conclusion. The real in 'those ideals of perfect womanhood' (p. 203) was exampled by Miranda, Imogen and Cordelia.

Trench asserted Shakespeare's 'intimate, in one sense profound, acquaintance with scripture', a subject upon which Charles

Wordsworth, the poet's nephew and Bishop of St Andrew's, who preached the afternoon sermon, wrote at length in *On Shakespeare's Knowledge and Use of the Bible* (1864). Wordsworth described Shakespeare as 'having been, in a more than ordinary degree, a diligent and devout reader of the Word of God' (p. 2), marshalling three types of evidence: 'First is the obvious reference to the facts and characters of the Bible which his plays contain; the second, the tone and colouring which pervade his moral and religious principles and sentiments; and third, the poetical thoughts or imagery which he appears to have borrowed more or less directly from the Scriptures' (p. 45). Wordsworth drew biblical examples from Parker's 'Bishops'' Bible (1568) and the Geneva Bible of 1560, those being the versions in commonest use in Shakespeare's day. Of *The Authorised Version of 1611* Wordsworth went so far as to suggest that 'it is probable that our translators of 1611 owed as much, or more, to Shakespeare than he owed to them' (p. 9) (Wordsworth accepted Malone's dating of two plays to after 1611). Certainly James I had experienced no conflict in extending his patronage to the Bible and Shakespeare's plays, both of which continued to resonate around Victorian churches and theatres. The Church and stage alike were inheritors and custodians of the finest creations of the English language. In 1870, the Convocation of Canterbury appointed committees to revise the Bible (Ensor, 1980, p. 143), but their remit was that 'changes were to be as few as possible' (Ollard and Crosse, 1912, p. 55). Thus even when their labours were completed – the New Testament in 1881, the Old Testament in 1884 – the Bible retained the character of *The Authorised Version* as its authentic voice. Given the period and stylistic similarities between *The Authorised Version* and Shakespeare's plays, a quotation such as 'happy are they that hear their detractions and can put them to mending' might well leave a congregation unsure of its origin. It is in fact from *Much Ado About Nothing* and was chosen by actor Squire Bancroft as his 'text' when, at the suggestion of Dr Boyd-Carpenter, Bishop of Ripon, he addressed the Church Congress on 'The art of speaking and reading' prompting 'some remarks about the affinity between the words of Shakespeare and the pages of Holy Writ. The same inspired truths abound throughout them both' (Squire Bancroft, 1925, p. 47). The Lord Chamberlain banned the Bible from the stage, but, from the tercentenary onwards, quotations from Shakespeare became increasingly unexceptionable in the pulpit. The problem with canonical texts, as Newman observed and the theatre knew, was that they could be subjected to contradictory interpretations. Even Shakespeare's knowledge and use of the Bible were susceptible to such treatment. Back in 1848 W. J. Birch examined Shakespeare's life and works to substantiate a very different view from Wordsworth's: 'We have therefore every a priori argument to suppose from his life what we have to confirm in the a posteriori examination of his works, that the tendency of Shakespeare's philosophy . . . and his views of religion were of a sceptical tendency' (Birch, 1848, pp. 14–15).

Wordsworth was convinced not only of Shakespeare's religious faith, but his 'conformity as a member of the Church of England' (Wordsworth, 1864, p. 228). How could the nation's bard have subscribed to other than the Established Church? Nevertheless, in proclaiming Shakespeare's God-given genius, the Church was also carrying out an act of appropriation for its own ends. For his tercentenary sermon, Wordsworth took the text 'All Thy works praise Thee, O Lord; and Thy Saints give thanks unto Thee' (Psalm 45. 10, Prayer Book version). If Coleridge's views were implicit in much of Trench's sermon, those of John Keble were explicitly cited in Wordsworth's. That 'the works of Shakespeare are plainly on the right side' was 'in accordance with the voice of one whose testimony upon such a point will be accepted as the highest and most unquestionable authority; I allude to the reverend author of the "Christian Year"' (Hunter, 1864, p. 211). In the Coleridgean vein, Wordsworth attributed 'the passages of a coarser sort . . . to the age in which he lived' (p. 212) and upheld Shakespeare's moral integrity. Unusually for the time Wordsworth referred to Shakespeare's theatre – 'but a hovel, all rude, and shapeless, and unadorned' – to make the point 'how little true greatness is dependent upon external circumstances' (p. 215). This was both a theological (cf. Newman's 'our true excellence' which came from within, not without) and a social point: Shakespeare 'debarred . . . from the higher classical education' (p. 215) had triumphed over this handicap, thereby providing an example of self-improvement to the unprivileged of Victorian England.

The common ground between Trench's and Wordsworth's sermons provides evidence of the establishment's attitude towards the uses of Shakespeare. His genius was derived from God, not from any other source; lapses into coarseness could be excused by the age in which he lived; his morality was sound and consistent with Christianity; he was no advocate of political disturbance, but an example of how someone from a humble background could achieve success despite unfavourable personal and social circumstances. Shakespeare had been reconstituted in the Victorian mould.

Deference to any lingering vestiges of religious prejudice against the theatre no doubt influenced the choice of Handel's *Messiah*, with a chorus of 500 including Holy Trinity choir, as the first performance in the Pavilion on 25 April. An audience of 2,000 packed the auditorium, with seats priced from 21s to 5s. For the plays (*Twelfth Night*, a double-bill of *Romeo and Juliet* and *The Comedy of Errors*, and *As You Like It*) later in the week, seats were 10s 6d, 5s and 2s 6d, but these prices were still high and effectively regulated the nature of the audiences. The exclusion by price of the less privileged members of society caused resentment; copies of a boldly printed handbill appeared around Stratford:

TIME! SHAKESPEARE THE POET OF THE PEOPLE

People of Stratford! Where are the seats reserved for you at the forthcoming festival? What part or lot have you who originated it, in the coming celebration? None! But you will be permitted to see the Fireworks, because they cannot let them off in the Pavilion; and you are promised something for yourself *after the swells have dined.* (Copy in the Shakespeare Centre Library)

A particular bone of contention was a pageant (the centre-piece of Garrick's jubilee), which the committee had refused to include in the festival on the grounds that 'a Boxing Night Crush must take place in every street in Stratford if any strong attraction were held out to the million on the first week of the celebration' (Hunter, 1864, p. 148). When the pageant took place on Monday 2 May, Stratford was thronged with 30,000 visitors transported thither by cheap train excursions from Warwick, Birmingham, Wolverhampton, Worcester, Bristol and Gloucester. During the week more elevating fare was officially provided with concerts and plays in the Pavilion, to which admission was 3s, 2s and 1s. Assiduous as he was in promoting cultural opportunities for his parishioners, including his own servants, Revd Julian Young must have received his coachman's account of *Othello* with mixed feelings:

Grinning from ear to ear with pleasurable reminiscences, he replied with infinitely more alacrity than his predecessor [the butler] – ''Twas really beautiful, Sir. I liked it unaccountable!' The cheerful face clouded over as I asked him what it was about. 'I don't ezactly know, Sir!' . . . 'Oh! I know, Sir, now; I know. It ran upon sweethearting! Aye that it did. And there were two gennelmen, one was white, and the other was black: and, what was more, both o' these gents was sweet on the same gal.' (Young, 1871, pp. 292–3)

Both in London and Stratford tercentenary celebrations had reflected tensions within society, with the emerging working classes asserting themselves rather than meekly accepting what their social superiors condescended to provide for them. Stratford was clearly the victor in the rivalry with London, but metropolitan disdain for the Warwickshire town was still rife when Charles Flower, assuming his father's mantle, launched the scheme for a permanent Shakespeare Memorial Theatre, the foundation stone of which was laid on 23 April 1877. At a luncheon for 800 that day Tom Taylor extolled the examples of the Duke of Saxe-Meiningen's Court Theatre and Charles Calvert at the Prince's Theatre where 'the whole population of Manchester and the surrounding hive of industry . . . receive . . . lessons of sound dramatic art'. Helen Faucit, who had withdrawn from the Stratford tercentenary celebrations in indignation at the engagement of French actress Stella Colas as Juliet, was present, seated between Charles Flower and the Vicar of Stratford. To her surprise and pain she heard her health being proposed, to which her husband made an impromptu response in which he alluded to the sympathetic attitude towards the theatre of the Bishop of Manchester – 'one of the most broadminded of our bishops' (Foulkes, 1992a, pp. 88–9).

In 1879 Helen Faucit returned to Stratford to appear as Beatrice at the opening of the Memorial Theatre. Prior to her performance she visited Holy Trinity Church and New Place 'where he [Shakespeare] died [and] a feeling more earnest, more reverential, came over me than I have experienced even in Westminster Abbey, in Santa Croce, or in any resting-place of the mighty dead' (Martin, 1900, p. 357). Once on stage Helen Faucit found her delight in the humour, wit and emotions of Beatrice 'doubled by the sensitive sympathy of my audience' (Faucit, 1887, p. 330). The auditorium in which the audience found themselves seated had none of the red-plush and gilding which characterised most late-Victorian theatres. It was stark to the point of austerity and with text inscribed below the dome was likened to a Nonconformist chapel (Bott, 1974, p, 9). The sense of earnestness rather than indulgence was reinforced when the adjoining library and picture gallery were completed.

Beatrice was the subject of one of Helen Faucit's essays collected in *On Some of Shakespeare's Female Characters* (1887). That essay was dedicated to John Ruskin, and other dedicatees (Geraldine Jewsbury – Ophelia, Portia, Desdemona; Anna Swanwick – Imogen; and Robert Browning – Beatrice) reflected, as they were no doubt intended to do, her influential social circle. Helen Faucit's conception of her characters was very much the ideal in the real. To her Portia had 'the essence of Christianity within her' and the actress projected the action beyond the play with Portia turning 'in pity towards the miserable and forsaken outcast [Shylock]' (p. 44). Imogen, Viola and Rosalind were 'pure women to the very core' (p. 265), though Beatrice's 'frequent repetition of the name of the Deity has struck most painfully upon my ear' (p. 305). On her husband's knighthood in 1880 Helen Faucit became Lady Martin; her book was 'respectfully dedicated by permission' to the Queen, who sent not only a wreath but also an accompanying equerry (Major Harbord) to the actress's funeral service in November 1898, affording 'evidence of the esteem in which the deceased actress was held by the Queen' (*Era* 5 November 1898). Possessed of what Macready called 'a holier charm' (J. C. Trewin, 1955, p. 168), Helen Faucit had contributed her advantageous marriage, a diligently cultivated circle of influential friends and her high moral and religious principles, as well as her undisputed talent as an actress, to the theatre. After her death Sir Theodore Martin was as uxorious a widower as he had been a husband. In addition to writing a laudatory biography, he set about memorialising his late wife. Mindful of the profound effect that Holy Trinity Church had had upon her and eager to enshrine her name there, Martin presented a marble pulpit, the front of which featured the figure of St Helen. On 18 October 1899 the Bishop of Worcester conducted a service of dedication which included 'an eloquent sermon . . . preached by Canon Ainger, Master of the Temple' (Martin, 1900, p. 407). How accurately the figure captured the features of St Helen it was impossible to judge, but its resemblance to Helen Faucit was all too evident. Henceforward preachers at Holy Trinity delivered their sermons from a pulpit embellished by what was effectively an image of an actress. In 1900 Martin sought to have John Henry Foley's marble relief of Helen Faucit – executed decades earlier – placed in the chancel of Holy Trinity. The popular novelist Marie Corelli, a colourful resident of Stratford-upon-Avon, led the opposition, as a result of which Martin presented the work to the Shakespeare Memorial Theatre, where it has remained ever since (Royal Shakespeare Theatre, 1964, p. 65).

By the time of Helen Faucit's death Shakespeare's place in the pantheon of immortal genius was beyond dispute and statues of him had been erected in London and Stratford-upon-Avon. A reproduction of Paul Scheemaker's statue of the bard was the centre-piece of Leicester Square and, in Stratford, Henry Irving had unveiled a statue in Rother Market and Lord Ronald Gower had presented his bronze group of Shakespeare surrounded by Hamlet, Prince Hal, Falstaff and Lady Macbeth to the town. The republican and unbeliever Frederic Harrison organised 'Obituary Celebrations' to 'do honour to the memory of some departed worthy' and pilgrimages 'to the home, or tomb, and associations of great men . . . The most elaborate of these visits were to

Stratford-upon-Avon' (Frederic Harrison, 1911, vol. II, pp. 288–90). Carlyle, with whom Harrison had clashed in early life (vol. I, p. 343), could not have foreseen the scale which hero-worship would reach. Harrison's 'Obituary Celebrations' were tantamount to a secular version of Keble's *The Christian Year* and his pilgrimages a stepping-stone between their medieval religious prototypes and the mass tourism of the late twentieth century.

The zeal with which the Church promoted the status of Shakespeare probably did it a disservice. In time the emphasis on God-given genius evaporated, leaving behind not a 'prophet of God', but an idol to challenge his putative creator. Although mid-Victorian clergymen generally venerated him as a poet, pointedly disregarding his work in the theatre, Shakespeare was the Victorian theatre's strongest asset. As late as 1892 Henry Irving wrote:

I daresay that it will appear to some readers a profanation of the name of Shakespeare to couple it with the title of playwright. But I have chosen this title for my introduction because I am anxious to show that with the mighty genius of the poet was united, in a remarkable degree, the capacity for writing plays intended to be acted as well as read. One often finds that the very persons who claim most to reverence Shakespeare, not only as a poet but also as a dramatist, carry that reverence to such an extent that they would almost forbid the representations of his plays upon the stage, except under conditions which are, if not impossible, certainly impracticable. (Henry Irving and Marshall, 1892, vol. I, p. lxxxi)

Once the poet and the man had been acknowledged, acclaimed and venerated, it was inevitable that opposition to his plays would gradually crumble. The timing of the Shakespeare tercentenary, like all such commemorations, was predetermined, but for the theatre it was wonderfully propitious, coinciding with other advantageous trends in society and religious thought to advance its cause.

CHAPTER 7

From Passion Play to pantomime

> a certain vigorously democratic clergyman . . . seized me and bore
> me off to the last night of the pantomime at 'the Brit.'
>
> G. B. Shaw

That the outbreak of plague in a small Bavarian village in the winter of
1632–3 should have an effect upon the theatre in Victorian England may
seem improbable, but from 1860 a succession of English visitors, many of
them clergymen, made their way to Oberammergau and reported on
their experience of seeing the Passion Play there. In July 1633 the villagers of Oberammergau took a solemn vow that, if they were relieved
from the plague, 'they would enact the Passion of the Redeemer every
tenth year with the utmost skill and devotion of which they were
capable' (Lane and Brenson, 1984, p. 26). True to their word, the villagers performed their play for the first time in 1634, and from 1680, at
the end of each decade. The text was successively revised – by Pater
Rosner in 1750, by Pater Knipfelberger in 1780, by Otto Weiss in 1810;
Rochus Dedler worked on what became the definitive music score
between 1811 and 1820; scenery became increasingly elaborate, reflecting trends in the professional theatre; certain families developed almost
hereditary connections with the principal roles (pp. 182–5). For the 1840
performances a theatre was constructed and 'It was in this year . . . that
English spectators came in large numbers' (Corathiel, 1950, p. 71).

Elisabeth Corathiel noted that 'Protestant countries, probably
because of their greater affluence, were among the first to recognize
Oberammergau Art, just as they have not been backward in acknowl-
edging the message of the Oberammergau Passion Play' (1950, p. 53).
Theological differences between the play's Roman Catholicism and
Protestantism were a concern for early Anglican visitors, but Elisabeth
Corathiel's point about affluence is no less, probably more, important.
Early English visitors were perforce well-to-do and though they gener-

ally commended what they saw they drew the line at extending the experience to their countrymen at large. In the mid nineteenth century the journey to Oberammergau was difficult and expensive. The railway line was extended – from Munich – to Weilheim in 1870, to Murnau in 1880 and to Garmisch in 1890; it reached Oberammergau in 1900.

In 1860 the English vanguard was led by Dean Milman and Revd Arthur Penrhyn Stanley. Milman corresponded with Stanley in October 1860, by which time he had read Stanley's account in *Macmillan's Magazine*: 'Your impressions and conclusions accord entirely with mine' (A. Milman, 1900, p. 265). Milman was especially impressed with 'the getting up' of the play – 'I have seen the operas in most of the great Continental opera-houses; but I never saw anything so fine as what the French call the *mise en scène*' (p. 265) – and by the *corps dramatique*, numbering 426, which he conceived 'in grouping and mode of half-mimical expression [to be] the exact counterpart of the Greek drama' (p. 265).

Arthur Penrhyn Stanley, a scion of the Stanleys of Alderley, was the untiring champion of Latitudinarianism. Educated at Rugby School during Thomas Arnold's headmastership he became his biographer as well as his disciple. At Oxford he won the Newdigate Prize in 1837 and obtained a first in classics in 1838; a supporter of university reform, he was appointed Professor of Ecclesiastical History in 1856. Stanley was a firm favourite with the royal family, who were instrumental not only in his preferment but also in his marriage in 1862 to the formidable Lady Augusta Bruce. Even his support for *Essays and Reviews* did not stand in the way of Stanley succeeding Richard Chenevix Trench as Dean of Westminster in 1864, an office which he held with renown until his death in 1881. Whilst Bishop of Norwich (1837–49), Stanley's father invited the singer Jenny Lind to stay at the palace 'as a compliment to her excellent character', as his son wrote to Mrs Arnold on 28 September 1848, continuing: 'the one epithet which characterises her . . . [is] gifted; but it is still more rare to see anyone possessed with such a perfect consciousness that it is a gift – not her own, but given by God' (Prothero, 1895, pp. 112–13). Jenny Lind became a personal friend of Stanley's sister, who married Revd C. J. Vaughan, headmaster of Harrow and later Master of the Temple and Dean of Llandaff (F. Archer, 1912, p. 187). Stanley himself admired fellow Rugbeian Macready (Prothero and Bradley, 1893, vol. I, pp. 204–6), and Rachel (pp. 393–4) and Helen Faucit whose friendship with Lady Augusta dated back to 1841 (Martin, 1900, p. 80).

Broad churchman though he was, Stanley felt the necessity of placing the Oberammergau play in the context of the Reformation, pointing out that Luther had endorsed such spectacles and that Milton's first sketch of *Paradise Lost* was a sacred drama: 'The repugnance, therefore, which has, since the close of the seventeenth century, led to the gradual suppression of these dramatic spectacles, is not to be considered a special offspring of Protestantism, any more than their origin and continuance was a special offspring of the Church of Rome' (*Macmillan's Magazine*, October 1860, p. 464). The Oberammergau play had only been saved from suppression 'by the prohibition of a Latitudinarian king [Max-Joseph]' (p. 465) and it did 'not contain what is distinctive of any peculiar sect of Christendom' (p. 476). Indeed 'The Virgin appears not more prominently or more frequently than the most rigid Protestant would allow' (p. 476) and the attitude of the Apostles 'in receiving, and of their Master in giving, the bread and wine of the supper, far more nearly resembles that of a Presbyterian than a Roman Catholic ritual. The cup is studiously given, as well as the bread, to all who are present' (p. 472). Stanley discussed at length the interpretation of Judas Iscariot, then, as he continued to be, the most contentious aspect of the play. The treatment had been progressively softened: 'internal development of motives has taken the place of the demons which the earlier machinery reproduced in outward shape' (p. 469). In 1860 the curtain fell on the yellow-robed Judas clambering up the fatal tree; even his piercing death-shriek was silenced. The elimination of physical devils in favour of internal remorse reflected developments in religious thought in Germany as well as England.

Stanley calculated that three-quarters of the Oberammergau audience consisted 'of the humbler grades of life' for whom it was (whatever it may be to their superiors in station) an 'edifying and instructive spectacle'. Their demeanour was grave, respectful and reverent throughout, exhibiting the same 'vision of rustic simplicity and high wrought feeling . . . [as was] exhibited in the Dionysian theatre' (p. 466). Stanley was insistent on 'the utter inapplicability of such a performance to other times and places than its own'; it 'cannot be transplanted' (p. 477). He placed his reliance on its 'inaccessible situation, its rude accompaniments, its rare decennial recurrence' as safeguards 'that it may never attract any large influx of spectators from distant regions or uncongenial circles' (p. 477).

In practice Stanley stimulated the very process which he sought to forestall, as Revd F. W. Farrar testified: 'What was said and written of it by Dean Milman, Dean Stanley, and Sir George Grove in 1860, gave the main impulse in England to its enormous popularity' (Revd F. W. Farrar,

1890, p. 91). The tide of visitors was delayed, but not stemmed, by the disruption of the Franco-Prussian war, as a result of which only sixteen performances were given in 1870 (Bentley, 1984, p. 55). Amongst the English visitors was Canon Malcolm MacColl, whose account (1870) ran into three editions before performances were resumed by 1871. In the meantime other European religious drama was attracting English visitors. In 1865 G. H. Lewes saw *Paradise Lost* at the Gaieté theatre in Paris with 'a stout ballet-girl in very scant clothing representing Eve; a well-shaved Adam in skins and fleshings' and a 'jovial and grotesque' Satan (1875, pp. 173–4). He proceeded to Antwerp where at the Théâtre des Variétés he encountered a Sunday performance of the Oberammergau play finding, as he believed any Protestant would – his 'first repulsion' overcome – that 'it was really religious . . . wholly beneficial' (p. 178). In 1867 Lewes journeyed to Spain, where in Barcelona he attended 'a day performance at one of the people's theatres [a large tent] of a mystery-play [*Los Pastores em Bethlehem* – 'The Shepherds of Bethlehem'] in the Catalonian dialect', which was 'interesting not only as a relic of the old past, but also as an amusement for the people which, while it gratified the dramatic instinct, touched their souls on finer issues than could be opened by the vast majority of modern plays' (p. 216). On 16 October 1871 Matthew Arnold addressed a capacity audience of 900 members of the Birmingham and Midland Institute in the Masonic Hall on 'A Persian Passion Play', a subject which proclaimed its abstruseness when 'the peasants of the neighbouring country, the great and fashionable world, the ordinary tourist, were all at Ammergau' (Super, 1970, p. 12).

Leading the fashionable world in 1871 were the Prince and Princess of Wales, who, though they travelled incognito, would not have needed the services of Thomas Cook and Sons, who initiated their tours to Oberammergau that year. Amongst the large contingent of Anglican clergymen, 'many of whom, I know, had never been within the walls of a theatre' was Revd Julian Young (1875, p. 70), whose religious sensitivity to the experience was tempered by his thespian family background. Young was sternly critical of much in the performance: 'the scenery was inferior . . . The music . . . anything but ravishing . . . The singing muffled . . . The mixture of colour in grouping was often infelicitous, and sometimes meretricious . . . the acting of the women was inferior' (p. 73). On the credit side Tobias Flunge as Pontius Pilate transcended acting, 'it was identification' (p. 74), and, as Judas Iscariot, Gregor Lechner manifested 'remorseful agitation' at the Last Supper (p. 77). At the conclusion of the play Young concurred with his wife 'in reverting, henceforward, to the

Passion-Spiel as the most practically helpful and edifying of homilies' (p. 85). The experience of seeing peasants scaling these dramatic heights must have put Young in mind of his efforts with their Warwickshire counterparts.

In 1880, Lord Houghton, also a veteran of the Stratford Shakespeare tercentenary celebrations, lodged in Oberammergau with '"the Christus", who has nothing of the traditional figure, but much dignity of his own' (Reid, 1890, vol. II, p. 394). He observed the debt to Van Eyck, Rubens and Raphael in the tableaux. Theatre manager John Hollingshead brought a professional eye to bear: 'The stage management, costumes and properties of the Passion Play were perfect. Much of this was doubtless due to tradition, but more to the teaching of Munich – that great and almost obtrusive art centre being within two hours of Oberammergau' (1895, vol. II, p. 174). Though the actors – 'discreet and inoffensive' – were amateurs, Hollingshead found that 'What was originally a solemn service had already become vulgarised and was on the rapid downward path to the showman's level' (pp. 173–4). With little if any experience of the theatre the clergymen observed by W. L. Courtney, Oxford don and later drama critic of the *Daily Telegraph*, did not share Hollingshead's perception, but 'showed their unbroken absorption in the spectacle' (1925, p. 145).

Also present in 1880 was Frank Harris, who returned in 1890, the idea having been planted by his long-term mistress, Laura: 'It would be a great holiday, I thought, so I proposed to take her and her mother for the opening performances in May' (1958, p. 282). Harris found the acting inferior to that of 1880, but fortunately Laura's mother, 'who disliked him [Harris]' (Brome, 1962, p. 80), was more impressed and 'with much difficulty I got one seat for her' to see the play a second time, 'so Laura came and spent the afternoon with me in my room – four hours never to be forgotten' (Harris, 1958, p. 284).

Such ulterior motives did not sully the expeditions of G. B. Shaw, Jerome K. Jerome, W. T. Stead, Elizabeth Robins, Mrs Alec Tweedie and Revd F. W. Farrar, all of whom visited and wrote about the 1890 performances. First they had the travel arrangements to make. Actress Elizabeth Robins agonised over a conflicting theatre engagement and the cost of the expedition before making her way to Thomas Cook and Sons whose first-class return fare was £11 0s 6d or £11 5s depending on the route (Tweedie, 1890, p. 117). Jerome K. Jerome, whose account of his journey to Oberammergau occupies two-thirds of his *Diary of a Pilgrimage*, also enlisted the services of Cook's agent: 'we all of us sneer at

Mr Cook . . . but I notice most of us appeal, on the quiet to [him] . . . , the moment we want to move abroad' (1891, p. 103). Once in Oberammergau lodgings had to be located – 'an airy apartment adorned with various highly-coloured wood-carvings of a pious but somewhat ghastly character' (p. 110). Elizabeth Robins 'was lodged with Stead's ally, King Herod' (1940, p. 309). Shaw's companion Sidney Webb 'had written to the Burgomaster . . . in terms which are only used in Germany in addressing the Emperor' (Laurence, 1965, p. 255), but this did not prevent some confusion. Farrar was privileged to stay at the home of Joseph Mayr 'who this year, for the third time at the age of forty-two, plays the character of the Christus' (Revd. F. W. Farrar, 1890, p. 47).

The next day began early: 'At six o'clock there is a full choral celebration of High Mass for all who are to take the chief part in the play' (1890, p. 55) and in the theatre itself 'after they are dressed for their parts, the great company assembles on the stage and the priest says a prayer and consecrates them to their work that day' (Robins, 1940, p. 318). Far from finding this incongruous Elizabeth Robins asked: 'Yet who among us of the stage has not framed many a desperate little prayer while waiting outside for an entrance cue?' (p. 318).

Individual members of the audience inevitably brought different perspectives to the Passion Play. Shaw, attending as music critic of the *World*, considered the singing variable in quality: 'Howbeit, considering that the population of the village is only thirteen hundred, they have not done badly' (Laurence, 1989, vol. II, p. 147). The music was irredeemably derivative (Mozart, Haydn, Spohr) and 'no more medieval than Regent-street' (p. 146). Though to some this inauthenticity was a failing, to others it was a relief: 'In the old days of the mysteries there was a certain tumultuous and almost comic element in this scene [Purge of the Temple], for the medieval sightseer expected to be provided with the ludicrous in connection with the pathetic. Now it is done with consummate reverence, and there is nothing which the most frivolous spectator could venture to smile at' (Revd F. W. Farrar, 1890, p. 83). Mrs Alec Tweedie delighted in this improved Medievalism:

Sitting among those simple surroundings, it seemed almost impossible to realise that one was living in the nineteenth century. Living in an age of machinery, steam, electricity and invention, an age when all is hurry and bustle, it is strange to be suddenly transported back, as it were, to the Middle Ages, when our forefathers were wont to witness religious dramas, inferior though they must have been to the ones of the present day. (1890, p. 80)

8. The Crucifixion in the Oberammergau Passion Play

In contrast, journalist W. T. Stead, whose *The Story that Transformed the World* sold 24,000 copies between July and November 1890 (1890, 'Preface'), far from being lulled into a purified neo-Medievalism, found the play redolent of contemporary issues. The money-changers in the temple reminded him of a recent deputation to the Home Secretary by shopkeepers complaining of their eviction from Trafalgar Square; Nathaniel, who suborned false witnesses, was 'the very image of the *Times* newspaper in a horned hat. It was the Parnell Commission all over again' (p. 159). Other contemporary parallels flooded into Stead's mind, including 'the Cause of Women and the Cause of the Poor' (p. 158). Elizabeth Robins, who in her Ibsen performance did much for the cause of women, cast a professional eye at the mechanics of the production, 'borrowed from the Munich Hof Theatre' (1940, p. 316), during rehearsal.

A mechanical device by which the spearhead left 'the semblance of a deep gash' was used to give 'tremendous realism' to the Crucifixion (illustration 8), which Farrar found 'overwhelmingly oppressive' (1890, p. 22). Mrs Alec Tweedie was similarly affected: 'The Crucifixion is most powerful, and I may add awe-inspiring' (1890, p. 96). In answer to his own question 'What is the total effect of the Play?' Farrar replied: 'It has been predominantly good . . . It has deepened their [the villagers'] religious character, stimulated their devotion, increased their knowledge and marvellously developed all their artistic and intellectual gifts' (1890, pp. 122–3). Yet despite these fulsome encomiums Farrar, like Stanley, was totally averse to any extension of the play to other spheres: 'The Ober Ammergau Play would be absolutely reprehensible except in connection with its history and natural surroundings' (*New Review*, 1893, vol. 8, p. 186).

The 1890 performance was the apogee of influential British interest in the Oberammergau Passion Play. A new theatre was completed for the 1900 performances providing a 'well-raked auditorium' (Hartnoll, 1958, p. 36) for audiences which included Johnston Forbes-Robertson, Arthur Bourchier with his future brother-in-law Kenneth Barnes, and Maria Trench, biographer of her father Richard Chenevix Trench, who published a translation of the play (1900). The fervour of a religious experience had given way to a cool appraisal of theatrical accomplishment; 'one looked for a primitive atmosphere, which was lacking' wrote Forbes-Robertson (1925, p. 196). The temptation to exploit the play commercially was enormous. Actors were recompensed only for loss of earnings – 'about fifty pounds' for Mayr as Christ in 1890 (Jerome, 1891, p. 118) – but the decennial infrequency of performances left scope for intervening performances elsewhere. Resistance to the 'reprehensible attempt to produce these performances' in London had provoked 'for once the unanimous voice of public opinion against it' according to playwright Henry Spicer (1881, p. 22). The Examiner of Plays, E. F. S. Pigott, took pride in having prevented London performances (Woodfield, 1984, p. 119). In 1898 Clement Scott told Robert Blathwayt: 'Imagine producing the Ober Ammergau Passion play in London. It would be too horrible; a religious play inevitably offends. Of course the producers of it say that they do it with a good motive. Rubbish! It is done in the hope that it will bring money to the manager's pocket' (Blathwayt, 1898, p. 8). Certainly financial gain lay behind the bizarre saga of Salmi Morse's *The Passion Play A Miracle Play in Ten Acts* in San Francisco and New York 1879–84 (Nielson, 1991). Eventually film provided the medium for extending the Passion Play's audience, reaching Wakefield's Opera House on Sunday 19 March 1899 'when a "musical pictorial service" included a screening of the Ober-Ammergau Passion Play and Life of Our Lord' (C. M. P. Taylor, 1995, p. 195).

The example of the achievements of the Bavarian peasants did encourage theatre-minded clergymen to stage religious dramas with their congregations. Mrs Alec Tweedie cited several examples: St Michael's, Shoreditch, St Peter's, London docks and Rous Lench near

9. Tableau of the Adoration of the Shepherds at
Christ Church Mission, Poplar

Evesham (1890, pp. 82 and 111). On 6 March 1896 the *Illustrated Church News* carried an account of the Christ Church Oxford Mission at Poplar (illustration 9), which had been founded 'to bring members of Christ Church face to face with different conditions of life amongst the poor of East London'. The late Rector of Poplar, Revd James Adderley, had realised the value of bringing colour into the drab lives of his parishioners and had instituted 'processions through the streets, with surplice and cassock, cross and banner' on Easter Day and other great festivals, in addition to which:

Every other year a series of Bethlehem tableaux are given, and with the exception of the Christus and the Blessed Virgin the characters are taken by parishioners. The singing is performed by a chorus of girls, who are placed in front of the stage. The gospel describing the picture is chanted by a priest. These *tableaux* have been very helpful in bringing home to the hearts and minds of many who have seen them the reality of our Saviour's earthly life. The demand for tickets [1,200] is always very great.

Alas such enterprises were not without their hazards. In November the *Illustrated Church News* (20 November 1896) reported the death of George Barnes, a lay-reader at St John's Church, Middlesbrough, as a result of 'an accident while carrying scenery which had been used in connection with some *tableau vivants* which he had organised for the purpose of raising funds for Church purposes'. At least the prospect of hell-fire, for so long held out to those engaged in theatrical activities, did not threaten Barnes.

The widespread attention directed to the Oberammergau Passion Play stimulated interest in indigenous medieval religious drama. Mrs Alec Tweedie referred to 'the learned William Hone' (1890, p. 3), whose *Ancient Mysteries Described, Especially from the English Miracle Plays* (1823) was recognised as a seminal work, making accessible many thereto obscure sources. Hone's tone was hardly that of an advocate: 'From the manifold corruptions of religion resulted the gross practices and delusions which are noticed in the ensuing pages without comment; for the work is a collection of facts, not of inferences. It commences with the Coventry Mysteries; the passages from the Apocrypha Gospel, whereon the scenes are founded, being printed beneath' (p. x).

Dean Milman gave due consideration to the drama in his *History of Latin Christianity*, tracing its development from Hroswitha to its eventual ejection from church buildings. Significantly he referred to 'Legend, like the gospels' (H. H. Milman, 1855, vol. VI, p. 495) being well-suited to dramatisation and acknowledged the 'unrestrained fun, mingled with sacred subjects' (p. 493) in the Mysteries. In his *A Church Dictionary A Practical Manual of Reference for Clergymen and Students* (1842) Walter Farquhar Hook judged that 'the coarseness of an unrefined age' would not be 'tolerated now' and described the Oberammergau Passion Play as 'a great improvement upon them [the Mysteries]' (1887, p. 512). Hook could be exonerated of any prejudice against the theatre. As a child he wrote the libretti for two of his father's operas and from Oxford, where he was a contemporary of the future seventh Earl of Carlisle, he wrote to his mother in June 1819 of his 'filial affection for the stage, corrupted, depraved and odious as it is now'. He looked forward to the abolition of the 'abominable monopoly of the two theatres' and to the realisation of his ambition 'to become a manager of some great theatre' (W. R. W. Stephens, 1880, p. 22). Instead he became a clergyman and in Leeds (1839–59) he was known, Tory though he was, as 'the working men's vicar', building a new parish church and promoting popular education. In 1859 he became Dean of Chichester and was one of the clerical patrons of the National Shakespeare Committee in 1864. In that year F. J. Furnivall founded the Early English Texts Society. Furnivall was also active in adult education, the object of Henry Morley's efforts as lecturer, editor and author. In his *Illustrations of English Religion* (1890) Morley discussed the texts, staging and audiences of Mystery plays. Readers of the *Nineteenth Century* (October 1883) and the *Theatre* (1 May 1887) were informed about medieval drama. In 1913 *The Religious Drama* by Gordon Crosse was accorded a place in the 'Arts of the Church' series.

Crosse instanced the revival of *Everyman* (1901) and Laurence Housman's *Bethlehem* (1902) as early examples of 'The Modern Revival' (chapter 8) of religious drama, though he might have cited R. H. Horne's *Bible Tragedies – John the Baptist* and *Judas Iscariot; A Mystery* (1848). Horne 'cast this Scriptural Tragedy [*Judas Iscariot*] in the form of the old English Mystery Play, as being the class to which it more legitimately belongs, and also with a view to remove it as far as possible from the dramatic literature of our own day, in reverence to the general bearings and atmosphere of the subject' (n.d., p. 112). Horne attributed his choice and treatment of subject to an Ordination Sermon by Archbishop Whateley who found 'no reason for concluding . . . that he [Judas] was influenced by the paltry bribe of thirty pieces of silver' (p. 109), but rather that he 'dared to act on his own conjectures' (p. 110) of what Christ would do. Adopting Whateley's views, Horne guarded 'against the evil of . . . making a sort of hero of so treacherous a disciple' (p. 111), but, in the path of Coleridge, he concentrated on remorse – 'his dreadful remorse' (p. 111) – and, like the Oberammergau revision, placed Judas's torment within him rather than externally. To the 'Distant sounds of the heavy blows of a hammer on Calvary' Judas cried out:

> Mine eyes spin webs of fire – Oh mercy, Christ!
> Mercy! for thou canst hear me from afar -
> Hear me scream 'Mercy!' (p. 189)

There was no prospect that Horne's play would be performed on stage. When Laurence Housman submitted *Bethlehem* to William Redford, Examiner of Plays, a licence was only granted 'on the condition that the Virgin was not to speak nor the Holy Child to be seen' (Housman, 1937, p. 188). Significantly, the first religious drama to be staged by William Poel, the pioneer of Elizabethan-style revivals of Shakespeare's plays, was *Everyman* which is not of biblical origin. Poel came from a devout family; his mother, 'intensely religious in the evangelical tradition' (Speaight, 1954, p. 16), was the daughter of Revd

Henry Gauntlett. As a child Poel was the model for Jesus in W. Holman
Hunt's *The Discovery of Christ in the Temple*, but did not visit a theatre until
he was twenty. As a young touring actor Poel 'went first to the Parish
Church, if possible during service time' (p. 38); in Waterford he took
exception to the Anglican bishop's remarks on the theatre: 'Why will the
votaries of religion and morals despise and denounce the stage as they
do? Where would those large numbers that never enter a church get
their instruction . . . if not from the stage?' (pp. 36–7). He listened atten-
tively and critically to the preaching of Manning, Kingsley and Stopford
Brooke. As manager of the Victoria, Poel had expressed his concern
about the ascendancy of instruction over entertainment and later wrote
that: 'The primary object, however, of all these entertainments [Mystery
plays, Moralities, Interludes and Masques] was not to edify or instruct,
but to amuse' (1920, p. 2). The choice of *Everyman*, the most didactic of
these dramas, 'was due to the suggestions of Dr Ward (then Master of
Peterhouse, Cambridge)' (Gomme, 1936, p. vii). A. W. Ward had previously been Professor of History and English Language and Literature at
Owen's College, Manchester, coinciding with Charles Calvert's management at the Prince's Theatre, and successively principal and vice-chancellor of the Victoria University. Ward's *English Dramatic Literature to the
Death of Queen Anne* (1875) was quoted in Poel's printed text and programme notes for *Everyman*: 'the sustained force of the general action
and the simple solemnity with which it is carried out from first to last are
unmarred by a trace of frivolity or vulgarity, and yet come straight home
from *Everyman* to everyman' (Poel, 1901, pp. 4–5).

The locations chosen by Poel for performances of *Everyman* were
hardly the haunts of every man: only after encouraging responses at the
Charterhouse (13–20 July 1901), University College, Oxford (9 August,
for the Delegacy summer school), the Dome at Brighton (30 October),
and St George's Hall (26 May 1902) was *Everyman* staged at a theatre –
the Imperial, in 1902. Even then the critic of the *Sketch* considered: 'It
[*Everyman*] is not exactly the piece to offer the general public [who] might
be inclined to mock at the religious aspect of the Mystery', but 'The
Elizabethan Society, which presented the piece, fortunately is a very
earnest body, and so is able to handle matter which under ordinary circumstances might seem horribly blasphemous . . . this is an entirely
admirable production' (2 April 1902). Poel's production of *Everyman* may
have been his 'most famous single achievement' (Speaight, 1954, p. 17),
but a play and production of such irreproachable earnestness hardly set
a precedent for the revival of other medieval drama.

Nevertheless it was during the reign of Queen Victoria that the principal Christian festival was inextricably linked with theatrical entertainment – the Christmas pantomime. English pantomime is a hybrid absorbing several traditions from ancient Greek theatre to *commedia dell'-arte* and vernacular forms. David Mayer identifies William Mountford's 1685 adaptation of Marlowe's *Dr Faustus* as 'the earliest piece to contain a characteristic of the pantomime, though not so identified . . . To the plot of Marlowe's play Mountford added the comic antics of Harlequin and Scaramouche, thereby uniting a popular tale with the stock masks of *commedia dell'arte*' (1969, p. 4). In its turn Marlowe's *Dr. Faustus* was indebted to earlier drama as Gãmini Salgãdo points out: 'The Good and Evil Angels who embody the struggle with Faustus' soul come straight out of medieval Morality drama' (1971, p. 138).

Writing in 1881 Leopold Wagner strongly asserted the link between pantomime and medieval drama. He identified the origins of 'the fairies in our Pantomimes' with the angels in the Mysteries and the 'demons in the Pantomimes' with the devils and evil angels (1881, pp. 27, 28) and pointed out that 'Beelzebub himself was introduced as the principal comic actor' (p. 23). Infernal scenes in pantomimes – 'up to a comparatively recent date, almost every one of the Pantomimes used to open with a "demon-scene" . . . strongly savouring of brimstone' (p. 28) – were the counterpart to the 'dark pitchy cavern from whence issued appearances of fire and flames . . . [and the] hideous yellings and noises . . . of the wretched souls tormented by the restless demons' (p. 23) in the Mystery plays, the purpose of which 'being to impart religious instruction to the dull masses' (p. 22). Wagner had no doubt that 'out of the Mysteries, the Moralities, the old Comedies and lastly, the Puppet-shows, sprang the elements of a rare old English pantomime, such as our grandfathers looked upon, and enjoyed themselves over' (p. 27). Though pantomime's debt to medieval drama had become less evident Wagner could still cite a living example: 'Indeed, anyone who has made a study of English Dramatic Literature would not fail to recognise, in a visit to the Britannia Theatre, as near an approach to the old Morality Plays as might be expected in the present generation' (p. 28). A later historian of the pantomime regarded Wagner's as 'a reasonable theory' (A. E. Wilson, 1934, p. 20) and identifies 'the spirit of Saturnalia' as the 'true origin of pantomime' (p. 23). J. R. Planché entitled the last of his numerous pantomimes *King Christmas: A Fanciful Morality* (1901, p. 458).

The attention of Victorian clergymen tended to be directed at what they considered to be improper aspects of pantomime as Bishop Fraser's advice to a lady correspondent, who 'was ashamed to sit in my place and allow my daughters to see the ballet' (*The Times* 4 October 1878), illustrated: 'My good friend, if you would only influence your friends and persuade them to influence all that they can influence to stay away from the pantomime for a single week, until the objectionable ballet, if it be objectionable, be withdrawn, I think the evil you complain of would be withdrawn.' Instead of relying on such a forlorn strategy, the bishop would have done better to look beneath the surface at the allegorical basis of pantomime.

Dean Milman's association of the scripture with legend – already noted – was taken up by Baden Powell in his contribution to *Essays and Reviews* (1860, p. iii) in which he quoted from *Latin Christianity*: 'History to be true must condescend to speak the language of legend' (H. H. Milman, 1855, vol. I, p. 388), and went on to argue that miraculous occurrences in scripture were no longer indispensable and should be discarded as a foundation of faith. In *The God of Miracles* (1875) Matthew Arnold advanced a similarly sceptical view of 'those unsaveable things, the Bible miracles' (Super, 1970, p. 170). He rejected both fundamentalist and rationalist interpretations of miracles, using the example of Cinderella's coach, of which the former, making some concession to the latter, would maintain that the fairy godmother 'actually changed the pumpkin . . . into a one-horse cab', and the latter that she paid for 'a cab for her godchild by selling her pumpkins' (pp. 170, 171). Arnold did not advance his own explanation, but Murray Roston postulates that it might have been that 'the godmother substituted a coach-and-six for the pumpkin so quickly that Cinderella imagined a miraculous transformation had occurred, although (he would add circumspectly) it was miraculous that a coach-and-six just happened to be standing by at the time' (1968, p. 236). The key word is 'imagined', for it was in the imagination, seminally defined by Coleridge, that Arnold's intuitive approach to interpreting scripture found its answer: 'Simple, flexible common-sense is what we most want, in order to be able to follow truly the dealings of that spontaneous, irregular, wonderful power which gives birth to tales of miracles – the imagination' (Super, 1970, p. 171).

It was in expanding their capacity for imagination that pantomime appealed to the Victorian mass audience, whose everyday lives were dominated by unrelenting toil and constrained domesticity. Charles Calvert's *Cinderella* (1873–4) at the Prince's Theatre in the heart of Bishop Fraser's Manchester diocese offered its audiences more heavenly visions than they were likely to have dreamt of:

Scene 2.   REALMS OF IMAGINATION IN MID AIR

In which the Fairy Godmammas discuss the fortunes of Cinderella. The arrival of the God Morpheus and the Prince. The vision of the Moon – the symbols of Asia, Africa, America, and Europe displayed in the skies.

Scene 5.   FAIRY CLOUDLAND IN BLUE ETHER
THE GLOBE'S ORBIT

In boundless space, – The Assembled Earth Fays Attending on Ceres, and the Haunt of Athena, and her Fairies of the Air, changing to

THE SOURCE OF THE SEAS

The abode of Amphitrite and her fairy Oceanides, changing to

THE PAVILION OF LIGHT,
GRAND BALLET OF THE ELEMENTS

and concluded with:

GRAND TRANSFORMATION SCENE
ENDYMION'S DREAM
FABLE

Endymion, a shepherd, having conceived a passion for the Goddess Juno, was condemned by Jupiter to an eternal sleep in a cavern. Diana, fascinated by the Shepherd's beauty, descending to earth as Luna, visited nightly.

ARGUMENT

The summit of Mount Latimus solemnly grand in the rays of the setting sun . . . Endymion is transfixed, a portion of the mountain is rent, and Jupiter full of majesty is present . . . and consigns him [Endymion] to eternal sleep in a cavern . . . The mountain is transformed into a cavern . . . An exhalation fills the cavern, and a charming realisation of the Shepherd's dream is manifested in the visiting of Diana and Endymion amidst the denizens of the star lit regions of the air.

(Programme in Manchester Central Library)

From 'The Globe's Orbit' to the Byronic peak of Mount Latimus, miraculously transformed into a cavern, Calvert's *Cinderella* encompassed visions of heaven and earth which must have stretched its audience's imagination far beyond anything in their experience. As Michael Booth has pointed out, such extra-terrestrial emanations were 'by no means an isolated theatrical phenomenon' (1991, p. 199), but also found expression in Thackeray's *The Rose and the Ring* (1853), Charles Kingsley's *The Water Babies* (1863) and Lewis Carroll's *Alice's Adventures in Wonderland* (1865). Pantomime was not completely divorced from the trials of contemporary living. At the Princess's Theatre in 1849 *King Jamie, or, Harlequin and the Magic Fiddle* represented hell – 'the Hell of Evil Spirits' – into which Alcohol had been exiled by the Irish apostle of temperance Father Matthew (Frow, 1985, p. 129).

Pantomime appealed to all classes in society and was as much a feature of Drury Lane as of provincial and suburban London theatres. Shaw wrote that 'the Superior Person – myself for instance' was inclined to 'disparage' pantomime amongst 'the mere silliness and levities of the theatre' (1932, vol. III, p. 21). On 23 January 1897 he attended Sir Augustus Harris's *Aladdin* arranged by Oscar Barrett, at Drury Lane, with Dan Leno as the Dame. Although Shaw found 'the traditional privileges of vulgarity . . . scrupulously respected by a manager whose reputation has been made by the comparative refinement of his taste and the superiority of his culture in spectacular and musical matters' (p. 34), the strains of *Siegfried* which accompanied Aladdin's combat with the genie of the lamp and the clown who played 'The Pilgrims' March' from *Tannhäuser* provided just such musical refinement for the more discerning members of the audience. Returning to Drury Lane for *The Babes in the Wood* on 27 December 1897, Shaw contrasted the 'dullness, senselessness, vulgarity, and extravagance' on show with 'the artistic possibilities of our Saturnalia' (p. 279).

Shaw found these possibilities realised at the Britannia Theatre, Hoxton, which Leopold Wagner had commended as 'a people's theatre' (1881, p. 28) where annual pantomimes captured the spirit of the Mystery plays. In the normal course of his duties Shaw would not have visited Hoxton, 'a neighbourhood in which the Saturday Review is comparatively little read', 'but for a certain vigorously democratic clergyman, who seized me and bore me off to the last night of the pantomime at "the Brit." . . . not far from Shoreditch Church' (p. 351). The clergyman was Revd A. W. Oxford; the pantomime that year (1897–8) was J. Addison's *Will O'The Wisp* (*Era* 1 January 1898). The Britannia was managed by Mrs Sara Lane, 'who played fairy queens longer than any woman who ever lived – barring immortals' (Disher, 1950, p. 46), to whom Shaw was presented. 'The clergyman's box, which was about as large as an average Metropolitan railway station, was approached from the stage itself' (Shaw, 1932, vol. III, p. 352), affording Shaw the opportunity to inspect 'the working of a star-trap by which Mr Lupino was flung up through the boards like a stone from a volcano' (p. 353). In the absence of stalls the occupants of the pit were directly in front of the stage on to which they threw flowers and confectionery, encouraging their favourite performer Topsy Sinden: 'Pick it up, Topsy' (p. 354). Having previously seen Topsy Sinden reduced to appearing in 'some unspeakably dreary inanity at the West End, to interpolate a "skirt dance"', when he had 'looked at her with cold hatred', Shaw was pleasantly surprised to find

that 'At the Britannia Miss Sinden danced, acted, and turned out quite a
charming person' (p. 354). Indeed the whole experience was such that
'decent ladies and gentlemen who have given up West End musical farce
in disgust will find themselves much happier at the Britannia pantomime' (pp. 353–4). The 'display of beauty was sufficiently voluptuous'
(p. 353), but not salacious, and 'Even the low comedians were not black-
guards, though they were certainly not fastidious, Hoxton being somewhat Rabelaisian in its ideas of broad humour' (p. 353). A high point was:

One scene in which the horrors of seasickness were exploited with great
freedom, made the four thousand sons and daughters of Shoreditch scream
with laughter. At the climax, when four voyagers were struggling violently for a
single bucket, I looked stealthily round the box, in which the Church, the
Peerage, and the Higher Criticism were represented. All three were in convul-
sions. (p. 353)

For the 'vigorously democratic clergyman' zealous for the moral well-
being of the audience there was Lupino's 'demon conflict with the
powers of evil, involving a desperate broad-sword combat, and the most
prodigious plunges into the earth and projections therefrom by volcanic
traps as aforesaid . . . conducted with all the tragic dignity of Richard III
and received in the true Aristotelean spirit by the audience' (p. 355).

Unpretentious, exuberant, robust and wholesome, with its roots
demonstrably in medieval religious drama, the Hoxton pantomime was
truly popular entertainment, in which all classes of society were bonded
together by the shared experience of theatrical communion. It represented the true spirit of the relationship between the stage and morality
far more authentically than the purged and derivative Oberammergau
Passion Play and the earnest Puritanism of William Poel's *Everyman*.

CHAPTER 8

The ancient universities

BRASSETT: Well, College gents'll do anything!
Brandon Thomas *Charley's Aunt*

The interest engendered in the theatre amongst John Mitchell Kemble's Cambridge contemporaries in the late 1820s through their friendship with him extended far beyond their youthful admiration for Fanny Kemble, the production of *Much Ado About Nothing* and the apprentice attempts at playwriting by Richard Chenevix Trench and John Sterling. Each member of that coterie who was granted a full span of years (Arthur Hallam and John Sterling were not) continued to engage directly or indirectly with the theatre from the position of professional eminence which he achieved. J. M. Kemble and W. B. Donne were both Examiner of Plays in the Lord Chamberlain's office, totalling thirty-four years in office (1840–74) between them. F. D. Maurice shrank back from direct involvement with theatre, but his challenge to the idea of an after-life of eternal hell-fire and his pioneering educational work at King's College, Queen's College and the Working Men's Colleges were formative of a more tolerant climate for the theatre. In addition to supporting Maurice in his educational ventures, Richard Chenevix Trench achieved distinction as a philologist, popularised the scientific study of language and initiated the proposal for setting up the *Oxford English Dictionary*. He gave his archiepiscopal support to the Shakespeare tercentenary celebrations in Stratford, where he was joined by Lord Houghton, formerly Richard Monckton Milnes, who also contributed, albeit in a 'deprecatory tone' (L. Irving, 1951, p. 355), to the banquet on the stage of the Lyceum Theatre to celebrate the one-hundredth performance of Irving's *The Merchant of Venice* on 14 February 1880. Later that year he visited the Oberammergau Passion Play. Three of Alfred Tennyson's plays were performed by Irving at the Lyceum – *Queen Mary* (18 April 1876), *The Cup* (3 January 1881) and *Becket* (6 February 1893). Without the contributions of J. M. Kemble,

W. B. Donne, F. D. Maurice, Richard Chenevix Trench, Lord Houghton and Alfred, Lord Tennyson, the chronicle of the nineteenth century, including its theatre, would have been significantly different.

The next theatre development in Cambridge, following the production of *Much Ado About Nothing* on 19 March 1830, was the formation of the Cambridge Garrick Club in 1835. Though it numbered a few graduates and dons in its ranks this was not a university club, as W. C. Macready condescendingly remarked: 'The president of the club is a solicitor, which seems the aristocratic of the club: I heard of no grade above it; an artist, an apothecary, stage-coachman, innkeeper, etc., make up the society' (Pollock, 1876, p. 395). The Cambridge Garrick Club's list of honorary members included 'the names of Charles Kemble, W. Macready, Sheridan Knowles, Liston and Douglas Jerrold' (Burnand, 1880, pp. v–vi) and the club did give a dinner in honour of Knowles. In August 1836 Macready appeared with the Garrick Club in the title-role of Sheridan Knowles's *Virginius* at the Barnewell Theatre, recording the occasion in his diary with characteristic irascibility:

August 2nd – I was as civil as I could be and prudently ordered my portmanteau from the inn, dined in my dressing-room, and had only time to array myself for the character of Virginius, when the play began. It went off better than I could have expected, and I was called for at the end, but shirked the coming, being anxious to betake myself early to bed. (Pollock, 1876, p. 395)

Macready returned to Cambridge in his retirement year to read *Hamlet* on 17 February 1851, as he did at Oxford the next day, 'after the Vice-Chancellor dilly-dallied . . . fearing perhaps that a player might harm the morals of the University' (J. C. Trewin, 1955, p. 232), and at Eton College on 21 February (Pollock, 1876, p. 651). The ancient universities were belatedly conferring some recognition on the achievements of the actor, who, as a young man, had hoped in vain to study at one of them.

When F. C. Burnand arrived at Trinity College, Cambridge, in 1855 his interest in drama had already been quickened at Eton, where Revd Gifford Cookesley took parties of 'his house pupils up to Windsor Theatre at night' (Burnand, 1904, vol. 1, p. 182). Burnand led a deputation to the Vice-Chancellor who 'declined to grant them sanction for a theatrical performance' (1880, p. 21), but nevertheless a meeting was held, attended by seventeen undergraduates (of whom six were Etonians and three Harrovians), as a result of which the Amateur Dramatic Club (ADC) was formed. Shortly afterwards Charles Donne, son of W. B. Donne the incumbent Examiner of Plays, became secretary and treasurer. Burnand's perception of the place of drama at the University of Cambridge was:

The idea of the ADC was an adaptation of the Cambridge Union Club, substituting dramatic entertainment for political debating. I now see that the Society, if recognised and directed by judicious authority, could work for a higher end, and for a far more important object, than was contemplated by its first founders, who will readily admit that their notion in starting the Club was to obtain a fair opportunity for the exercise of their dramatic talents, thus affording themselves novel and intellectual recreation, and their friends a considerable amount of amusement. Dramatic Art requires that its leading professors in every department should be men of education, of taste, of refinement. (1880, pp. xii-iii)

The first efforts of the ADC were distinctly recreational – *Did you ever send your wife to Camberwell?* – which the authorities were willing to indulge. Burnand recounted the Proctor's attitude:

He was much interested, considerably amused, owned that our object was laudable, and our efforts, not only harmless, but absolutely beneficial. And I daresay he recounted to Several Dons in Hall, or in the common room, that evening, his visit to the 'ADC', and expressed his wish to see, unofficially, one of our performances. At all events, before we parted, he gave us his positive assurance that, as long as we continued on the path of virtue, as long as we stuck to our professed object of amusing the undergraduate public with our theatrical entertainments, and did not permit orgies, or suppers, or Bacchanalian gatherings in our Club rooms, so long we might be quite certain of not being interfered with by the authorities, that is, as far as he could speak for them. *He* at all events did not expect Cox and Box to be Fellows of Trinity, and did not wish us to be performing musty old Greek and Latin plays like the Westminster scholars. (p. 57)

The ADC was tolerated by the university authorities – 'we were never once molested, or warned'; 'Dons came to us: dropping in . . . saying no more about it to their stricter clerical brethren', regarding its activities as preferable to undergraduates 'losing more than they could afford at loo, or at billiards, drinking at wines' (p. 57). Clearly the basis of this indulgence was that theatre was a relatively harmless form of recreation; no status was being accorded to it and it was certainly not being endorsed as a prospective career for undergraduates.

The presence of the Prince of Wales in Cambridge, as part of the rigorous education devised for him by his father, was seized upon by the ADC, who invited him to attend a performance on 2 March 1861. The programme was comprised of five light pieces, one written by Burnand. For the first time the actors played under their own names: 'It was a hazardous venture, and one which received deep consideration, but it was attended with great success' (p. 215). With the royal seal of approval, the ADC was emboldened to extend invitations to future productions to heads of colleges, Professor and Mrs Charles Kingsley and the Bishop of Worcester. Regular in his attendance was Revd Robert Phelps, Master of Sidney Sussex College, together with his family, who thus gave public support in his own university to the art of which his brother Samuel was such a distinguished luminary. When, in 1880, F. C. Burnand wrote his *Personal Reminiscences* of the ADC the book was dedicated 'By Permission To His Royal Highness The Prince of Wales To Whose Most Goodnatured Encouragement The Club is Mainly Indebted for Its Present Recognised Position'.

On leaving Cambridge F. C. Burnand, as already recounted, had considered taking holy orders, deciding instead on the theatre – and journalism – as a career. That Burnand remained alert to religious matters is demonstrated by his curious contribution to the controversy surrounding Bishop Colenso of Natal's *The Pentateuch and Book of Joshua Critically Examined* (1862–3). Burnand 'could not but be struck by the utter absence of any authoritative utterance which should be universally accepted by Anglicans of all parties, ritualistic, high, moderate, low and lowest, as decisive of, or as temporarily silencing, the controversy' (1904, vol. II, p. 266). In a couple of hours Burnand wrote an eight-page pamphlet, thousands of copies of which – at threepence each – were soon sold. *Bishop Colenso Utterly Refuted and Categorically Answered by Lord Dundreary* (Burnand, 1862) is written in the persona of Lord Dundreary, from Tom Taylor's *Our American Cousin*, a part made famous by E. A. Sothern's hugely popular performance. Lord Dundreary is described as having 'first distinguished himself as an artist and careful student in a theological examination at the SISTER UNIVERSITY, where he finished (and very quickly too) his educational course' (p. 268). The pamphlet is couched in Lord Dundreary's distinctively puzzle-headed, lisping and stuttering style. Thus on the exodus of the Israelites: 'Tho the Bishop findth a lot of difficulty in the number of people who went out of Egypt, all the – all the huthbandth and wiveth, and daughterth, and thonth, and all their thonth and their daughterth, and their fatherth and m – m – motherth for thome – thomething like to twenty-two mileth' (p. 269).

The prevailing light-heartedness of the ADC stood Burnand in good stead in his career as the writer of burlesque and humorous journalism. He was the long-serving editor of *Punch*, 1880–1906, and was knighted in 1902.

The attitude of the Cambridge graduate (already quoted) who wrote to Charles Kean in the 1850s – 'I am the son of a clergyman, and lately a member of the University of Cambridge . . . and I see nothing before me save the stage or enlistment' (J. W. Cole, 1859, vol. II, p. 20) – was perpetuated. Charles Brookfield was the son of Revd W. H. Brookfield, friend of Carlyle, Tennyson, Thackeray and Dickens. He succeeded in persuading his family that he was too delicate to remain at Westminster School and spent a couple of years attending 'a few lectures at King's College, London' (Brookfield, 1902, p. 21) and frequenting theatres in that city and Paris, before going up to Trinity College, Cambridge, in 1875. There his 'solitary distinction was the Winchester Reading Prize' (p. 51) despite the fact that the adjudicators 'considered my reading of the Scriptures rather too dramatic – that I had given different voices to the various persons, which was considered almost irreverent' (p. 52). Having embarked on law as a career Brookfield turned to the theatre:

It was early in 1879 that I made up my mind to go upon the stage – if I could. I don't think it was Vanity that prompted me – at least not Vanity alone – although this may have thrown out to me an occasional word of encouragement. I was 'eating my dinners' at the Inner Temple . . . but I felt I ought to try to Earn an income sooner than I had any prospect of doing at the Bar. Mrs Alfred Wigan counselled me to join a stock company so as to get plenty of hard work and experience. (p. 91)

Through the agency of Henry Kemble, Brookfield met fellow clergyman's son Charles Wardell, Ellen Terry's second husband, for lunch at the Garrick Club. Matters were swiftly arranged in a profession in which personal recommendation and mutual liking counted for more than professional training or experience, and in October 1879 Brookfield set off on a tour with Kelly (Wardell's stage name) and Ellen Terry. Though Brookfield does not seem to have betrayed much seriousness of character himself he found the antics of the company on the Sunday trains 'appallingly playful' (p. 96). Nevertheless, he thought 'on the whole I was wise, situated as I was, to go on the stage . . . I wanted to earn a living at once. I had achieved no scholarly distinction at Cambridge and the stage appeared to be the only craft which one was paid to learn' (p. 92).

It was at Oxford that a more elevated and dedicated attitude towards the theatre gradually developed. A key figure who straddled the worlds of the university and the theatre was Charles Reade. Born on 8 June 1814 at Ipsden Manor House, some sixteen miles from Oxford, Reade came from a well-to-do family and duly entered Magdalen College, Oxford: 'Mother kissed me, gave me a valedictory blessing, bade me be a good boy and make haste to be a bishop!' (Coleman, 1903, p. 35). Although taking only a third-class degree in Greats, Reade was awarded a fellowship, becoming college bursar in 1844 and vice-president in 1851. Unusually for a don at the time, Reade did not take holy orders and his mother, 'still bent on my being a Bishop', realised that he 'had found a paradise elsewhere – a forbidden one, 'tis true, for the beastly stage-door barred my way to fame' (p. 58). To Reade's mother 'The Theatre' was 'that pit of perdition' (p. 59).

Reade's first performed play was *The Ladies' Battle*, an adaptation from the French, at the Olympic Theatre on 7 May 1851. John Coleman recorded Reade's identification with the authors of the Moralities, *Gammer Gurton's Needle*, Elizabethan plays – 'most of the players and playwrights of Elizabethan times were varsity men' – and Henry Hart Milman, 'but I [Reade] believe this is the first case on record of a Vice-Chancellor [vice-president] having written and produced a play during his term of office, a circumstance of which I was not a little proud' (p. 90). Reade was aware of the potential for creating a common culture shared by the universities and the population at large. Reade proceeded to write twenty plays and twenty-seven novels, as well as serials, short stories, pamphlets and journalism. He collaborated with Tom Taylor on four plays including *Masks and Faces* (Haymarket Theatre, 20 November 1852); he was a member of the Garrick Club where he spent many of his leisure hours; and was friendly with Dickens and Bulwer Lytton.

In preparation for his novel *It Is Never Too Late to Mend* (1856) Reade visited Durham, Oxford and Reading gaols, writing of Reading:

Went to-day to the chapel of Reading Gaol. There I heard and saw a parson drone the liturgy and hum a commonplace dry-as-dust discourse to two hundred great culprits and beginners . . . He droned away as if he had been in a country parish church. He attacked the difficult souls with a buzz of conventional commonplaces that have come down from book of sermons to book of sermons for the last century, but never in that century knocked at the door of a man in passing – nor ever will . . . Well, I'm not a parson; but I'll write one, and say a few words, in my quiet temperate way about this sort of thing. (p. 161)

Reade adapted *It Is Never Too Late to Mend* for the stage. It was first performed in Leeds in March 1865 and then at the Princess's Theatre, London, on 4 October 1865. The brutality of life inside prison is depicted with stark realism, anticipating John Galsworthy's *Justice* (1910). The set for act 2 scene 2 is 'A line of cell doors in a corridor of the borough gaol' with references to 'the great *separate and silent system*', 'the crank . . . ; only done 3,350 revolutions out of your 3,500', and 'the punishment jacket'. Despite the unfavourable impression created by the chaplain at Reading Gaol, Reade's Revd Eden is a sympathetic figure:

EDEN: I am here to see the laws of heaven and of man respected. And it is my painful duty to tell you that they are constantly violated by your order. (Hammet, 1986, p. 135)

and one of the inmates, Tom Robinson, says:

ROBINSON: I hate the human race; and but for good Mr Eden I should hate Him who made them the heartless miscreants I find them here. (p. 136)

Martin F. Tupper, educated at Christ Church, Oxford, and author of the hugely popular *Proverbial Philosophy* (1838–76), wrote of *It Is Never Too Late to Mend*: 'Despair of good is the great and evil antagonist, which so long as there is Life and Hope, it is worth any Man's while to try and conquer, and you possibly have done more good by your acted morals at the Princess's than many bishops in many cathedrals' (Coleman, 1903, p. 250).

In an article, 'The pulpit and the stage', which he contributed to the *Theatre* (1 April 1882), Tupper considered that: 'There has been a great levelling-up so far as play-actors are concerned, even if there has not been also, perhaps unfortunately, considerable levelling-down on the clerical side in the matter of renouncing and denouncing pomps and vanities.' He reasserted the power of 'acted morals':

We will name no names, but are bold to say that many of the most exemplary, not only in morals, but also in religion, may be found among professional players; and further (of course excepting obvious exceptions), we will express our belief that many English plays of our time, so long as they are free of French taint, convey excellent social lessons, and are full of generous sentiments, as truly as, if not more than, may be heard from many pulpits.

Reade himself believed that, in addition to its potential for pleasure and delight, 'it surely cannot be even questioned that the Drama is the most potent educational medium in existence' (Coleman, 1903, p. 258). Certainly 'social lessons' were part of his purpose both as a novelist and playwright. A fervent teetotaller, Reade adapted Zola's *L'Assommoir* as *Drink* (Princess's Theatre, 2 June 1879) of which William Archer wrote: 'If ever there was a drama which would cause instant conversion from evil ways, *Drink* was that drama' (in Hammet, 1986, p. 25). Though Reade remained a layman, his college position still placed the obligation of celibacy upon him, but from 1856 he lived in Mayfair with Mrs Seymour, a former actress, with whom he shared the management of the St

James's Theatre in 1854–5. Of their relationship Ellen Terry wrote: 'Between Mrs Seymour and Charles Reade there existed a friendship of that rare sort about which it is easy for people who are not at all rare, unfortunately, to say ill-natured things. Charles Reade worshipped Laura Seymour, and she understood and sympathised with his work and his whims' (Craig and St John 1933, p. 85).

Charles Reade seems to have been equally understanding about Ellen Terry's personal predicament in the early 1870s. As a result of a chance encounter – she with a broken pony-cart, he in hunting pink riding to hounds – in which he urged her to 'Come back to the stage', she did so as Philippa Chester in his play *The Wandering Heir* in 1874 at a salary of £40 a week (p. 69). Although Reade had no reservations about persuading Ellen Terry to return to the stage, following Mrs Seymour's death in 1879 he himself experienced profound doubt about his own involvement in the theatre: 'A month or two later, with his usual inconsistency, he went to the opposite extreme, and informed me with great *empressement* that he did not intend to write for the Theatre again, and henceforth he would devote himself entirely to Biblical studies!' (Coleman, 1903, p. 397). Apparently finding an example in the piety of Sheridan Knowles's later years Reade urged Coleman 'to quit the Stage and take to the Church . . . you'd make a splendid popular preacher' (p. 398). Reade came strongly under the influence of Revd Charles Graham, Baptist minister of Avenue Road Church, Shepherd's Bush, who wrote of Reade's conversion in *The Christian*. Reade, with his brother, first attended Graham's church in early December 1879 and the following Sunday 'after the service asked for a personal interview, in which he frankly and fully opened his mind in relation to his spiritual state. Throughout the month these interviews were repeated several times each week. He had the deep conviction of his state as a sinner condemned by the righteous law of God' (Graham, 1884, p. 9). Graham furnished Reade with scriptural texts (Leviticus 1. 4; 2 Corinthians 5. 20; 1 John 5. 10–11) which 'gave him a foundation on which he felt he could securely stand' (p. 10). Clearly his lengthy involvement in the theatre lay at the heart of Reade's spiritual torment:

Early in 1880, Mr Reade asked my advice in relation to his connection with the theatre. My reply was that he had found a new Master, from whom it was both his privilege and duty to seek guidance. Soon after, he said to me, 'I have now cut off the right hand and cast it from me: I am done with the theatre.' But it is only right to say that in the meshes of that evil net he allowed himself to be again entangled.

Of his sin in this entanglement my valued friend soon became convinced. Confined to his room by one of his severe bronchial attacks, I called on him, when immediately he said to me, 'I have backslidden from God; I have returned to the world. Is there mercy for me?' (p. 13)

Reade died on 11 April 1884; the inscription on his coffin lid read: 'CHARLES READE, Dramatist, Novelist, and Journalist'. John Coleman's interpretation was: ' "Dramatist" first – always first! At his own request the words were placed thus. The ruling passion was strong in death, and to the very last he remained faithful to his first and early love – the Drama' (1903, p. 417). Whatever Charles Reade's final thoughts about the theatre were, the doubts which assailed him during his last five years demonstrated the continuing power of religious opposition to the theatre even for a man of independent mind and spirit, whose plays had been widely acknowledged as a strong force for good.

When Charles Dodgson dined at Magdalen College, Oxford, on 19 October 1856, his host, mathematics fellow James Barnby, strongly advised him 'to read *Never too late to mend*, a novel by one of their Fellows, Charles Reade' (Green, 1971, vol. I, p. 93). Charles Dodgson was born on 27 January 1832, the eldest of Canon Charles Dodgson's eleven children. As a child Charles Dodgson built a marionette theatre with the help of the village carpenter, but though his father was indulgent towards home theatricals he 'never relaxed his principled objections to the stage and none of his daughters ever attended a commercial theatre' (Lennon, 1947, p. 25). After Rugby School, under both Dr Arnold and his successor Archibald Tait, Dodgson went up to Christ Church, Oxford, in 1851 and stayed there for the remaining forty-seven years of his life, becoming a member of the teaching staff in 1856. During the 1850s Dodgson regularly attended London theatres, taking particular delight in Charles Kean's Shakespeare revivals at the Princess's. As a don, Dodgson was expected to take holy orders, but though he was ordained deacon on 22 December 1861, he never proceeded to priest's orders. Dodgson was much concerned at the time of his ordination by the attitude of the Evangelical Bishop of Oxford, Samuel Wilberforce, towards priests attending the theatre:

The Bishop of Oxford, Dr Wilberforce had expressed the opinion that the 'resolution to attend theatres or operas was an absolute disqualification for Holy Orders', which discouraged him very much, until it transpired that this statement was only meant to refer to the parochial clergy. He discussed the matter with Dr Pusey and with Dr Liddon. The latter said that 'he thought a deacon might lawfully, if he found himself unfit for the work, abstain from direct ministerial duty'. And so, with many qualms about his own unworthiness, he at last decided to prepare definitely for ordination. (Green, 1971, vol. 1, pp. 152–3)

Dodgson's speech impediment was undoubtedly a major obstacle to him performing full priestly duties, but he availed himself of the freedom which his non-parochial status gave him to attend the theatre. Not only did Dodgson attend the theatre but he also fostered friendships in the theatrical fraternity, especially amongst young actresses. Ellen Terry described Dodgson as 'one of my earliest friends among literary folk. I can't remember a time when I didn't know him' (Craig and St John, 1933, p. 142). He gave Ellen and her sisters a copy of *Alice in Wonderland* – 'He always gave any new young friend "Alice" at once' (p. 142). The friendship was interrupted by Ellen Terry's matrimonial breakdown with G. F. Watts and her liaison with E. W. Godwin but resumed after her marriage to Charles Wardell and continued through her golden years as Irving's leading lady at the Lyceum: 'Mr Dodgson was an ardent play-goer. He took the keenest interest in all the Lyceum productions, frequently writing to me to point out slips in the dramatic logic which only he would ever have noticed!' (p. 142). Dodgson's large circle of theatrical friends included Tom Taylor to whom, on 25 January 1866, he sent 'a sketch of a domestic drama' (Green, 1971, vol. 1, p. 239). With the success of *Alice in Wonderland* Dodgson became involved in stage adaptations, contributing an article on 'Alice on the stage' to the *Theatre* on 1 April 1887.

On that day Dodgson wrote to Clement Scott about another 'paper' which 'I am meditating and may offer to you', seeking assurance that 'in the first instance' it would be read by 'no one but yourself. In the event of its not being accepted, I should very much prefer its not having been seen by any one else' (Cohen, 1979, vol. II, p. 670). Such unassuming modesty was as unnecessary as it was touching. Scott duly published 'The stage and the spirit of reverence' by Lewis Carroll (Dodgson) on 1 June 1888. Carroll began his article by stating that he was addressing his reader 'as a man: not as a churchman, not as a Christian, not even as a believer in a God – but simply as a man who recognises (*this*, I admit, is essential) that there is a distinction between good and evil'. He cited examples of audiences demonstrating their awareness of this distinction: 'the low fierce hiss' directed at Skinner, 'The Spider' (played by E. S. Willard) in *The Silver King* – 'they see Sin in all its hideousness and shudder at the sight'; the sympathetic ripple of applause for the comical old greengrocer Mr George Barrett in *The Golden Ladder*; and their rapport with Frederick Robson – 'the greatest actor our generation has seen' – in *The Porter's Knot*.

To 'reverence' Carroll gave a broad application: 'reverence is due to subjects connected with religion, I wish to give to this word a broader sense than the conventional one. I mean by it simply a belief in some good and unseen being above and outside human life as we see it, to whom we feel ourselves responsible.' Of profane language he 'did not think the worst instances occur on the stage', but in 'popular literature' (Barham's *The Ingoldsby Legends*) and 'fashionable society', including 'the utterances of *reverend* jesters'. Stage oaths he found profane when 'lightly and jestingly uttered', but 'used gravely and for a worthy purpose, they are at any rate not to be condemned by any appeal to the *Bible*'. The act of prayer and the depiction of places of worship on stage were accept-able if reverent and free from vulgarity. He even thought that the 'exquisite taste and reverent handling in the church-scene in "Much Ado" at the Lyceum' might encourage some, 'to whom the ideas of God, or heaven, or prayer, were strange' to think '"Is *this* what church is like? I'll go and see it for myself!"' Carroll heartily wished that Irving would transfer the 'dialogue between Beatrice and Benedick, with all its deli-cate banter and refined comedy . . . to the *outside* of the church'. Impersonations – even unflattering ones – of ministers of religion were tolerable: 'I would not seek to shield them from ridicule *when they deserve it*'; evil spirits – Irving's Mephistopheles – were legitimate, but needed to be treated seriously and 'The same claim, for seriousness of treatment, may be made as to the subject of Hell and future punishment' – W. S. Gilbert's chorus of little girls singing 'He said "Damn me!" He said "Damn me!"', failing on that count:

Put the two ideas side by side – Hell (no matter whether *you* believe in it or not: millions do), and those pure young lips thus sporting with its horrors – and then find what *fun* in it if you can! How Mr Gilbert could have stooped to write, or Sir Arthur Sullivan could have prostituted his noble art to set to music, such vile trash, it passes my skill to understand.

Carroll concluded with an outline of how the parable of the Prodigal Son might be turned into 'a most effective play', but, as he well knew, a play on such a subject would not be licensed for the stage. However in the freedom which he allowed to the theatre in its treatment of religious matters, and in the examples of 'the Spirit of Reverence' which he cited, Carroll showed how far toleration between the Church and the stage had progressed, but as an Oxford don his liberal attitude towards the theatre had limits. On 1 April 1883 he visited the vice-chancellor of the university, Dr Benjamin Jowett, 'to speak about the backs I wish to give to the seats in the gallery at St Mary's. I also talked about Vance ["the Great Vance", Alfred Peck Stevens . . . one of the most famous of Music Hall Singers and Comedians] whom I want him to forbid in Oxford' (Green, 1971, vol. II, p. 415). Benjamin Jowett was then at the pinnacle of his lengthy career, which had begun as a Balliol undergraduate in 1836 (while Tait was a fellow) and progressed to the Regius Chair of Greek in 1855, Master of Balliol in 1870 and vice-chancellor, 1882–6. Ordained by Samuel Wilberforce, Bishop of Oxford, in 1845, Jowett, a contributor to *Essays and Reviews* (1860), was a Broad churchman of liberal persuasion, a close confederate of Dean Stanley. In 1877 his former pupil W. H. Mallock had drawn a scarcely veiled portrait of Jowett as Dr Jenkinson in *The New Republic or Culture, Faith and Philosophy in an English Country House*. Indeed all of the principal characters in *The New Republic* were easily recognisable: Mr Storks (Huxley), Professor Stockton (Tyndall), Mr Herbert (Ruskin), Mr Luke (Matthew Arnold), Mr Rose (Walter Pater), Donald Gordon (Carlyle) and Lady Grace (Mrs Mark Pattison).

Bishop Fraser spent the evening of 19 November 1877 at the Athenaeum leafing through *The New Republic* and making the appropriate identifications for 'the *dramatis personae*': 'Stanley, I hear, is very angry at the book, for its satire on Jowett. Matthew Arnold is, I am told, not at all displeased at being presented as Mr Luke' (Diggle, 1889, p. 446). Geoffrey Faber describes Mallock's portrait of Jowett as 'very maliciously intended . . . Every farcical device is used to ensure that Jenkinson appears ridiculous' (1957, p. 376) and yet Faber concedes that 'a recurring and perplexing note of respect somehow queers the intention'. For all its satirical intentions Mallock's portrait conveys the essence of Jowett's contribution to the religious debate of his day.

The first incongruity is the setting for Dr Jenkinson's sermon – 'a complete miniature theatre' (Patrick, 1950, p. 66):

The scene that met their eyes was certainly not devotional. The whole little semicircle glittered with heavy gilding and with hangings of crimson satin, and against these the stucco limbs of gods and goddesses gleamed pale and prominent. The gallery rested on the heads of nine scantily-draped Muses, who, had there been two less in number, might have passed for the seven deadly sins; round the frieze in high relief reeled a long procession of Fauns and Bacchanals; and half the harem of Olympus sprawled and floated on the azure ceiling. Nor was this all. The curtain was down, and, brilliantly illuminated as it was displayed before the eyes of the congregation Faust on the Brocken, with a long plume with the young witch, who could boast of no clothes at all. (p. 66)

Dr Jenkinson enters 'in his ordinary dress . . . selecting the central stall as a kind of *prie-Dieu*, he knelt down facing his congregation' (p. 66). Beginning with a passage from the Koran, he 'then went on to the Confession, the Absolution, and a number of other selections from the English morning service, omitting, however, the creed, and concluded with a short prayer of St Francis Xavier's' (p. 67). The eclecticism of Jenkinson's liturgy chimes with the incongruity of the setting, which does not seem to disconcert him at all. He accepts with alacrity the proposal that he should deliver his sermon from the stage and the curtain is raised to reveal him 'standing in the middle of a gorge in the Indian Caucasus – the remains of a presentation of Prometheus Bound which had taken place last February' (p. 61). For his text Dr Jenkinson has selected Psalm 3, verse 10 – 'The fear of the Lord is the beginning of wisdom' – proceeding to a discourse on Plato: 'There is, for instance, no doctrine more often selected for attack by those who oppose Christianity upon moral grounds, than that of which my text is an expression. I mean the doctrine of a morality enforced by rewards and punishments' (p. 69). Having undermined the idea of a religion based on fear, Jenkinson proceeds to the Bible: 'to understand the meaning of my text, we must try to see what, from his position and education, the writer could have meant by it' (p. 73), thus:

'We now see that, in the face of recent criticism, we cannot even be sure about any of the details of the divine life of our Lord. But in all this' – the Doctor's voice here became still more aërial, and he fixed his eyes upon the painted ceiling of the theatre, as though he were gazing on some glorious vision – 'in all this there is nothing to discompose us. We can be quite sure that He lived, and that He went about doing good, and that in Him we have, in the highest sense, everlasting life.' (p. 75)

Rejecting the idea of absolute evil, Dr Jenkinson speaks of the growth of Christianity 'through an admixture of what we now recognise as evil . . . It has been said that it is the part of the devil to see in good the germs of evil. Is it not also the part of the devil not to recognise in evil the germs of good? . . . And so, may we not recognise in all things the presence and the providence of God?' (p. 77). Doctor Jenkinson 'took the whole congregation quite aback' (p. 80) by concluding with the Apostles' Creed, after which 'Faust and the young witch again covered the preacher from the eyes of his congregation' (p. 81).

Like all effective satire *The New Republic* has a foundation of truth and Dr Jenkinson's sermon distils the essence of progressive religious thought during the preceding four decades – the challenge to 'a morality enforced by rewards and punishments' (concomitant with Maurice's revisionary concept of hell); reading the Bible as one would other great works of literature; the de-mystification of miracles; and the rejection of 'absolute evil'. All these developments had been conducive to creating a more sympathetic climate for the theatre, thereby rendering the apparently incongruous setting of 'a complete miniature theatre' for Dr Jenkinson's sermon surprisingly apt. In any case Mallock's book appeared in the year in which an Anglican bishop (Fraser) had conducted services in two theatres.

In the country houses which he actually visited Jowett did meet actors. At Tennyson's Haslemere home on 12 January 1885 the company included Frank Archer, there on a mission from Henry Irving to discuss *Becket* (F. Archer, 1912, pp. 258–60); a couple of years earlier in West Malvern, Jowett encountered Lady Martin (Helen Faucit) with whom he discussed Shakespeare (Abbott and Campbell, 1897, vol. II, p. 179). Jowett was 'more than enthusiastic about Shakespeare' (Tollemache, 1904, p. 102), though his choice, according to Swinburne, of *The Merry Wives of Windsor* as his favourite play (Faber, 1957, p. 369) was unorthodox. Jowett's preference for Shakespeare was reflected in the charter granted to the Oxford University Dramatic Society in 1884: 'one play by Shakespeare each year – but nothing else' (Wickham, 1977, p. 115).

Near to the end of his term of office as vice-chancellor of the University of Oxford, Jowett invited Henry Irving to give the Commemoration lecture in the Examination Schools on 26 June 1886. Over 4,000 applications were received for the 1,500 places to hear Irving speak on 'Four great actors': Richard Burbage, Thomas Betterton, David Garrick and Edmund Kean. As befitted the occasion Irving concentrated on his stated subject, but he did allow himself the observation that 'I have not had the advantage – one that very few members of my profession in the past, or even in the present times have enjoyed – of a university education' (J. Richards, 1994, p. 52), adding that for many years Oxford had banned actors in term-time.

Jowett began his own speech with a tribute to the 'great services which he [Irving] has rendered to the world and to Society by improving and elevating the stage'. He cautioned 'some young aspirants to the stage' that the life of a great actor is 'not such a heaven upon earth' as they dreamed of. He illustrated his remark that 'things which we hear with our own ears and see with our own eyes make a far deeper impression on us than what we read' by recalling the enduring impression made upon him by Macready's Lear forty years ago. Of the Puritan prohibitions of drama he said:

It is an old quarrel between the stage and the Church; and there is a quarrel older still between the stage and Greek philosophy. For Plato, as you know, banishes from his Utopia, first the drama and then the poets, on the grounds that they are twice removed from truth, and that by acting weak and effeminate parts men become assimilated to what they act.

Jowett took issue with Plato and Puritans alike as taking up 'arms against human nature, they do not see that there is a piece of drama in us all, the games of primitive tribes, the plays of little children are a refutation of them'. To the other camp, who upheld drama as 'a great instrument of popular education', he replied 'we do not expect to find sermons in plays':

But in general the influence of the theatre is indirect, it is not intended to teach us that vice is always punished, and virtue triumphant, but to present a fair picture of human nature . . . although the first purpose of the drama is not to point a moral; the indirect influence of the theatre is very great, and tends to permeate all classes of society, so that the condition of the stage is not a bad index or test of a nation's character. We in England are in part what we have been made by the plays of William Shakespeare. Our literature, our manners, our religion, our taste have been to a very great extent affected by them. (*Oxford Chronicle and Berks and Bucks Gazette* 3 July 1886)

Jowett concluded by applauding not the actors of Irving's lecture, but two 'noble benefactors' – W. C. Macready and Irving himself. Prior to his lecture, Irving had sent Jowett a copy of Pollock's *W. C. Macready; Reminiscences and Selections from his Diaries and Letters* (L. Irving, 1951, p. 475).

Arthur Bourchier, of Christ Church, founder of the Oxford University Dramatic Society, presented Irving with an Address, and T. H. Maclean, of New College, ex-president of the University Boat Club, gave him a handsomely bound copy of Fleay's *Life of Shakespeare and his Works*. In response Irving proffered his sincere thanks – 'such catholic acts as the Vice-Chancellor's were great incentives to men who in the battle of life were sometimes exposed to prejudice and narrow-mindedness'. The next day the university pulpit was occupied by Dr William Boyd-Carpenter, Bishop of Ripon, whose friendship with Squire Bancroft and sympathy for the theatre exempted him from such charges. The bishop and the actor were fellow week-end guests of the vice-chancellor.

'Performance of Shakespeare or of Greek plays in the Theatre at Oxford' had been number fifteen (out of seventeen) on Jowett's 'Agenda, 1881–1886, during my Vice-Chancellorship' (Faber, 1957, p. 390). As Charles Reade knew, drama had been strongly represented in the university in Tudor times, but thereafter it had been officially discouraged.

10. Benjamin Jowett and the *Agamemnon* cast, Oxford

In 1847 an amateur group was founded at Brasenose College, which co-opted from Christ Church Frank Talfourd, the son of Sir Thomas Noon Talfourd, author of *Ion*, whose burlesque of *Macbeth* they performed (Carpenter, 1985, p. 11). Charles Dodgson attended various amateur dramatics – tableaux for the Prince of Wales during the royal family's visit in December 1860 (Green, 1971, vol. i, p. 163) and Christ Church theatricals on 5 December 1863 (p. 207). Officially the university banned drama and in 1869 'the fateful fiat went forth in . . . the shape of the Vice-Chancellor's decree. There were to be no more theatricals, amateur or otherwise within the jurisdiction of the university' (Mackinnon, 1910, p. 39). Nevertheless on 5 December 1879 the Philothespian Society was formed at Christ Church; and in 1880–1 a young New College don, W. L. Courtney, and undergraduate Frank Benson secured the consent of Jowett for a performance of Aeschylus's *Agamemnon* in the original Greek in the new hall at Balliol College (illustration 10). In 1883 the Philothespians staged *The Merchant of Venice* with Etonian Arthur Bourchier as Shylock, then in 1884 the Oxford University Dramatic Society was formed. Their opening production on 9 May 1885 was

1 Henry IV preceded by a prologue written by George Curzon and spoken by Cosmo Gordon Lang, dressed as a Doctor of Divinity, with an audience which included the Bishop of Oxford, the Deans of Westminster and Christ Church and Jowett himself. The OUDS *Twelfth Night* on 13 February 1886 was the opening production in the newly constructed Theatre Royal – generally known as the New Theatre – which for many years served the society as a permanent home.

These significant achievements owed a great deal to the authority and enthusiasm of Jowett, but they would not have happened had there not been a ground-swell of support amongst undergraduates and dons. Of the latter the most important was W. L. Courtney of New College – 'To him Oxford largely owed its New Theatre' (T. E. Courtney, 1930, p. 13). Courtney belonged to a new generation of dons, of whom ordination and celibacy were no longer required. They lost 'the traditional social rank of the clergyman' which 'had served to compensate for the lack of high status in the role of teacher itself' (Engel, 1983, p. 10), but brought to the university a more liberal and open-minded outlook on activities such as drama. Courtney remained a don for only thirteen years, becoming a journalist as drama critic and book reviewer for the *Daily Telegraph*.

Traditionally there had been extensive interchange between the ancient universities and the leading public schools. In the public schools too the tradition of masters being in holy orders was being eroded. T. W. Bamford identifies 'the first significant number of lay appointments for Eton, Harrow and Rugby' occurring in the 1850s (1967, p. 55). By 1890, 80 per cent of masters at 22 leading schools were not in holy orders, though the tradition of the clerical headmaster survived for considerably longer. As 'the clerical collar lost its dominating influence' (p. 54) so the number of pupils entering the Church also declined, the combined total for Rugby and Harrow dropping from 36 in 1830 to 9 in 1880 (p. 210). The attitude towards recreation in public schools also changed. In place of the unregulated free use of leisure, as depicted by Tom Hughes in *Tom Brown's School Days*, schools increasingly put non-classroom hours on an ordered footing with organised games and hobbies, in which producing magazines and acting plays were included. Thus by the 1880s undergraduates arrived at the universities with an expectation of involving themselves energetically and purposefully in non-academic pursuits, whether it be on the cricket field or the stage (see Motter, 1929).

When Arthur Bourchier arrived at Christ Church, Oxford, in 1882 he 'had already decided while at Eton that he was going to be a professional actor' (Carpenter, 1985, p. 27). Frank Benson came to New College from

Winchester with his prowess as an athlete established and his interest in acting already developed by Revd Charles Halford Hawkins at the Shakespeare Reading Society (F. Benson, 1930, p. 58) in which he had taken Ophelia, Rosalind and Constance (J. C. Trewin, 1960, p. 5). H. B. Irving had been sent to Marlborough College, established principally for sons of the clergy, where his 'dramatic genius' had been acclaimed for his recitations in the Penny Readings regularly held there (*Marlburian* 2 December 1886). Henry Irving hoped that, with the benefits of Marlborough and New College, Oxford, behind him, his son would pursue a profession other than the theatre, but at Oxford Harry soon came under the influence of that 'pliant Christian' W. L. Courtney, thanks to whom 'the climate of Oxford was becoming more favourable to stage-struck young gentlemen than anywhere else in England' (L. Irving, 1967, p. 135) and enlisted in OUDS.

One undergraduate, arriving at Balliol College in October 1882, whose father would have shared Henry Irving's apprehensions about his son becoming immersed in university drama, though from a very different perspective, was Cosmo Gordon Lang, the son of a Church of Scotland minister. On a youthful visit to London, Cosmo Gordon Lang had agonised about entering the Lyceum Theatre:

There was also the theatre, hitherto a forbidden territory. Might he go and see *Othello*? Irving and Booth were playing and, after all, Shakespeare was different. 'Now don't be alarmed . . . sooner than go to a modern comedy I would cut off my head.' There spoke the Manse. The answer is unrecorded, but must have been favourable, for Cosmo went, to his ample gratification, so entering a world that would mean much to him a little later. (Lockhart, 1949, p. 21)

At Oxford such inhibitions swiftly faded, as Lang recalled: 'I was one of the founders, with Arthur Bourchier, James Adderley, Alan McKinnon and others . . . It fell to me to open the first performance – Henry IV (First Part) – by reciting a prologue written by George Curzon, a rather dull and bombastic composition' (p. 36). *The Times* judged that Lang delivered the prologue 'fairly', expressing puzzlement over why he was dressed as a doctor of divinity. Perhaps it was prophetic, for Lang became Archbishop of Canterbury; his cousin Alexander Matheson Lang became an actor. According to W. Macqueen-Pope, 'His Grace always said that Alexander would have made a better archbishop than he, but that he, the archbishop, was the better actor' (1951, p. 280). Certainly Cosmo Gordon Lang carried the aura of the actor into his ecclesiastical duties, leading to suspicion of insincerity in some quarters, as Dr Webb recorded:

Lang's instinctive sense of the dramatically or spectacularly appropriate made him a wonderful performer in great ceremonies and the like; but of course a wonderful performer is not in the least of a humbug, or without a deep and serious interest in what he is doing. Yet it is not always easy to convince a certain kind of man that this is so. (in Lockhart, 1949, p. 202)

J. G. Lockhart regarded Lang's dramatic flair in a positive light:

Lang was fully aware of his gift and of its uses. His sense of the theatre never left him. But to say that he was a great actor is very far from saying that he was a great humbug. Indeed, the opposite is true, for without an essential sincerity no acting can be great. He had a clear picture of what an Archbishop should be, how he should look and behave and live. As a man might school himself to play Hamlet or Othello he schooled himself to play the part; and in time, like any good actor, he merged himself in it and became what he was playing. That is, in large measure, the story of the next twenty years. (p. 202)

As the butler Brassett lugubriously observes of the antics of the undergraduates of St Olde's College, Oxford, in Brandon Thomas's *Charley's Aunt* (1892): 'Well, College gents'll do anything!', which might well include a future Archbishop of Canterbury performing with OUDS. That so little incongruity should be attached to such a conjunction was due to the lead taken by Oxonians in the second half of the nineteenth century in breaking down prejudice against the theatre. Though assailed by doubts in later life Charles Reade revived the tradition of university dramatists and invested his plays with strong moral purpose. Charles Dodgson maintained a lifelong enthusiasm for the theatre and, whether or not the identification – amongst others – of the Dormouse with F. D. Maurice and the Tiger-lily with Ellen Terry (Jones and Gladstone, 1995, pp. 222, 274) is accepted, he undoubtedly facilitated the two-way traffic between the university and the theatre. Benjamin Jowett's contribution was at least threefold: as a liberal churchman he advanced ideas which were helpful to the theatre; as the pre-eminent Plato scholar of his day he dismissed Plato's opposition to the theatre; and as vice-chancellor of the University of Oxford he took an active role in promoting undergraduate drama and in proclaiming the respectability of the profession of which Henry Irving was the leader, thereby aligning the university with an art form which was part of the national culture.

CHAPTER 9

Actresses

Ellen in Heaven

Henry Irving

The Church and the theatre were both leading, but contrasting, spheres of activity for Victorian women. The Anglican parish offered no professional opportunities for women, but as Bishop Fraser's confirmation figures reveal (73,754 women to 44,050 men – Bishop J. Fraser, 1880, p. 7), they were in the majority in congregations. Charitable and social activities were inevitably dominated by middle-class women, not least the incumbent's own family, unfettered by the need to earn a living. As late as 1908 Frederic Harrison wrote:

> When we say that we would see the typical work of women centred in her personal influence in the Home, we are not asking for arbitrary and rigid limitations. We are not calling for any new legislation or urging public opinion to close any womanly employment for women. There are a thousand ways in which the activity of women may be of peculiar value to the community, and many of these necessarily carry women outside their own houses and into more or less public institutions. The practice of the ladies connected with our Church alone would satisfy us how great is the part which women have to play in teaching, in directing moral and social institutions, in organising the higher standard of opinion, in inspiring enthusiasm in young and old. We are heartily with such invaluable work; and we find that modern civilization offers to women as many careers as it offers to men. (1908, p. 76)

Harrison asserted that 'The career of women is to dignify and elevate the life of men . . . Their real career is a moral one to ennoble and purify the entire life of mankind' (pp. 124–5). He conceded that 'As doctors, artists, poets, philosophers, leaders of political and social movements, there are doubtless occasional spheres for a few exceptional women' (p. 123). That Harrison omitted the theatre from the 'occasional spheres' suitable for 'a few exceptional women' was a reflection of his disdain for it: 'I have, indeed, a settled resolution never to enter a London theatre'

(1911, vol. 1, p. 338). Opposed as Harrison was to women's suffrage, actresses' support for the movement, culminating in the formation of the Actresses' Franchise League in December 1908 (Holledge, 1981, p. 47), would have alienated him further from the theatre. One actress who had no doubt that women's time had come was Florence Farr: 'This is to be the Woman's century. In it she is to awake from her long sleep and come into her kingdom' (1910, p. 7).

Florence Farr traced 'the degradation of women in the past' to 'the religion of the country round Mount Ararat. The lowering of their status occurred when the white races adopted the Syrian Semites' Scriptures. The Christian religion brought us that curse cowering behind its gospel of glad tidings; and it is most remarkable to trace the way in which the Jews' religion crept into Europe under the cloak of Christianity' (p. 8). She referred to the 'unpleasant details about Adam and Eve . . . in the Prophetic narrative' as a result of which 'the blame of all social evils' was fixed on Eve (p. 9). As well as biblical prejudice, Miss Farr had her sights fixed on the contemporary social lot of women, pointing out that of the 13,000,000 women past childhood in England and Wales (out of a total of 17,000,000 females) 'about 4 million are engaged in occupations and trying to make their own living'. She observed that 'Women find it hard to get any professional income out of the Government offices, the Church, or the law courts' (p. 25). For women pursuing a career in the theatre the rewards were widely divergent: 'the most successful London actress may receive a salary of £5000 a year . . . I suppose the average successful singer is delighted with £1000 a year, the average successful actress with £500 a year' (p. 25).

Divergent though incomes in the theatre were, they were based on talent rather than gender. Far from being in competition with men for the same work (acting roles), women were indispensable in the theatre with the result, as Michael Baker writes, that 'in no other trade or profession were women treated on such favourable terms in relation to their male colleagues' (1978, p. 95). The massive increase in the size of the acting profession enumerated in chapter 3 opened up opportunities for more women. Tracy C. Davis has analysed the sex ratio of performers in England and Wales from 1841 to 1911 in Table 9.1.

This gives 'an astounding aggregate increase of 2958 per cent in the seventy year period from 1841–1911' (1991, p. 40). Such a massive increase could not have been generated from within the existing ranks of the acting profession; it was brought about by an influx of new recruits from non-theatrical families. For such families an acting career for a

Table 9.1. *The acting profession in England and Wales, from census enumerations 1841–1911*

year	Enumerations			Ratios female:male	Census increase (N)			Census increase (%)		
	female	male	total		female	male	total	female	male	total
1841	310	1,153	1,463	26.89:100						
1851	643	1,398	2,041	45.99:100	333	245	578	107.42	21.25	39.51
1861	891	1,311	2,202	67.96:100	248	−87	161	38.57	−6.22	7.89
1871*	1,693	1,895	3,588	89.34:100	802	584	1,386	90.01	44.55	62.94
1881	2,368	2,197	4,565	107.78:100	675	302	977	39.87	15.94	27.23
1891	3,696	3,625	7,321	101.96:100	1,328	1,428	2,756	43.92	65.00	60.37
1901	6,443	6,044	12,487	106.60:100	2,747	2,419	5,166	74.32	66.73	70.56
1911	9,171	9,076	18,247	101.05:100	2,728	3,032	5,760	42.34	50.17	46.13

Note

*The figures in the 1871 divisional table of 'Occupations of the People' do not tally with the county or overall national tables. The amended figures here are derived from the county tables which distinguish actors from showmen and persons employed in and about theatres. (T. C. Davis, 1991, p. 10)

Source: Published censuses of England and Wales

daughter 'was a version of the Fall from virtue' (p. 72), however the process was both encouraged and ameliorated by the enhanced respectability achieved by actresses from long-established theatrical families. The contributions of Fanny Kemble and Helen Faucit have already been amply illustrated; other prominent examples were Marie Wilton, Madge Robertson and Ellen Terry.

The father of Marie Wilton (1839–1921) 'was originally intended for the Church; but that idea was soon abandoned for he was infatuated with an early love for the stage' (Mr and Mrs Bancroft, 1889, p. 1). Robert Pleydell Wilton's decision was received with horror by his family, which included several clergymen – amongst them his maternal grandfather and an uncle, both Revd William Wise and both fellows of St John's College, Oxford. To them Robert Wilton 'had been defiled and nothing could wash him clean again' (p. 3). As a child performer Marie Wilton encountered religious hostility – and indeed hypocrisy – when she took part in an amateur entertainment in aid of church-building. Afterwards she was petted by the ladies present, who started a collection 'to buy me a toy, as a souvenir of the occasion' until they discovered that she was the daughter of an actor when 'the smiles vanished, and the expressions changed in a way to have turned lemons sour. The bags were closed with a cold relentless click' (p. 6). Marie Wilton did not allow this experience to taint her attitude towards religion in later life.

In 1867 Marie Wilton married Squire Bancroft who, by his own admission 'was brought up in some luxury, and surrounded by all the gentle influences one could wish' (p. 58). As a married couple the Bancrofts enjoyed the society of several clerics – Bellew, Archdeacon Wilberforce and Dr Boyd-Carpenter, Bishop of Ripon (Squire Bancroft, 1925, pp. 38–47). In 1882 the Bancrofts visited the English church at Engadine – a health resort in Switzerland – the opening of which was attended by the Bishops of Bedford and Gloucester and Bristol, the latter 'a well-known mountaineer' (p. 340) whose friendship they had enjoyed in England. The Prince and Princess Christian gave a handsome altar-cloth and amongst the other donations were three 'which brought the Church and Stage in further union, for Mr Arthur Cecil gave the books, Mr Bancroft the bell, while Mrs Bancroft erected a beautiful memorial window above the altar to the memory of her mother' (Mr and Mrs Bancroft, 1889, p. 341). Another visitor to the English church at Engadine was Fanny Kemble who wrote 'Anything more extraordinary than some of the English church services I have attended since I have been at Engadine cannot well be imagined' (1890, vol. II, p. 113). In subscribing to such an exclusive place of worship actors were meeting their social as well as their devotional needs. If actors were to become part of the social establishment, membership of the Established Church, preferably at its socially most prestigious level, was an important part of the process.

In 1897 Squire Bancroft became the second actor-knight. In their long and eminently respectable retirement the Bancrofts contemplated their last rites. According to A. E. W. Mason, Squire Bancroft 'had the Victorian passion for funerals' and of his first visit to Golders Green crematorium reported: 'The relatives were kind enough afterwards to ask me to go behind' (1935, p. 135). Lady Bancroft, who was personally devout, stipulated that 'the hour and place of her funeral were [to be] kept secret, . . . known only to immediate members of the family and four friends' (Squire Bancroft, 1925, p. 237). Nevertheless her funeral was followed immediately by a memorial service in St Martin-in-the-Fields at which Revd W. H. Elliott, Vicar of Holy Trinity, Folkestone, delivered a eulogy:

And the thought of that man at the back of the gallery – what she could do for him, to make him forget his cares and have his part in the sunshine and merriment of life, to take away the frown and to wear the smile – was for her, I believe, the true motive and the abiding inspiration of her art. Such a task, one cannot but think, is very much according to the mind of Him who gives the wayside flower a robe that Solomon might envy, that we may see it and be glad. (p. 239)

The foundation stone of the Bancrofts' success was their innovative and influential productions of Tom Robertson's plays at the Prince of Wales Theatre in the mid 1860s. Tom Robertson came from a large family and of his reportedly twenty-one siblings his sister Madge (1848–1935) achieved greatest distinction, becoming in 1926 the third theatrical Dame of the British Empire under her married name of Kendal. Like Marie Wilton, Madge Robertson was a child performer, making her stage debut at the age of four. As a girl she sang in the choir of a Roman Catholic church in Bristol, but her father resisted the priest's suggestion that she should convert to Roman Catholicism: 'My father said, "No. When she herself realises what real religion means, she can follow her own inclinations!"' (Kendal, 1933, p. 21). This she certainly did. In her teens she took the radical politician Henry Labouchere to task on the subject of registry office marriages: 'The registrar's office was, however, not designed for people to be married in' (p. 24). She was equally forthright on the subject of divorce – 'How often I have implored women never to divorce the father of their children! It handicaps them and throws over them a shadow seldom lifted' (p. 24) – and on marriages between partners: 'holding different religious views . . . No, mixed marriages never succeed' (p. 25). Her views were put to the test and borne out by her younger daughter Dorothy, who married B. A. Meyer in a registry office and was subsequently divorced.

In her conventional views on marriage Madge Kendal was aligning herself – and her profession – with one of the fundamental social and religious tenets of Victorian society. Her own marriage to actor William Kendal (Pemberton, 1900, p. 2), who changed his name from Grimston on joining the profession, was eminently respectable. Madge's father had made it a condition of his consent to her marriage 'that as long as we acted, we should never be parted' (Kendal, 1933, p. 66), thereby committing Kendal to what Shaw described as 'a Perpetual Joint' (p. 70). On 23 September 1884 Madge Kendal addressed the Congress of the National Association for the Promotion of Social Science in Birmingham with a paper on 'The drama'. She reflected that 'The Theatrical Profession is acknowledged to be a high and important one', with other professions '"overstocked" . . . too many clergy men, too many lawyers, too many doctors and the fact that the terms actor and gentleman may now be regarded as synonymous seems to have sent the "overdraft" of all those other professions head-long onto the stage'. For their younger sons, 'well-to-do parents hailed the present social position of the actor with delight', and though they might not have been so enthusiastic on their daughters' behalf:

How many educated girls, finding themselves, through force of circumstances, suddenly compelled to face the world on their own account, have turned with a sigh of relief from the prospect of the stereotyped position of 'companion' or 'governess' to the vista that an honourable connection with the Stage holds out to them. From these, and from other sources, the Theatrical Profession also runs the risk of becoming 'overstocked'. (p. 188)

T. H. S. Escott judged the Bancrofts and Kendals as at 'the apex of the theatrical profession from a social point of view – sons at Eton, houses in fashionable quarters, villas on the Thames, shooting-boxes in Scotland, horses and carriages, visiting lists, fine friends, an endless round of entertainment – whatever, in fact, lends distinction or respectability to life belongs to them' (1885, pp. 297–8). The actress 'who ten or fifteen years ago was dancing a breakdown on the burlesque stage, finds herself seated today, between the Premier and a prelate, at the dinner-table of a peer' (p. 299). Not merely seated beside a prelate: 'they might be the wives of barristers or bishops. They are the incarnation of everything that is orthodox in British matronhood. Mrs. Kendal, one of the best artists of her sex on the London stage, is in private life the very epitome of all domestic virtues and graces' (p. 297).

One actress widely regarded as the epitome of grace, though not of conventional virtue, was Ellen Terry (1847–1928). Like Marie Bancroft and Madge Kendal, Ellen Terry came from a theatrical family (see Steen, 1962), making her debut aged nine as Mamillius in Charles Kean's *The Winter's Tale* in June 1856, when Lewis Carroll 'especially admired the acting of the little Mamillius, Ellen Terry, a beautiful little creature who played with remarkable ease and spirit' (Green, 1971, vol. I, p. 88). At sixteen the beautiful little creature married painter George Frederick Watts, thirty years her senior, at St Barnabus's Church, Kensington, on 20 February 1864 (Manvell, 1968, p. 48). Formal separation followed swiftly on 26 January 1865; divorce was delayed until September 1877, when Watts maintained that his motive for marriage had been 'to remove an impulsive young girl from the dangers and temptations of the stage' (Auerbach, 1987, p. 116). By then Ellen Terry had borne two children (Edy, 6 December 1869, and Teddy, 16 January 1872) to architect E. W. Godwin. In 1877 she married actor Charles Wardell, separating from him in 1881 and becoming a widow on his death in April 1885. In 1907 Ellen Terry married actor James Carew, but they lived together for only two years. Even leaving aside the disputed nature of her relationship with Henry Irving, Ellen Terry was no model of Victorian womanhood.

A gauge of society's attitude to Ellen Terry is to be found in the account given by Lewis Carroll to Mrs J. B. Baird in April 1894:

I honestly believe her position was, from her point of view, this:

I am tied by *human* law to a man who disowns his share of what ought to be a mutual contract. He never loved me and I do not believe, in God's sight, we are man and wife. Society expects me to live, till this man's death as if I were single and to give up all hope of love for which I pine and shall never get from *him*. This other man loves me as truly and faithfully as any lawful husband. If the marriage ceremony were *possible* I would insist on it before living with him. It is *not* possible and I will do without it. (Cohen, 1979, vol. II, pp. 1015–16)

Whilst Ellen Terry was living with Godwin, who later deserted her, Carroll 'held no communication with her. I felt that she had [so] entirely sacrificed her social position that I felt I had no desire but to drop the acquaintance' (p. 1016). The change came when she married Charles Wardell, whose stage name was Kelly, the actor son of 'a clergyman, vicar of Winlaton, Northumberland – a very charming parson of an old-fashioned type' (Craig and St John, 1933, p. 115) who performed the marriage ceremony. Whether Ellen Terry was primarily motivated by a strong physical attraction to Wardell or the desire to give respectability to her children, she did achieve the latter. There was a reconciliation with her own mother and in Carroll's words 'This second marriage put her, in the eyes of Society, once more in the position of a respectable woman' (Cohen, 1979, vol. ii, p. 1016). Wardell drank and had a violent temper, there was a judicial separation in 1881, but after Wardell's death Ellen Terry was a widow and although her third marriage was short-lived it was never formally terminated. That there was a craving for respectability in Ellen Terry is indicated by her account of Edy's confirmation by Dr Bickersteth, Bishop of Exeter, in Exeter Cathedral on 11 January 1887: 'A private ceremony by the Bishop for Edith. Strange! Over thirty years ago Father and Mother (with Kate and me) *walked* (necessity!) from Bristol to Exeter, and now my child is given half-an-hour's talk with the Bishop before her confirmation' (Melville, 1987, p. 126).

Michael Booth has written of Ellen Terry's appeal:

She expressed through a combination of physical appearance, movement, voice and indefinable *presence* a poetic and aesthetic ideal of Victorian womanhood, representing not so much the domestic or chastely maidenish side of that ideal common in fiction and drama as a more physical temptress, whose sexuality was made acceptable and to an extent distanced by the conventions of poetic imagery and pictorial art. (1986, p. 83)

'Our Lady of the Lyceum' as Oscar Wilde dubbed her, Ellen Terry achieved the status of an icon on the stage and in portraits by Watts, Millais and Sargent, amongst others. Henry Irving described W. Graham Robertson's 1891 pastel study (illustration 11) with the rapt expression and tousled, still drying, hair, bordered on one side by lilies as 'Ellen in Heaven' (Robertson, 1931, opp. p. 144, and p. 159). For all her waywardness few could imagine that her maker would deny a place in heaven to one of his most ethereal creations. Earthly recognition came with the DBE in 1925.

In succession to Helen Faucit and Fanny Kemble, Marie Bancroft, Madge Kendal and Ellen Terry provided powerful role models for young women considering a career in the theatre. Unlike other professions, such as medicine, teaching or the law, the theatre had no recognised means of entry. In 1879–80 *Punch* fancifully proposed the establishment of Curtain College – to which 'Girton College would form an annexe' (27 December 1879) – with Ben Webster as Chancellor and Stewart Headlam as 'the official Visitor'. It was not until 1904 that the Royal Academy of Dramatic Art was founded by Herbert Beerbohm Tree.

11. 'Ellen in Heaven', pastel study of Ellen Terry by W. Graham Robertson

Opportunities were expanding for young women, who increasingly sought professions, for which their education had equipped them. The curriculum considered to be suitable for girls was weighted towards liter-ature, music, the arts and domestic studies (Maurice, Kingsley, Johnson *et al.* 1855). In his lecture delivered in Hanover Square Rooms on 29 March 1848 F. D. Maurice outlined the objectives and aims of Queen's College, which had originally been conceived as an establishment for governesses, though taking inspiration from Tennyson's *The Princess* (1847). Drawing, music, mathematics, natural philosophy, Latin, language and grammar were to have their places on the syllabus 'But the master key . . . is assuredly *English Literature*. By that word I mean the books of really great Englishmen . . . Shakespeare and Milton.' Maurice continued:

These authors, I hope, will be read in the strictest sense of the word; read by the pupil as well as the teacher. The real force of an author's work, the structure of his sentences, still more his rhythm, which, in prose as well as in poetry, is often such a help in understanding his character, can scarcely be appreciated until he is read aloud. (Tweedie, 1898, p. 13)

Maurice seems to have been blessed with more attentive pupils at Queen's College than he was at King's. Caroline and Mary E. Hullah remembered: 'Mr Maurice reading us . . . the death of Falstaff, and saying "I shall not say anything about it, because I want you to think it over for yourselves." He made a great deal, in a very quiet way, of the line, "I hope there was no need to trouble himself with any such thoughts yet."' (p. 69). On the staff of Queen's College, Maurice gathered around him William Sterndale Bennett, Professor Hullah, Charles Kingsley, Tom Taylor, Richard Chenevix Trench and – later – William Benham, Arthur Stanley and Henry Morley. Kingsley lectured on English Composition and English Literature, stating in the former that words themselves were given by God 'who vindicated language as His own gift, and man's inventions, in that miracle of Pentecost' (Revd F. D. Maurice, Kingsley, Brasseur *et al.* 1849, p. 31); every principle of composition 'which is true and good, that is which produces beauty, is to be taken as inspiration from above, as depending not on the will of man but of God; not on any abstract rules of pedants' invention, but on the eternal necessities and harmony, on the being of God Himself' (p. 31). Thus: 'The critical examination of good authors, looking at language as an inspiration, and its laws as things independent of us, eternal and divine, we must search into them as we would into any of the set of facts, into nature, or the Bible, by patient introduction' (p. 31). This approach would be applied to Norman poetry, Chaucer, 'then to the use of the Drama; then to the poets of the Elizabethan age. I shall analyse a few of Shakespeare's masterpieces' (p. 40). Shakespeare also had his place in Kingsley's English Literature syllabus and he looked forward to authors yet unborn:

For the true literature of the 19th century, the literature which shall set forth in worthy strains the relation of the two greatest facts, namely of the universe and of Christ, which shall transfigure all our enlarged knowledge of science and of society, of nature, of art, and man with the eternal truths of the gospel, that poetry of the future is not yet here but is coming, aye even at the door; when this great era shall become conscious of its high vocation, and the author too shall claim his priestly calling, and the poets of the world, like the kingdoms of the world, shall become the poets of God and of His Christ. (p. 50)

Amongst the many remarkable women who attended Queen's College and in whom, therefore, the principle of reading aloud and the idea of the author's 'priestly calling' were inculcated were actresses Maud Holt (Mrs – later Lady – Beerbohm Tree); Esmé and Felicity Beringer; Florence Farr – 'one of the decidely more unconventional students' (Kaye, 1972, p. 180); Dorothy Kendal Grimston – Madge Kendal's younger daughter; Cicely Courtneidge; and Henzie Raeburn. In time, reading aloud developed into elocution (Professor Owen Bredon) and then the staging of both English and Greek plays: *As You Like It* (December 1884), *Macbeth* (January 1885), *Much Ado About Nothing* (June 1885), and *Antigone* (December 1890) (*Queen's College Magazine*, and Gryllis, 1948, pp. 58–9). An enthusiasm for the theatre was fired in Maud Holt and her contemporary the future Mrs Alec Tweedie, whose own declaration that she wanted to go on the stage drew this response from her father, physician Dr George Harley: 'During the next four years I will try to show you what going on the stage really means, and the labour it entails' (1904, p. 3). Miss Harley subsequently made her mark as a travel-writer with books on Mexico, Finland, Iceland, Norway, Denmark (*Danish versus English Butter-Making*) and of course Oberammergau, but she also wrote *Behind the Footlights*: 'The Church and Stage cast their fasci-nating meshes around most folk some time during the course of their existence. It is scarcely strange that such should be the case, for both hold mystery, both have their excitements and man delights to rush into what he does not understand' (1904, p. 6).

Mrs Tweedie was alert to 'the perils on the stage, to which of course only the weak succumb, but the temptations are necessarily greater than in other professions' (p. 16). In answer to her own question 'Why do women crowd the stage?', Mrs Tweedie replied: 'The answer is a simple one – because men fail to provide for their own. If every man, willing and able to maintain a wife, married, there would still be over a million women left' (p. 302).

Amongst the other professions which beckoned was teaching. Two former Queen's College pupils who carried its principles forward in other institutions were Dorothea Beale and Frances Buss at Cheltenham

Ladies' College and the North London Collegiate School (Scrimgeour, 1950) respectively: 'The actual reading – specially of poetry – was a delight to both reader and hearers. Miss Beale had a strong dramatic instinct, a keen enjoyment of poetry and the right use of words. She had also a wonderful voice, which she managed well, and though always quiet and restrained in manner, carried her audience with her unwearriedly' (Raikes, 1908, p. 262). As well as reading aloud, Miss Beale also upheld Maurice's and Kingsley's view of literature as a source of moral instruction:

The subject became the vehicle for much teaching that it was not convenient to give in Bible lessons. She sought to interest her class in books, in reading in noble thoughts, in true prose and poetry. But this was by no means all. She sought primarily to give views of life, conduct, and character such as would enable her hearers to go from the school into a larger world, already prepared to know what to find . . . knowledge of character, she would often say, is so important for women. Hence she liked, if possible, once a year to read and lecture upon one of Shakespeare's great plays to the first class. (p. 261)

Miss Beale expressed her views on *King Lear* in a paper which she sent to John Ruskin, who replied (24 March 1887): 'It is one of the subtlest and truest pieces of Shakespeare criticism I ever saw', going on to express severe reservations: she had missed 'the key note. You never enter into the question of what it is that drives Lear mad. And throughout you fall into the fault which women nearly always commit if they don't err on the other side, – of always talking of love as if it had nothing to do with sex' (p. 208). On 8 June he wrote even more stringently:

Especially, I could not tell you anything of your paper on Lear, because I think women should never write on Shakespeare, or Homer, or Aeschylus, or Dante, or any of the greater powers in literature. Spenser, or Chaucer, or Molière, or any of the second and third order of classics – but not the leaders. And you really had missed much more in Lear than I should like to tell you. (p. 208)

As a pioneer of women's education Miss Beale was hardly acquiescent to being denied 'the greater powers in literature'. In 1898 the Princess Hall was opened taking its name from the Princess of Wales and Tennyson's *The Princess*, of which an adaptation by elocution mistress Miss Chute had been staged in the town's old theatre by the College Guild (former pupils) in 1890 (Clarke, 1953, p. 59). The Princess Hall 'was first used on February 8, 1898, on the occasion of the Bishop of Gloucester's annual address to the College' (Steadman,1931, p. 150), but the presence of a leading actor would have been no less appropriate for the hall combined the features and function of a theatre and a place of worship (illustration

12. The Princess Hall, Cheltenham Ladies' College

12). The proscenium arch is flanked by a stage box and hymn-board on one side and an organ on the other. The proscenium curtain provides a backcloth for an altar and crucifix, surmounted by a fresco – *A Dream of Fair Women* – by J. Eadie Reed, depicting Andromache, Alcestis, Cato's Portia, the Lady in *Comus, inter alia*. The galleried auditorium accommodates congregations and audiences alike. If any single late-Victorian structure can be said to embody the union of Church and stage it must be the Princess Hall at Cheltenham Ladies' College.

Miss Beale encouraged the Guild to stage productions – often dramatisations of poetry – with *Comus* in 1896 and *Scenes from the Life of Dante* in 1900: 'She had a keen dramatic sense, and delighted in watching rehearsals and personally coaching some of the individual actors . . . The Guild plays were of course chosen, like the subjects of her literature lessons, with a view to elevate rather than entertain' (Raikes, 1908, p. 332). Miss Beale's attitude to the professional theatre was equivocal. Frank Benson's company visited the college annually from the 1880s, but as Constance Benson recalled: 'Miss Beale was the headmistress, and a real autocrat. She would not allow the girls to visit the theatre, so the performance had to take place in a small classroom, without scenery or furniture. Among the numbers of girls present, only one man was allowed, a clergyman, who sat in the middle of the front row of seats' (1926, p. 60). In *Macbeth*, 'the witches, in full evening-dress, solemnly marched round a chair as they chanted their words'; in *The Merchant of Venice*, 'the part of Jessica had to be much cut, as Miss Beale thought the character a bad example' (Kamm, 1958, p. 115); in *Julius Caesar*, Caesar 'died muffling up his face in one of Miss Beale's white damask dinner cloths' – but the girls 'were absolutely thrilled by these performances' (Steadman, 1931, p. 38). From upholding the moral force of great literature and reading it aloud, to Benson's unadorned performances, elocution classes and the Guild plays, Cheltenham Ladies' College under Miss Beale illustrates the progression of drama within a leading girls' school committed to instilling strong religious principles in its pupils.

Constance Benson (*née* Fetherstonhaugh) came from the sort of family (Indian army) whose daughters attended Cheltenham Ladies' College. Her decision to go on the stage was prompted by her mother's loss of 'the greater part of her money . . . owing to bad investments', but 'my mother had unwittingly fostered in me since babyhood, by constantly reading aloud to me from Shakespeare's works, and teaching me the speeches of many of the characters' (1926, pp. 23–4) the desire to be an actress. The Fetherstonhaughs had lived in Oxford where 'Lewis Carroll was another friend of my childhood', presenting Constance with copies of the 'Alice' books which remained 'my most treasured possession' (p. 23).

It was to Lewis Carroll (Revd Charles Dodgson), bachelor cleric and don with an abiding interest in the theatre, that parents of several aspiring actresses turned for advice. One such was Revd Reginald Barnes, Vicar of Heavitree and Prebendary of Exeter Cathedral, who had been a college contemporary of Dodgson. In his case there was no innate hostility to the theatre – 'Vicarage at Christmas time; when a theatrical performance by the children of the house was the centre of attention' (Hartnoll, 1958, p. 2) – but when his elder daughter declared her wish to go on stage, 'at that time unheard of', Revd Barnes 'felt the situation poignantly and was tormented by his conviction of the dangers Violet would encounter entering such an unknown world' (Vanbrugh, 1948, p. 12). Violet made her debut at Toole's Theatre in 1886, and in 1888 she and her younger sister Irene joined Sarah Thorne's company at Margate, which had a reputation as a training ground for entrants into the profession from well-to-do families. Both sisters adopted the surname Vanbrugh on stage and Irene's 'first professional London engagement came through a college friend of my father's, the Revd C. L. Dodgson – better known as Lewis Carroll' (p. 18) who secured the role of the White Queen in a stage version of *Alice in Wonderland* for her at the Globe Theatre in December 1888. In 1941 the 'White Queen' became a Dame of the British Empire.

Another family which called upon Dodgson's services was the Bairds. As with the Barnes there was no hostility to the theatre as such: John Baird, at Rugby under Arnold and then Trinity College, Cambridge, had written a burlesque, *The Enchanted Lake! or The Fisherman and the Genie*, which shared the bill with Bulwer Lytton's *Richelieu* in which Henry Irving made his stage debut at the New Royal Lyceum Theatre, Sunderland, on 29 September 1856 (L. Irving, 1967, p. 31); he was a member of the Garrick Club. In 1854 John Baird had married Emily Jane Brinton, of the Kidderminster carpet-manufacturing family, who was 'a deeply religious woman; in the home she made for her husband no day would begin without family prayers' (p. 28). It was into this home that the couple's sixth daughter Dorothea (Dolly) Frances was born in 1873. She attended South Hampstead High School for Girls, where she won prizes for scripture and recited a passage from *Coriolanus* on speech day. In her school holidays Dolly Baird was much in the company of her sister Emily and her husband, E. T. Cook, secretary to the London University Extension Lectures programme, who became something of a surrogate father to her. With the Cooks, Dolly Baird saw *Macbeth* at the Lyceum Theatre. In 1893 Mrs Baird moved to Oxford, where amateur dramatists were much in vogue and Dolly performed with the Christmas Dramatic Wanderers and met Charles Dodgson.

In his letter to Mrs Baird of 12 April 1894, Dodgson wrote:

There are two questions that I want to put before you for consideration.

The first is as to that friend of mine to whom Dolly wishes to be introduced. I have now introduced to her four of the daughters of my friends of ages between 18 and 25; but in every case, before doing so, I told the mother the history of my friend and asked her whether, now she knew all the circumstances, she still wished her daughter to be introduced. In each case the answer was 'Yes' – so now, before giving any more promises to Dolly, I would like to know what you think about it. (Cohen, 1979, vol. II, pp. 1014–15)

The second question was 'may Dolly come and dine with me?'; the friend was Ellen Terry and it was to this letter that Dodgson appended the account of her private life already quoted. On 26 May Dolly, her mother and Dodgson saw *Faust* at the Lyceum Theatre. The experience did not deter Dolly Baird from going on the stage, but she decided to make her own way rather than to rely on Dodgson's influence. Shortly afterwards she took an engagement with Ben Greet, who 'was extremely particular about the morals of the young people in his companies' (Isaac, 1964, p. 18), at 10s a week, providing her own wardrobe.

It was Ben Greet, whose respectability, if not his munificence, was beyond doubt, whom Flora Mayor's eldest brother Robin recommended to her 'Just for amateur acting' (Oldfield, 1984, p. 60). Flora Mayor was the daughter of an Anglican cleric who successively held chairs of Classics and Moral Philosophy at University College, London; she was educated at Surbiton High School and Girton College, Cambridge. Her parents were both opposed to a stage career for her, her mother 'on snobbish grounds', her father 'on spiritual grounds' (p. 59). In February 1897 Flora Mayor took an engagement with an obscure theatre company in Hastings, of which she wrote to her twin sister, Alice: 'The dressing rooms are rather horrid gloomy little holes . . . Conversation . . . is not inspiring. The play I think is rather a questionable one. It really does seem to me rather immoral in places, and the tone is low throughout' (p. 60).

Flora Mayor persevered for a time, but then abandoned the stage. As another aspiring actress from a privileged background, Harriet Taylor's daughter Helen, had found – despite in her case the co-operation of her mother and John Stuart Mill – the social environment of the theatre was intolerable. That was in 1856; by the late nineteenth century there were congenial theatre companies – Benson's, Sarah Thorne's, Ben Greet's, with schools attached, and the West End – in which the discerning and/or well-advised aspirant could embark on her career.

One such was Sybil Thorndike, who made her professional debut with Ben Greet's Pastoral Players – Matheson Lang as leading man – in the grounds of Downing College, Cambridge, on 14 June 1904 – a reassuring configuration for a clergyman's daughter. The eldest of Revd Arthur Thorndike's four children, Sybil took part in amateur theatricals in the family home in Minor Canon Row, Rochester Cathedral, from the age of four. Her brother Russell 'never lost the thrill of Sybil's tragic performance of Abraham on the nursery table' (Thorndike, 1929, p. 12). Her parents were admirers of Henry Irving and Ellen Terry and, although they had expected Sybil to become a concert pianist and her brother Russell, a clergyman, they accepted their children's choice of theatre 'with surprising equanimity' (S. Morley, 1977, p. 23). When asked by Michael MacOwan, 'There's a long connection, isn't there, between the church and the theatre?', Dame Sybil Thorndike replied:

Oh yes. We always used to think that father, in the pulpit, looked like Forbes Robertson. And another technical thing that was wonderful, father had the most tremendous long breath, only beaten by Larry Olivier. Father could do the general exhortation, 'Dearly beloved brethren, the scripture moveth us', one and a half times through in one breath; Larry could do it twice. We used to notice father in church, Russell used to nudge me and say, 'Father's doing the collect all in one breath.' (Burton, 1967, p. 51)

That their weekly, or more frequent, childhood exposure to church ritual, with their own father in the leading role, should encourage any latent dramatic tendencies in clergymen's children is not surprising. Indeed they were likely to witness their father performing far more regularly and frequently than were the children of actors.

The distinction between 'families of the stage, those well-known people or generations of play-actors' and 'the hundreds of young people, especially of the opposite sex, who have so unhealthy a craving for matters theatrical, and who enter upon the life with an absolute ignorance of all that is hidden by its glittering exterior' was made by Clement Scott in the controversial interview 'Does the theatre make for good?' with Raymond Blathwayt who 'was originally in holy orders' (Swears, 1937, p. 61), first published in the Evangelical Christian magazine *Great Thoughts* in 1897 (Blathwayt, 1898, pp. 3–4). Scott, drama critic of the *Daily Telegraph* since 1871, was the son of the Vicar of Christ Church, Hoxton, and had been educated at Marlborough College and at King's College, London, evening classes. In his school holidays from Marlborough in the 1850s he had 'been made welcome as a mere lad by Revd Henry Hart Milman' at the deanery, 'the rendez-vous of literature and fine arts', where on Sunday evenings 'Thackeray was a lion' (Scott, 1897, p, 49). Despite his impeccable Anglican pedigree, Scott converted to Roman Catholicism in later life.

Reactionary though he was as a drama critic, Scott's condemnation of the stage as a career for outsiders, especially women – 'It is nearly impossible for a woman to remain pure who adopts the stage as a career' (Blathwayt, 1898, p. 4) – carried considerable weight, coming as it did from such an informed source. In the welter of correspondence which followed, actors and clergymen weighed in with their views, those of Revd Hugh Price Hughes reflecting the damage which Scott had done to the theatre in certain quarters: 'The effect of reading the interview is to convince me that the modern theatre in London is in a worse condition than I had ventured to hope' (p. 20).

One of Scott's main strictures against the theatre was that: 'The worst of the theatrical is that it induces the vain and egotistical that is in all of us to a degree that would be scarcely credited by the outsider. Actors, and very particularly actresses, cannot bear a word of dispraise, as I have frequently said' (p. 5). This was the tenor of 'Mummer Worship' (1888) by George Moore, whose novel *A Mummer's Wife* (1885) had explored the clash between inherited Puritanism and the bohemian life of travelling actors. Moore summarised his objections to the theatre: 'Our contention is a threefold one; first that acting is the lowest of the arts, if it be an art at all; secondly, that the public has almost ceased to discriminate between bad and good acting . . . ; thirdly that the actor is applauded not for what he does, but for what he is' (Moore, 1939, p. 219). On Moore's assessment Macready's goal, that like other professions the theatre should confer dignity on the initiated, had proved hollow in the attainment: 'For the last ten years the actor has not only demanded acclamation for what he does, but he has striven to obtain, and has succeeded in obtaining, praise for what he is, thus emulating all priests and sacred apes' (p. 218). As John Stokes writes, to Moore: 'Respectability was but one manifestation of vanity' (1972, p. 128) – 'the mummer grew ashamed of his hose and longed for a silk hat, and above all a visit from the parson' (Moore, 1939, pp. 212–13). Moore surveyed the lot of the modern mummer:

his villa in St John's Wood; his boys educated at Eton; his wife, a portly lady on the verge of forty-five and society, tells her visitors of the many acts of Christian charity she is performing and the luncheon parties to which she has been asked. The mummer's house is full of letters from eminent people, cuttings from newspapers, and portraits of himself and his wife; for as he was civilized (up or down, which is it?), his vanity has grown as weed never grew before: it overtops all things human, and puts forth religious blossom. (p. 213)

Such respectability, mocked though it was by Moore, was not attained by all members of the profession. He hypothesized Ethel, Harriet and May singing a chorus 'Put us on the stage, mamma' and prophesied their fate: 'Ethel returns to London, where she is sometimes engaged to play small parts at a salary of five pounds a week. Harriet married an actor; she is now divorced. May ran away with a banker, who promised to marry her, but didn't, . . . now she is drinking herself to death' (p. 227). Moore resurrected all the old prejudices about actresses, sparing them only the identification with prostitution. By the 1890s the mores of society into which actors had so long sought admittance were sexually lax. Lillie Langtry, whose father, the Dean of Jersey, 'had the true histrionic gift' and whose mother was much admired by Charles Kingsley (Langtry, 1925, p. 17), may have enjoyed the favours of the Prince of Wales, but that distinction was not reserved for members of her profession. Liaisons between actresses (or show-girls) and the upper classes were prevalent. Even when the relationship was formalised into marriage, the bride's motive was often regarded as suspect and the outcome not infrequently was unhappy. Horace Wyndham lists 22 alliances between actresses and the peerage between 1884 and 1906 (1951, p. 174). That contracted between the 21-year-old Viscount Dunlo and actress and unmarried mother Belle Bilton was challenged in the courts by his father and prompted a leading article in *The Times*: 'It is devoutly to be hoped that our gilded youth are generally possessed of a will they can call their own, have a stronger sense of honour and are more fastidious about their companions' (p. 98). In fact the marriage of the Earl and Countess of Clancarty, as they became, was serenely happy, unlike that between convent-educated Miss May Yohé and Lord Francis Hope, heir pre-sumptive to the Duke of Newcastle, which ended in divorce.

Though the Matrimonial Causes Act of 1857 provided for divorce, the Church's commitment to marriage as one of its sacraments was undiminished. Nevertheless individual cases were treated not unsympathetically, as was shown by that of Ellen Terry. No one could question Fanny Kemble's profound religious beliefs and sense of pro-priety, yet she had divorced her American husband, Pierce Butler. Unhappy was the fate of the beautiful and talented actress, Adelaide Neilson. Her mother was an actress on a northern circuit; rumour had it that her father was a Spaniard. A diligent scholar at the Wesleyan Methodist Sunday School, at twelve Adelaide Neilson was sent to work as a fuller at Green Bottom Mill, Guiseley, whence she escaped to London where 'she was engaged as a ballet girl . . . Her superiority to the other ballet girls in the same theatre was soon made manifest; and one interested in the theatres – Philip Lee – a graduate of Brasenose College, Oxford, who had been at Rugby, was so attracted by the girl that he fell in love with her' (Scott, 1899, vol. II, p. 227). Lee paid for Adelaide Neilson to receive a good education and subsequently married her. Miss Neilson was welcomed by Lee's parents at their home at Stoke Bruerne in Northamptonshire, where Mr Lee was rector. Westland Marston attended a dinner there at which many of the guests were clergymen: 'Mr and Mrs Lee seem to have accepted their son's marriage with a then unnoted actress in a very liberal spirit. They were devoted to her' (Marston, 1890, p. 352). Adelaide Neilson's career prospered in London and North America; she was particularly admired as Isabella in *Measure for Measure*: of her performance Joseph Knight wrote; 'In all essentials

Miss Neilson's interpretation was admirable. Our stage has supplied us during late years with few instances of exposition more ample and more satisfying' (Knight, 1893, pp. 112–13). Like Isabella's novitiate with the votaries of Saint Clare, Adelaide's marriage did not endure. She and Lee were divorced in 1877; she died in 1880, aged only thirty-two.

For many actresses marriage marked the end of their career. This was a reflection of their sex's life pattern and the demands and opportunities of their profession. Tracy C. Davis cites the 1881 census returns showing that 75 per cent of actresses in Liverpool and 63 per cent in Glasgow were 'in the 15- to 29-year-old age group' (1991, p. 42). Returns for Lambeth show that 'The vast majority of 25- to 29-year-old married actresses (74.43 per cent) had a spouse in some branch of theatrical or musical employment, and only 8.34 per cent of married actresses aged 30 or over had spouses who were not connected with the performing arts' (1991, p. 43). One trend for theatrical couples was smaller families. J. A. Banks showed that the mean number of children born to actors dropped from 4.17 in marriages contracted between 1871 and 1881 to 3.15 in those contracted between 1881 and 1891 (1981, p. 100).

Unions within the profession not only held out the best prospect for the wife continuing a career, but also for the endurance of the marriage. This was true of the Bancrofts and the Kendals and to incomers Dorothea Baird and Violet and Irene Vanbrugh, who married respectively H. B. Irving, Arthur Bourchier and Dion Boucicault the Younger. In 1899 Leopold Wagner wrote:

Not a few of the most admired actresses of our time developed their early taste for the drama amid influences very far removed from the theatre, namely at the convents where they received their education. The periodical dramatic entertainments superintended by the gentle sisterhood within the convent walls are in all respects excellent. Mrs Beerbohm Tree took part in a Greek play before Mr Gladstone during her Queen's College days. (1899, p. 3)

Mary Susan Etherington, 'so respectably nurtured, sent to that carefully chosen convent in Belgium' (Bolitho, 1936, p. 17), was taken by her grandmother to Number 10 Downing Street to seek Gladstone's advice on her intended stage career:

He spoke of the Greek Drama, and then of the monkish Mysteries and Moralities, of the Restoration Drama, and then cleverly introduced by the grand preamble, he spoke of the advent of women on the stage. He frowned as he suggested the depravity of the life I wished to live. He talked of Macready, of Helen Faucit and Kean and Irving. He forgot his moralising for a moment and spoke of the power for good of the dramatist and actor. Then he looked at me again, remembered his mission and drew all he had said into a final argument. (p.19)

Her grandmother beamed with relief assuming that Mary Susan would now give up her mad idea, but instead another actress-Dame of the future left Number 10 that day – Marie Tempest.

The traffic was not entirely one-way. Isabel Bateman (1936) left the stage to join the Community of St Mary the Virgin in Wantage, of which she became Reverend Mother General. The Community of St Mary the Virgin had been founded in 1848 as part of the movement to establish Anglican sisterhoods encouraged by Edward Pusey and John Mason Neale (Geoffrey Rowell, 1983, p. 110). Mary Anderson forsook the stage for the rural peace of Broadway, where her home contained a private chapel (Anderson, 1936, p. 80), 'the vestments made from her original "Juliet" gowns' (C. Benson, 1926, p. 245). Symbolic, or merely frugal, as Mary Anderson's needlework may have been it was but a change of costume compared to the change of heart which other actresses wrought in clerical attitudes towards their profession. At a farewell banquet on 16 July 1889 to mark the Kendals' departure for New York Joseph Chamberlain presented Mrs Kendal with a diamond brooch; he spoke of the fate of a gifted French actress, who 'at her death was denied by churlish priests the rites of the Church to which she belonged', continuing:

And, if now, evidences of such bigotry and intolerance have almost disappeared from amongst us it is largely owing – chiefly owing – to those who, like Mrs Kendal, have shown how to combine the values of a woman with the talents of the actress, and who have ennobled the profession to which they belonged by the personal dignity and by the weight of character which they exhibited. (Kendal, 1933, p. 216)

The contribution of actresses such as Fanny Kemble, Helen Faucit (Lady Martin), Lady Bancroft and Dame Madge Kendal to the *rapprochement* between Church and stage was indeed formidable. They conducted themselves in a manner consistent with contemporary ideals of womanhood and motherhood. They became 'ladies connected with our Church', not on the margins, but as valued members of fashionable congregations, where their managerial acumen and attraction as celebrities were assets in charitable work. In return the theatre was vested with the respectability which the approval of the Church could bestow. In society at large other forces were at work which were conducive to bringing the daughters of professional families onto the stage.

Educational provision for girls expanded, with a curriculum in which English Literature was the 'master-key', providing the reassurance of moral teaching with the opportunity to read, recite and perform. Daughters of clergymen were predisposed to respond to these opportunities. Their upbringing had not only exposed them repeatedly to the ritual of church services, with their father performing a leading role, but, unlike the daughters of other professionals, clergy-daughters were accustomed to going out into the world, encountering parishioners from different walks of life. As an apprenticeship for the stage, the early life of a clergyman's daughter had much to commend it.

CHAPTER 10

Headlam, hell and Hole

No, parsons, go to the theatre, if possible go often, and let your acts
be seen.

Ben Greet

Of all the Victorian clerics who espoused the theatre's cause, Revd
Stewart Headlam staked most. He was born on 12 January 1847 at
Wavertree, near Liverpool, one of underwriter Thomas Duckworth
Headlam's four children. The Headlam household was Evangelical.
The children learnt their catechism and passages from the Bible; theatre
and playing-cards were proscribed, but Thomas Headlam 'was a great
hand at charades . . . very fond of poetry . . . and he also gave us
Shakespeare readings' (Bettany, 1926, p. 6), albeit from a bowdlerised
version. Like many such families who placed the theatre out of bounds,
the Headlams attended readings, such as those by the German Reeds:
'From the home point of view theirs was not a theatrical show' (p. 6). As
Doreen Rosman has shown this was common practice amongst
Evangelicals whose 'aversion to the theatre' by far exceeded their objections to 'other worldly amusements' (1984, p. 75), largely because of the
contaminating company and the glitter of costumes and scenery.
Stripped of these and within the safety of the family home 'the drama
was no more dangerous than any other literary genre' (p. 177).

In 1860 Stewart Headlam went to Eton where his fag was Crauford
Tait, son of Revd Archibald Tait, Bishop of London at the time.
Amongst Headlam's Eton masters was William Johnson Cory, formerly
a King's scholar and participant in Long Chamber theatricals (Warre-
Cornish, 1897, pp. 2–3). Cory, who achieved recognition as the author of
Ionica (1858) and 'The Eton Boating Song', numbered Charles Kingsley,
F. D. Maurice and J. M. Ludlow – 'our greatest man' (p. 57) – amongst his
friends. Another Eton master at the time, Revd W. A. Carter, extended
his 'patronage' to productions of *She Stoops to Conquer* (31 July 1862) and

The Rivals (30 July 1863) – Lord Randolph Churchill played Lucy in the latter, but Headlam was not a participant (Tarver, 1898, p. 200).

When Headlam left Eton for Trinity College, Cambridge, in 1865 he already 'held ultra-democratic, if not Socialist, views' (Bettany, 1926, p. 12). He was predisposed to coming under the influence of F. D. Maurice, whose lectures as Professor of Casuistry and Moral Philosophy were no more popular amongst undergraduates than his classes at King's College, London, had been – 'while not a dozen men attended Maurice's lectures on moral and metaphysical philosophy, all the horsey men used to crowd into Kingsley's lecture on history' (p. 21). From Maurice, Headlam took two guiding principles: emancipation from the popular notion of hell and a belief in the brotherhood of man. F. G. Bettany described Maurice as 'the greatest influence on Headlam's life; Cambridge, in fact, as he recalled it, meant Maurice and little more' (p. 19). After Cambridge, Headlam became one of the 'Doves' which Revd C. J. Vaughan collected around him as Master of the Temple; he was ordained deacon in 1870 and priest in 1872. His first curacy was at St John's, Drury Lane (1870–3), followed by St Matthew's, Bethnal Green, under Revd Septimus Hansard, during which time (1873–8) he came under the influence of Father Nihill at the Tractarian stronghold of St Michael's, Shoreditch.

The location of St John's in Drury Lane brought Headlam into direct contact with theatres, which hitherto he had only entered furtively – looking in for an hour to see Adelaide Neilson in the balcony scene of *Romeo and Juliet*. He saw Irving's *Hamlet* at the Lyceum and Madame Titiens at Covent Garden, but 'in these days began his passion for the ballet and ballet-dancing' (p. 28). One evening he recognised on stage two girls who were communicants at St John's, but when he spoke to them afterwards: 'They implored him not to let other church attendants know how they made their living, because if the nature of their work were once known they would be cold-shouldered in the church' (p. 28).

The dancers' anxiety to conceal their profession implied that the congregation at St John's included some disapproving and better-off parishioners. Bethnal Green was overwhelmingly working-class. It had been the particular object of Bishop Blomfield's church-building pro-gramme, its population having increased to 70,000 in 1837: 'Ten churches were then built in as many years, all free from pew-rents' (Macleod, 1974, p. 104). Building churches was one thing; filling them with congregations another. In 1846 Blomfield referred to Bethnal

Green as 'the spot where it is said that we have sown our seed in vain' (p. 104). Material inducements were no answer: 'In the hand to mouth economy of large parts of the local population, the church was chiefly seen as a source of material help' (p. 112). Nevertheless the Church had to extend its ministry to the leisure time (the culture) of its parishioners; lectures, debates and sport were part of the counter-offensive against the public house and the lower forms of amusement. This called for a particular type of parish priest and in such cases as Stewart Headlam's there was a reciprocity between the priest's personal needs and those of the community:

To those like Stewart Headlam, who founded the Guild of St Matthew when he was a curate at Bethnal Green parish church in the 1870s, life as an East End parson was a form of liberation, a means of asserting a counter-conception of church and 'priest' to that prescribed by convention. As Shaw put it, he belonged to 'a type of clergy peculiar to the latter half of the nineteenth century ... They wanted the clergyman to be able to go to the theatre, to say damn if he wished to do so, to take a large interest in political and social questions, to have dancing in his house if he chose, and to affirm the joyousness and freedom and catholicity of the church at every turn.' (p. 111)

The Guild of St Matthew was founded on St Peter's Day 1877 with a membership of 40, which increased to 364 by 1895. The objectives of the Guild were:

1 To get rid, by every possible means, of the existing prejudices, especially on the part of Secularists, against the Church, her sacraments and doctrines, and to endeavour to 'justify God to the people'.
2 To promote frequent and reverent worship in the Holy Communion and a better observance of the teaching of the Church of England, as set forth in the Book of Common Prayer.
3 To promote the study of social and political questions in the light of the Incarnation. (Leech, 1968, p. 63)

The essence of Headlam's theology was that it combined the sacramentalism of the Tractarians and the earthly concerns of Christian Socialists. Edward Norman defines Headlam's fundamental conviction: 'that all men were in Christ, that there was no distinction between the sacred and the secular because all work was God's work and all human experience conveyed divine truth' (1987, p. 107). Given that large sections of the Church and society generally still refused to accept that the theatre was God's work it was not surprising that actors, and more especially dancers, became the object of Headlam's attention.

Headlam's first public intervention on behalf of the theatre was a lecture entitled 'Theatres and Music Halls' given at the Commonwealth Club on 7 October 1877 and subsequently published both in the *Era* and pamphlet form. Headlam attacked the Puritan notion of the theatre as an ante-room of hell and proclaimed actors, singers and dancers as God's creatures. Not only did he admit – unashamedly – his own attendance at theatres, but positively encouraged others to follow his example: 'I really think if I were in authority over any such [young women], instead of saying, as so many good parents say, "I don't hold with your going to such places", I should make it my duty to send every young woman whose name was Dull to see these young women who are so full of life and mirth' (Bettany, 1926, p. 44).

Headlam based his exaltation of the divine joyousness of dancing and singing on the Psalms, prefacing the published version of his lecture with 'The singers and the dancers, yea, and all my fresh springs shall be in Thee', though he had in fact substituted 'dancers' for 'players on instruments' in the *Authorised Version* and 'trumpeters' in the *Book of Common Prayer* (p. 97). Such a scriptural emendation added to an offence which was already rank in the eyes of Headlam's superiors. He was banned from preaching in Hansard's church and on 4 January 1878 received notice to leave (D. O. Wagner, 1930, p. 188). Never one to favour conciliation to conflict when he perceived an issue of principle to be at stake, Headlam locked horns with his diocesan bishop, the Evangelical and generally tolerant Revd John Jackson, with whom he remonstrated:

> I can't help thinking . . . that a large majority of the regular church-goers at the West End, to whom your Lordship preaches, are also theatre-goers, and does it not minister to hypocrisy and the worst kind of priestcraft to let the people go unblamed and make the clergy stay away?
>
> It is not for me to judge my brethren of the clergy, but I feel so strongly myself the great wrong which the clergy do, who cut themselves off from the public amusements of the people, the immense opportunity for raising their characters which they lose by what would be merely Pharisaic isolation, that I cannot feel that my lecture is harmful. That evil people, whether religious or worldly, will make an evil use of it is quite possible. (p. 59)

For Headlam, Jackson remained a lost cause up to the end of his episcopacy (and his life) in 1885. The succour which the Established Church denied to Headlam came from other quarters. At the Unitarian Chapel, Essex Street, the Strand, in October and November 1878, Revd J. Panton Ham delivered a series of seven discourses on 'The theatre and the theatrical profession', in one of which he cited 'the Bishop of Manchester – that good brave man' for his sympathetic attitude towards the theatre. Nevertheless, the bishop withheld his support from the Church and Stage Guild, which Headlam founded on 30 May 1879: 'I am afraid that the Church and Stage Guild has not recommended itself to me as an institution likely to be productive of much good. If you will not be angry with me for speaking plainly, the whole idea seems too fantastic' (Bettany, 1926, p. 102).

The objective of the venture which Bishop Fraser judged to be 'too fantastic' was to remedy the failings which Headlam itemised as follows:

I We have failed to recognise the enormous educational power which there is in the Drama. Educational power which is useful for all, but which is especially useful when brought to bear on those whom we call the vast masses of our population, and whom (it is our constant complaint) *we* have utterly failed to reach . . .

II But, secondly, we have failed to recognise the importance, especially in this hard-working age and city of ours, of genuine amusement and bright spectacle. The singer and the dancer are, in their vocation and ministry, truly and godly serving God.

III And if we have adopted towards the Stage . . . this clerical policy of isolation . . . it has been doubly harmful as fostering the very evils which every true artist is found to deplore in some theatrical circles . . . our indiscriminate abuse of the stage has done much to foster popular opinion that all theatrical causes are lost. (*Era* 1 June 1879)

Headlam's case for the theatre rested therefore on three arguments, none of which he was the first to advance: its educational value – especially for the vast masses of the population; the godliness of the theatrical calling; and the destructiveness of isolationism and indiscriminate abuse of the stage. Such a case might have been expected to commend itself to the theatre profession at large, if not to all shades of Church opinion, but his ensuing remarks suggest that Headlam anticipated some resistance even there: 'We shall meet together absolutely as equals in it [the Church and Stage Guild]; if there is any converting to be done it will have to be done quite as much by the theatrical members as by the clerical.' Later Headlam wrote:

There was one thing we always repudiated as a Guild, and that was having any idea of undertaking a mission to the dramatic profession. Such a notion would have seemed to us an impertinence. Rather, we used to say, should there be a mission among the clergy to teach them right understanding of the stage and the player, and to preach to them of a broader charity. (Bettany, 1926, pp. 101–2)

Possibly influenced by his own Evangelical upbringing, Headlam was well advised to avoid any suggestion of 'a mission to the dramatic profession', particularly if he wished to enlist the support of its leaders. In 1873 Revd and Mrs Courthope-Todd had founded the Theatrical Mission as a letter mission, sending a letter each month to girls in touring companies 'asking for a reply if any assistance was needed' (Heasman, 1962, p. 277). Later it provided actresses with letters of introduction to benevolent-minded ladies connected with the Mission, who would take an interest in them during their sojourn in a particular provincial town. The Mission subsequently acquired premises in King Street: 'a comfortable club room for the poorer members of the profession and a cheerful playground and temporary nursery for the little mites who are qualifying for such novelties as the "Infantile Hornpipes"' (*Era* 3 May 1884). The demand for the Mission's services was reflected by average attendances of 320 per week, but the profession's mouthpiece, the *Era*, voiced two objections: the first that the Mission's leaders 'have placed themselves in antagonism to the profession by the confident assumption of its evil nature'; and second that 'the very existence of the Mission . . . smacks of insult'. The only other classes subject to missions were sailors, domestics and fallen women; there were no missions to lawyers or stockbrokers, professions to parity with which the theatre aspired.

In reality the theatre was the broadest of professions, requiring for its members many – contrasting – mansions. The Mission was relocated to Henrietta Street, Covent Garden, where its premises were known as Macready House. There it was favoured with the presidency of the Dean of Norwich, but it eschewed a strictly denominational base and sought widespread co-operation, especially with Nonconformists. The Mission's facilities were well used: 'During the year the advantages of the mission had been used by over 1,500 ladies and girls of the theatrical and music-hall stage and over 150 girls had boarded in the house' (*Illustrated Church News* 22 May 1896). In 1901 the Theatrical Mission moved to Charlotte Street where it remained until 1923, becoming subsumed in a YWCA hostel for theatrical employees around 1912.

The Theatrical Mission exposed social tensions within the acting profession, the leaders of which baulked at association with indigent colleagues who were the objects of proselytizing charity. The hard-won status now enjoyed by the theatre's brightest luminaries, who regarded themselves as the equals – at least – of lawyers and stockbrokers, was tarnished if their humbler colleagues were treated like sailors and fallen women. If actors needed support in illness, hard times and old age they should support the Actors' Benevolent Fund and the – Royal from 1853 – General Theatrical Fund, the centenary of which in 1933 was attended by Cosmo Gordon Lang, Archbishop of Canterbury (W. Trewin, 1989, p. 133).

Headlam repined that the Church and Stage Guild's 'professional members never included the leaders of the stage. Mrs Kendal came to one or two of our early meetings, but soon left us. Henry Irving proved a disappointment' (Bettany, 1926, p. 101). This stand-offishness was a matter of status, not only within the legitimate theatre, but also between it and other forms of entertainment, notably the music-hall, whose members were encouraged by Headlam to join the Guild. Another important consideration for the likes of Mrs Kendal and Irving was that association with Headlam would have been detrimental to the cordial relations which they were successfully cultivating with senior church-men, who regarded Headlam as a renegade on more grounds than his espousal of the stage. Nevertheless the priest and the actor extolled each other's virtues. Headlam proclaimed Irving's acting gifts as 'the messages which God sends men' (p. 102) and in later life Irving was reported as saying: 'People sometimes maintain that the stage is indebted to me for the greater esteem in which it is now held, but really, did they but know it, actors owe far more to that man Headlam' (pp. 103–4).

Despite the stand-offishness of the stage's leaders, within a year of its formation the Church and Stage Guild numbered 172 actors amongst its 470 members, of whom 91 were clergymen. Theatrical members included W. H. Kendal, Mrs Kendal, Rose Leclerq, Herman Merivale, Genevieve Ward, Charles Warner and, interestingly, dramatist Charles Reade who was succumbing to doubts about his involvement with the stage. Augustus Harris was sympathetic, making the foyer of Drury Lane Theatre available for the purposes of *conversaziones*; Johnston Forbes-Robertson was a supporter, but 'Ben Greet was all along the staunchest of allies' (p. 101). Born aboard his father's ship HMS *Crocodile* on 24 September 1857, 'His parents wished him to become a priest of the Church of England' (Isaac, 1964, p. 15). Greet never attained the rank of great actor, but as a principled and respected manager he did much to advance his profession. Following the success of Poel's production of *Everyman* at the Imperial Theatre, Greet performed it in countless the-atres, churches and open spaces on both sides of the Atlantic; during the First World War he was Lilian Baylis's doughty adjutant at the Old Vic. A life-long friend of the devout Mary Anderson, Greet was regarded by middle-class fathers, not least clergymen, as an eminently respectable manager to whom they could confidently entrust their stage-struck daughters. Greet's knighthood in 1929 was for services to drama and education. In December 1892 he gave a paper to the Church and Stage Guild on 'Parsons and playhouses', in which he extolled the late Cardinal Newman's encouragement of plays at the Birmingham Oratory and the attendance of the Vicar of Margate at Sarah Thorne's theatre. He exhorted clergymen to visit theatres: 'No, parsons, go to the theatre, if possible go often, and let your acts be seen. So you will help to preach the gospel of love to men of good will' (*Era* 7 January 1893).

In the rigidly hierarchical organisation of the Church of England the natural inclination of the average clergyman was to defer to authority and he received no encouragement to support the Church and Stage Guild from his superiors. Matters did not change when Frederick Temple was appointed by Gladstone to succeed Jackson as Bishop of London in 1885. As a contributor to *Essays and Reviews,* Temple was no stranger to controversy. His previous episcopal appointment to the see of Exeter in 1869 had produced a tumult in deference to which he withdrew his essay from any subsequent editions of *Essays and Reviews.* Hopeful of a more sympathetic response from Temple than from Jackson, 'Ben Greet suggested that Dr Temple should be invited to one of its [the Church and Stage Guild's] meetings [*conversazioni*] in Drury Lane' (Leech, 1968, p. 76). Temple declined, but agreed to meet Headlam.

On a hot July day in 1885 Headlam led a Church and Stage deputation, which included Ben Greet and two dancers, to Fulham Palace. Dancers were generally regarded as the most suspect of performers – Bishop Fraser had taken exception to their short skirts – so, by including dancers in the deputation, Headlam was characteristically confronting the most entrenched form of religious anti-theatrical prejudice head-on. Not surprisingly therefore the discussion centred on dancers. Temple, like Fraser, objected to dancers' short skirts and went on to express his concern for young men whose passions were aroused by such sights and who left the theatre in search of gratification for their lusts. In reply Headlam tried 'in vain to make the bishop think of dancing as an art of motion, and not merely as an opportunity to display' (Bettany, 1926, p. 67). Headlam claimed that some good did come out of the encounter in that, when the bishop bade farewell to Miss Wooldridge, one of the dancers, he said, 'I am sure you are a good woman; I hope you don't imagine I think any harm of you', to which, startled and indignant, she replied: 'I should hope not.' Headlam maintained that in strict accordance with his views the bishop should have said: 'You have done much harm by following a calling which leads young men astray. You wear a dress when you dance in public of which I disapprove. You belong to a profession the morals of which I suspect.' That the bishop did not so express himself proved to Headlam that: 'Knowledge of, or actual meeting with, a dancer broke down prejudice even here. The bishop virtually recanted – was converted thanks to that very association of Church and Stage which we as a Guild advocated and wished to make general' (pp. 68–9).

Temple's continuing hostility towards the Church and Stage Guild belied a full-scale conversion, but his tone towards the dancers themselves lent some credence to Headlam's interpretation. In a letter of October 1885, Temple wrote:

Now I believe the evil to be great. I believe there is much on the stage, and, in particular, in the ballet, which does grave mischief to many young men, possibly to many young women . . . My own personal experience of young men is very considerable, and I have no doubt whatever that a very large number of spectators of the ballet, even if they are quite able to prevent impurity from going into art, are nevertheless led into most disastrous sins of imagination . . . I acquit the dancers from all share of the evil which affects the spectators. The dancers begin young and . . . grow up thinking no harm . . . The innocency of the dancers, however, does not prevent the mischief to the spectators. (Sandford, 1906, vol. II, p. 130)

The exchanges between Headlam and Temple rumbled on, fuelled by accounts in the *Church Reformer*, which Headlam owned. The two men held fundamentally different concerns – Headlam for the dancers, Temple for young and impressionable members of the audience, especially, it must be said, young men from well-to-do backgrounds. Between the two men there was a social, as well as a cultural and religious, divide. Headlam, the Etonian Christian Socialist, identified with the workers; Temple, the former headmaster of Rugby School, with the ruling class. On 30 July 1887 Temple reiterated his views to Headlam: 'I am confident that to the vast majority of young men and young women the sight of such dancing is a very grievous temptation' (Bettany, 1926, pp. 69–70).

Another antagonist of the Church and Stage Guild was Revd Henry Parry Liddon. From 1854 to 1859 Liddon had been vice-principal of Cuddesdon College, the Oxford diocesan training college for clergy, founded by Bishop (Sam) Wilberforce. Thither F. C. Burnand had repaired and was 'in amazement lost' at the sight of Liddon, 'an Italian-looking ecclesiastic', with his 'persuasive style' and 'insinuating manner'. Liddon's 'imitations of "Sam" Wilberforce's peculiarly unctuous manner showed that, as a professional mimic, the Vice-Principal of

Cuddesdon might have turned this talent to some account' (Burnand, 1904, vol. 1, pp. 306–7). The account to which Liddon put his talent was preaching, earning general recognition for his pulpit performances of long, rhetorical and extempore sermons. Liddon declined many offers of preferment not only in the Church (the deanery of Salisbury, the bishoprics of Edinburgh and St Albans), but also, in 1868, the Wardenship of the newly founded Keble College. He divided his time between Oxford, where from 1862 until his death in 1890 he had rooms in Christ Church and from 1870 was Ireland Professor of Exegesis, and London, where he was Canon of St Paul's. Though a Tractarian ritualist and an exceptionally gifted preacher, possessed of a talent for mimicry, Liddon was set against the theatre and upheld the Oxford Churchmen's Union ban on its members attending performances. Alerted to the formation of the Church and Stage Guild by Charles Dodgson, Liddon wrote to Revd John Oakley, Dean of Manchester, on 15 May 1879:

Speaking for myself, there is no form of entertainment which I should so entirely enjoy, as good acting. But I have never been inside a theatre since I took orders in 1852, and I do not mean to go into one, please God, while I live . . . there can, I apprehend be no sort of doubt that a clergyman who goes to theatres forfeits moral influence to a certain extent with all classes, and quite irretrievably with some . . . When the world at large hears of our 'asserting the right of Churchmen to take part in theatrical amusements', it will say that the real motive of the aesthetic element of Church services is at last apparent. It will argue that Religious Ceremonial has been all along – not an aid to enable the soul to mount to the Unseen and the Supersensuous – an aid to be used and then forgotten – but an indulgence of a taste which is only and really to be satisfied in the theatre. (J. O. Johnson, 1904, pp. 282–3)

In addition to these objections Liddon's opposition to the Church and Stage Guild rested on his conviction 'that the influence of the theatre, in the case of the *average* human nature and character, lies in the direction of sin' (p. 284). Even attendance at the eminently respectable Lyceum Theatre could lead down a slippery slope: 'And it is surely much better that young people should not go even to Mr Irving than that they should gradually learn a taste for performances which would be as unwelcome to Mr Irving as they are to ourselves' (p. 285).

Liddon stuck to the Catholic doctrines of sin, repentance and the prospect of punishment in the after-life, in opposition to the liberal theology of F. D. Maurice and Revd F. W. Farrar, whose sermons on 'Eternal Hope' at Westminster Abbey in October and November 1877 stirred up controversy: 'I am sure that the true and adequate reply to Farrar, etc., lies in a very full statement of the doctrine of the Intermediate State, with its practical corollary of Prayers for the Faithful departed. The mass of people do not think about the texts of scripture which, *pace* Farrar, do prove that lost souls are punished eternally' (p. 287).

The great schools of nineteenth-century religious thought were no longer self-contained. Liddon and Headlam both drew inspiration from the Oxford Movement, sharing a commitment to sacramentalism and ritual and an admiration for Keble in particular, but in their views on the after-life they diverged completely, with Headlam subscribing whole-heartedly to Maurice's doctrines on that subject. In 'Christian Socialism A Lecture' delivered to the Fabian Society on 8 January 1892 Headlam declared 'so far at any rate as the teaching of Jesus Christ Himself is concerned, you will find that He said hardly anything at all about life after death, but a good deal about the Kingdom of Heaven, or the religious society to be established on earth' (1892, p. 2). In his Church and Stage Guild lecture on 'The function of the stage', Headlam had said: 'The more eager we are to improve the material condition of the people, the more important does it become for us to remember that man does not live by bread alone . . . giving men those other things . . . which though not material, are absolutely essential for men, if they are to live full lives and develop all their god-given faculties' (1889, p. 7).

He quoted Keble's *The Christian Year* – 'with Thee all beauty glows' – in support of his assertion that:

No, our [the Church and Stage Guild's] whole strength consists in this, that the contemplation of what is beautiful, and the enjoyment of what is pleasurable is right and good in itself. The moral ministry of the stage depends upon the fact, that we can be made better people by being made brighter and happier people: and actors, singers, dancers are members of the Church, not because they are good, but because they have been admitted into that society in the ordinary way – a way which consecrates their calling as it does every other calling. In fact, our guild is a little part of that great spreading movement which, instead of confining the sphere of the Church to religion and the next world, maintains that the Church is to be the kingdom of heaven upon earth; a kingdom of which we are all present inheritors, and not merely future heirs, in which all human faculties are to be fully developed, in which all callings are consecrated. (pp. 9–10)

Given that the moral ministry of the stage rested upon the enjoyment of the pleasurable, the contemplation of beauty and the belief that 'all callings are consecrated', Headlam asserted that the Puritans

must, then, either agree with the teachings of the Hebrew Psalmist and John Keble, and say, 'The singers and the dancers, yea, and all my fresh founts of joy, are in Thee', 'There is no light but Thine: with Thee all beauty glows'; or they must denounce these things as evil. I suggest to you, therefore, that the dancers are equally with the actors in tragedy and comedy, ministering to the well-being of humanity. (p. 19)

Headlam's commitment to 'the well-being of humanity' was put to the test in the case of Oscar Wilde. When he was approached by Selwyn Image to advance £1,225 for Wilde's bail, Headlam, whom Wilde had privately dubbed 'the heresiarch' (Ellmann, 1988, p. 438), had met the man accused of sodomy only twice. Nevertheless Headlam swiftly recognised a cause worthy of his support and, though he was fearful of accusations of *seeking* notoriety, notoriety itself held no fears for him. Nevertheless he later admitted 'But of all public difficulties I have been in this was the most painful' (Bettany, 1926, p. 130). Each morning Headlam met Wilde and went with him to the court and returned with him in the evening. True to his promise Headlam, 'as irreproachable at the end of Wilde's prison sentence as he had been before it began' (Ellmann, 1988, p. 491), met Wilde on his release from Reading Gaol and took him to his home, where Wilde changed and drank his first cup of coffee in two years. Wilde expressed his appreciation by giving Headlam an inscribed copy of *The Ballad of Reading Gaol*, other recipients of which included Laurence Irving, Shaw and William Archer.

Headlam's prospects of rehabilitation in the Church of England were as remote as Wilde's in English Society. He devoted the later years of his life to local politics and education (the London Shakespeare League with Ben Greet, Day Continuation Schools and Working Men's Institutes), thereby advancing another of F. D. Maurice's great causes. The passage of time did see the inexorable rise up the Church hierarchy of Headlam's 'cautious supporter' (Hole, 1934, p. 16), Randall Davidson, who advanced from chaplain to Archibald Tait, whose daughter Edith he married, to Dean of Windsor (1883), Bishop of Rochester (1891 – Sybil Thorndike 'recited Brutus' for him in the drawing room: Thorndike, 1929, p. 55), Bishop of Winchester (1895) and ultimately Archbishop of Canterbury (1903). Davidson had 'intervened on Headlam's behalf in his struggles with the Bishop of London (Dr Jackson) over a telegram which Headlam had sent to Charles Bradlaugh, the radical free thinker, in prison' and wrote warmly to Headlam during his last illness in October 1924 (Bell, 1935, vol. 1, p. 47). Davidson's co-biographer of Tait was Canon William Benham, a disciple of Maurice and supporter of the stage. As Archbishop of Canterbury Davidson addressed the Actors' Church Union 'and paid a warm tribute to the work of Stewart Headlam in his vindication of the Stage' (Hole, 1934, p. 16). Davidson's own biographer was Bishop Bell of Chichester, who, as Dean of Canterbury, 'invited John Masefield the poet, Gustav Holst the composer and Charles Ricketts the designer to create a play for Canterbury Cathedral, . . . in the climate of 1928 his innovation was sensational' (Browne, 1979, p. 1). The year of 1928 also saw Cosmo Gordon Lang, a theatre enthusiast from his days at Oxford, succeed Davidson as Primate of All England. Following the performance of *The Coming of Christ* in Canterbury Cathedral the Religious Drama Society was founded, leading to the religious dramas of T. S. Eliot, Charles Williams and Christopher Fry. Thus a trajectory can be described from Headlam's advocacy of the theatre in the Church and Stage Guild to the greatest religious drama of the twentieth century – T. S. Eliot's *Murder in the Cathedral*, first performed in the Chapter House of Canterbury Cathedral on 15 June 1935 (Browne, 1970, p. 63).

Headlam himself achieved the status of dramatic immortality as Revd James Mavor Morell in Shaw's *Candida*. Shaw knew Headlam well – he lectured to the Guild of St Matthew and the Church and Stage Guild, they were fellow Fabians and Shaw campaigned for Headlam in London County Council and London School Board elections (Laurence, 1972, p. 190) – but he was always evasive about his model for Morell, pointing out that he knew practically all the leading Christian Socialist clergy (Stopford Brooke, Canon Shuttleworth and Fleming Williams) too (W. S. Smith, 1963, p. xvii). Nevertheless, as Warren Sylvester Smith says: 'A good case can be made for the theory that he [Morell] was drawn directly from the figure of Stewart Headlam' (p. xvii). In *Candida*, the bookshelves of St Dominic's Parsonage in the Hackney-Hoxton district contain Maurice's *Theological Essays* and Morell, 'a Christian Socialist clergyman . . . an active member of the Guild of St Matthew' (Shaw, 1961a, p. 95), 'bursts open the cover of The Church Reformer . . . and glances through the Mr Stewart Headlam's leader and the Guild of St Matthew's news' (p. 97).

Brought up in Dublin as a member of the Anglican Church of Ireland in a predominantly Roman Catholic culture, Shaw's education encompassed the Wesleyan Connexional School, the non-sectarian Central Model Boys' School and the Protestant English Scientific and Commercial Day School (Holroyd, 1988, pp. 33–6). As drama critic of the *Saturday Review* in the 1890s Shaw cast an informed eye over the religious subject matter which featured in so many plays of the period.

Shaw dealt with religion as a theme in many of his plays (see Abbott,

1965): *Mrs Warren's Profession* (1894) with its unflattering portrayal of the 'pretentious, booming, noisy, important' Revd Samuel Gardner, 'the fool of the family dumped on the Church' (1961b, p. 327); Revd Anthony Anderson in *The Devil's Disciple* (1897); *Man and Superman* (1905); the Salvation Army in *Major Barbara* (1906); the Bishop of Chelsea in *Getting Married* (1908); *Androcles and the Lion: An Old Fable Renovated* (1912); *Back to Methuselah: A Metabiological Pentateuch* (1921); and *Saint Joan* (1923). The collective title of 'Three Plays for Puritans' (covering *The Devil's Disciple*, *Caesar and Cleopatra* and *Captain Brassbound's Conversion*) indicates that, like Matthew Arnold and H. A. Jones, Shaw was conscious of the long-standing 'absence of the rich evangelical English merchant and his family' (1962, p. 9) from the stalls and was in the business of enticing them into the theatre.

In the epistle dedicatory of *Man and Superman*, Shaw addressed Arthur Bingham Walkley _ 'You once asked me why I did not write a Don Juan play' (1951, p. vii) – and went on to survey the treatment by Molière, Mozart and Byron of a subject for which the prototype was 'invented early in the XVI century by a Spanish monk' (p. xi). It was the old Spanish play on the Don Juan theme entitled *Atheista Fulminato* which Coleridge had discussed at length in his review of Revd Maturin's *Bertram* in 1816. In writing a play about Don Juan, Shaw was adding his contribution to a lengthy and distinguished tradition, but in a characteristically untraditional way. Act 3 of *Man and Superman* is located in the Sierra Nevada, but the setting which Shaw describes is not so much a recreation of the natural terrain as a reconstruction of a Byronic image or a Martin canvas: 'Higher up, tall stone peaks and precipices, all handsome and distinguished. No wild nature here: rather a most aristocratic mountain landscape made by a fastidious artist–creator. No vulgar profusion of vegetation' (p. 115). The foreground consists of 'one of the mountain amphitheatres of the Sierra' (p. 115). As night falls a transformation scene is effected: 'The peaks shew unfathomably dark against the starry firmament: but how the stars dim and vanish; and the sky seems to steal away out of the universe. Instead of the Sierra there is nothing: omnipresent nothing. No sky, no peaks, no light, no sound, no time nor space. Utter void' (p. 131). The amphitheatre remains in place. Hell, therefore, is an amphitheatre in a void. True to tradition from the Mystery plays to Britannia Theatre pantomimes, the Devil rises from a trap in the stage floor, into a scarlet halo, to the accompaniment of great chords in which 'Mozart's music gets grotesquely adulterated with Gounod's' (p. 142). The Devil is described as 'very Mephisthophelean', though he is 'getting prematurely bald' and is 'peevish and sensitive when his advances are not reciprocated' (p. 142). Given Shaw's propensity for scoring points off Henry Irving he would not have been disconcerted if those familiar with Irving's *Faust* had been reminded of it, indeed the 'Don Juan in Hell' episode can be seen as a cerebral riposte to the visual excesses of the Brocken scene at the Lyceum Theatre.

Though Shaw deploys the stage-trap later for the Devil's exit ('This way, Commander. We go down the old trap' p. 182) and calls for another transformation scene ('One sees, with a shock, a mountain peak shewing faintly against a lighter background' p. 183), the substance of the 'Don Juan in Hell' episode is a debate, which includes a discussion of the nature of heaven and hell. Ever the iconoclast, Shaw advances Maurice's and Farrar's ideas of heaven and hell antithetically. Heaven is 'the icy mansions of the sky' (p. 143) whence the Statue takes refuge in hell: 'Nobody could stand an eternity of heaven . . . [it] is the most angelically dull place in all creation' (p. 145). Heaven, far from being the coveted reward of the deserving, is 'intolerable' to all but 'the rows of weary people', who 'sit there in glory, not because they are happy, but because they think they owe it to their position to be in heaven. They are almost all English' (p. 147). When Ana asks incredulously: 'Can anybody – can *I* go to heaven if I want to?', the Devil replies 'rather contemptuously': 'Certainly, if your taste lies that way' (p. 145). In *Man and Superman* therefore Shaw reinvents the story of Don Juan; places the Devil and hell on stage, depicting hell as an amphitheatre complete with a stage-trap; and takes nineteenth-century thinking on the after-life, if not to its logical, then to its most extreme, conclusion.

Shaw's earthly span of years was exceptionally lengthy, that of the Church and Stage Guild was not – it faded out of existence in 1900. However, even before it had quite expired, another organisation came into being which in some respects carried its purposes forward. This was the Actors' Church Union which emerged during 1898–9 under the leadership of Revd Donald Hole, who contrasted its fortunes with those of the Church and Stage Guild: 'The battle which Headlam had to fight was principally against bishops. Of the Actors' Church Union it may be said that the bishops were its nursing fathers' (1934, p. 22). The Actors' Church Union may have been more fortunate in its bishops than the Church and Stage Guild had been, but Headlam's antagonism of his episcopal superiors often seemed to be driven by his own temperament rather than the interests of the Guild.

Benefiting from changing attitudes – described by Hole as 'almost miraculous' (p. 22) – in the Church, the Actors' Church Union was very much a response to changing work practices in the theatre. In London long runs had become the order of the day and in the provinces a network of touring theatres had replaced the stock companies of former years. The reasons for these developments were social, economic and technological. With its vastly increased population – much of it with time and money to spare – and more visitors, London had sufficient theatre-goers to sustain a popular play for months. As productions became more elaborate and costly, managers needed longer runs to recoup their investment. The railway system made it possible to tour a production up and down the country, closing in one town on Saturday night and opening in another – hundreds of miles distant – on the following Monday. For London actors, as H. B. Irving observed, 'the life of an actor is unfortunately, in these days of long runs, one that tends to a good deal of idleness and waste of time; unless a man or woman be very determined to employ their time profitably' (1906, pp. 135–6). The devil finds work for idle hands. For actors employed in touring companies, as Jerome K. Jerome wrote: 'Sunday is the great travelling day . . . Sunday travelling is most unpleasant. I can assure Sabbatarians that it brings its own punishment' (1885, p. 128). Some managers did their best to shield their companies from this unpleasantness. As Lillah McCarthy recalled, Wilson Barrett booked 'special carriages . . . and hampers were placed in our carefully-guarded private compartments . . . He believed that an actress should maintain an air of reserve and aloofness' (1933, p. 43).

Actors fortunate enough to be employed by such a considerate manager still faced the prospect of arriving in a strange town on a Sunday evening; church-goers amongst them would almost certainly have to forgo attendance at Sunday service – they would be unfamiliar with local places of worship and unknown to ministers of all religions; any individual unfortunate enough to suffer anything untoward had no obvious source of help and advice. It was one such case which came to the attention of Revd Donald Hole:

The story was this. A young girl, touring the provinces in a theatrical company, was in great trouble and distress of mind. I don't know exactly what the trouble was; it was connected, I believe, with her father who was ill, but anyway she stood in sore need of practical advice and sympathy and help. She was in a strange town, far away from home, and she knew no one to whom she could turn. In the company, of course, she had friends, and the other girls in her dressing room found out that something was a matter, and tried to comfort her. Said one, 'Why don't you go to the Vicar here, and ask him to write a letter for you?' But the other girls exclaimed, 'Oh! that would be no good; the Vicar wouldn't do anything for us, *we don't belong to his parish.*' (1934, p. 24)

It was to address this problem and to provide pastoral care for touring actors generally that the Actors' Church Union was formed. Its principal objective was for:

Every town in the Provinces to have its Chaplain, who shall visit lay members as his temporary parishioners, and render them every service in his power; also to notify to local Managers of Theatres his willingness at all times to be of service to members of travelling Companies while in the town. Permission to be obtained for the Chaplain's address to be posted in the Theatre, with a list of services at all the Churches. (p. 27)

The scheme relied on the co-operation of the local theatre managers, the support of the Actors' Association – established in 1891 (Macleod, 1981, p. 72) – and, most crucially, parish priests. By the end of 1899 the Actors' Church Union had 13 chaplains – from Sunderland to Southend (*Actors' Church Union Report 1899*, p. 6); in 1902 the number had risen to 72 (*Actors' Church Union Report 1902*, pp. 14–18) and in 1905, to 153 (*Actors' Church Union Report 1905–6*, p. 3). Chaplains were of course registering their personal sympathy for the theatre, but that so many did so in dioceses all over the land indicated that episcopal disapproval of the theatre was waning. The first president of the Actors' Church Union (from 1899 until his death in 1934) was Revd Edward Stuart Talbot (Stephenson, 1936, pp. 138–9), successively Bishop of Rochester (1895), Southwark (1905) and Winchester (1911–24). Part of Talbot's task in creating the separate see of Southwark out of the Rochester diocese was to convert St Saviour's church into a cathedral (Mansbridge, 1935, p. 16). Southwark was rich in historic associations for actors. In St Mary Overy (a contraction of 'over-the-river'), 'near London Bridge, a stone's throw from the Globe Theatre' (Schoenbaum, 1978, p. 29), on New Year's Eve 1607, William Shakespeare's brother Edmund was interred, as, in time to come, were John Fletcher and Philip Massinger.

In 1869, at the age of only twenty-five, Talbot had been appointed as the first Warden of Keble College, Oxford, a position which he held for eighteen years. Talbot was a true son of the Oxford Movement to which Hole ascribed credit for the Church's changed attitude towards the stage:

It may, I think, be said with truth that the great change which has taken place in the attitude of the official Church towards the Stage, has been the result of the

Oxford Movement. It is true that the early Tractarians, personally, showed little sympathy with the Stage, and that some of them even retained an inherited strain of Puritanism, which was quite averse from things theatrical. But they built better than they knew, and the great Sacramental principle, for which they stood, bore fruit which they themselves had not seen. The emphasis laid upon the Incarnation, by which God had become Man, and had entered into human relationships and had sanctified all material things, was bound to react upon all human life and activities. The principle of Sacramentalism extended beyond the Seven Sacraments of the Church, and revealed a spiritual meaning underlying the material expression of beauty and art. (1934, p. 11)

In his address on 'The aims and objects of the Actors' Church Union', delivered at St Paul's Church, Knightsbridge, on Sunday 2 April 1905, Talbot had proclaimed the common ground between clergymen and actors, particularly as 'close students of human life' (1905, pp. 10–11), and he had roundly rejected the view of the stage as an instrument of evil: 'it is and it has been in times past a moral cruelty to deliver to Satan, as it were, all those by whose life and labour the stage was maintained' (p. 12).

The Oxford Movement had adopted a strict policy on the obligations of Church membership; but the Actors' Church Union was more indulgent: 'Membership of the Actors' Church Union should not necessarily imply even nominal membership of the Church of England, it should imply one thing only, namely a desire to come into touch with the local chaplains' (p. 29). The recruitment of actors gathered pace from 5 in 1899 to 66 in 1902 and 190 in 1905 (*Actors' Church Union Reports*). Their modest subscriptions – and donations – were needed to cover running costs, though, with the chaplains as unpaid volunteers, these too were modest. Although the Actors' Church Union was accessible to, and committed to serving, the humblest member of the profession, it succeeded, where the Church and Stage Guild had failed, in attracting leading actors. This was no doubt because it did not court controversy and did set out to address a genuine need in a practical way. The membership list shows that amongst the actors who joined before 1905 were George Alexander, Alfred Bishop, Lilian Braithwaite, Mrs Edward Compton, Gertrude Elliott (Mrs Forbes-Robertson), Winifred Emery (Mrs Cyril Maude), Ben Greet, Cyril Maude, Ellen Terry, Sybil and Russell Thorndike, Irene Vanbrugh and Sir Charles Wyndham.

Annual conferences were held, customarily at the president's home, in Kennington, preceded by Holy Eucharist in his private chapel. Apologies were formally received – Henry Irving's and Frank Benson's regularly, though neither appears on the list of members. Proposals were made, such as Ben Greet's on 24 June 1902 that St Paul's Covent Garden should be the headquarters church. The year's work was reported, with particular pride in the expansion of Actors' Church Union centres, which numbered 120 by 1905. Clergymen and actors addressed the assembly, John Martin Harvey doing so on 10 July 1906. Harvey, who strove 'at regular intervals throughout his life . . . to make the theatre serve to express a religious ideal' (Disher, 1948, p. 193), recalled that:

In my travels I have had the good fortune to meet many of the Chaplains of the Actors' Church Union – the initiative, I am bound to say has always been on their side – and I can speak heartily of their tact, their good fellowship and their sympathy with the workers of my profession, a profession which perhaps in its essentials so closely resembles the calling of a priest. (*Actors' Church Union Report 1905–6*, p. 15)

Harvey proposed that 'on the anniversary of the death of our beloved chief, Sir Henry Irving . . . [who] himself took a keen interest in the formation of our union . . . a memorial service should be held at which, upon the invitation of the Actors' Church Union, the whole dramatic profession should be asked to attend' (p. 16). The walls of St Paul's Covent Garden are lined with commemorative tablets to members of the theatrical profession, for many of whom memorial services were held there. From its office in the upper storey of the church the Actors' Church Union continues its work amongst the profession at large.

Mario Borsa, however, wrote disparagingly of the Actors' Church Union:

The English Church which, like St Thomas Aquinas, considered actors to be outside the pale of religion, has founded one of the most curious associations imaginable, the Actors' Church Union, the object of which is to reclaim actors and actresses who have strayed from the right path by the mere fact of having taken that which leads to the stage! In every provincial city the Union has its delegates, whose office is to approach artists who may visit their town, keep a watch on their conduct, keep them company – especially at night when they leave the theatre – and speak to them of life eternal, of its punishments and its rewards. Sunday especially – Sunday, which good English Churchmen are supposed to spend between church and their arm-chair, between the Bible and the Sunday paper – is fraught with danger for the unlucky actors, who are bound to utilize the only day on which the theatres are closed, for travelling. And it is on Sunday that the activity of the Actors' Church Union is most fervid and most acceptable to Heaven! (1908, pp. 21–2)

Modest in its tone, non-discriminatory in its membership and practical in its endeavours, the Actors' Church Union has proved to be a durable organisation. It took its inspiration from the belief that the actor's art was 'acceptable to Heaven', and, though the number of actors seeking such assurance has diminished, it survives as a living testimony to the long struggle for reconciliation between Church and stage.

CHAPTER 11

Henry Arthur Jones and Wilson Barrett

It's *profane*, Mr Jo – o – ones.

Mrs Patrick Campbell

At the beginning of 1896 two plays opened in London, which, in their very different ways, contributed significantly to the Church-and-stage debate: *The Sign of the Cross* by Wilson Barrett at the Lyric Theatre on 4 January and *Michael and his Lost Angel* by H. A. Jones at the Lyceum Theatre on 15 January. The authors of these two plays were no strangers to each other. Back in March 1879 Jones and Barrett had corresponded about the revision of the former's play *It's Only Round the Corner*, which had been performed at Exeter in the previous year and which Barrett later (August 1879) produced at the Grand Theatre, Leeds, as *Harmony Restored*. Barrett wrote to Jones: 'All oaths should be expurgated; "this is your darnation old mother again" would probably provoke and certainly deserve a hiss, all the expletives do not strengthen but disfigure a charming piece. I do not think Barry's conversion and singing the Moody and Sankey hymns advisable – I abhor cant as much as any man living' (M. Thompson, 1957, p. 42).

Barrett also proffered advice to Jones on *A Clerical Error*, his one-act piece about a middle-aged vicar's delusion that his pretty young ward, Minnie, loves him: 'You must beware of the tendency to coarseness. How could a lady finish an act with such a speech as Muriel's "Neither in earth nor in heaven nor in hell"? They would howl at it in London. And that is but one expression among many' (p. 43).

Jones heeded Barrett's advice and *A Clerical Error* was successfully presented at the Court Theatre on 13 October 1879. Two years later (30 October 1881) Barrett was pressing Jones for a new play:

The public are pining for a pure English comedy – with a pure story, in which the characters shall be English, with English ideas, and English feelings, honest, true men and tender, loving women, and from which plague, pestilence, adultery, fornication, battle, murder and sudden death shall be banished. The author who can do in three acts what you have done in 'A Clerical Error' will take as strong a stand now as Tom Robertson took years ago.

The characters must not *preach* virtue, let them act it, not spout self-denial, but show it. The public taste is depraved, no doubt, the more depraved the greater certainty of success for the man who will try to raise it. (p. 44)

Barrett's prescription for 'a pure English comedy' from which adultery and fornication were banished indicated the way in which he thought the reform of the theatre should be effected, showing no prescience of the wave of new drama which was to sweep the theatre in the wake of Ibsen and in which Jones was to feature prominently. Such a comedy as Barrett envisaged was not forthcoming from Jones, whose first full-length play, *His Wife*, a sensational seduction drama, was staged at the Sadler's Wells Theatre on 6 April 1881. Undeterred, Barrett still pressed Jones for a play, but now a melodrama instead of a comedy. The result was *The Silver King*, first staged at the Princess's Theatre on 16 November 1882. *The Silver King* draws on the conventions of melodrama, whilst eschewing its excesses. Jones used a short story 'Dead in the Desert' by H. C. Pauling, 'which had powerfully impressed me in my childhood' (D. A. Jones, 1930, p. 68). Henry Herman was credited with co-authorship, but Jones later discounted his contribution as he did Barrett's authorial claims to the play (pp. 69–73). *The Silver King* tells of Wilfred Denver (played by Barrett), a dissipated, but good-hearted, young man who, having been convinced that he has committed murder, flees the country – in disguise – leaving his wife and children in the care of his faithful old servant Jaikes. Having made his fortune in Nevada, Denver returns to save his family, but cannot reveal his identity until he discovers that the real murderer is Skinner – 'the Spider'. Russell Jackson has explored the evolution of *The Silver King* (Jackson, 1982, pp. 220–4), during which the religious tone of certain passages was modified and moralising references to drink and gambling were cut. The most contentious and powerful speech remained Denver's, at the Chequer's Inn (act 2, scene 4), fleeing from his supposed crime:

DENVER: And yesterday at this time I was innocent! Yesterday he was alive – and I could laugh and play the fool, and now! Oh God! put back Thy universe and give me yesterday! Too late! Too late! Ah, my wife, how thoughtful she was. Shall I ever see her again – and my children? Ah, Heaven, work out some way of escape for me – not for my own sake, not to shield me from the just consequences of my crime, but for the sake of my dear wife and innocent children who have never done any wrong. Spare me till I have made atonement. (p. 61)

The resonance of 'Oh God! put back Thy universe and give me yester-day!' was such as to send some members of the audience searching their Bible.

From the outset *The Silver King* was hailed as a superior form of melo-drama. George Augustus Sala described it as 'a rift in the clouds, a break of blue in the dramatic heavens' and the critic of the *Theatre* wrote that the play was 'pitched in a much higher key than the ordinary melodra-mas of the day, and, in truth . . . must not be confused with the sensa-tional panoramas which nowadays so often pass for plays' (pp. 5–6). For Jones it was the opinion of Matthew Arnold that mattered most. Jones had been greatly impressed by Arnold's 1879 essay 'The French play in London' and had written to him enclosing copies of his two plays to date (Super, 1974, p. 479). Three years later Jones asked Arnold to attend the opening of *The Silver King*. Arnold replied from the Athenaeum on 2 November 1882 that 'I will certainly come and see your play, but do you care particularly about my coming to the first representation?' (D. A. Jones, 1930, p. 62). He indicated that he would prefer to see it in December or 'the early part of next year' when he would be in London. In the event, by 19 November Arnold had seen *The Silver King* and wrote to John Morley, recently appointed editor of the *Pall Mall Gazette*:

Shall I write you a letter with the impressions called forth by the first representa-tion of *The Silver King*? . . . I know nothing of the author personally, but he wrote saying he had nourished himself on my works and wished I would go to his first representation. I resisted, but went at last, expecting to be bored, but am highly pleased. I should sign 'An Old Playgoer'. (Super, 1974, pp. 479–80)

The regular reviewer had already given warm praise to Jones's play, but Arnold's impressions were published on 6 December – for a fee of £3. As befitted 'An Old Playgoer', Arnold recalled seeing Macready at the Princess's 'some five-and-thirty years ago', when, although the actor's 'intellect, study, energy and power' were admirable, 'he was ill-sup-ported, the house was shabby and dingy, and by no means full; there was something melancholy about the whole thing' (p. 94). In 1882 he found the Princess's 'another world':

The theatre itself was renewed and transformed; instead of shabby and dingy, it has become decorated and brilliant. But the real revival was not in the paint and gilding, it was in the presence of the public. The public was there; not alone the old, peculiar public of the pit and gallery, with a certain number of the rich and refined in boxes and stalls, and with whole, solid classes of English society conspicuous by their absence. No, it was a representative public, furnished from all classes, and showing that English society at large has now taken to the theatre. (p. 95)

In the place of 'a single powerful and intelligent performer', though 'Mr Wilson Barrett, as Wilfred Denver, is so excellent that his primacy cannot be doubted', there was 'a whole company of actors, able to speak English, playing intelligently, supporting one another effectively' (p. 95). Of the play itself Arnold wrote, 'It is not Shakespeare', and he could not agree with those who had praised it as 'a drama of a new and superior kind, bordering upon poetic drama, and even passing into it' (p. 95). *The Silver King* relied 'for its main effect upon an outer drama of sensational incident', but for that, 'no less than for the inner drama', 'there is needed exposition by means of words and sentiments' (p. 95). The significance of *The Silver King* was that 'the diction and sentiments do not overstep the modesty of nature':

Instead of giving to their audience transporting diction and sentiments, Messrs Jones and Herman give them literature. Faults there are in 'The Silver King'; Denver's drunkenness is made too much of, his dream is superfluous, the peasantry are a little tiresome, Denver's triumphant exit from Black Brake Wharf puzzles us. But in general throughout the piece the diction and sentiments are natural, they have sobriety and propriety, they are literature. It is an excellent and hopeful sign to find playwrights capable of writing in this style, actors capable of rendering it, and a public capable of enjoying it. (p. 96)

The importance of what Matthew Arnold beheld at the Princess's Theatre that night was every bit as great as he proclaimed – the combination of a worthy play, a thoroughly competent acting company and a responsive and socially representative audience had been the aspiration of the Select Committee nearly half a century earlier. The key words are 'Messrs Jones and Herman give them literature'. The neo-Elizabethan verse dramas of the first half of the century had proved to be a false start, but here was a play of literary quality in the dominant genre of the contemporary theatre. The question which faced the theatre for the remainder of the nineteenth century and through the twentieth was whether the appeal of plays of literary worth would extend to 'English society at large' or only to the better-educated, socially privileged, discerning theatre-goers.

The heir to many of his father's ideas Matthew Arnold, in his sphere of activity as H. M. Inspector of Schools from 1851 to 1886, was concerned with the education, not of a social élite, but of the masses. In his *General Report for the Year 1852* he upheld the study of great literature, as a means not only of elevating and humanising young people, but also of creating a bond of intellectual sympathy between the classes:

I attach little importance to the study of languages ancient and modern, by pupil-teachers . . . but I am sure that the study of portions of the best English authors, and composition, might with advantage be made a part of their regular course of instruction to a much greater degree than it is at present. Such training would tend to elevate and humanise a number of young men, who at present, notwithstanding the vast amount of raw information which they have amassed, are wholly uncultivated; and it would have the great social advantage of tending to bring them into intellectual sympathy with the educated of the upper classes. (Marvin, 1908, p. 17)

In his *General Report for 1861* Arnold commended 'The learning by heart extracts from good authors' (p. 88). He considered 'three hundred lines of good poetry' annually (p. 186) to be appropriate and stressed the importance of selecting passages 'of signal beauty and effectiveness' such as the 'judgement scene in the *Merchant of Venice*' (p. 203).

Arnold's experience as an inspector of schools informed his writing on culture, pre-eminent amongst which is *Culture and Anarchy* (1869). The objective of culture, as exampled by literature, was not to indoctrinate the masses with a particular creed, but to encourage them to use ideas freely and to become part of 'the social ideal' which stretched 'from one end of society to another':

The ordinary popular literature is an example of this way of working on the masses. Plenty of people will try to indoctrinate the masses with sets of ideas and judgments constituting the creed of their own profession or party. Our religious and political organisations give an example of this way of working with the masses. I condemn neither way; but culture works differently. It does not try to teach down to the inferior classes; it does not try to win them for this or that sect of its own, with ready made judgments and watchwords. It seeks to do away with classes; and to make the best that has been thought and known in the world current everywhere; to make all men live in an atmosphere of sweetness and light; where they may use ideas, as it uses them itself, freely, – nourished and not bound by them.
This is the *social idea*; and the men of culture are the true apostles of equality. The great men of culture are those who have a passion for diffusing, for making prevail, for carrying from one end of society to the other, the best knowledge, the best ideas of their times . . . (J. D. Wilson, 1963, p. 70)

As Raymond Williams points out, Matthew Arnold's 'recommendation of the State as the agent of general perfection' (1987, p. 119) was central to his strategy. This was as true for the theatre as it was for education. Matthew Arnold's most sustained piece of writing on theatre, 'The French play in London', first published in the *Nineteenth Century*, 6 August 1879, was occasioned by the six-week visit by the Comédie Française to the Gaiety Theatre in 1879. Arnold recalled 'in my youth', seeing 'the divine Rachel' as Hermione in Edinburgh: 'I followed her to Paris, and for two months never missed one of her performances' (Super, 1973,

p. 65). Arnold was amongst 'the company that used to gather round the Martins' [Helen Faucit's] dinner-table' in Onslow Square (Simpson and Braun, 1913, p. 326).

The inspector of schools, encouraging pupils to learn 300 lines of poetry annually, could be detected in Arnold's remarks about the superiority of 'the majestic English iambic' over the 'incurable artificiality' of the rhyming Alexandrine and his assertion that: 'Poetry is simply the most delightful and perfect form of utterance that human words can reach' (Super, 1973, p. 68). Despite the superiority of its verse form and the example of Shakespeare, the English theatre had 'no modern drama at all', but instead 'we have numberless imitations and adaptations from the French' (p. 78). Arnold advanced as explanations for this the state of British society – 'our vast society is not at present homogeneous enough' (p. 78) – and the inheritance of Puritanism, 'the prison of Puritanism', as a result of which 'our middle class forsook the theatre' (p. 79). He recalled seeing the Haymarket company in Shrewsbury twenty years earlier when 'The real townspeople, the people who carried forward the business and life of Shrewsbury, and who filled its churches and chapels on Sundays, were entirely absent . . . a good example . . . of the complete estrangement of the British middle class from the theatre' (p. 80). George Augustus Sala made the same observation of the audiences at theatres in country towns in *Twice Round The Clock*, adding 'We may pretend to despise the Puritan world . . . but it is folly to ignore the vast numerical strength of these same Puritans' (1859, p. 294). At last Arnold detected 'a signal change is coming over us', reflected in the existence of forty theatres in London – a belated, though direct, consequence of the 1843 legislation. The upper and middle classes were showing 'an increased liking . . . for the theatre', a reflection of changing religious attitudes towards it:

Our French friends would say that this class [middle], long petrified in a narrow Protestantism and in a perpetual reading of the Bible, is beginning at last to grow conscious of the horrible unnaturalness and ennui of its life, and is seeking to escape from it. Undoubtedly the type of religion to which the British middle class has sacrificed the theatre, as it has sacrificed so much besides, is defective. But I prefer to say that this great class, having had the discipline of its religion, is now awakening to the sure truth that the human spirit cannot live aright if it lives at one point only, that it can and ought to live at several points at the same time. The human spirit has a vital need, as we say, for conduct and religion; but it has the need also for expansion, for intellect and knowledge, for beauty, for social life and manners. The revelation of these additional needs brings the middle class to the theatre.

The revelation is indispensable, the needs are real, the theatre is one of the mightiest means of satisfying them, and the theatre, therefore, is irresistible. That conclusion, at any rate, we may take for certain. We have to unlearn, therefore, our long disregard of the theatre; we have to own that the theatre is irresistible. (Super, 1973, pp. 80–1)

Arnold perceived the middle class 'beginning to arrive at the theatre again after an abstention of two centuries and more; arriving eager and curious, but a little bewildered' and 'finding the English theatre without organisation, or purpose, or dignity' (p. 81). Interestingly Arnold located the origin of the return of the middle class to the theatre in their 'need ... for expansion, for intellect and knowledge, for beauty, for social life and manners', not in the enhanced attractions provided by a theatre which had reformed itself. In modern parlance the process was consumer-driven. He argues that the theatre should organise itself, or rather the state should organise the theatre, to provide for this new audience. Although Arnold acknowledged that the abolition of the patent theatres was inevitable, it was to them that 'our stage owes the days of power and greatness ... So far as we have had a school of great actors, so far as our stage has had a great tradition, effect, consistency, and a hold on public esteem, it had them under the system of the privileged theatres' (p. 84). The system had its faults:

but then instead of devising a better plan of public organisation for the English theatre, we gladly took refuge in our favourite doctrine of the mischief of State interference, of the blessedness of leaving every man free to do as he likes, of the impertinence of presuming to check any man's natural taste for the bathos and pressing him to relish the sublime. We left the English theatre to take its chance. Its present state of impotence is the result. (p. 84)

In place of free trade and the Benthamite refusal to ascribe superiority to certain kinds of amusement, Arnold advocated state support for the higher forms of theatre:

Forget ... your clap-trap, and believe that the State, the nation in its collective and corporate character, does well to concern itself about an influence so important to national life and manners as the theatre. Form a company out of the materials ready to hand in your many good actors or actors of promise. Give them a theatre in the West End. Let them have a grant from your Science and Art Department ... Let the conditions of the grant be that a repertory is agreed upon, taken out of the works of Shakespeare and out of the volumes of the *Modern British Drama*; ... as to new pieces, let your company use its discretion. Let a school of dramatic elocution and declamation be instituted with your company ...
When your institution in the West of London has become a success, plant a second of like kind in the East. The people *will* have the theatre; then make it a

good one. Let your two or three chief provincial towns institute, with municipal subsidy and co-operation, theatres such as you institute in the metropolis with State subsidy and co-operation. So you will restore the English theatre. (pp. 84–5)

The debate about a National Theatre intensified in the late 1870s, but it could be traced back to the proposal made in 1848 by Effington Wilson, a supporter of mechanics' institutes, who published 'the early works of Jeremy Bentham when nobody else dared to do so' (Elsom and Tomalin, 1978, p. 6). As befitted an advocate of popular education, Wilson's concept of a National Theatre was anti-élitist: educating the public by popularizing good drama, particularly Shakespeare. Tom Taylor, another exponent of popular education, was also an advocate for a National Theatre (Whitworth, 1951, p. 26). In March 1878 William Gladstone advocated the creation of a National Theatre in an open letter to the *Theatre* (13 March 1879); in October both George Godwin and Henry Irving joined in the debate with contributions to the Congress of the Social Sciences Association. Godwin stressed 'the ameliorative influence of education in art'; but though he was sure that 'any government which gave, under wise supervision, a moderate allowance to the theatre would act wisely', he was equally sure that 'no Government will attempt it' (1878, p. 6). Irving counselled that it was 'at present unadvisable to touch upon the subject of state subsidy with reference to the British stage' (p. 28) and J. R. Planché thought that it was 'hopeless to expect government subsidy as in France' (1879, p. 4).

The view that the theatre had an educational function and that it could be a force for moral good commanded growing, though by no means universal, assent in influential circles by 1879. There was an awareness that a new public, escaping from 'the prison of Puritanism', was extending, if not transferring, its patronage to the theatre and that it would need, expect even, a prevailing tone of morality there, as a reinforcement or substitute for what the Church provided. Whether England, like other European countries, should add a National Theatre to its state institutions, of which of course the Established Church was one, was not to be resolved positively for nearly 100 years, thereby leaving in abeyance the question of whether the purpose of such a theatre would be to popularise drama or to serve an educated élite.

Henry Arthur Jones was no stranger to 'the prison of Puritanism'; he was born on 20 September 1851 in Grandesborough, Buckinghamshire, the son of a tenant farmer of Welsh Nonconformist extraction. Jones's parents 'in reality . . . were Puritan' (D. A. Jones, 1930, p. 28); for his mother, 'the informing motive of her whole life was an unusually deep religious belief' (p. 26). When Jones went to school 'the little boys whose parents were Dissenters had to sit on a bench away from the Orthodox Church of England lads' (p. 27). Aged twelve, Jones was sent to live with an uncle – 'the deacon of a Baptist chapel, who kept a shop in Ramsgate' (p. 31). He received no further schooling and was pressed into becoming a teetotaller (he would receive £5 after three years). Theatre-going was prohibited and although he wrote a play at sixteen, he was eighteen before he saw one – the Kendals in *Leah*. The effect of this upbringing on Jones was counter-productive; he caused his mother great concern 'because he was not a believer' (p. 27). He did however marry in church – St Andrew's, Holborn – and attended services with a critical ear to the preaching. He described Spurgeon, 'the Boanerges of the Baptists [who] ... declared that a playgoer ceased to be a member of a Christian community' (Cordell, 1932, p. 12), as having 'a good deal of the low comedian about him' (D. A. Jones, 1930, p. 47). From the services and preaching of Revd H. R. Haweis he derived 'the rarest pleasure' (p. 47) and he declared the Bishop of Ripon 'the preacher he most admired' (p. 48). Both Haweis and the Bishop of Ripon, Boyd-Carpenter, had made public their support for the theatre.

By his own admission Jones 'had nourished himself' on the works of Matthew Arnold, whose influence is apparent in 'The theatre and the mob' with its allusions to philistinism, Mr Bright and 'The French play in London'. Jones shared Arnold's aspiration for literary drama, but had doubts about its appeal to the mass of play-goers:

Among the many hopeful signs of a real and permanent dramatic revival in England there are only too many assurances that, while on the whole playgoers may be said to desire literature and poetry, the great body of them also much more desire many much less worthy things – sensation, realism, noise, tricks of surprise, huge scenic effects, tawdry dresses, foolish songs – anything but the quiet, steady, faithful portraiture of character in natural fitting language. (*Nineteenth Century*, September 1883, p. 441)

Given this predominating preference, for 'much less worthy things', 'on the whole the modern English drama remains, in its literary aspect, as far as ever from attaining the grandeur and dignity of a great national, noble, self-respecting art' (p. 441). The problem was that: 'The great majority of playgoers never have come to the theatre, and in no period of time that can be safely reckoned upon, are they likely to come to the theatre, for literature and poetry, for any kind of moral, artistic, or intellectual stimulus, or for any other purpose than mere amusement and pastime' (p. 442). The question was how far the elevation of drama was compatible with a socially diverse audience. Jones used the image of 'the Siamese-twin condition':

We find everywhere a growing interest in drama as an art, in opposition to the drama as a popular entertainment of the circus or music-hall type. Not that dramatic art seeks to deprive the masses of their amusement, not that it demands that they shall be dull, but that they shall laugh with the beneficent, side-shaking, heart-easing mirth of wise men, instead of with the withering, heart-hardening laughter of fools. It insists that if the Siamese-twin connection with popular amusement is to be preserved, its unwholesome brother shall get himself purged and shrived, and render himself amenable to discipline; it insists on dragging popular entertainment up to its level, and refuses to be dragged down to the level of popular amusement. And the end is not to rob the people of their pleasure but to increase and rationalise and elevate it. (p. 451)

Jones's belief in the higher form of pleasure to be derived from literary drama was combined with the desire to convert 'the great majority of playgoers'. Like Arnold, Jones saw the arrival of the erstwhile prisoners of Puritanism in the theatre as a significant development. In 'Religion and the stage' he wrote:

The present attitude of religious persons towards the stage is a somewhat curious one. For some two hundred years religious opinion in England has been more or less antagonistic to the theatre. But gradually the far-seeing and more liberal-minded teachers in the different sects have become alive to the fact that the theatre is immensely popular, and must be tolerated and reckoned with. It threatens to become a powerful influence in the moral life of the nation. And religious persons are fast discovering that, in the huge sempiternal dullness and mechanical routine of English life, theatre-going is not an unpleasant way of spending the evening. Like Dame Purecraft in the matter of eating pig, they would like to have it made as lawful as possible. So they come timorously, with the old notion still clinging to them that they are in 'the tents of the wicked'. How welcome to weak consciences have been the various entertainments that, under some convenient name or cloak, have afforded to religious persons a satisfaction of the ineradicable dramatic instinct, and saved them the sin of going to a theatre. How ludicrous is the spectacle of religion, shivering on the brink of Shakespeare at the Lyceum or Princess's, and turning away to regale itself at the Christy Minstrels or the Chamber of Horrors! What a blank and stupefying denial of all the genial humane qualities of our nature is implied in the wholesale condemnation of that Boanerges of the Baptists! But the truth is that religious persons, after having vilified the theatre for two centuries, are fast coming back to it. Not all Mr Spurgeon's shouting to his flock to stay and batten in his sheep-pens on the dismal moor of hyper-Calvinism will long keep them from straggling to the green pastures and broad waters of the nation's intellectual life. (*Nineteenth Century*, January 1885, p. 158)

Although these stragglers from the sheep-pen of religion expected the theatre to maintain standards of moral decency they were resistant to the treatment of religion itself as a dramatic theme. They 'come timidly to the theatre with a vague sense of wrong-doing, and are shocked if there is any mention of religious subjects. Their views of life are such, that there is no general reconciliation possible between the two ideas of religion and the theatre, and so they wish to keep them utterly apart' (p. 158). Jones's objective was not merely that church-goers should come to the theatre, but that they should be confronted there with dramatic explorations of religious subjects. Shaw recognised Jones's assault on this barrier in *Michael and his Lost Angel*: 'The real objection to Mr Jones's play is the objection to Michael's treatment of religion as co-extensive with life: that is, as genuinely catholic. To the man who regards it as only a watertight Sunday compartment of social observance, such a view is not only inconvenient, but positively terrifying' (1932, vol. II, p. 23).

Jones realised that the attitude of the 'much larger proportion of simply indifferent persons', who pay merely 'the ordinary Englishman's ear and lip reverence to the current creed' was no more propitious. Having dispensed with religion 'to a great extent in regulating their lives, they think it may very well be allowed to remain in its present condition of honoured and respected superannuation, as an affair of Sundays, and parsons, and churches and chapels' (*Nineteenth Century*, January 1885, p. 159).

Thus, for all the softening of religious attitudes towards the theatre, the resistance to the treatment of 'religion and politics' on stage was still formidable 'because these are the subjects upon which counter opinions are most rife and popular feelings most easily raised' (p. 157). This restriction was an obstruction to drama achieving its rightful potential: 'It is quite certain, however, that the existence of such a restriction upon the dramatist forbids the hope of English drama ever reaching forward to be great art, and condemns it to remain as it is, the plaything of the populace, a thing of convention and compromise' (pp. 159–60).

In 'The Bible and the stage', originally published in the *New Review* in February 1893, Jones pressed for the theatre's right to deal with religious subjects on an equal footing with 'the painter, the poet, and musician' (H. A. Jones, 1895, p. 119), pointing to the Mystery plays as a precedent. He asserted:

But I see no reason why the great human stories of the Bible should not be utilised on our stage. I am speaking here with the utmost reverence for a Book, or rather Books, which I have dearly loved and constantly studied from my childhood, which have been my classics . . . It is with the greatest love for these books that I hold it to be quite lawful to treat certain of their stories upon the modern stage. Lawful, I say – the question of expediency is one that must be applied to each individual case as it arises. The English theatre could not possibly make a worse use of the Bible than the sects have done, or misunderstand it so completely. (p. 123)

Later that year – August 1893 – also in the *New Review*, Jones speculated on 'The future of English drama', acknowledging that not only had 'ordinary subjects been treated in a more serious and daring manner, but many matters that ten or twenty years ago were considered to be outside the sphere of the theatre altogether have been dealt with during the past few years' (1895, p. 129). He prophesied that 'Religion, politics, science, education, philosophy, are likely to be dealt with on the English stage during the next generation' (p. 129) and drew attention to the advent of 'a slightly more intellectual public' (p. 125) who demanded higher standards than 'the last generation' of 'the great body of playgoers', who 'had not emancipated themselves from Puritan prejudices' (p. 126). He postulated that 'This smaller section of cultivated playgoers is likely to be largely reinforced from the greater public', but acknowledged that 'this line of severance between dramatic art and popular amusement has been made more definite during the last few years' and that 'there has been a concurrent movement in the opposite direction, and the music halls have made more and more successful invasions of the theatres' (p. 127). For all his hopes to the contrary, Jones was describing not the creation of a homogeneous theatre, but the split into the literary and the popular. He concluded the essay: 'The more the Church becomes an archaeological museum of fossil dogmas, the less hold and command it will have upon the religion and morality of the nation. If the pulpit loses its power, will the Drama take its place?' (p. 181).

If the elevation of drama was to take the popular audience along with it, education was an important ally. In his inaugural address – 'The relations of the drama to education' – at the reopening of the City of London College on 12 October 1893, with Revd Prebendary Whittington in the chair, Jones began with a question: 'Has the drama any relation to education?', answering that a perusal of the prospectus revealed none save a class on elocution. He claimed 'that there should be very strong relations between the drama and education' (1895, p. 289). The goal of education was not 'how to scramble for material advantages and to outwit each other in the race for money', but to develop 'the science of living' (p. 291) and it was 'this wide knowledge of life and mankind' that 'the drama can give in a transcendent manner' (p. 293). The power of drama exceeded that of books, other art and mere spoken address: 'Now in this great power of presenting life and the realities of life in such a way as to give the spectator the same knowledge of them as he would possess after years of observation and experience, the stage is supreme' (p. 293).

Jones's perception of the drama's educational function was on the same lines as Matthew Arnold's principles for liberal education, which should not indoctrinate the masses 'with ready made judgments and watchwords':

I hope our chairman will not take it unkindly if I dare to suggest that the stage has an advantage over the pulpit not only in the matter but also in the methods of its teaching. The pulpit is a direct, an absolute teacher. So are all other teachers who come here to instruct you. The drama is not. I am going to give you a paradox, yet a profound truth. The drama does teach, must teach, is a potent influence and also a great art in proportion as it does teach, yet *the moment it takes the professorial chair, the moment it assumes the professorial robes, it stultifies itself, it usurps a function and an authority that it has no right to or business with, and it becomes a meddler and a bungler. The drama cannot directly and explicitly affirm or teach or solve or prove anything.* (p. 302)

Great plays – *Hamlet, Othello* – transcended a single, simple response: 'What does *Hamlet* prove? Nothing, no more than life itself. What does it teach? Just whatever you please; just whatever you like to read into it' (p. 304).

This is the paradox of life and it is equally the paradox of art – that though it must have a meaning and an end, they always elude you when you search for them. Therefore I say that the drama is following life, is following nature, when it teaches in the same way, not directly, not absolutely, not for an immediate result, but hiddenly, silently, implicitly, and with results and consequences that are removed and far-reaching, and not obvious at first glance to the average man. (p. 304)

With regard to 'the average man' Jones protested that 'I am often misrepresented as being an enemy of popular amusements' (p. 305), but though he affirmed his 'greatest sympathy for all forms of entertainment that have for their object the lightening of the burdens and the easing of the hearts of our overworked city populations' and had been 'constantly in favour of removing all restrictions from those who provide entertainment for the people, whether in theatre or music-halls', he could not help recognising:

that we shall never have an English drama worthy of a great nation while the mere entertainment of the masses is the only object of our plays. The pursuit of mere amusement defeats its own ends. The more you pander to the lower tastes of the public, the more you have to pander to them, the less and less satisfaction you give it, until at the last if it does not turn and rend you, it despises and forgets you. (p. 306)

In his refusal to compromise artistic integrity in the pursuit of popularity Jones was adopting – no doubt unconsciously – Newman's position in the Tamworth Reading Room debate: that those who defer to facile distractions 'will find themselves outbid in the market for gratifications much closer at hand, and on the level of the meanest capacity' (1891, p. 267).

Jones collected his articles, lectures and prefaces (to *Saints and Sinners* and *The Case of Rebellious Susan*) into book form as *The Renascence of the English Drama* (1895), to which he wrote a preface. He referred to the emergence, between 1882 and 1894, of 'a body of cultivated playgoers' and 'the gradual change . . . both in the constitution of our audiences and in their way of regarding a play' (p. vi). Of the goals for which he had striven in the preceding ten years, foremost was:

a recognition of the distinction between the art of the drama on the one hand and popular amusement on the other, and of the greater pleasure to be derived from the art of the drama. I have been constantly misrepresented as seeking to deprive theatre-goers of their enjoyment, yet all my aim has been to show them how they may increase it. There is not a lecture or paper in this book that does not contain a statement explicit or implicit, repeated ad nauseam, that the theatre exists for the one end of giving pleasure, and that it can instruct and educate only as the other fine arts do; that is, incidentally and indirectly, never with any set purpose. (p. vii)

Jones affirmed 'that popular amusement is one thing and the art of the drama another. That time is fighting to separate them may be seen from a glance at the history of the stage during the last thirty years' (p. viii). The 'best of our West-End houses' were now as free from the suspicion of impropriety 'as our churches and chapels' (p. x).

Jones's analysis of the state of English drama and theatre drew together many strands of thought running through the nineteeth century. He asserted the essentiality of literary quality in drama, as had his mentor Matthew Arnold, like many – Charles Kemble, H. H. Milman, amongst others – before him. He observed the return of the middle classes to the theatre as a consequence of the erosion of religious prejudice. He proclaimed the dramatist's right to treat religious subjects and the theatre's power to educate 'hiddenly, silently, implicitly'. He affirmed the theatre's 'great power of presenting life and the realities of life', thereby extending the spectator's knowledge beyond his own experience and observation, a point made by F. D. Maurice in his preface to Kingsley's *The Saint's Tragedy*. He tacitly refuted Bentham's view that the value of amusements lay only in the amount of pleasure derived from them by their participants, claiming instead that greater pleasure 'was to be derived from the art of the drama' than from 'popular amusement'. He held out the hope that 'the greater public' would reinforce the 'smaller section of cultivated playgoers', thereby creating in the theatre that cultural homogeneity for which Matthew Arnold longed. Jones's wish for the theatre to be both 'popular and profound', as F. D. Maurice had characterised Shakespeare's plays, was unquestionable, but in his ultimate refusal to compromise 'the art of the drama' with 'popular amusement' he showed a resolution worthy of Newman.

Concurrently with writing and lecturing on the theatre, Jones was putting his ideas into practice as a dramatist. *Saints and Sinners* at the Vaudeville Theatre on 25 September 1884, in Gerald Weales's words, 'reintroduced the possibility of religion as a serious consideration in the English drama' (1961, p. 4). The play ran for almost 200 nights, but its London first night (it had previously been performed in Margate and Greenwich) 'received a very mixed reception, as some of the pit and other parts of the house objected to the scriptural quotations used by the characters, and the audience hissed and booed loudly' (D. A. Jones, 1930, p. 89). In this piece Jones did make a concession to public taste. Letty Fletcher, the daughter of a dissenting minister, is seduced by Captain Eustace, an aristocratic bounder. Her father makes public confession of her sin from his pulpit, as a consequence of which the two are banished, to be rescued by Letty's first love, farmer George Kingsmill, recently returned, rich, from Australia. In the original version Letty dies, but in the revised version she survives to marry Kingsmill. Matthew Arnold attended the play and commended it, except 'that the marriage of the heroine to her farmer does not please me as a dénouement' (H. A. Jones, 1895, p. 323).

On 21 May 1890 Jones's *Judah* was performed at the Shaftesbury Theatre. Amongst Jones's notes for the play, Richard A. Cordell located 'a sketch for a play he names "Coleridge"' (1932, p. 64) – an enticing prospect indeed. In the event, *Judah* revolves around a fanatical Welsh clergyman, Judah Llewellyn, who falls in love with a young girl, Vashti Dethic, who, at her father's instigation, deceives people into believing that she can cure them by fasting and faith-healing. Judah discovers the truth but, after initially protecting the girl, makes a public confession. *Judah* was well received, the *Star* describing the third act as 'all pure, unadulterated, spiritual drama' (22 May 1890).

Controversy attended *Michael and his Lost Angel* both before and after its short run at the Lyceum Theatre from 15 to 25 January 1896. Jones offered the roles of Revd Michael Feversham and his 'Lost Angel' Audrie Lesden to Irving and Ellen Terry (Griffin, 1991, p. 39), but Irving, whose preferences always prevailed in their professional partnership, did not like it. Instead Johnston Forbes-Robertson and Mrs Patrick Campbell were cast. Mrs Patrick Campbell, the daughter of a Roman Catholic mother and a father who was 'a cheerful believer in Darwinian theory' (Campbell, 1922, p. 11), had already run the gauntlet of religious susceptibilities as Agnes Ebbsmith, who hurls a Bible into a wood-burning stove in act 3 of Pinero's *The Notorious Mrs Ebbsmith* at the Garrick Theatre (13 March 1895). She 'came to rehearsal only for Forbes's sake (she said)' (Peters, 1985, p. 122) and soon clashed with Jones, carolling 'It's *profane*, Mr Jo – o – ones' (p. 122); she wanted cuts to be made, but Jones was adamant – not only must Mrs Patrick Campbell play Audrie as written, but she must also do it in the manner he pre-scribed. She left the cast and was replaced by Marion Terry. Mrs Patrick Campbell had hated the church scene (act 4); Forbes-Robertson, upon whom the chapel services of his schooldays at Charterhouse had left an enduring impression (Forbes-Robertson, 1925, p. 18), experienced great anxiety with his character, but regarded the play 'as the finest serious play that gifted author wrote' (p. 166).

In *Michael and his Lost Angel,* Jones returns to the themes interdicted in Wilson Barrett's letter of 30 October 1881, which he had explored in *Saints and Sinners* and *Judah:* adultery, sin, repentance and forgiveness. The first act is set in the vicarage parlour of Cleveheddon, the incum-bent of which is Revd Michael Feversham, educated at Eton and Oxford, the author of *The Hidden Life*, who, in his father's words, 'is shaping religious thought throughout England today' (Hamilton, 1925, p. 14). Feversham has obliged Rose, the daughter of his secretary Andrew Gibbard, to make public confession of her adultery. Feversham himself has fallen in love with Audrie Lesden, whom he believes to be a widow. In act 2 she follows him to Saint Decuman's Island, where she is stranded with him for two nights. Michael proclaims 'I love you with all my being' and Audrie, showing 'great delight', says 'It's an awful delight to think that a man would dare risk hell for one' (p. 41). She determines to leave him – 'I will leave you':

MICHAEL: You will? Yes it cannot be so! My work, my vows – I cannot, may not taste of earthly love. Oh it's cruel to dash the cup from my lips! (*Pause: then very calmly.*) You are right! I feel that we are choosing heaven or hell for both our souls this night! Help me to choose heaven for you, and I'll help you to choose heaven for me. (p. 42)

Their resolution is undermined by the breakdown of Audrie's arrangements to leave the island. Back at the vicarage in act 3, Feversham is a man 'trying to realize that he has committed a great and irrevocable sin' (p. 44), heightened by the discovery that Audrie's husband is still alive. Act 4 is set in the opulently restored (by Audrie's donations) Minster Church of St Decuman, painstakingly delineated by Jones, the stage set for which Shaw described as 'an appalling example of the worst sort of German "restoration"' (1932, vol. II, p. 21). There Michael is joined by Audrie and, though he avows 'You are the holiest thing on earth to me' (Hamilton, 1925, p. 73), he proceeds to make his – now predictable – confession, from the altar steps: 'I have broken the sanctity of the marriage vow' (p. 76). The final act finds Michael in the reception room of San Salvatore at Majano in Italy where he is preparing for conversion to Roman Catholicism under the instruction of his uncle, Father Hilary. Thither the portrait of his mother – an emblematic good angel – previously seen in the vicarage has followed him, as has his 'Lost Angel' Audrie, 'her face wasted and hectic' (p. 82). Though Audrie is now a widow, earthly union is not to be theirs – 'she drops dead', leaving Michael to deliver the closing speech of the play to Father Hilary:

MICHAEL: Take me! I give my life, my will, my soul, to you! Do what you please with me! I'll believe all, do all, suffer all – only – only persuade me that I shall meet her again!

(*Throws himself on her body.*) (p. 85)

Shaw, amongst others, detected the influence of Nathaniel Hawthorne's *The Scarlet Letter*, 'In a new Puseyite mode' (1932, vol. II, p. 20), which Jones denied: 'I did not draw the theme or character of Michael in *Michael and his Lost Angel* from *The Scarlet Letter*' (in Cordell, 1932, p. 121). Kerry Powell has pointed out resemblances between Hawthorne's novel and Oscar Wilde's *A Woman of No Importance*, including Mrs Arbuthnot's name – 'can it be fortuitous that this sign of her shame begins with an "A?"' (1990, p. 59). Audrie's name also begins with 'A', the symbol for adultery in *The Scarlet Letter*. Forbes-Robertson had tried to persuade Jones to change the title of the play to *Michael and*

Audrie, 'telling Jones that "lost angel" had been a term for a lady of pleasure for many years' (Peters, 1985, p. 122). As Patricia S. Kruppa has shown, images of Mary Magdalene pervaded Victorian culture (1992, p. 117). When Wilkie Collins's *The New Magdalen*, his dramatisation of his own novel first staged in 1873, was revived in October 1895, Shaw wrote:

> Where Wilkie Collins really struck the new movement was in his sketch of the Reverend Julian Grey, who might have been a stagey forecast of the Reverend Stewart Headlam, though he was probably a reminiscence of some earlier pioneer of Christian Socialism. You will find hundreds of such parsons now: in fact the Guild of St Matthew is a Guild of St Julian Grey. (1932, vol. 1, p. 232)

It took Henry James, in *Guy Domville* at the St James's Theatre, 5 January 1895, to 'give us a hero who sacrifices his love to a strong and noble vocation for the Church' (p. 7).

In *Michael and his Lost Angel,* Jones had strayed far from the 'pure story' with 'tender loving women' void of 'adultery, fornication' which Wilson Barrett had extolled to him in 1881. In doing so Jones had embraced the social, moral and religious mores of the 1890s, as characterised by Holbrook Jackson:

> Every physical excess of the time went hand in hand with spiritual desire. The soul seemed to be trying the way of the flesh with calamitous desperation. Long years of Puritanism and rationalism had proved the folly of salvation by morality and salvation by reason, so in a fit of despair the unsatisfied spirit of the age sought respite in salvation by sin. The recognition of sin was the beginning of the revolt against rationalism and the beginning of the renewal of mysticism. (1913, pp. 159–60)

Though the theme of 'salvation by sin' may have struck a particular chord in 'the unsatisfied spirit' of the 1890s it had its antecedents in Coleridge's play *Remorse* and his prose-poem *Cain*.

Sophisticated critics hailed Jones's success. William Archer considered that 'In *Michael and his Lost Angel* Mr Henry Arthur Jones has enriched, not our theatre only, but our literature, with a beautiful love-story' (1897, p. 16). He acclaimed 'Mr Jones's finely-inspired romance' as 'by far – oh, very far! – the best thing he has done' (p. 18). Shaw declared 'Its art is in vital contact with the most passionate religious movement of its century, as fully quickened art always has been' (1932, vol. II, p. 15). On this point the *Illustrated Church News* was less sure, finding the play 'full of inconsistencies and improbabilities'. It acknowledged 'passages of considerable literary merit', but was puzzled: 'What precise moral, if any, Mr Jones intended to convey, it is not easy to determine' (24 January 1896). For

Jones, a play 'in vital contact with the most passionate religious movement of its century', possessing 'passages of considerable literary merit',
but without a 'precise moral' was true to his own stated objectives for
drama. On this count *Michael and his Lost Angel* could be counted a
success, but it was withdrawn after only ten performances and has not
received a major stage revival. The critical and box-office responses to
Michael and his Lost Angel reflected the divide between the theatre of the
intellect and popular appeal.

In 'The Bible and the stage' H. A. Jones wrote:

Not that I object to people saving their souls, even at the theatre if they wish, but
there are different ways of doing it, and I would prefer not to save mine through
the medium of religious chromo-lithographs, or religious magazines, or religious melodramas. I do not say that I would rather be damned, but I would
make it a matter of careful deliberation. (1895, p. 121)

It was in the genre of 'religious melodramas' that Wilson Barrett
excelled. Born William Henry Barrett near Chelmsford on 18 February
1846, Wilson Barrett was one of four children of George Barrett, a
gentleman farmer, and his wife Charlotte. The Barretts were 'a devout
churchgoing family' (J. Thomas, 1984, p. 11); the young William
attended Sunday school and when the family moved to London – St
Pancras – in 1857, he joined the choir of St Peter's Church. Enthused by
his youthful theatre-going, Barrett joined the profession, spending his
early years – and indeed many of his later ones – in the provinces. In
Aberdeen, Barrett met and in due course – 21 July 1866 – married
actress Caroline Heath, nine years his senior and illegitimate. The
wedding was conducted by Miss Heath's clergyman brother, but kept
secret from her family because of the disparity in the couple's ages. Miss
Heath supported her husband in his career and became Reader to
Queen Victoria.

The success of *The Silver King* encouraged Barrett into authorship. He
found a collaborator in Thomas Henry Hall Caine with whom he wrote
Ben-My-Chree (Princess's, 17 May 1888), adapted from Caine's novel *The
Deemster*, and *The Manxman* (Leeds 22 August 1894; the Shaftesbury
Theatre, 18 November 1895), from Caine's novel of the same title. Born
in Runcorn on 14 May 1853, Caine (Kenyon, 1901) cultivated a life-long
association with the Isle of Man. However Liverpool was the nursery of
his talent – there, as a young man, he took part in readings, corresponded with John Ruskin and became 'a Christian Socialist a good
many years before the name was known' (H. H. Caine, 1908, p. 39). In
fact Caine left the Church of England to become a Baptist; he strongly

espoused and supported causes such as teetotalism and the rescue of 'fallen women'.

Having first corresponded with him, Caine met Dante Gabriel Rossetti in 1880 and the next year moved into the poet's Cheyne Walk home, becoming, in William Gaunt's phrase, 'A Boswell from the Isle of Man' (1965, p. 215). He met Rossetti's friends and imbibed his reminiscences: 'When we were very young we helped Frederick Denison Maurice at his Working Men's Colleges, and there Charles Kingsley and others made speeches and delivered lectures' (H. H. Caine, 1908, p. 120). Caine worked as a journalist, sending reviews of London plays to the *Liverpool Mercury*, as a result of which Wilson Barrett wrote to him saying 'I think you could write a play' (p. 255). The two men were well suited as collaborators, sharing strong religious convictions and a populist belief in the theatre's capacity to do good. Caine had first-hand experience of the theatre's power to convert and captivate its detractors. His own father had 'an attitude of determined hostility' towards the theatre until, aged sixty, he saw Irving as Hamlet and 'at the triumphant moments he looked as if he wanted to say "Glory be to God!"' (p. 356). His mother was similarly carried away by Irving in *Louis XI*. Caine, who acclaimed 'the efforts made towards the redemption of the stage by Mr Irving' (1877, p. 7), was asked by the actor to write a play for him on Mahomet, but 'a protest came from the Indian Moslems and the office of the Lord Chamberlain intervened' (Caine, 1908, p. 351, and Stoker, 1906, vol. II, pp. 120–1).

Caine continued to write Christian melodramas after the breakdown of his partnership with Barrett, caused by a dispute over *The Christian* which had a chequered history from its première in New York on 10 October 1898 to the revised version at the Lyceum Theatre with Matheson Lang on 31 August 1907 (see *Play Pictorial*, vol. II, no. 65, pp. 26–7). The titles of Caine's plays are indicative of their content: *The Eternal City* (1902), *The Prodigal Son* (1905) and *The Bondman* (1906). The *Era* reported Caine's address to the Philosophical Institution in Edinburgh on 'Moral responsibility in the novel and the drama' in November 1894: 'Mr Caine makes a very earnest and plausible protest against the exclusion of religious and political subjects from the stage' (10 November 1894). From 1885 until his death in 1931 Caine worked on a 'Life of Christ' which, though uncompleted, ran to 3 million words. It was eventually edited by his sons and published in 1938, totalling 1,250 pages. More modest was Caine's *Life of Samuel Taylor Coleridge* in the 'Great Writers' series (1887), a sound and, within its scope, comprehensive volume, conducive towards the poet's rehabilitation, after the decades during which his reputation had been overshadowed by the stigma of his opium addiction.

Hugely popular and honoured (knighted in 1918, appointed a Companion of Honour in 1922) in his lifetime, Hall Caine drew together several important strands in the relationship between the Church and stage: the Nonconformist ethic, Christian Socialism, Coleridge and the theatre's command of a mass audience for religious purposes.

Mass appeal was certainly Wilson Barrett's aim and achievement with *Claudian* by W. G. Wills and Henry Herman (1883) and his own *The Sign of the Cross*, which was 'performed by Barrett or by one of his companies more than 10,000 times' and which during its London run (1896–7) 'was attracting audiences at the rate of 70,000 per week' (Mayer, 1994, p. 109). Souvenirs including postcards, large coloured prints, illustrated programmes and copies of Edward Jones's hymn 'Shepherd of Souls' were bought in large quantities. That this was more than sheer commercialism is indicated by the heading – 'The mission of the stage' – of an article in the *Era* (12 August 1893) reporting Barrett's recent 'chat' with a journalist in Southampton. Wilson Barrett was quoted as saying:

I do not think that the bulk of the people present at a theatrical performance of one of Shakespeare's plays go there to hear *him*. They go to *see* his plays mounted in an attractive manner, and to hear an actor or actress who has made a reputation in a particular part.

The stage masses as to time and place nearly all arts and nearly all talents, such as poetry, painting, music, elocution, sculpture, and acting as animated atatuary [statuary]. It needs the highest powers of the dramatist, the archaeologist, and the historian in writing and costuming of the plays; the highest knowledge of architect and scientist in constructing and ornamenting the theatre, and the most cunning ingenuity of the mechanic in the construction of machinery and devices necessary for the spectacle and the scenery. The production of light and colour necessitates an accurate knowledge of chemistry. The fact is that there is not an art or science whose help or aid the stage does not require.

Wilson Barrett maintained that 'the higher, the finer, and purer the sentiment expressed and absorbed . . . the greater the rest, the strength, the vigour it gives to mind and body', but his emphasis – with reference to Shakespeare – on the visual ('to *see* his plays'), rather than the auditive, signalled that the play itself was not paramount, but was one element in the overall theatrical experience. Thus William Archer, who had hailed *Michael and his Lost Angel* as literature, described *The Sign of the Cross* as 'A Salvationist Pantomime': 'a combination of the penny dreadful and the Sunday-school picture book . . . My business is with the drama as a form of art, and art has nothing to say to this series of tawdry tableaux, with their crude appeal to the shallowest sentiments and lowest instincts of the mob' (1897, pp. 9–10).

Put simply, *The Sign of the Cross* – the title was Clement Scott's suggestion – tells of the assault by Marcus, Prefect of Rome, on the virtue of the Christian slave Mercia. The final scene is set in 'A dungeon under the amphitheatre' with 'the roars of hungry beasts' and 'the equally merciless howls of the blood thirsty populace' as the background to the Christian hymn-singing (Mayer, 1994, p. 181). Mercia enters 'with her arms crossed on her breast. A bright light falls on her' (p. 184); she is joined by Marcus, who offers her Nero's pardon 'on one condition . . . That thou dost renounce this false worship' (p. 185). In reply to Marcus's assertion 'There is no afterlife', Mercia replies (illustration 13):

MERCIA: Art thou so sure of that? Ask thyself, are there no inward monitors that, in thy more thoughtful moments, silently teach thee there is a life to come.
MARCUS: All men have wishes – for a life to come – if it could better this.
MERCIA: It will better this – if this life be well lived. Hast thou lived well? (p. 185)

These sentiments strike home to Marcus, who proclaims: 'The brute is dead in me – the man is living – thy purity, that I would have smirched, hath cleansed me – Live, Mercia, live (*kneels*) – and be my wife' (p. 185). Mercia confesses 'I have no shame in telling thee I love thee next to Him' and the play ends:

MARCUS: Return to Caesar – Tell him Chrystos has triumphed – Marcus, too, is a Christian – (*Drawing her closer to him*) Come, my bride –
MERCIA: My bridegroom –
MARCUS: Thus, hand in hand, we go to our bridal (*they ascend the steps*) – There is no death for us, for Chrystos hath triumphed over death. The light hath come. Come, my bride. Come – to the light beyond. (*Exit hand in hand, into the arena*) (*Curtain*) (p. 187)

William Archer wrote that 'A curious essay might be written on the theology of melodrama, with illustrations from recent productions [*The Silver King* and *Claudian*] at the Princess's Theatre' (1886, p. 87). The theology, if it could be dignified as such, of *The Sign of the Cross*, was based, not on 'salvation by sin', but on the defence of purity, and the resistance of temptation, reinforced by the reality of the afterlife. Wilson Barrett contrasted Pinero's Paula Tanqueray (in *The Second Mrs Tanqueray*) – 'the newest Magdalen' – with Mercia 'emblematic of Christianity . . . beautiful with a half-divine loveliness and an exquisite soul', who 'steadfast in her faith resists all temptation' (*Idler*, 1896, 264–6). Writing of *The Sign of the Cross*, G. W. Foote recalled a melodrama at the Britannia Theatre in

13. Wilson Barrett, *The Sign of the Cross*

the 1870s, with the villain's belated appeal to heaven in the last moments of the play. He might have invoked Revd Maturin's *Bertram*, about which Coleridge had written so contemptuously seventy years earlier, for Marcus's conversion belonged to the same order of contrived morality as Bertram's.

As Foote observed, Barrett's play was crudely painted in black and white: 'All the pagans are wicked people – tyrants, sycophants, intriguers, assassins, drunkards, thieves, and prostitutes. All the Christians are good people – pure, benevolent and merciful' (1896, p. 11). He contrasted the methods of 'proselytising and didactic plays' with 'the poet's method', the former being 'direct', the latter 'indirect . . . An organic whole, like one of Shakespeare's tragedies, suggests as life itself suggests, the lesson is borne in upon us unobtrusively yet irresistibly, like a lesson of our personal experience' (p. 10). Barrett's was the former method; Jones's the latter.

So unambiguous was the message of *The Sign of the Cross* that, the scanty costumes not withstanding, it gained almost universal approbation from all religious denominations. Historical though its setting was, the play was addressed to the society of its day. The conversation about divorce between Marcus and the patricians Glabrio and Philodemus in act 1 has a racy contemporaneity about it. The analogues between the decadent Roman Empire and Britain in the 1890s were spelt out; as David Mayer puts it 'An Empire that cannot accommodate Christianity will fail, collapsing in upon itself' (Mayer, 1992, p. 73).

Shaw, who in *Androcles and the Lion* (1912) was to break the stereotypes of toga-drama and elevate the genre to the status of literature, acknowledged: 'It [*The Sign of the Cross*] is a tremendous moral lesson' (1932, vol. II, p. 13). Harold Child instanced the case of his father who was vehemently opposed to the stage: 'He soon had reason to change that opinion. Moreover after he had come up to London to see *The Sign of the Cross*, he thought the stage might do some good in the world after all' (1939, p. 15). Far from denouncing the play, clergymen – such as Revd Sydney Fleming, Vicar of St James's, Croydon – positively urged their congregations to see it (Mayer, 1994, p. 109). G. W. Foote recorded:

When I saw the performance at the Lyric Theatre I was struck by the novel character of the audience, which might be called a congregation. It seemed to be the emptyings of the churches and chapels of London. Most of the people appeared to be unused to such surroundings. They walked as though they were advancing to pews, and took their seats with an air of reverential expectation. Clericals, too, were present in remarkable abundance. There were parsons to the right of me, parsons to the left of me, parsons in front of me. (1896, p. 8)

The *Illustrated Church News*, perplexed and censorious about Jones's *Michael and his Lost Angel*, had no difficulty with *The Sign of the Cross*, which it hailed as 'a modern miracle play':

Such a play must do great good . . . Mr Wilson Barrett has done a service to all who are engaged in Christian teaching or Church work, and the spirit of entire reverence in which he has written his play, and in which it is acted by himself and all concerned, removes it far from beyond the reach of cavil or prejudice. It is emphatically a play to be seen, and even those who do not ordinarily attend the theatre may well make an exception in favour of *The Sign of the Cross*. (10 January 1896)

G. W. Foote acknowledged Barrett's 'striking success from a popular and managerial point of view': 'By appealing to the sentimental and religious public, instead of to the more limited public with some dramatic taste and experience, he has drawn crowds to hear his fine if somewhat monotonous voice, and witness his statuesque posings in the scanty clothing of ancient Rome' (1896, p. 8).

Foote's distinction between 'the sentimental and religious public' and 'the more limited public with some dramatic taste and experience' crystallised the difference between the constituency for Henry Arthur Jones's plays and that for Wilson Barrett's. Both men shared the mission to break down 'the prison of Puritanism' and to treat religion as a dramatic subject, but their objectives and methods were fundamentally different. Jones's sphere was the play of ideas, aspiring to the status of literature and eschewing a 'precise moral'; Barrett's sphere was the spectacular melodrama, susceptible to only one interpretation. Barrett's theme was the resistance of temptation; Jones's the possibility of 'salvation by sin'. Barrett upheld the sanctity of marriage; Jones explored the consequences of adultery. Jones hoped that 'the greater public' would join 'the smaller section of cultivated playgoers'; Barrett appealed unabashedly and directly to 'the greater public'.

January 1896 was a high point in the relationship between Church and stage, but, though it marked a significant advance, it also revealed a fission. The hopes of Matthew Arnold and others that the theatre would provide a common culture for all sections of society were, in the respect of drama, faltering. Instead of helping to create a broad church the advent of the prisoners of Puritanism militated towards theatrical sectarianism. At this point the writing on the tablets which were to inform the theatre's evolution could be deciphered: one theatre for 'the smaller sections of cultivated playgoers' and another for 'the greater public'. But there was time yet for one man to transcend this division – not a dramatist, but an actor – Henry Irving.

CHAPTER 12

Henry Irving

BECKET: Into Thy hands, O Lord – into Thy hands!

Tennyson *Becket*

In his upbringing, his turn of mind, his personal appearance and bearing, his social habits, and the nature of his genius as an actor and the roles in which this found expression on the stage, Henry Irving was uniquely fitted to effect the summation of the reconciliation between the Church and the stage. Born John Henry Brodribb at Keinton Mandeville in Somerset on 6 February 1838, his parentage held out little promise of what the future had in store: 'Weighed against the balance of heredity, the child's chances of worldly success seemed small. On his father's side a long line of sturdy but unimaginative Somerset farmers, on his mother's side an obscure line of Cornishmen who never appear to have set the Fal on fire. Of material fortune there was none' (L. Irving, 1951, p. 31). Methodism was the ruling force in the family: regular attendance at chapel, visits from the minister Mr Southey, and 'The child's first consciousness was the sound of his mother's voice reading from the Bible' (p. 32). When John Henry Brodribb was four, even such material security as the family had possessed was under threat and, like many country people at the time, the Brodribbs turned to city life (initially Bristol) for their livelihood. Instead of taking their son with them, the Brodribbs entrusted him to his maternal aunt, Sarah Penberthy, who lived in the mining village of Halsetown above St Ives in Cornwall. There the principles of Methodism, teetotallism and daily Bible readings were strictly enforced, though lightened by Aunt Sarah's lively and tolerant humour. Aunt Sarah's 'cherished hope' for her nephew was 'of his entering the ministry' (p. 37), but aspects of the boy's behaviour caused her concern: his recitations of Shakespeare and the curious episode when he and his cousins 'Hideously disguised in masks, horns and tails . . . had appeared at the bedside of an old woman who had for too long persecuted the village children with threats of brimstone and hellfire' (p. 37). The minister, Mr Wallington, reassured Aunt Sarah of young Henry's Christian devotion: 'Her anxiety, however, was finally allayed when, shortly after his tenth birthday, the lad, during a service, fell into an ecstasy and professed his conversion, the sincerity of which the minister never for a moment doubted' (p. 37). Whether or not the manner of the ten-year-old's conversion owed anything to his incipient acting talent can only be a matter of speculation, but 'It seemed, indeed, as though her nephew was able to reconcile play-acting with piety' (p. 37). This reconciliation of play-acting and piety was to be an abiding theme of Henry Irving's life.

Following the death of Aunt Sarah's husband Isaac in 1848 John Henry joined his parents in London. He attended the City Commercial School where he excelled in the elocution class taught by Dr Pinches, the headmaster, and took full advantage of the opportunity for public recitation at the annual speech days, after one of which he was introduced to – and congratulated by – the actor William Creswick. Shortly afterwards John Henry wrung from his reluctant parents their hard consent to attend a theatre – Sadler's Wells, with Samuel Phelps as Hamlet: 'Only two years had passed since the boy had openly professed a spiritual conversion in the chapel at Halsetown. That night at Sadler's Wells, he inwardly underwent a second conversion, as intense and heartfelt as the first. He became confirmed in a faith, hitherto only vaguely understood, which he knew was his enduring inspiration' (p. 46). For John Henry Brodribb there was no incompatibility between his two conversions. He joined Henry Thomas's City Elocution Class, but also – perhaps less enthusiastically – accompanied his mother to the Albion Chapel, London Wall. His mother's religion was less accommodating: 'his strict Methodist mother cast him off when he went on the stage regarding it as a sinful occupation, and she had nothing further to do with him' (J. Richards, 1994, p. 19). Like many entrants to the stage from strict religious families, John Henry Brodribb adopted a stage name; his choice of Irving was not without significance: 'His stage name was adopted partly in honour of a celebrated preacher Edward Irving' (p. 17). The name of Irving certainly carried the association of Edward Irving's reputation as a preacher, but for Henry Irving it may have held an additional attraction. Following his tutelage of the future Jane Welsh Carlyle, a 'little scholar' imbued with 'a dramatic instinct' (Oliphant, 1864, p. 22), Edward Irving moved from Haddington to Kirkaldy. Revd Julian Young recounted:

I have been told that, somewhere about the year 1811, he [Edward Irving] acted in Ryder's Company in Kirkaldy, Fifeshire, and that he was at that time devoted to the stage, but the obliquity of his vision, the strangeness of his dialect, and the awkwardness of his gait exposed him to so much ridicule that he quitted the stage in disgust for the pulpit. (1871, p. 315)

The only manifestation of Edward Irving's leaning towards the stage recorded by Mrs Oliphant was requiring his class to read Milton and to learn 'large portions of *Paradise Lost* by heart' (1864, p. 32). One of his pupils inadvertently discovered the extent of her teacher's absorption in the poem:

It is said that one of his older pupils came on one occasion to this same Milton class before the arrival of her companions, and on reaching the door of the class-room, found Irving alone, reciting to himself one of the speeches of Satan, with so much emphasis and so gloomy a countenance, that the terrified girl, unable to conceal her fright, fled precipitately. (p. 32)

Obliquity of vision, strangeness of dialect and awkwardness of gait were physical characteristics which Henry Irving shared with his adopted namesake, as he did a fascination with the Satanic. Thus, for Henry Irving, the choice of his stage name may have extended beyond the popular association with preaching to a more powerful sense of identification and a determination to overcome his own physical disadvantages in the profession from which the preacher had been deterred.

Though in retrospect his first words as Gaston, Duke of Orleans, in Bulwer Lytton's *Richelieu* (at the New Royal Lyceum Theatre, Sunderland, on 29 September 1856) – 'Here's to our enterprise' – were imbued with prophecy, early success did not attend upon Henry Irving, actor. During the next twelve years of unrelenting toil in the provinces, the young actor's inner resolve and belief in the Nonconformist work ethic were put to the sternest test. Several years of unexceptional London engagements preceded the legendary first night of *The Bells*, under the Batemans, at the Lyceum on 25 November 1871, and a further seven passed before he took over the management, inaugurating his regime with *Hamlet* on 30 December 1878.

On 15 July 1869 Henry Irving married Florence Callaghan at St Marylebone parish church. She was the daughter of Surgeon General Callaghan, whose opposition to her marriage to an actor 'only served to add the charm of a clandestine romance to mutual attraction' (L. Irving, 1951, p. 143). Theirs was a textbook case of the hazards of an actor marrying outside the profession, especially into a higher social rank. Two sons,

Henry (Harry) Brodribb (5 August 1870) and Laurence Sidney (21 December 1871), were born, the latter not until after their parents' dramatic and irreconcilable separation on the first night of *The Bells*. Relations between Irving and his estranged wife remained bitter to the end, but, true to the mores of Victorian society, divorce was not considered. Irving lavished upon his sons – to invoke Lady Bracknell – 'every luxury that money could buy, including christening' and, as his fortunes prospered, education. Though Irving's motive was undoubtedly to give the boys the best possible start in life, it contained another element: the repudiation of his wife's insinuation of the social inferiority of the theatre. His sons' upbringing facilitated Irving's *entrée* into a social world into which members of his profession had hitherto rarely gained admission.

During his lengthy professional apprenticeship Henry Irving had ample opportunity to contemplate the nature of his calling and his contribution to it. In addition to his 'peculiarities of gait and speech', the impression created by Irving on Mrs Charles Calvert in Manchester in the early 1860s was of a thoughtful disposition: 'He had refined thoughts, lofty ideals, and he and his stage manager [Charles Calvert] were soon on friendly terms. They were kindred spirits . . . we would adjourn to the kitchen, where with our feet on the fender, we would discuss Shakespeare, dramatic art and poetry' (1911, pp. 61–2). Throughout his life Irving's private conversation often took a philosophical turn. H. Chance Newton recalled: 'he and I were wont to drift into talk about religion. We each knew the other had the deepest reverence for the theme of themes and an abiding sense of man's need for a vital faith to sustain him' (1927, p. 69). Irving would recall his aunt Sarah Penberthy: 'In many cases, however, the dear old soul didn't cause many round her to walk with God! She frightened us by her terrible "iron-bound" Calvinism; her awful theories as to its being necessary to be "Elect" to be saved, and all that kind of awful anti-Christian theology' (p. 70). His own creed was more tolerant:

Irving, indeed, was always very strongly in favour of the Larger Hope views of the *In Memoriam* of his old friend and sometime play-provider Tennyson. This view had, I found, been much deepened in Irving by his association with the wise and worthy, if not too-well-treated cleric, Dean Farrar, of whose noble book, *Eternal Hope*, Irving had ever the deepest and most sympathetic appreciation. (p. 69)

It was from his 'sometime play-provider Tennyson' that Irving received *Becket*, the play with which, above all others in his repertoire, he established the closest bond of personal identification. However, after he had prevailed on Bateman to stage *The Bells,* Irving exercised great influence over the Lyceum repertoire which reflected his abiding interest in the enactment of the spiritual on the stage, whether it be the saintly or the guilt-ridden. Peter Thomson has written: 'The literature of guilt had remained plentiful after the death of Byron and the dotage of Wordsworth and Coleridge, but it had lost its philosophical bite . . . When he performed in it, *The Bells* was as profound a study of the human conscience as *Lord Jim*' (1986, p. 100).

Typically for the period, *The Bells* was an adaptation – by an English solicitor, Leopold Lewis – of a French play, *Le Juif Polonais* by Emile Erkmann and Pierre Alexandre Chatrian. In the original play and in an earlier English version by F. C. Burnand, the guilt of the burgomaster Mathias for the murder of a Polish Jew fifteen years earlier is only gradually revealed and is not wholly certain until the final act. Lewis made one crucial alteration as David Mayer observes:

The Bells differs in the particular that the guilt of Mathias is explicit by the end of the first act. His crime is visibly recalled in the 'vision scene' which closes the act, and this difference between a suggestion of guilt and the certainty that the burgomaster is concealing his guilt is an element which reached into the unconscious fear of Victorian audiences. (Mayer, 1980, p. 4)

As David Mayer says '*The Bells* offered to theatre audiences the opportunity to share vicariously the experience of criminal action, guilt, fear of discovery, and eventual retribution' (p. 5), but in its enactment of the agonising and ultimately fatal effects of guilt – Mathias's convulsive death is brought about by his dream of his own trial and sentence to hang – it is also profoundly moral. Certainly Revd John Llewelyn Jones-Evans and his wife had no compunction about attending the Grand Theatre, Boscombe – he in 'his customary clerical evening attire' – and taking with them their seven-year-old son Eric, upon whom the vision scene, indeed the whole of Henry Irving's performance, left an enduring impression: 'And in the famous "dream scene" in which he re-enacted the murder of the Polish jew, the bestial blood-lust in his face and eyes, as he struck the fatal blow went far beyond acting and mere effect. At these moments Irving was a man possessed by a devil from the pit of hell' (p. 23).

That Irving's version of 'The Polish Jew' should focus on the effect of guilt rather than mere proof was a reflection of what fascinated him as an actor and as a man. A survey of Irving's repertoire at the Lyceum furnishes other explorations of the theme of guilt and remorse, for which *Eugene Aram* (19 April 1873), *Vanderdecken* (18 June 1878) and *Faust* (19

December 1885) may stand as examples. These plays were all written by W. G. Wills (with some input from Percy Fitzgerald on *Vanderdecken*), who, as the Lyceum house dramatist, tailored his work to fit Henry Irving. Wills was the son of an Anglican clergyman in Ireland and attended Trinity College, Dublin, before seeking his fortune in England.

The story of Eugene Aram, the schoolmaster driven to crime by poverty and later tormented by remorse, was already familiar in Thomas Hood's poem and Bulwer Lytton's novel, but Wills showed 'his wonted independence of fact. The murderer was in reality hanged, and the crime was without the extenuating circumstances with which his pen invested it' (Wills, 1898, p. 133). In Wills's version, Aram, having confessed his crime to his beloved Ruth, dies without the intervention of any outside agent, lying amongst the tombstones to the strains of faint music wafting from the nearby church. As with Mathias, for Irving the fascination of Aram lay in the effect of guilt on the criminal's mind. Clement Scott described Irving's performance:

It is not, perhaps, a play that will please the multitude. It is no *ad captandum* succession of surprises, situations and trick scenes. Eugene Aram is not tried for his life. We have no barristers and courts, and judges and docks. We have no 'forensic eloquence' with Mr So-and-So, in a wig and gown. We have no ghastly gibbet with Eugene Aram hanging in chains on Knaresborough Heath. There is little for the posters, but much, very much, for the imagination. We have here photographed the mind of Eugene Aram, the mind of a man who has murdered another fourteen years ago, the mind of a wretch who had hoped to live down conscience, the mind of a poor devil who is flung once more amongst the roses and love, and just as he is smelling the flower it falls to pieces in his hand. (1896, pp. 26–7)

Retribution does not depend upon the investigative efficiency of the forces of law and order or the administration of the judicial system, it comes from within and is inescapable. The fruitlessness of wrongdoing is underscored by the sense of irretrievable loss. *Eugene Aram* concludes: 'As Aram dies the music in the church peels out, and morning, which has been breaking, strikes out with level beams under the great yew-tree, and shreds a wan redness round the church, awakening the matin song' (Wills, 1898, p. 132).

The legend of 'The Flying Dutchman' had attracted writers from its first appearance in *Blackwood's Magazine* in May 1821: Edward Fitzball's Adelphi melodrama for T. P. Cooke (6 December 1826), Heine's poem and Wagner's opera. The story of the impious mariner destined to beat about the storm-tossed Cape of Good Hope until the day of judgement was proposed by Percy Fitzgerald 'and Mr. Irving was irresistibly attracted to the subject' (p. 134). Fitzgerald contributed the narrative construction to *The Flying Dutchman*, but Wills penned most of the dialogue including the whole of Irving's part of Vanderdecken. In the last scene Thelka, enamoured of Vanderdecken, is carried to the phantom ship and, awakened from her trance, learns the secret of her beloved's existence: he can only be released from his awful judgement by a woman's love:

> VANDERDECKEN: What is my doom?
>   Worse than Hell! Eternal loneliness!
>   Eternal silence! and in that awful silence
>   The worm of memory gnawing at my heart,
>   Anguish of thought within my brain, sleepless, intense,
>   Just hope enough to keep despair awake! . . .
>   Then the old frenzy rises in my brain,
>   Wild curses to my lips, and in the thunder
>   Sounds that do curse again shriek out -
>   'Sail on! Sail on!' until the Judgement Day,
>   'Unless that woman come!'

Thelka throws in her lot with Vanderdecken 'and on the night-air comes the whisper, "Pardon"' -

> The wind a melody
> Is laden with the murmur of God's pity.   (pp. 139-41)

The concept of hell as 'Eternal loneliness!/Eternal silence!' reflected trends in religious thought away from hell-fire, and the concluding whisper of 'Pardon' postulated a God of pity and forgiveness for the wrongdoer.

With *Faust* Wills and Irving were following in the footsteps of Marlowe, Goethe and, more recently, Gounod. In New York on 15 March 1888 Irving addressed the prestigious Goethe Society on 'Goethe and the theatre', having already published an account of his Mephistopheles: 'He is not the Satan of Milton, but a "waggish knave". He represents not the grandeur of revolt against the light, but everything that is gross, mean and contemptible. He delights not in great enterprises, but in perpetual mischief. Sneering, prying, impish, he is the heartless sceptic of modern civilization, not the demon of medieval superstition' (J. Richards, 1994, p. 126).

For Henry James the waggishness of Irving's Mephistopheles was excessive: 'He strikes us, however, as superficial – a terrible fault for an archfiend – and his grotesqueness strikes us as cheap' (Wade, 1957, p. 222). James was unimpressed by the great spectacle of the Brocken, a visual realisation of Goethe's Walpurgis Night scene: 'We attach also but the slenderest importance to the scene of the Witches' Sabbath, which has been reduced to a mere bald hubbub of capering, screeching, and banging, irradiated by the irrepressible blue fire, and without the smallest articulation of Goethe's text. The scenic effect is the ugliest we have ever contemplated' (p. 222). However, as Michael Booth has demonstrated, James was not typical and 'the Brocken Scene set audiences absolutely agog' (illustration 14):

Mephistopheles summoned his spirits once more, and the mad dancing briefly resumed. Thunder rolled again; the red glasses of twenty-five limelights shining through the background and upon openings in the rocks from which steam rose conveyed the impression that earth and sky were aflame. The rocks became molten and a rain of fire fell from the sky, scattered from bridges high over the stage by men with baskets of gold tinsel. At this sign of the supreme power of hell the weird host of revellers fell to their knees and raised their arms to their great leader, who stood alone on the summit in Miltonic majesty, his right hand flung aloft, outlined in relief against the background of fire. Thus ended a scene, which, in its combination of spectacle, mass force and power, grandeur, and nightmare, many reviewers said had never been equalled on the stage.
The Brocken scene was one of the great spectacles of nineteenth-century theatre, and probably the most extraordinary scene of its kind ever performed on the English stage. (1981, p. 120)

If Henry Irving was ever visited by recollections of childhood nightmares of hell-fire induced by Aunt Sarah's '"iron-bound" Calvinism' he purged them in his spectacular Brocken scene in *Faust*, as perhaps he had been trying to do when, 'Hideously disguised in masks, horns and tails', he and his cousins had appeared at the bedside of the old woman of Halsetown who had 'too long persecuted the village children with threats of brimstone and hellfire'. Irving's own creed had moved on to 'the Larger Hope views' of Tennyson's *In Memoriam* and Farrar's *Eternal Hope* and this was the note on which his *Faust* ended:

> FAUST: I promise, Margaret, but thou shalt not die.
> Upon my knees I beg of thee to come:
> Thy prison doors are open: let us fly.
> MARGARET: Ah! I feel death, like a delivering angel
> Sent straight from God, descending on my heart;
> Perchance, in mercy, I might die tonight.
> Nay let us kneel and pray that God may strike
> The chains of sin from our despairing souls.
> Because of our great love and all my sorrow,
> He may have pity, and may save us both.

14. Lyceum Theatre, *Faust*

Mephistopheles enters:
>   What is this mad delay? My horses stand
>   In the chill morning air; force her away.

Margaret flies to the foot of the cross, and clings to it for shelter; the fiend plucks
Faust away with the cry, 'Hither to me!' and the curtain falls on
Margaret lying dead, and a flight of shining angels come to her succour.

(Wills, 1898, p. 212)

As Michael Booth writes: 'With this tableau the play ended, a beautiful morality painting of the frustration of evil and the salvation of good' (1981, p. 123).

Byron's *Werner*, Colman's *The Iron Chest* and *Macbeth* could profitably be added to Mathias, Eugene Aram, Vanderdecken and Mephistopheles as examples of Irving's capacity to capture weird and haunted existences on stage. This sample of Irving's repertoire shows that 'the literature of guilt', for which Coleridge and Byron were the fountainhead, was given new life in theatrical terms by Irving. Peter Thomson describes Irving as Heathcliff in a dramatisation of *Wuthering Heights* as 'an appealing thought'. No less appealing is the prospect of Irving as the Ancient Mariner or as Cain, if Coleridge's prose-poem had reached completion in dramatic form. To Irving was granted the ineffable capacity to realise both the irredeemable earthly despair of remorse and the unquenchable comfort of the 'Larger Hope' in the after-life.

The polarities of good and evil, innocence and guilt featured in diptych roles in which Irving doubled brothers of contrasting personalities: Dubosc and Lesurges in *The Lyons Mail* and Fabien and Louis dei Franchi in *The Corsican Brothers*. As Dr Primrose in *Olivia*, W. G. Wills's adaptation of Goldsmith's *The Vicar of Wakefield* (27 May 1885), Irving embodied an essentially benign character, but even here he seized on the cleric's sense of guilt that he had allowed his love for his daughter to dominate over his love for God: '"She came between me and my love for God; I am punished for it at last." This is the one strong point on which Mr Irving evidently leans. It is the resignation to the Divine will, shown all through, that gives such beauty and interest to Mr Irving's fine study of paternal affection' (Scott, 1896, p. 281).

As Richelieu, Wolsey and Becket, personal considerations were intertwined with the politics of Church and state. Irving's physique and bearing were generally reckoned to be well suited to the embodiment of eminences of the Church. Joseph Harker considered that 'he would have made a most imposing archbishop' (1924, p. 129); William Archer wrote that 'His cast of countenance, his expression, his manner, are all prelatical in the highest degree. Nature designed him for a Prince of the Church' (1894, p. 49); and Mrs Aria said 'He looked like all the best bishops ought to look' (1922, p. 89). To many, Irving bore a striking resemblance to Cardinal Manning (L. Irving, 1951, p. 543). Augustin Filon considered that there was 'only one other man who could have represented Becket nearly as well [as Irving], and that was Cardinal Manning' (1897, p. 188).

Irving's Richelieu did not eclipse memories of Macready and Phelps in the role. The preparation for the production of *Henry VIII* (5 January 1892) was immense and Joseph Harker regarded it as Irving's most spectacular production: 'What a picturesque Wolsey he made! Rome was scoured for the silk for the cardinal's robes, which were a glorious red, and cost, I was credibly informed, some hundreds of pounds' (1924, p. 89). Clement Scott described the effect:

The first splendid effect is made with the entrance of Cardinal Wolsey, then in the fulness of his power, his wealth, and dignity. The silver trumpets sound, and amidst monks, retainers, servitors, choristers, and retinue, under a gorgeous baldaquin, the haughty Cardinal appears. Never before in our memory has Mr Irving made so wonderful a picture. He is swathed from head to foot in what is miscalled the cardinal's scarlet. It is not scarlet at all, but an indescribable geranium-pink, with a dash of vermilion in it. The biretta on his head is of the same blush-rose colour, and it hides every inch of hair, bringing into relief the pale, refined, and highly intellectual face. (1896, p. 338)

Irving made Wolsey 'the most refined and delicate-minded man at Court' and in his hands Wolsey's farewell to all his greatness 'is not so much the regret of a strong and ambitious man baffled, but that of a keenly sensitive man disappointed in his friend' (p. 340).

The progress of Tennyson's *Becket* to the stage was indeed lengthy, stretching from 1879 to its first night on 6 February 1893. The piece was published in 1884 and, though Tennyson had not written it for the stage, he and Irving shared the conviction that 'there was a play in it' (Stoker, 1906, vol. 1, p. 209). Irving persevered, taking *Becket* with him on his American tours of 1884–5 and 1887–8, but he could still not 'unearth it' (p. 211). In the spring of 1890 Irving and Bram Stoker visited the poet and conversation turned on Tennyson's poetry and his views of eternity. As befitted a long-time friend of F. D. Maurice, Tennyson said: 'You know I don't believe in an eternal hell, with an All-merciful God. I believe in the All-merciful God! It would be better otherwise that men should believe they are only ephemera' (p. 219).

After that meeting Irving began to work on *Becket* again. Stoker visited

Tennyson at Farringford on the Isle of Wight in September 1892 and broached some changes to which the poet replied: 'Irving may do whatever he pleases with it' (p. 225). Eleven days after Stoker's visit, Tennyson was dead; he was buried in Poets' Corner, Westminster Abbey, on 12 October. *Becket* reached the Lyceum stage on 6 February 1893, Irving's fifty-fifth birthday; Irving subsequently played it 318 times. The acting version of *Becket*, which inevitably shed much of Tennyson's original, was shaped by Irving's sense of theatrical practicability and dramatic effectiveness. He lavished upon the production the scenic talents of W. Telbin, Hawes Craven and Joseph Harker, the music of the composer favoured by Tennyson – Villiers Stanford – and the acting strength of his company with William Terriss as Henry II, Genevieve Ward as Eleanor of Aquitaine and Ellen Terry as Rosamund de Clifford. Irving's own performance as Becket (illustration 15) silenced even his most persistent critics. He transcended the peculiarities of his elocution: 'Every line, every sentence, every syllable, falls with rhythmical measure on the delighted ear' (Scott, 1896, p. 356). Becket's progress from statesman to saint was marked by a sublime serenity – 'half divine with the sense of coming martyrdom' – beneath which lay the fire and resolve of a man convinced of the rightness of his cause. In the final scene the 'old martial spirit' flashed forth when Becket dispatched Fitzurse headlong (*Era* 11 February 1893). Augustin Filon described the climax thus:

Those who saw Irving, mitred and crozier in hand, totter under the blow, and fall upon the altar steps, whilst the chanting of the monks came in gusts from the church above – mingled with the cries of the people beating against the door, and the rumbling of the thunder shaking the great edifice to its foundations – experienced one of the strongest emotions any spectacle ever gave. (1897, pp. 188–9)

To Irving, *Becket* was more than a play, as Laurence Irving wrote:

Never having forgotten the stern religious precepts of Aunt Penberthy, having striven all his life to wring from the Church a benediction on his art, he persuaded himself that in the performance of Becket, spanning the gulf between Church and Stage, he and his audience united in an act of worship. Irving was a simple man; he could have arrived at this make-believe state of grace in all sincerity, without being subjected for one moment of unctuous humbug. (1951, p. 560)

For Irving to span the divide between Church and stage was both a personal and a professional need. Personally he needed to synthesize his vocation with his religious convictions; professionally he regarded the Church's approval as essential to the respectability which he craved for

15. Henry Irving as Becket

the theatre. The royal command to perform *Becket* in the Waterloo Chamber at Windsor Castle in March betokened the approval not only of his sovereign, but also of the head of the Established Church. In addition to members of the royal family (the Queen, the Prince of Wales, the Empress Frederick of Germany) the audience included the Dean of Windsor, Revd Canon Dalton, Revd Canon Gee, the headmaster of Eton and Hallam Tennyson (*Era* 25 March 1893).

Becket also provided the *entrée* to the hallowed precincts of the Chapter House of Canterbury Cathedral. There, at the invitation of the Dean, Revd F. W. Farrar, Irving gave a reading of *Becket* in aid of the cathedral restoration fund, in May 1897. Amongst the 600 present were Church and civic dignitaries, visiting Americans, Irving's two sons, Henry Arthur Jones and, despite her disapproval of the occasion (L. Irving, 1951, p. 608), Ellen Terry and her daughter Edy Craig. Dean Farrar prefaced the reading with a short speech:

he [Sir Henry Irving] has throughout all his life endeavoured to purify the stage and to make it what it has been in past ages and other nations, what it may be and now constantly is among us, not only a source of pleasure and amusement, but a stimulus to the imagination and an element of thoughtful teaching, brought more vividly home to the mind through the medium of the eyes. We shall now have the high pleasure of hearing our foremost living actor interpret for us the drama of the late Laureate, the foremost poet of our age. (*Daily News* 1 June 1897)

Sir Henry Irving advanced to the small temporary platform, upon which was placed a pedestal covered with purple cloth, and proceeded to give his reading from a large quarto manuscript volume. Irving's text that day represented a further condensation of Tennyson's play amounting to a selection of the more important scenes. As in the theatre, Irving

was perhaps at his best in the scenes in the last act, bringing into strong relief all the terror and pathos of the Archbishop's end, and winding up with a magnificent outburst of defiance of his assassins until strength fails and the Archbishop sinks to his death. A notable circumstance, during the recital of these passages which held the assembly in breathless silence, was the muffled sound of the distant organ in the choir of the Cathedral. It was merely an ordinary incident of the afternoon service, but it seemed to have a peculiar fitness to the great tragedy described in the poet's dialogue. (*Daily News* 1 June 1897)

Earlier Irving had 'melted his audience to tears in the scenes in which Rosamund is engaged' (*Daily Telegraph* 1 June 1897). That observer was put in mind of his visit to the Oberammergau Passion Play, as Farrar himself may have been. Farrar had been appointed Dean of

Canterbury, on the Earl of Rosebery's recommendation, two years earlier. Then aged sixty-four Farrar had waited long for a senior appointment, as F. C. Burnand observed:

Farrar represented the 'Broad Church', and on more than one occasion his views were found to be somewhat broader than those of the Church to which he belonged. But nothing came of it. He was passed over whenever there was a bishopric vacant, for not even the great friendliness shown him by Queen Victoria could put a mitre on the head of a clergyman whose orthodoxy had been questionable. So he had been made Dean of Canterbury. (1904, vol. II, p. 206)

Farrar's delayed promotion may have been due not only to his liberal theology, but also to his flamboyant preaching style, which put both Burnand and Clement Scott in mind of Revd J. C. M. Bellew. Scott recalled listening to Farrar's sermons when he was a pupil at Marlborough College:

His [Bellew's] sermons were even more ornate than those of Dean Farrar, at the time that he, as a very young man, used to delight us boys, sitting under him in the chapel at Marlborough, long before he was headmaster, in the days when he had just come, full of honours and prize poems, from Cambridge, and always joined in our games of football and cricket. (1899, vol. I, p. 401)

Farrar drew on his experience as a master at Marlborough College and Harrow School, as well as his own schooldays at King William's School, Isle of Man, for his enormously successful and edifying story of school life *Eric, or Little by Little* (1858). After King William's, Farrar had attended King's College, London, where he came under the influence of F. D. Maurice and, through him, of Coleridge: 'it was from his [Maurice's] books that he [Farrar] learnt the germ of those convictions to which he gave utterance in his sermon on "Eternal Hope"' (R. Farrar, 1904, p. 26). At Cambridge (Trinity College), Farrar was a member of the Apostles and on graduating (in 1854) he was recruited by Revd G. E. L. Cotton who was in the process of reviving the fortunes of Marlborough College. He stayed there only a year before moving to Harrow School, of which Revd C. J. Vaughan was then headmaster. Whilst at Harrow, Farrar edited *Essays on a Liberal Education* (1867), to which Lord Houghton was a contributor. Farrar returned to Marlborough College as Master (headmaster) in 1871, leaving to become a canon of Westminster Abbey and Rector of St Margaret's, Westminster, in 1876; he was appointed Archdeacon of Westminster in 1883.

Farrar's sermons were an immense attraction. T. H. S. Escott described him as 'the most extensively admired of pulpit declaimers. His eloquence is inexhaustible and ornate. He deluges his congregation with magnificent words and splendid images. But his is the genius rather of the popular journalist than of the traditional school of Anglican preachers' (1885, pp. 165–6). As a preacher Farrar was noted for his 'prodigality in the use of quotations' (R. Farrar, 1904, p. 256). In one sermon at Great St Mary's, Cambridge, he was reckoned to have 'used altogether upward of eighty different quotations' (p. 257). In the range of his references, Farrar recalled Mallock's Dr Jenkinson and, like him, he did preach in theatres: at the Royal Victoria Coffee Hall in the mid 1880s (p. 280). Farrar's tour of the United States and Canada in 1885 was as triumphant a progress as Henry Irving's in those countries. For his lecture on the 'Educational value of philosophy' to Johns Hopkins University, the Baltimore Academy of Music had to be hired and 'about 3000 people filled stalls, pit, boxes and gallery to the roof' (p. 299). For his American admirers visiting England, attendance at a Farrar sermon was an essential part of their itinerary.

Farrar's most famous and controversial sermons were the series of five on 'Eternal Hope' delivered in Westminster Abbey in October and November 1877 and subsequently published (1878), running into numerous editions. These sermons were prompted in part at least by a series of articles by W. H. Mallock on the theme 'Is life worth living?', which Farrar took as one of his titles. In the 'Eternal Hope' sermons Farrar was taking up the baton from F. D. Maurice. In the first sermon, 'What heaven is', Farrar concluded 'Heaven means holiness; "Heaven means principle", Heaven means to be one with God' (1892, p. 25). In his third sermon, '"Hell" What it is not', Farrar said 'What the popular notion of hell is, you my brethren are all aware. Many of us were scared with it, horrified with it, perhaps almost maddened by it in our childhood . . . never-ending agony, physical tortures' (p. 55). These were experiences with which Henry Irving could identify, as he could with the quotations from Dante, Shakespeare, Milton and Coleridge with which Farrar laced his sermon. In his fifth sermon, 'Earthly and future consequences of sin', Farrar addressed the problem of morality without the strictures of hell-fire: 'The virtue which has no better basis than fear of Hell is no virtue at all' (p. 120). He warned against 'willing sin' (p. 131) committed by those who 'on the grounds of a possible hope beyond the grave try to make light of sin' (p. 130). Farrar trod, perhaps not entirely convincingly, a tight-rope: 'The punishment of sin is certain' (p. 134); 'The path to repentance may never be closed to us' (p. 153). Amongst the consequences of sin Farrar cited '*Fear*', as an example 'not of the physical, but of the moral workings of the law of punishment' (p. 143):

Take *Fear*, for instance. You have heard of haunted houses: have you ever heard of haunted men? Are there any here who are groaning under the burden of undetected sin? If so will they not recognise themselves as suffering this Nemesis of fear? As there are some men whose sins are open, going before to judgment – marshalling them in undisguised array to the very judgment-seat – so there are some men whose sins follow after. There are men everywhere – there are probably men here now – who ever, as they walk through life, hear footsteps behind them; for whom 'the earth is made of glass,' – on whom the stars seem to look down as spies; men whose pulses shake at every sudden ring of the door-bell – whose faces blanch if they be suddenly accosted – who tremble if a steady gaze be fixed upon them. Have not such men, – abject in the dismay and weakness to which sin has reduced them – thousands of times betrayed themselves by their own unreasonable fears, and by imagining that *their* sin was being spoken of, when something quite different was being spoken of? (pp. 144–5)

Farrar seems to be on the point of extending his 'prodigality in the use of quotations' to *The Bells*; the manifestations of fear which he describes were specifically evidenced in Henry Irving's Mathias: the shaking pulse ('at every sudden ring of the door-bell'), the blanched face, and the constant risk of self-betrayal.

It may have been because of Farrar that Henry Irving chose Marlborough College, to the Governing Council of which Farrar was appointed in 1876, for his sons' education. Given his professional and social status, Irving was almost bound to send his sons to one of the leading public schools which had either expanded or been established to cater for the demand for such education amongst the burgeoning middle class. Founded in 1843, 'The main aim, then, which the founders of Marlborough had in view was a first-class education at a low price for the sons of clergymen' (Bradley, Champneys and Baines, 1893, p. 54). In the College's charter, dated 21 August 1845, the Archbishop of Canterbury was designated as visitor and the Bishop of Salisbury as chairman of the Council consisting of twelve clergymen and thirteen laymen. Initially the sons of laymen were not to exceed one third of the roll and they were charged higher fees, though these were abolished in 1871. When the Irving boys entered Marlborough in September 1882, twenty-four of the intake of seventy boys were sons of clergymen (*Marlborough College Register*, 1910, pp. 423–8), though only seven, two of them not clergymen's sons, went on to take holy orders. If a conventional religious upbringing had been the extent of Henry Irving's aspirations for his sons, any public school would have served his purpose. His choice of Marlborough suggests a positive preference for forging clerical connections. If this was so, he succeeded. Shortly after arriving at Marlborough, Harry Irving wrote to his mother: 'I am getting now into the ways of the school. There is a fellow named Tate [*sic*] who is a relation of the Archbishop . . . he is my best friend and we often buy grub and go up to the forest together' (L. Irving, 1967, p. 119).

Harry Irving wrote of E. F. Benson, later the author of the Mapp and Lucia novels: 'He is a prefect, intensely amusing, fond of acting and the Old Bailey, and recommends himself to me' (p. 125). E. F. Benson's father, Revd Edward White Benson, had been appointed by Gladstone to succeed Tait as Archbishop of Canterbury in 1881. The two boys consolidated their friendship with the result that young Irving often spent the first day of the school holidays lunching at Lambeth Palace. In 1885 Frank Marshall, in an article on 'The stage and its detractors', wrote 'What the Archbishop of Canterbury's opinions are upon the stage we do not know' (*Theatre* 1 November 1885). In the summer of 1889 Archbishop Benson and Henry Irving were fellow guests of Joseph Sebag Montefiore at Eastcliff near Ramsgate. The prelate showed his awareness of and interest in one aspect of the theatre: 'I had a long and animated controversy with Irving and Leighton as to the theatrical children, in which we went over the whole ground' (A. C. Benson, 1899, vol. II, p. 274). A less controversial subject would have been Cornwall – Benson had been appointed the first Bishop of Truro in 1877, and during his episcopate had expended boundless zeal to transform the parish church into a cathedral. Benson described Irving's face as 'striking – it suggests Hamlet of itself', adding laconically 'God guide us in this strange world' (p. 274).

In 1886 a new chapel was consecrated and opened at Marlborough College by the Bishop of Salisbury, Revd John Wordsworth, another episcopal scion of the poet's family. Irving had 'subscribed handsomely' (L. Irving, 1967, p. 129) towards the building and took his dearest friend J. L. Toole, Laurence Irving's godfather, to view the results. However it was not the chapel, but the Bradleian Hall which provided the principal forum for the Irving boys. The Bradleian Hall had been opened during Farrar's headmastership – in commemoration of his predecessor Revd G. G. Bradley, who succeeded Stanley as Dean of Westminster in 1881; it 'directly led to the institution of "Penny Readings", – entertainments got up and conducted by the boys themselves' (Bradley, Champneys and Baines, 1893, p. 203). H. B. Irving's contributions to these Readings were acclaimed by his school fellows, who were no doubt primed by his father's reputation to hail his acting ability:

Next came H. B. Irving's recitation 'Sheltered'. Irving recited this melodramatic piece with great feeling. His dramatic genius called into life-like being, the murderer Anderson, as he lay crouching on the cottage floor bespattered with mire from his pursuers. The audience was spell-bound, the encore was vociferous, and Irving in response gave a reading from Artemus Ward, 'Charles F. Brown's Agricultural Experiences', in which he brought out every point, making each more pointed with his humorous intonation. (*Marlburian* 2 December 1886)

On 2 July 1887, in a programme arranged by E. F. Benson, H. B. Irving followed in his father's footsteps by reciting Hood's 'Dream of Eugene Aram', 'in his best form and he gave his recitation with immense dramatic force and thrilling effect' (*Marlburian* 25 July 1887). On 19 November 1887 H. B. Irving 'gave one of the Ingoldsby Legends, in which his versatile and dramatic powers appeared to great advantage', following this later in the evening with two scenes between Brutus and Cassius from *Julius Caesar*, with his younger brother Laurence: 'His [H. B. Irving's] representation of Brutus was very carefully studied. The younger Irving, though a rising light, is not as good as his brother: his delivery is too fast, and by no means distinct' (*Marlburian* 30 November 1887).

Though Harry Irving 'enjoyed a . . . well-delivered sermon' (L. Irving, 1967, p. 130), regular chapel attendance and association with parsons' sons did nothing to diminish his inclination towards religious scepticism:

When the time came to submit himself to the routine preparation for confirmation, he managed to conceal from his pastor his disbelief in most of the avowals he was called upon to make. Inwardly he resisted any attempt to instil in him fear of eternal punishment or hope of apparently uncongenial consolations after death. In due course, however, he knelt before the visiting Bishop and later made his first communion, with sceptical resignation. (p. 131)

When Harry Irving went up to New College, Oxford, where his tutor W. L. Courtney was a friend of his father, he was more conspicuous in the ranks of OUDS than in the college chapel. He was hauled before the college dean, Dr Spooner, who cautioned him: 'You seem, Mr Irving, to be very regular, very persistent, in your absence from chapel' to which Irving replied: 'Believe me, I've never been regular, never been persistent in my life.' Irving's fellow-culprit, later Canon Meyrick of Norwich, recalled Irving's delivery of these words: 'It was all so natural that it disarmed criticism. In anyone else's mouth, the reply would have been sheer insolence' (Brereton, 1922, p. 20). Dr Spooner was not equipped to detect the actor's art in Irving's insouciance; he had attended the theatre only once – to see Pepper's Performing Horses (L. Irving, 1967, p. 146).

As with his confirmation, Harry Irving deferred to the formalities of the Church for his marriage to the devout Dorothea Baird at St Pancras Church on 20 July 1896. Ben Greet read the lesson resoundingly, but the address by William Hulton of St John's College, Oxford, was 'perfectly attuned to the sentiments of that heterodox assembly' (p. 275) with its references to *As You Like It*, *Cymbeline*, *The Tempest* and George Herbert. Harry Irving's personal agnosticism was reinforced by his resentment towards the attitude of some clergy to the theatre. In his address to the OP Club in April 1901 on 'The art and status of the actor' H. B. Irving spoke of:

Those reckless and uncharitable charges levelled against men and women of the dramatic profession by unblushing Pharisees who would hold up their hands in horror if you asked them to enter a theatre, but who yet continue to unsparingly denounce the sins and follies of actors and actresses. These teachers and preachers who, I am sorry to say, number among them more than one religious minister of respectable eminence, seem to forget, in their fervid zeal, that there is no sin more ugly and unchristian than want of charity, no proceeding more dishonest than to accuse without investigation and to judge without audience. (1906, p. 80)

When H. B. Irving accepted an invitation to preach at St Martin-in-the-Fields he chose as his subject 'The amusement of the people' and launched a fierce attack on the Church: 'When one thinks of all the harm that has been done on this world in the name of religion by kings, and princes and statesmen, really of all human employment, the theatre seems to be the most innocent, the least susceptible of mischief and perversion' (Aria, 1922, p. 150).

As Mrs Aria observed: 'No prelate, however enlightened, could perhaps be expected to be quite pleased' (p. 150). Harry Irving's attitude to religion and the Church stands as a monument to the vanity of parental wishes. His father's abiding goal in life had been to effect the reconciliation between Church and stage, but his sons' education, calculated to further this process, had, in Harry's case at least, produced diametrically opposite results. Happily for Henry Irving his son's strident dissent could not undo the reconciliation between Church and stage to which he had so assiduously devoted himself. The earnestness with which Henry Irving campaigned on behalf of his profession is vouchsafed by the essays, addresses and lectures collected by Jeffrey Richards

(1994). An early speech indicative of Henry Irving's zeal was that to the Church of England Temperance Society at Shoreditch Town Hall on 31 March 1876, subsequently published in *All the Year Round* (22 April 1876). Irving entitled his talk simply 'Amusements', but in it he argued forcibly for the social and moral value of the theatre, not least as a corrective to the Church's waning power. He drew attention to 'how little the masses of our great towns are under the active influence of religion; to what poor extent they are educated; how limited is their reading, and, comparatively how much they frequent the galleries and pits of minor theatres' (Richards, 1994, p. 162). He asked 'what influences are really operative in raising the masses from the low levels of sordid occupations, and the lower deep of debasing pleasures?' The home was 'too often a scene of dirt and fretfulness'; religion 'for the millions it means nothing, or it means narrowness'; poetry 'is simply not read': 'It is from the theatre, from the Legitimate theatre – from English tragedy, comedy, and drama – that the commonality of all classes derive, more than from any other source, the food and stimulants which the higher nature requires' (p. 163).

Having established the centrality of the theatre for the population at large, Irving analysed the nature of its morality along the lines of Matthew Arnold and H. A. Jones. The stage 'must not be homiletic or didactic'. Evil was part of human existence and as such a proper subject for literature and drama:

If there be any who are for veiling from human sight all the developments of evil, they indeed must turn from the theatre-door, and must desire to see the footlights put out. But they must also close Shakespeare, avoid Fielding, Dickens, Thackeray, George Eliot; pronounce Kingsley immoral; and, so far as I can understand, read indeed but parts of the Bible. It is not by hiding evil, but by showing it to us alongside of good, that human character is trained and perfected. (p. 164)

Irving acknowledged that many theatres fell short of the ideal, but shared Arnold's vision of the theatre as a means of achieving social cohesiveness: 'What we want is an entertainment which the middle classes and the lower classes can enjoy together, and happily the dramas most in credit amongst us precisely answer that description' (p. 165). Irving diverged from Jones and Arnold in their emphasis on literature, to him 'every kind of managerial enterprise, spectacular or otherwise' (p. 165) offered opportunities for the attainment of the theatre's highest potential.

Mindful of his audience, Irving drew a distinction between the theatre and drink: 'The worst performances presented in our theatre cannot be so evil as the spending of a corresponding period of time in a gin palace or a pot-house' (p. 165). He offered his 'cordial contribution' to the cause of temperance and in return asked his auditors to use 'their influence for the purification, rather than the suppression or tabooing of the stage' (p. 165). In the Nonconformist creed, drink and the theatre were perceived as twin evils: 'In England attendance at a theatre – I know this well, for I was brought up in Cornwall – is too commonly regarded as a profession of irreligion' (p. 165). He offered the prospect of 'the happiest encouragements to individual and domestic virtues' (p. 166).

Irving's commitment to popular education was reflected in his acceptance of the presidency of the Perry Barr Institute and in the address which he gave there on 6 March 1878. He spoke of the advantages of the stage not only for the intellectual few, but also for 'the unimaginative many of all ranks', who 'even if they read works of poetic and dramatic fancy, which they rarely do, . . . would miss' passion, poetry and refinement 'on the printed page' (pp. 170–1). Like H. A. Jones, Irving pointed to the stage as a means of extending the experience of its audiences: 'the theatre is the only channel . . . through which are ever brought the great sympathies of the world of thought beyond their immediate ken' (p. 171). Resoundingly Irving proclaimed his enthusiastic theory of stage morality: 'A sort of decency sets in upon the coarsest person even in entering the roughest theatre. I have sometimes thought that, considering the liability to descent and the facility of descent, a special Providence watches over the minds and tone of our English stage' (p. 174).

The publication in 1888 of George Moore's 'Mummer Worship' incensed Irving to indignant ripostes in Edinburgh and Manchester in October 1888. Though in 1883 he had declined Gladstone's offer of a knighthood, in which Lord Coleridge had been the prime mover, Irving acquitted himself with the sense of duty befitting the leader of a worthy profession. Some of his speaking engagements were prestigious (the universities of Oxford, Cambridge where he was awarded an honorary degree in 1898, and Harvard), but others were modest – there was little kudos to be gained from addressing the Walsall Literary Institute, as did on 26 September 1894, or even from opening the Dulwich library, on ground given by Alleyn's foundation of Dulwich College, on 24 October 1896.

The audience depicted in Alfred Bryan's drawing of the Lyceum auditorium (*World* 12 December 1878, reproduced in A. E. Wilson, 1952, p. 201) represented the cream of Victorian society: the Prince and

Princess of Wales, Benjamin Disraeli who had voiced his support for the theatre in the House of Commons back in 1839, Gladstone and Cardinal Manning. Gladstone's conversion to the theatre has been remarked upon already; Manning's presence at the Lyceum amounted to nothing less than a *volte-face*. His hostility to the theatre had continued unabated after his conversion to Rome and in 1885 Frank Marshall still identified him as one of the theatre's most intransigent detractors:

We now come to Cardinal Manning . . . His enmity to the stage, as is popularly believed, almost amounts to fanaticism. It is no secret that he would gladly, if he could, put an end to those dramatic performances at Roman Catholic public schools, which have given so much innocent pleasure, and have encouraged so much study of Shakespeare and the higher class of dramas among the pupils of those schools. (*Theatre* 1 November 1885)

If, as Irving suggested, providence was watching over the English stage, he was its greatest bounty. If 'Every good gift and every perfect gift is from above, and cometh down from the Father of lights' (Chenevix Trench in his tercentary sermon (fo. 101), citing James 1.17), then Irving had been propitiously endowed, but he had also put those gifts to fruitful employment. Coleridge allowed the quality of genius to acting as an art and to David Garrick as its practitioner. The goal of being both popular and profound is as legitimate for the actor as it is for the poet, the painter, the musician and the dramatist. As Shaw frequently pointed out, the contemporary plays in which Irving appeared were not works of literary distinction, but his performances elevated pedestrian plays to the level of great theatre and in his exploration and portrayal of guilt and remorse he achieved insights into human nature as profound as those in other more durable arts. His was, in Coleridge's words, 'an insight into human nature at its fountainhead, which exists in those creations of Genius alone'. Early in the century Coleridge had written: 'We may then hope for a second Garrick or of an approach to a Shakespeare where we find the knowledge of Man united to an equal knowledge of Men, and both co-existing with the power of giving Life and Individuality to the products of both' (Ashe, 1888, pp. 337–8). In Shaw, Wilde, Pinero and Jones the late nineteenth century got nearer to 'an approach to a Shakespeare' than had been achieved for a century or more, but in Henry Irving it achieved 'a second Garrick'.

In 1895 Henry Irving became the first actor-knight. Under Irving's leadership the theatre had finally – though not permanently – achieved pre-eminence in the cultural life of the nation. In contrast: 'The heights of the Church of England's mid-Victorian strength and security sloped away to inconsequential lowlands' (Marsh, 1969, p. 289). In large measure the roles of the Church and stage had been reversed. The Church had become the suitor, seeking through an alliance with the theatre a place in, and influence over, the nation's increasingly secular culture. Irving was as indisputably head of his calling as the Archbishop of Canterbury was of the Church of England. Indeed man (Irving) for man (Tait, Benson, Temple) providence had been more generous to the theatre than it had to the Church. Furthermore Irving could claim that his primacy rested not on the patronage of one man – the Prime Minister – but on the broad foundation of the nation's theatre-goers, drawn from all classes, creeds and communities. For these faithful disciples Irving created visions of heaven and hell, conjured up the spectre of the remorse-laden fruits of sin and yet held out the consolation of 'the Larger Hope'. As befitted the high priest of his, and indeed any national, ministry Irving talked with sovereigns and princes, but did not lose the common touch.

It was meet therefore that Irving's final years were spent not in the metropolis, in his beloved high temple of the theatre the Lyceum, but principally amongst his flock in the provinces. His farewell tour began in Cardiff on 19 September 1904, followed by Swansea where at the end of a performance 'the audience sat still in their places and seemingly with one impulse began to sing . . . it was a strange and touching effect when the strains of Newman's beautiful hymn, "Lead Kindly Light", filled the theatre' (Stoker, 1906, vol. II, p. 345). That his performance should prompt such an expression of Christian witness must have reassured Irving that he had accomplished the concord between Church and stage. The tour was cut short in February 1905 when Irving was taken ill in Wolverhampton, but from April to June he played his farewell London season at Drury Lane and made his metropolitan valediction at His Majesty's Theatre on 15 June; then, in October, back to the provinces: Sheffield, followed by Bradford on 9 October. During the ensuing week a sense of presentiment pervaded the company: 'It had seemed to them, during the past ten days, as though he was consciously dying – they had spoken openly of this to one another' (L. Irving, 1951, p. 669). Nevertheless, when he came to the theatre for the performance of *Becket* on Friday 13 October, 'Irving seemed much better and stronger' (Stoker, 1906, vol. II, p. 355). In his scene with Edith Wynne Matthison as Rosamund in the third act:

Edith Wynne Matthison made a rhythmic slip – pronounced armed as a monosyllable. Her mistake did not pass unnoticed by Irving. With the ghost of a twinkle in his eye, he murmured: '. . . Armèd, my dear, armèd'. Disconcerted, she stumbled again, substituting his own words: 'And so farewell' for 'And so return'. The repetition of his earlier line seemed to strike a chord in his spirit. 'Pray for me too – much need for prayer have I', he said, and then added, 'Farewell – farewell', as she left the stage, with such profundity of meaning that it seemed as though he was on the brink of eternity and was striving to tell her so. (L. Irving, 1951, p. 669)

Irving proceeded to the play's ending, speaking what were to be his last words on the stage: 'Into Thy hands, O Lord – into Thy hands!'

Irving returned to the Midland Hotel, in the entrance hall of which he collapsed and, at ten minutes to the midnight hour, died. Mario Borsa attached significance to the place in which Irving departed this life: 'And in Bradford – one of those Northern cities where Puritanism has always fought the stage as enthusiastically as it has fought the Devil – he died. He fell on the enemy's very outworks, at the moment of victory, with the cheers still ringing in his ears' (1908, p. 269).

The capital claimed the earthly remains of the nation's first actor-knight. Whilst his body lay in state in the house of the Baroness Burdett-Coutts, leading members of his profession set about arranging his funeral. According to Laurence Irving, the Dean of St Paul's was approached without success, but, in any case, Westminster Abbey, where David Garrick and John Henderson were buried, was more appropriate. Dr Armitage Robinson, Dean of Westminster, despite his sister's remonstrance 'No actors – no actors!', agreed, after the intervention of Sir Anderson Critchett, the oculist to whom he was beholden for saving his sight: 'The only condition made was that the body should be cremated' (Stoker, 1906, vol. II, p. 361).

At noon on 20 October the funeral service of Sir Henry Irving took place in Westminster Abbey, where his great contemporaries Tennyson and Gladstone had also been laid to rest. The service, at which the King was represented, began with Chopin's Funeral March and ended with 'The Dead March in "Saul"'. It included Tennyson's 'Crossing the Bar':

> Twilight and evening bell,
> And after that the dark!
> And may there be no sadness of farewell
> When I embark;
> For tho' from out our bourne of Time and Place
> The flood may bear me far,
> I hope to see my Pilot face to face
> When I have crost the bar.   (1905, p. 894)

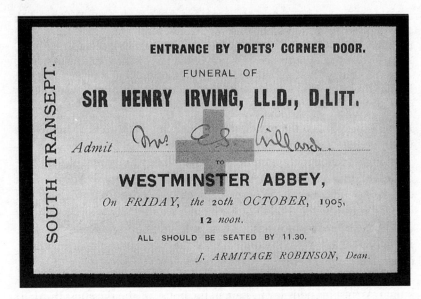

ENTRANCE BY POETS' CORNER DOOR.

FUNERAL OF

SIR HENRY IRVING, LL.D., D.LITT.

SOUTH TRANSEPT.

Admit _____

TO

WESTMINSTER ABBEY,

On FRIDAY, the 20th OCTOBER, 1905,

12 *noon.*

ALL SHOULD BE SEATED BY 11.30.

J. ARMITAGE ROBINSON, Dean.

16. Admission card for Henry Irving's funeral

That Henry Irving had harboured such a hope throughout his earthly years, from his Cornish childhood to the stage of the Theatre Royal, Bradford, was beyond doubt. Mrs Aria, the companion of Irving's later life, quoted 'his own words in testimony of his tenets': 'I believe in immortality, and my faith is strengthened with advancing years; without faith in things spiritual life would indeed be a weary waste' (1922, p. 142).

Upon Irving's coffin lay the pall of laurel leaves, the inspiration of Mrs Aria. Encircled in rays of autumn sunlight it caught the eye of the woman who had shared the high summer of Irving's greatness with him – Ellen Terry:

How terribly I missed that face at Henry's funeral. I kept on expecting to see it, for indeed it seemed to me that he was directing the whole most moving and impressive ceremony. I could almost hear him saying, 'Get on! get on!' in the parts of the service that dragged. When the sun – such a splendid tawny sun – burst across the solemn misty grey of the Abbey, at the very moment when the coffin, under its superb pall of laurel leaves was carried up the choir, I felt that it was an effect which he would have loved. (Craig and St John, 1933, p. 263)

Epilogue

MANLEY: Why, thou art a latitudinarian in friendship, that is, no
friend; thou dost side with all mankind, but wilt suffer for none.
William Wycherley *The Plain Dealer*

In certain respects the nineteenth-century schools of religious thought
have a counterpart in late twentieth-century academic theories.
Adherents to a particular theory apply it with the single-mindedness of a
religious zealot, dismissive of other viewpoints. The chronicle of the
Church and stage in Victorian England could no doubt be interpreted in
a variety of ways ranging from the deeds of heroes to the tide of social
history, but to do so would be to simplify and diminish it. In this context
this book is irredeemably latitudinarian.

The ideas (theories) which provided the driving force for the political
reforms of the second quarter of the nineteenth century were those of
Jeremy Bentham. Roman Catholic emancipation and the findings of the
1832 Select Committee on drama were forms of free trade. Thereafter,
although it retained its status as the Established Church, the Church of
England had to defend, justify and promote its primacy in the religious
life of the nation. Similarly the abolition of the patent theatres' monopoly left the capital without any established home for legitimate drama.
Thereafter individual actors achieved such status through their own
industry and talent within a competitive, commercial system. In due
course the case for a state-subsidised National Theatre was pressed, but
was not brought to fruition until the next century was well advanced.
Uniquely England had a national Church, but no National Theatre.

The Church and the theatre were therefore both confronted by the
consequences of deregulation. They both strove for a recognised position amongst the nation's institutions. They both served – geographically
and socially – the population at large. They both faced the challenge of
the huge new industrialised conurbations. They both sought to uphold

237

their traditions in an increasingly democratic society and mass culture. They both aspired to preserve and to popularise, to maintain their integrity and to bring the newly emancipated classes into their fold. They both saw themselves as forces for cohesion within an increasingly fragmenting society.

The movements which came into being to re-energise the Church for its task served, largely unintentionally, to facilitate the theatre's aspirations to the same goals. The Oxford Movement asserted the non-negotiable requirements of Church membership, but it also proclaimed that all callings were acceptable to – indeed derived from – God. This and the movement's revival of ritual were positive developments for the theatre. F. D. Maurice, the leading light of Christian Socialism, delivered his and succeeding generations 'from the incubus of Hell-fire' (Somervell, 1929, p. 116) upon which religious opposition to the theatre had traditionally relied. His dedication to building the kingdom of heaven on earth brought the temporal condition of men, including their amusement and those who provided it, within the Church's ambit. Amongst Latitudinarians, Jowett advocated reading scripture 'like any other book' and, as a Greek scholar, disavowed Plato's fundamental objections to the theatre. Broad churchman Bishop Fraser, the citizen-bishop, sought to involve himself and his Church in all aspects of the life of his vast Manchester diocese. The impact of Evangelicalism, traditionally inveterate in its opposition to the theatre, was often counter-productive. Two key figures, Henry Irving and Stewart Headlam, reacted strongly against the forms of Evangelicalism in which they had been brought up. Evangelical assumptions about the evil nature of the theatre were progressively undermined; missions directed at the theatre, even though they met a – social rather than spiritual – need amongst young female performers, were widely resented.

The fountain-head for so much nineteenth-century thought was Samuel Taylor Coleridge. Samuel Smiles castigated Coleridge as 'infirm of purpose . . . he wanted the gift of industry and was averse to continuous labour' (1905, p. 396), but as poet, dramatist, literary and dramatic critic, and religious and social thinker Coleridge was not only fecund in himself, but the cause of fecundity in others. Coleridge's treatment of sin, guilt, remorse, punishment and the after-life opened up a rich seam for others to explore. His psychological approach to character and his recognition of the oblique morality of art were signposts for the century. A witness to genius on stage, he advanced the idea of a clerisy to disseminate high culture amongst the population at large. The conjunction of religion, education and the theatre present in Coleridge's writing was both fused and diffused to the service of each component.

In many respects education was the broker in the marriage between Church and stage. In the wake of reforms at the ancient universities and Forster's Education Act of 1870 the Church of England fought tenaciously to maintain its role in the education of the population. The expansion of education (elementary schools, adult education of various kinds and the enfranchisement of women) brought with it the introduction of new subjects, of which English literature was pre-eminent and within which Shakespeare was paramount. Given the religious foundation of most of these educational initiatives it was inevitable that the curriculum should be vested with moral purpose. At the time when Benjamin Jowett was arguing for the interpretation of the Bible like any other book, literary classics were being scrutinised for the moral precepts contained within them. Oratory, traditionally taught at public schools as a training for the Church, politics, the law and, only inadvertently, the stage, found its popular counterpart in elocution. The progression from reading a play, to reciting it, seeing it and acting it was to be expected. As Henry Irving observed 'the natural effect of reading a good play is a desire to see it acted' (J. Richards, 1994, p. 196). The inherent affinity between preaching and acting was increasingly recognised, and the levelling of status between the Bible and the bard brought the latter within the compass of many a preacher's prescribed texts.

As the theatre was invading the schoolroom and the Church, so too was religion making its way onto the stage. The ban on dramatisations of the Bible was still absolute, unless they were so heavily disguised as to be, technically at least, unrecognisable, but with Henry Arthur Jones and Wilson Barrett in the vanguard the theatre secured its right to treat religious subjects, as other arts had done for centuries. This development was concurrent with the arrival in the theatre of the respectable middle classes, until recently incarcerated in the prison of Puritanism. The drama did not prove to be a vehicle of social cohesion in the theatre. Instead it evolved into literary and popular genres serving different sections of the population.

Nevertheless, the theatre was increasingly prominent in cultural life nationally. Several social factors were at work to promote this process. Urbanisation and industrialisation created large concentrations of population. Even the less well-off had some leisure in which to seek respite from their drudgery. The Church was faced with a dilemma. It could either reject this secular culture and thereby alienate large

numbers of people, whom it was its mission to serve, or it could countenance it, seek to influence it and become part of it. As J. H. S. Kent has
suggested 'persistent memories of having been part of the dominant
culture in the past' (1973, p. 158) influenced many clergymen to take the
latter course. Whether in so doing they served the long-term interest of
the Church is debatable, but in the short term the theatre, amongst
others, was a beneficiary.

The state regarded the Established Church as a means of regulating
society and increasingly both it and the Church perceived that the
theatre could fulfil a similar function. Given that the population must be
entertained, it was preferable that their amusements should be of the
higher order – Bentham was here o'erthrown. The monarch – and
Supreme Head of the Church of England – did not need much persuasion. Queen Victoria was a natural devotee of the stage, though without
the encouragement of Prince Albert she may not have regarded it in
such elevated terms. The factors resulting in Gladstone's conversion to
the theatre were no doubt personal, religious, social and political. The
endorsement of a convert always carries extra conviction amongst
waverers, rarely more so than with a man of Gladstone's moral and religious zeal. Few, if any, prime ministers have carried out their role in
making senior Church appointments as assiduously as Gladstone did. It
was Gladstone who advanced Irving's knighthood.

The leaders of the stage had succeeded in throwing off the stigma of
rogues and vagabonds. In his personal – if not his professional – life
Macready was beyond reproach: in Tennyson's words 'moral, grave,
sublime' (1905, p. 578). He conducted his household on the most rigorous
code of the Victorian *paterfamilias*, instilling religious principles in his
family and wrestling with current theological issues and mixing socially
with leading churchmen. Charles Kean carried the credentials of an
Eton education and with it a network of school contemporaries, several
of them prominent in the Church. Though he was the last man to
exploit the fact, Samuel Phelps had a brother who was an eminent
Cambridge don in holy orders, but his achievements at Sadler's Wells
drew the unsolicited approbation of Archibald Tait on their own merit.
Actresses faced sterner religious and social prejudice than actors, but
Fanny Kemble, Helen Faucit, Marie Bancroft and Madge Kendal disarmed criticism as they demonstrated that the pursuit of a stage career
was reconcilable with the ideals of family life, personal devotion and
social intercourse with dignitaries of the Church. That such indulgence
was extended to the wayward Ellen Terry provided the measure of the

advance which the theatre had made in its pursuit of acceptability and respectability.

If a celestial scribe had penned the drama of Church and stage in Victorian England he could not have created a character more suited to effect its summation than Henry Irving. His upbringing, his bearing, his turn of mind, his social discourse and, pre-eminently of course, the nature of his genius as an actor combined to make Henry Irving the supreme embodiment of his profession's aspirations to bond with the religious life of their countrymen. In his life and in his art Irving was popular and profound. It was granted to an actor, rather than a dramatist, to realise that elusive social cohesion which lay at the heart of Coleridge's idea of a clerisy and Matthew Arnold's writing on culture. Irving was accorded a funeral in Westminster Abbey at which the nation's leaders were present or represented, but he was mourned across the land. Charles Forshaw collected a volume of *Poetical Tributes in Memory of the Late Sir Henry Irving* (1905), the contributors to which included a dozen clergymen. In his foreword Sir Albert Kaye Rollit wrote of 'a loss the sense of which it [the nation] has most worthily marked by the decree of its supremest approach to the gift of immortality by entombment in Westminster Abbey'.

That the theatre which, at the beginning of Queen Victoria's reign, was widely regarded as the lowliest of the arts, if one at all, should see its departed leader so revered was a remarkable transition. If 'Every good gift and every perfect gift is from above and cometh down from the Father of lights', then the Father of lights had been generous in his gift of Henry Irving to the theatre. Be that as it may, the fact that Irving's pilgrimage through life ended in Westminster Abbey was due to religious, social, cultural and educational shifts, to which he contributed and from which he benefited, but which had a momentum of their own.

References

Abbott, Anthony S. 1965. *Shaw and Christianity*, New York.

Abbott, Evelyn and Campbell, Lewis, eds. 1899. *Letters of Benjamin Jowett, MA, Master of Balliol College Oxford*, London.

Actors' Church Union Reports, 1899, 1902 and *1905–6,*London.

Allen, Peter. 1978. *The Cambridge Apostles. The Early Years*, Cambridge.

Allen, Shirley. 1971. *Samuel Phelps and the Sadler's Wells Theatre*, Middletown, Conn.

Anderson, Mary. 1936. *A Few More Memories*, London.

Archer, Frank. 1912. *An Actor's Notebooks*, London.

Archer, William. 1886. *About the Theatre*, London.

 1890. *William Charles Macready*, London.

 1894. *The Theatrical World of 1893*, London.

 1897. *The Theatrical World of 1896*, London.

Aria, Mrs. 1922. *My Sentimental Self*, London.

Arundell, Dennis. 1965. *The Story of Sadler's Wells Theatre*, London.

Ashe, T., ed. 1888. *Table Talk*, London.

Auerbach, Nina. 1987. *Ellen Terry*, London.

Bailey, Peter. 1978. *Leisure and Class in Victorian England. Rational Recreation and the Contest for Control, 1830–1885*, London.

Baker, Michael. 1978. *The Rise of the Victorian Actor*, London.

Bamford, T. W. 1967. *The Rise of the Public Schools*, London.

Bancroft, Mr and Mrs. 1889. *Mr and Mrs Bancroft. On and Off the Stage*, London.

Bancroft, Squire. 1925. *Empty Chairs*, London.

Banham, Martin, ed. 1985. *Plays by Tom Taylor*, Cambridge.

Banks, J. A. 1981. *Victorian Values. Secularism and the Size of Families*, London.

Barham, Revd D. H. 1880. *Life of Rev. Richard Harris Barham*, London.

Barham, Revd R. H. 1896. *The Garrick Club. Notices of One Hundred and Thirty-Five of its Former Members*, London.

Barish, Jonas. 1981. *The Anti-theatrical Prejudice*, London.

Barker, Kathleen. 1985. Thirty years of struggle: entertainment in provincial towns between 1840 and 1870. In *Theatre Notebook*, 33:1, 25–31:2, 68–75:3, 140–9.

Barnes, J. H. 1914. *Forty Years on the Stage*, London.

Bateman, Isabel. 1936. *From Theatre to Convent: Memories of Mother Isabel Mary CSMV*, London.

Battiscombe, Georgina. 1963. *John Keble A Study in Limitations*, London.

Bebbington, D. W. 1982. *The Nonconformist Conscience Chapel and Politics, 1870–1914*, London.

Bell, Revd G. K. A. 1935. *Randall Davidson Archbishop of Canterbury*, 2 vols. Oxford.

Bellew, J. C. M. 1863. *Shakespeare's House at New Place, Stratford-upon-Avon*, London.

Benson, A. C. 1899. *The Life of Edward White Benson Sometime Archbishop of Canterbury*, 2 vols. London.

Benson, Constance. 1926. *Mainly Players Bensonian Memoirs*, London.

Benson, Frank. 1930. *My Memoirs*, London.

Bentley, James. 1984. *Oberammergau and The Passion Play*, Harmondsworth.

Benzie, William. 1983. *Dr F. J. Furnivall Christian Scientist*, Norman, Okla.

Best, Geoffrey. 1989. *Mid-Victorian Britain 1851–75*, London.

Bettany, F. G. 1926. *Stewart Headlam: A Biography*, London.

Birch, W. J. 1848. *An Inquiry into the Philosophy and Religion of Shakspere*, London.

Black, Eugene, ed. 1973. *Victorian Culture and Society*, London.

Blaiklock, E. M., trans. 1983. *The Confessions of Saint Augustine*, London.

Blathwayt, R. 1898. *Does the Theatre Make for Good?*, London.

Blomfield, Alfred. 1863. *A Memoir of C. J. Blomfield*, 2 vols. London.

Boas, Guy. 1948. *The Garrick Club*, London.

Bolitho, Hector. 1936. *Marie Tempest*, London.

Booth, Michael. 1965. *English Melodrama*, London.

   1981. *Victorian Spectacular Theatre 1850–1910*, London.

   1986. Pictorial acting and Ellen Terry. In Foulkes, 1986a, pp. 78–86.

   1991. *Theatre in the Victorian Age*, Cambridge.

Borsa, Mario. 1908. *The English Stage Today*, London.

Bott, John. 1974. *The Figure of the House*, Stratford-upon-Avon.

Bowring, John, ed. 1962. *The Works of Jeremy Bentham*, 11 vols. London, New York.

Bradley, A. G., Champneys, A. C. and Baines, J. W. 1893. *A History of Marlborough College During Fifty Years From its Foundation to the Present Time*, London.

Brereton, Austin. 1922. *'H. B.' and Laurence Irving*, London.

Briggs, Asa. 1968. *Victorian Cities*, Harmondsworth.

British Parliamentary Papers, Stage and Theatre 1, 1968, Shannon.

   Education in England: Education General 4, 1969, Shannon.

   Stage and Theatre 2, 1970, Shannon.

Brome, Vincent. 1962. *Frank Harris*, London.

Bromley, J. 1959. *A Man of Ten Talents: Richard Chenevix Trench*, London.

Brooker, Peter and Widdowson, Peter. 1987. A literature for England. In *English Politics and Culture 1880–1920*, ed. Robert Colls and Philip Dodd, pp. 116–63. London.

Brookfield, Charles H. E. 1902. *Random Reminiscences*, London.

Brown, C. K. Francis. 1953. *A History of the English Clergy 1800–1900*, London.

Browne, E. Martin. 1970. *The Making of T. S. Eliot's Plays*, Cambridge.

   1979. *Fifty Years of Religious Drama*, Leicester.

Bulwer Lytton, Edward. 1833. *England and the English*, 2 vols. London.

Bunn, Alfred. 1824. *A Letter to the Rev. J. A. James of Carr's Lane Meeting House, with notes Critical, Religious and Moral*, London.

1840. *The Stage Before and Behind the Curtain*, 2 vols. London.

Burnand, F. C. 1862. *Bishop Colenso Utterly Refuted and Categorically Answered by Lord Dundreary. With a short memoir and a few notes by his Lordship's sincere admirer, F. C Burnand Esq. B. A., Barrister at Law*, London.

1880. *The 'ADC' Being Personal Reminiscences of the University Amateur Dramatic Society, Cambridge*, London.

1904. *Records and Reminiscences Personal and General*, 2 vols. London.

Burton, Hal, ed. 1967. *Great Acting*, London.

Caine, G. R. Hall and Caine, Derwent Hall. 1938. *The Life of Christ by Hall Caine*, London.

Caine, Henry Hall. 1877. *'Richard III' and 'Macbeth' The Spirit of Romantic Play in Relationship to the Principles of Greek and of Gothic Art, and to the Picturesque Interpretations of Mr. Henry Irving. A Dramatic Study*, London.

1887. *Life of Samuel Taylor Coleridge*, London.

1908. *My Story*, London.

Calcraft, J. W. 1838. *A Defence of the Stage*, Dublin.

Calvert, Mrs Charles. 1911. *Sixty-eight Years on the Stage*, London.

Calvert, F. B. 1822. *A Defence of the Acted Drama In a Letter Addressed to the Rev. Thomas Best MA of Sheffield*, Hull.

1852. *Principles of Elocution by Thomas Ewing Thoroughly Revised and Greatly Improved*, London and Edinburgh.

1869. *The Art of Reading and Preaching Distinctly. A Letter to The Rev. Dean Ramsay, LLD, MA, FRSE Incumbent of St John's Edinburgh*, London, Oxford and Cambridge.

Campbell, Mrs Patrick. 1922. *My Life and Some Letters*, London.

Carlyle, Thomas. 1857. *Life of John Sterling*, London.

1915. *Chartism*, London.

1967. *On Heroes, Hero-Worship and the Heroic in History*, London.

Carpenter, Humphrey. 1985. *OUDS A Centenary History of the Oxford University Dramatic Society*, Oxford.

Chadwick, Owen. 1966 (vol. I) and 1970 (vol. II). *The Victorian Church*, London.

Cheity, Susan. 1974. *The Beast and the Monk. A Life of Charles Kingsley*, London.

Child, Harold. 1939. *A Poor Player*, London.

Clarke, A. K. 1953. *The Story of Cheltenham Ladies' College*, London.

Close, Revd Frederick. 1877. *The Stage Ancient and Modern. Its Tendencies on Morals and Religion. A Lecture*, London.

Cohen, Morton N., ed. 1979. *The Letters of Lewis Carroll*, 2 vols. London.

Cole, G. D. H., ed. 1927. *A New View of Society and other Writings by Robert Owen*, London.

Cole, J. W. 1859. *The Life and Theatrical Times of Charles Kean FSA*, 2 vols. London.

Coleman, John. 1903. *Charles Reade As I Knew Him*, London.

Coleridge, Derwent, ed. 1852. *Dramatic Works of Samuel Taylor Coleridge*, London.

1876. *Poems of John Moultrie*, London.

Coleridge, Derwent and Coleridge, Sara, eds. 1852. *Poems of Samuel Taylor Coleridge*, London.

Coleridge, S. T. 1917. *Biographia Literaria*, London.

Collier, Jeremy. 1698. *A Short View of the Immorality and Profaneness of the English Stage With the Sense of Antiquity upon this Argument*, London.

Colmer, John, ed. 1976. *On the Constitution of the Church and State*, London.

Cooper, Thomas. 1872. *The Life of Thomas Cooper written by Himself*, London.

Corathiel, Elisabeth. 1950. *Oberammergau and its Passion Play*, London.

Cordell, Richard A. 1932. *Henry Arthur Jones and the Modern Drama*, New York.

Courtney, T. E. 1930. *The Making of An Editor W. L. Courtney 1850–1928*, London.

Courtney, W. L. 1925. *The Passing Hour*, London.

Cox, Jeffrey. 1982. *The English Churches in a Secular Society Lambeth, 1870–1930*, Oxford.

Craig, Edith and St John, Christopher, eds. 1933. *Ellen Terry's Memoirs*, London.

Crosse, Gordon. 1913. *The Religious Drama*, The Arts of the Church, London.

Crump, Jeremy. 1986. The popular audience for Shakespeare in nineteenth-century Leicester. In Foulkes, 1986a, pp. 271–82.

Dale, Revd Thomas. 1828. *An Introductory Lecture Delivered in The University of London*, London.

Dann, F. 1994. This multiform modern evil: the annual admonitions of the Revd Thomas Best of Sheffield. In Foulkes, 1994, pp. 90–7.

Darbyshire, Alfred. 1907. *The Art of the Victorian Stage*, London.

Davidson, Revd Randall T. and Benham, Revd William. 1891. *Life of Archibald Tait*, 2 vols. London.

Davies, Edwina. 1990. The life and work of James Fraser, unpublished Ph.D. thesis, University of Manchester.

Davis, Jim, ed. 1992. *The Britannia Diaries of Frederick Wilton*, London.

Davis, Tracy C. 1991. *Actresses as Working Women*, London.

Deelman, Christian. 1964. *The Great Shakespeare Jubilee*, London.

Denman, John. 1835. *The Drama Vindicated*, Cambridge.

Diggle, John W. 1889. *The Lancashire Life of Bishop Fraser*, London.

Disher, M. Willson. 1948. *The Last Romantic. The Authorised Biography of Sir John Martin-Harvey*, London.

1950. *Pleasures of London*, London.

Dixon, J. M. 1879. *The Pulpit and the Stage*, Hull.

Downer, Alan S. 1966. *The Eminent Tragedian. William Charles Macready*, London and Cambridge, Mass.

East, Revd John. 1844a. *The Pulpit Justified and the Theatre Condemned. A Letter to some members of the Association for Increasing the Attractions and Promoting the Improvement of Bath*, London.

1844b. *The Theatre. A Discourse on Theatrical Amusements and Dramatic Literature*, London.

Ellmann, Richard. 1988. *Oscar Wilde*, London.

Elsom, John and Tomalin, Nicholas. 1978. *The History of the National Theatre*, London.

Engel, A. J. 1983. *From Clergyman to Don. The Rise of the Academic Profession in Nineteenth-Century Oxford,* Oxford.

Ensor, R. C. K. 1980. *England 1870–1914,* Oxford.

Era Almanack, The, 1880, London.

Escott, T. H. S. 1885. *Society in London,* London.

1897. *Social Transformations of the Victorian Age,* London.

Esher, Viscount, ed. 1912. *The Girlhood of Queen Victoria,* 2 vols. London.

Essays and Reviews, 1860, London.

Evers, C. R. 1939. *Rugby,* London.

Faber, Geoffrey. 1957. *Jowett – a Portrait with Background,* London.

Farr, Florence. 1910. *Modern Woman: Her Intentions,* London.

Farrar, Revd F. W. 1890. *The Passion Play at Oberammergau 1890,* London.

1892. *Eternal Hope. Five Sermons,* London.

Farrar, Revd F. W., ed. 1867. *Essays on A Liberal Education,* London.

Farrar, Reginald. 1904. *The Life of William Farrar,* London.

Faucit, Helena, Lady Martin. 1887. *On Some of Shakespeare's Female Characters,* London.

Fielding, K. G., ed. 1960. *The Speeches of Charles Dickens,* London and Oxford.

Filon, Augustin. 1897. *The English Stage,* London.

Foot, M. R. D., ed. 1968. *The Gladstone Diaries,* vol. 1. London.

Foote, G. W. 1896. *The Sign of the Cross. A Candid Criticism of Mr Wilson Barrett's Play,* London.

Forbes-Robertson, Johnston. 1925. *A Player under Three Reigns,* London.

Forshaw, Charles E. ed. 1905. *Poetical Tributes in Memory of the Late Sir Henry Irving,* London.

Foulkes, Richard. 1979. Adult education and the theatre: the early years. In *Studies in Adult Education,* 1979, 30–41.

1984. *The Shakespeare Tercentenary of 1864,* London.

1985. The Royal Dramatic College. In *Nineteenth Century Theatre Research,* 13:2, 63–85.

1992a. *The Calverts: Actors of Some Importance,* London.

Foulkes, Richard, ed. 1986a. *Shakespeare and the Victorian Stage,* Cambridge.

1986b. Charles Kean's *King Richard II*: a Pre-Raphaelite drama. In Foulkes, 1986a, pp. 39–55.

1992b. *British Theatre in the 1890s. Essays on Drama and the Stage,* Cambridge.

1994. *Scenes from Provincial Stages. Essays in Honour of Kathleen Barker,* London.

Francis, T. K., trans. 1912. *Keble's Lectures on Poetry 1832–1841,* 2 vols. London.

Fraser, Hilary. 1986. *Beauty and Belief. Aesthetics and Religion in Victorian Literature,* Cambridge.

Fraser, Bishop James. 1872. *Charge Delivered at His Primary Visitation,* Manchester.

1876. *Charge Delivered at His Second Visitation,* Manchester.

1880. *Charge Delivered at His Third Visitation,* Manchester.

Froude, James Anthony, ed. 1883. *Letters and Memorials of Jane Welsh Carlyle,* 3 vols. London.

Frow, Gerald. 1985. *'Oh, Yes It Is!' A History of Pantomime,* London.

Ganzel, Dewey. 1982. *Fortune and Men's Eyes. The Career of John Payne Collier*, Oxford.

Garnett, Richard and Garnett, Edward. 1910. *Life of W. J. Fox*, London.

Gaunt, William. 1965. *The Pre-Raphaelite Tragedy*, London.

Godwin, George. 1878. *On the Desirability of obtaining a National Theatre*, London.

Golden, James L. and Corbett, Edward P. J., eds. 1968. *The Rhetoric of Blair, Campbell, and Whateley*, New York.

Gomme, Allan. 1936. William Poel. A chronological record of his published writing, unpublished typescript in the Theatre Museum, London.

Graham, Charles. 1884. *The Late Charles Reade: The Story of his Conversion*, London.

Green, Roger Lancelyn, ed. 1971. *The Diaries of Lewis Carroll*, 2 vols. Westport, Conn.

Griffin, Penny. 1991. *Arthur Wing Pinero and Henry Arthur Jones*, London.

Gryllis, Rosalie Glynn. 1948. *Queen's College 1848–1948*, London.

Haigh, Alan. 1984. *The Victorian Clergy*, London.

Hamilton, Cicely and Baylis, Lilian. 1926. *The Old Vic*, London.

Hamilton, Clayton, ed. 1925. *Representative Plays by Henry Arthur Jones*, 4 vols. Boston, Mass.

Hammet, Michael, ed. 1986. *Plays by Charles Kean*, Cambridge.

Hardwick, J. M. D., ed. 1954. *Emigrant in Motley*, London.

Hare, A. 1986. Shakespeare in a provincial stock company. In Foulkes, 1986a, pp. 258–70.

Hare, Julius. 1848. *Essays and Tales of John Sterling*, 2 vols. London.

Harker, Joseph. 1924. *Studio and Stage*, London.

Harris, Frank. 1958. *My Life and Adventures*, London.

Harrison, Brian. 1967. Religion and recreation in nineteenth-century England. In *Past and Present*, 38 (December 1967), 98–125.

Harrison, Frederic. 1908. *Realities and Ideals*, London.

1911. *Autobiographical Memoirs*, 2 vols. London.

Harrison, J. F. C. 1954. *A History of the Working Men's Colleges*, London.

1961. *Learning and Living 1790–1960*, London.

Hartley, A. J., ed. 1970. *Sketches of Contemporary Authors*, New York.

Hartnoll, Phyllis, ed. 1958. *Welcome, Good Friends. The Autobiography of Kenneth R. Barnes*, London.

Haweis, Revd H. R. 1878. *Shakespeare and the Stage*, London.

Headlam, Revd Stewart. 1889. *The Function of the Stage. A Lecture*, London.

1892. *Christian Socialism. A Lecture*, London.

Hearnshaw, F. J. C. 1929. *The Centenary History of King's College, London, 1828–1928*, London.

Heasman, Kathleen. 1962. *Evangelicalism in Action*, London.

Hempton, D. 1996. *Religion and Political Culture*, Cambridge.

Hole, Revd Donald. 1934. *The Church and the Stage. The Early History of the Actors' Church Union*, London.

Holledge, Julie. 1981. *Innocent Flowers: Women in the Edwardian Theatre*, London.

Hollingshead, John. 1895. *My Lifetime*, 2 vols. London.

Holroyd, Michael. 1988. *Bernard Shaw Volume 1. 1856–1898. The Search for Love*, London.

Hone, William. 1823. *Ancient Mysteries Described, Especially from the English Miracle Plays*, London.

Hook, Revd Walter Farquhar. 1887. *A Church Dictionary A Practical Manual of Reference for Clergymen and Students*, London.

Horne, R. H. 1840. *Gregory VII*, London.

   1844. *A New Spirit of the Age*, 2 vols. London.

   n.d. *Bible Tragedies*, London.

Houghton, Walter E. 1973. *The Victorian Frame of Mind*, London.

Housman, L. 1937. *The Unexpected Years*, London.

Howell, Margaret J. 1982. *Byron Tonight. A Poet's Plays on the Nineteenth Century Stage*, Windlesham.

Hughes, Thomas. 1887. *James Fraser Second Bishop of Manchester*, London.

Hunter, Robert. 1864. *Shakespeare and Stratford-upon-Avon Together with a Full Report of the Tercentenary Celebration*, London.

Irving, H. B. 1906. *Occasional Papers Dramatic and Historical*, London.

Irving, Henry and Marshall, Frank A. 1892. *The Works of William Shakespeare*, 8 vols. London.

Irving, Laurence. 1951. *Henry Irving. The Actor and his World*, London.

   1967. *The Successors*, London.

Isaac, Winifred F. E. C. 1964. *Ben Greet and The Old Vic A Biography of Sir Philip Ben Greet*, London.

Jackson, Holbrook. 1913. *The Eighteen Nineties A Review of Art and Ideas at the Close of the Nineteenth Century*, London.

Jackson, Russell, ed. 1982. *Plays by Henry Arthur Jones*, Cambridge.

Jerome, Jerome K. 1885. *The Stage – and Off. The Brief Career of a Would-be Actor*, London.

   1891. *Diary of a Pilgrimage*, London.

Johnson, Catherine B. 1905. *William Bodham Donne and His Friends*, London.

Johnson, J. O. 1905. *Life and Letters of Henry Parry Liddon*, London.

Jones, Doris Arthur. 1930. *The Life and Letters of Henry Arthur Jones*, London.

Jones, Edmund D., ed. 1956. *Nineteenth Century English Critical Essays*, Oxford.

Jones, Henry Arthur. 1895. *The Renascence of the English Drama. Essays, Lectures and Fragments*, London.

Jones, Jo Elwyn and Gladstone, J. Francis. 1995. *The Red King's Dream or Lewis Carroll in Wonderland*, London.

Jowett, Benjamin. 1860. On the interpretation of Scripture. In *Essays and Reviews*, pp. 320–433. London.

Jowett, Benjamin, trans. 1888. *The Republic of Plato*, Oxford.

Kamm, Josephine. 1958. *How Different from Us. A Biography of Miss Buss and Miss Beale*, London.

Kaye, Elaine. 1972. *A History of Queen's College*, London.

Keble, Revd John. 1827. *The Christian Year*, London.

Kelly, Thomas. 1957. *George Birkbeck. Pioneer of Adult Education*, Liverpool.

1962. *The History of Adult Education in Great Britain*, Liverpool.

Kemble, Frances [Fanny]. 1878. *Records of a Girlhood*, 3 vols. London.

1882. *Records of a Later Life*, 2 vols. London.

1890. *Further Records*, 2 vols. London.

Kendal, Dame Madge. 1933. *Dame Madge Kendal by Herself*, London.

Kent, Revd J. H. S. 1973. The role of religion in the cultural structure of the later Victorian city. In *Transactions of the Royal Historical Association*, 5th series, 23, 153–73.

Kenyon, C. Fred. 1901. *Hall Caine The Man and the Novelist*, London.

Kingsley, Charles. 1873. *Plays and Puritans and other Historical Essays*, London.

1877. *Charles Kingsley His Letters and Memories of his Life, edited by his wife*, 2 vols. London.

1879. *Alton Locke*, London.

1889. *Poems*, London.

Knappen, M. M. 1939. *Tudor Puritanism*, Chicago.

Knight, Charles. 1864–5. *Passages of A Working Life*, 3 vols. London.

1893. *Theatrical Notes*, London.

Knights, Ben. 1978. *The Idea of the Clerisy In the Nineteenth Century*, Cambridge.

Knowles, James Sheridan. 1873. *Lectures on Dramatic Literature Delivered by James Sheridan Knowles During the Years 1820–1850*, London.

Kruppa, Patricia S. 1992. 'More sweet and liquid than any other': Victorian images of Mary Magdalene. In *Religion and Irreligion in Victorian Society*, ed. R. W. Davis and R. J. Helmstadter, pp. 117–32. London.

Krutch, Joseph Wood. 1949. *Comedy and Conscience after the Restoration*, New York.

Lacy, T. H. 1840. *The Theatre Defended, chiefly in reference to the last Annual Sermon of the Rev. Thomas Best against Theatrical Amusements*, Sheffield.

Lane, Eric and Brenson, Ian, eds. 1984. *The Oberammergau Passion Play*, London.

Lane, R. J., ed. 1870. *Charles Kemble's Shakespeare Readings*, 3 vols. London.

Langtry, Lillie. 1925. *The Days I Knew*, London.

Laurence, Dan H., ed. 1965. *Bernard Shaw Collected Letters 1874–1897*, London.

1972. *Bernard Shaw Collected Letters 1898–1910*, London.

1989. *Shaw's Music. The Complete Music Criticism of Bernard Shaw*, 2 vols. London.

Leech, Kenneth. 1968. Stewart Headlam, 1847–1924 and the Guild of St Matthew. In *For Christ and the People*, ed. Maurice B. Reckitt, pp. 61–81. London.

Lejeune, A. 1984. *The Gentlemen's Clubs of London*, London.

Lennon, Florence Becker. 1947. *Lewis Carroll*, London.

Lewes, G. H. 1850. *The Noble Heart*, London.

1875. *On Actors and the Art of Acting*, London.

Lobb, Kenneth Martyn. 1955. *The Drama in School and Church*, London.

Lock, Walter. 1893. *John Keble A Biography*, London.

Lockhart, J. G. 1949. *Cosmo Gordon Lang*, London.

Lowder, Charles, ed. 1888. *Richard Chenevix Trench Letters and Memorials*, 2 vols. London.

Lyte, Sir H. C. Maxwell. 1911. *A History of Eton College*, London.

MacColl, Canon Malcolm. 1870. *The Ammergau Passion Play*, London.

Mackerness, E. D. 1979. Bigotry and the bard; the case of the Sheffield Shakespeare Club. In *Theatre Notebook*, 33:3, 109–16.

Mackinnon, Alan. 1910. *The Oxford Amateurs. A Short History of the Theatricals at the University*, London.

Macleod, Hugh. 1974. *Class and Religion in the Late Victorian City*, London.

Macleod, Joseph. 1981. *The Actor's Right to Act*, London.

Macqueen-Pope, W. 1951. *Ghosts and Greasepaint. A Story of the Days that were*, London.

Manning, Revd H. E. 1842. *Sermons*, 2 vols. London.
   1865. *Essays on Religion and Literature*, 3 vols. London.

Mansbridge, Albert. 1935. *Edward Stuart Talbot and Charles Gore*, London.

Manvell, Roger. 1968. *Ellen Terry*, London.

Marchand, Leslie A. 1971. *The Athenaeum A Mirror of Victorian Culture*, New York.

Marlborough College Register 1843–1909, 1910, Marlborough.

Marsh, P. T. 1969. *The Victorian Church in Decline. Archibald Tait and the Church of England 1868–1882*, London.

Marshall, Dorothy. 1977. *Fanny Kemble*, London.

Marston, Westland. 1890. *Our Recent Actors*, London.

Martin, Sir Theodore. 1889. *Essays on the Drama*, London.
   1900. *Helen Faucit (Lady Martin)*, London and Edinburgh.

Marvin, F. S., ed. 1908. *Reports on Elementary Schools 1852–1882 by Matthew Arnold*, London.

Mason, A. E. W. 1935. *Sir George Alexander and the St James's Theatre*, London.

Maurice, F. D. 1834. *Eustace Conway, or The Brother and Sister*, 3 vols. London.
   1838. *The Kingdom of Christ*, 3 vols. London.
   1853. *Theological Essays*, London.

Maurice, Revd F. D., Kingsley, Revd Charles, Brasseur, Isidore *et al*. 1849. *Introductory Lectures delivered at Queen's College, London*, London.

Maurice, Revd F. D., Kingsley, Revd Charles, Johnson, George *et al*. 1855. *Lectures to Ladies on Practical Subjects*, Cambridge.

Maurice, Frederick. 1884. *The Life of Frederick Denison Maurice*, 2 vols. London.

Mayer, David. 1969. *Harlequin in his Element. The English Pantomime, 1806–1836*, Cambridge, Mass.
   1992. Toga plays. In Foulkes, 1992b, pp. 71–92.

Mayer, David, ed. 1980. *Henry Irving and 'The Bells'*, Manchester.
   1994. *Playing out the Empire. 'Ben Hur' and Other Toga Plays and Films. A Critical Anthology*, Oxford.

McCarthy, Lillah. 1933. *Myself and Friends*, London.

Meeks, Leslie. 1933. *Sheridan Knowles and the Theatre of His Time*, Bloomington.

Meisel, Martin. 1983. *Realizations Narrative and Theatrical Arts in Nineteenth-Century England*, New Jersey.

Meller, J. E. 1976. *Leisure and the Changing City*, London.

Melville, Joy. 1987. *Ellen and Edy*, London.

Messenger, Gary S. 1986. *Manchester in the Victorian Age. The Half-Known City*, Manchester.

Milman, Arthur. 1900. *Henry Hart Milman DD Dean of St Paul's. A Biographical Sketch*, London.

Milman, H. H. 1815. *Fazio. A Tragedy*, London.

  1855. *The History of Latin Christianity to the Death of Nicholas V*, 6 vols. London.

Mirror of Parliament, The, 1833, London.

Mirror of Parliament, The, 1839, London.

Moody, Jane. 1994. Writing for the metropolis: illegitimate performances of Shakespeare in early nineteenth-century London. In *Shakespeare Survey*, 47, 61–9.

Moore, George. 1939. *Confessions of a Young Man*, London.

Morley, Henry. 1890. *Illustrations of English Religion*, London.

  1891. *The Journal of a London Playgoer*, London.

Morley, Sheridan. 1977. *Sybil Thorndike. A Life in the Theatre*, London.

Motter, T. H. Vail. 1929. *The School Drama in England*, London.

Murray, Christopher. 1986. James Sheridan Knowles: the Victorian Shakespeare? In Foulkes, 1986a, pp. 164–79.

Newman, J. H. 1891. *Discussions and Arguments on Various Subjects*, London.

Newton, H. Chance. 1927. *Cues and Curtain Calls*, London.

Nicholson, Watson. 1906. *The Struggle for a Free Stage in London*, London.

Nielson, Alan. 1991. *The Great Victorian Sacrilege. Preachers, Politics and The Passion 1879–1884*, London.

Norman, Edward. 1987. *The Christian Socialists*, London.

Oldfield, Sybil. 1984. *Spinsters of This Parish The Life and Times of F. M. Mayor and Mary Sheepshanks*, London.

Oliphant, Mrs. 1864. *The Life of Edward Irving*, London.

Ollard, S. L., assisted by Crosse, Gordon 1912. *A Dictionary of English Church History*, London.

Paley, William. 1794. *A View of the Evidences of Christianity*, London.

Palmer, David. 1965. *The Rise of English Studies*, Oxford.

Parker, John W., ed. 1858. *Essays on the Drama. William Bodham Donne*, London.

Patrick, J. Max, ed. 1950. *The New Republic or Culture, Faith and Philosophy in an English Country House*, Gainesville, Fla.

Patterson, Annabel. 1989. *Shakespeare and the Popular Voice*, Oxford.

Paxton, Sydney. 1917. *Stage See-Saws or The Ups and Downs of an Actor's Life*, London.

Pemberton, T. Edgar. 1900. *The Kendals A Biography*, London.

Penley, W. S. 1884. *Penley on Himself. The Confessions of a Conscientious Artist*, Bristol.

Peters, Margot. 1985. *Mrs Pat. The Life of Mrs Patrick Campbell*, London.

Phelps, W. May and Forbes-Robertson, Johnston. 1886. *The Life and Life-Work of Samuel Phelps*, London.

Planché, J. R. 1879. *Suggestions for Establishing an English Art Theatre*, London.

  1901. *Recollections and Reflections*, London.

Poel, William. 1920. *What Is Wrong With the Stage*, London.

Poel, William., ed. 1901. *Everyman*, London.

Pollock, Sir Frederick, ed. 1876. *Macready's Reminiscences*, London.

Powell, Kerry. 1990. *Oscar Wilde and the Theatre of the 1890s*, Cambridge.

Prothero, R. E. ed. 1895. *Letters and Verses of Arthur Penrhyn Stanley DD*, London.

Prothero, R. E. and Bradley, G. G. 1893. *The Life and Correspondence of Arthur Penrhyn Stanley*, 2 vols. London.

Pugh, P. D. Gordon. 1970. *Staffordshire Portrait Figures*, London.

Pugin, A. W. N. 1841. *Contrasts*, London.

Quennell, Peter, ed. 1969. *Mayhew's London*, London.

Raikes, Elizabeth. 1908. *Dorothea Beale of Cheltenham*, London.

Raysor, Thomas Middleton, ed. 1960. *Samuel Taylor Coleridge Shakespearean Criticism*, 2 vols. London.

Reader, W. J. 1966. *Professional Men. The Rise of the Professional Classes in the Nineteenth Century*, London.

Reid, T. Wemyss. 1890. *Life, Letters and Friendships of Richard Monckton Milnes*, 2 vols. London.

Richards, Denis. 1958. *Offspring of the Vic. A History of Morley College*, London.

Richards, Jeffrey, ed. 1994. *Sir Henry Irving. Theatre, Culture and Society. Essays, Addresses and Lectures*, Keele.

Roberts, R. E., ed. 1865. *Sermons on Theatrical Amusements Delivered in St James's Church, Sheffield by the Late Rev. Thomas Best, MA Oxon.*, London.

Robertson, W. Graham. 1931. *Time Was*, London.

Robins, Elizabeth. 1940. *Both Sides of the Curtain*, London.

Rosman, Doreen M. 1984. *Evangelicals and Culture*, London.

Roston, Murray. 1968. *Biblical Drama in England From the Middle Ages to the Present Day*, London.

Rouse, W. H. D. 1898. *A History of Rugby School*, London.

Rowell, Geoffrey. 1974. *Hell and the Victorians*, Oxford.
    1983. *The Vision Glorious Themes and Personalities of the Catholic Revival in Anglicanism*, Oxford.

Rowell, George 1978. *Queen Victoria Goes to the Theatre*, London.
    1993. *The Old Vic Theatre. A History*, Cambridge.

Rowell, George, ed. 1960. *Nineteenth Century Plays*, Oxford.

Royal Shakespeare Theatre. 1964. *Catalogue of Pictures and Sculptures*, Stratford-upon-Avon.

Sala, George Augustus. 1859. *Twice Round the Clock*, London.

Salgãdo, Gãmini. 1971. Christopher Marlowe. In *English Drama to 1710*, ed. Christopher Ricks, pp. 118–47. London.

Sandford, E. G., ed. 1906. *Memoirs of Archbishop Temple*, London.

Scharf, George, Jr. 1867. *Observations on the Westminster Abbey Portrait of Richard II*, London.

Schoenbaum, S. 1978. *William Shakespeare. A Compact Documentary Life*, Oxford.
    1991. *Shakespeare's Lives*, Oxford.

Scott, Clement. 1896. *From 'The Bells' to 'King Arthur'*, London.
    1897. *The Wheel of Fire. A Few Memories and Recollections*, London.
    1899. *The Drama of Yesterday and Today*, 2 vols. London.

Scrimgeour, R. M., ed. 1950. *The North London Collegiate School 1850–1950*, London.

Shattuck, Charles H. 1948. E. B. Lytton and Victorian censorship. In *Quarterly Journal of Speech*, 34, 65–72.

Shaw, Bernard. 1932. *Our Theatres in the Nineties*, 3 vols. London.

  1946. *Androcles and the Lion*, Harmondsworth.

  1951. *Man and Superman*, Harmondsworth.

  1961a. *Plays Pleasant*, Harmondsworth.

  1961b. *Plays Unpleasant*, Harmondsworth.

  1962. *Plays for Puritans*, Harmondsworth.

Simpson, Harold H. and Braun, Mrs. Charles. 1913. *A Century of Famous Actresses*, London.

Smiles, Samuel. 1880. *Duty*, London.

  1903. *Thrift*, London.

  1905. *Self-help*, London.

Smith, Adam. 1838. *An Inquiry into the Nature and Causes of the Wealth of Nations*, London.

Smith, Edward. 1844. *The Theatre. A History and Moral Tendency*, London.

Smith, H. P., ed. 1960. *Literature and Adult Education A Century Ago: Pantopragmatics and Penny Readings*, Oxford.

Smith, Warren Sylvester. 1963. *The Religious Speeches of Bernard Shaw*, Pennsylvania.

  1967. *The London Heretics*, London.

Smyth, Charles. 1949. *Dean Milman 1791–1868*, London.

Solly, Henry. 1856. *Gonzaga di Capponi*, London.

  1867. *Working Men's Social Clubs and Educational Institutes*, London.

  1893. *These Eighty Years, or The Story of an Unfinished Life*, 2 vols. London.

  1896. *Herod the Great*, London.

  1898. *The Life of Henry Morley, LLD*, London.

Somervell, D. C. 1929. *English Thought in the Nineteenth Century*, London.

Speaight, Robert. 1954. *William Poel and the Elizabethan Revival*, London.

Spicer, Henry. 1881. *Church and Stage*, London.

Staplyton, H. E. C. 1863. *The Eton School Lists from 1791–1850*, London.

Stavisky, Aron Y. 1969. *Shakespeare and the Victorians: Roots of Modern Criticism*, Norman, Okla.

Stead, W. T. 1890. *The Story that Transformed the World, or The Passion Play at Ober Ammergau in 1890*, London.

Steadman, F. Cecily. 1931. *In the Days of Miss Beale. A Study of Her Work and Influence*, London.

Steen, Marguerite. 1962. *A Pride of Terrys*, London.

Stephens, John Russell. 1970. William Bodham Donne. Some aspects of his later career as Examiner of Plays. In *Theatre Notebook*, 25:1, 25–32.

  1980. *The Censorship of English Drama 1824–1901*, Cambridge.

Stephens, W. R. W. 1880. *The Life and Letters of Walter Farquhar Hook DD, FRS*, London.

Stephenson, G. 1936. *Edward Stuart Talbot 1844–1934*. London.

Sterling, John. 1843. *Strafford A Tragedy*, London.

Stewart, Robert. 1985. *Henry Brougham 1778–1868*, London.

Stockholm, Johanne M. 1964. *Garrick's Folly The Stratford Jubilee of 1769*, London.

Stoddard, R. H., ed. 1874. *Personal Reminiscences by Chorley, Planché and Young*, New York.

Stoker, Bram. 1906. *Personal Reminiscences of Henry Irving*, 2 vols. London.

Stokes, John. 1972. *Resistible Theatres. Enterprise and Experiment in the Late Nineteenth Century*, London.

Stottler, J. F. 1970. A Victorian stage censor: the theory and practice of William Bodham Donne. In *Victorian Studies*, 13:3, 253–82.

Styler, W. E., ed. 1968. *Learning and Working*, London.

Super, R. H., ed. 1960–74. *Complete Works of Matthew Arnold*, London.

    1970. *God and the Bible*, vol. VII of Super, 1960–74.

    1973. *English Literature and Politics*, vol. IX of Super, 1960–74.

    1974. *Philistinism in England and America*, vol. X of Super, 1960–74.

Swears, Herbert. 1937. *When All's Said and Done*, London.

Tait, Bishop Archibald. 1858. *A Charge to the Clergy of London*, London.

Talbot, Bishop Edward. 1905. *The Aims and Objects of the Actors' Church Union*, London.

Tarver, F. 1898. Acting at Eton. In *Amateur Clubs and Actors*, ed. W. G. Elliott, pp. 193–220. London.

Taylor, C. M. P. 1995. *Right Royal Wakefield Theatre 1776–1994*, Wakefield.

Taylor, Tom. 1871. *The Theatre in England Some of its Shortcomings and Possibilities*, London.

Temple, Revd Frederick. 1860. The education of the world. In *Essays and Reviews*, pp. 1–49. London.

Tennyson, Alfred. 1905. *Works*, London.

Thomas, Brandon. 1892. *Charley's Aunt*, London.

Thomas, J. 1984. *The Art of the Actor-Manager Wilson Barrett and the Victorian Theatre*, Epping.

Thompson, Elbert N. S. 1903. *The Controversy between the Puritans and the Stage*, New York.

Thompson, Marjorie. 1957. Henry Arthur Jones and Wilson Barrett. Some correspondence 1879–1904. In *Theatre Notebook*, 11:2, 42–50.

Thomson, Peter. 1986. 'Weirdness that lifts and colours all': the secret self of Henry Irving. In Foulkes, 1986a, pp. 97–105.

Thorndike, Russell. 1929. *Sybil Thorndike*, London.

Tollemache, Lionel A. 1904. *Benjamin Jowett Master of Balliol*, London.

Tolles, Winton. 1940. *Tom Taylor and the Victorian Drama*, New York.

Tomalin, Claire. 1991. *The Invisible Woman. The Story of Nelly Ternan and Charles Dickens*, Harmondsworth.

Toynbee, William, ed. 1912. *The Diaries of William Charles Macready, 1833–1851*, 2 vols. London.

Tracts for the Times, 1834–41, 6 vols. London.

Trench, Maria. 1900. *The Passion Play at Ober-ammergau*, London.

Trewin, J. C. 1955. *Mr Macready*, London.

1960. *Benson and the Bensonians*, London.

Trewin, Wendy. 1989. *The Royal General Theatrical Fund A History: 1838–1988*, London.

Tulloch, John. 1885. *Movements of Religious Thought in Britain During the Nineteenth Century*, London.

Tweedie, Mrs Alec. 1890. *The Oberammergau Passion Play 1890*, London.

1904. *Behind the Footlights*, London.

Tweedie, Mrs Alec, ed. 1898. *The First College for Women*, London.

Vanbrugh, Irene. 1948. *To Tell My Story*, London.

Wade, Allan, ed. 1957. *Henry James. The Scenic Art*, New York.

Wagner, Donald O. 1930. *The Church of England and Social Reform Since 1854*, New York.

Wagner, Leopold. 1881. *The Pantomimes and All About Them*, London.

1899. *How to Get On the Stage*, London.

Walker, James. 1787. *The Melody of Speaking Delineated*, London.

1801. *The Academic Speaker*, London.

1816. *A Rhetorical Grammar*, London.

Warnock, Mary, ed. 1972. *Utilitarianism*, London.

Warre-Cornish, F. W. 1897. *Extracts from the Letters and Journals of William Cory*, Oxford.

Weales, Gerald. 1961. *Religion in Modern English Drama*, Westport, Conn.

Wheeler, Michael. 1990. *Death and the Future Life in Victorian Literature and Theology*, Cambridge.

Whitworth, Geoffrey. 1951. *The Making of a National Theatre*, London.

Wickham, Glynne. 1977. The revolution in attitudes to the dramatic arts in British universities 1880–1980. In *Oxford Review of Education*, 3:2, 115–21.

Wilkinson, Revd C. Allix. 1888. *Reminiscences of Eton (Keate's Time)*, London.

Willey, Basil. 1964. *Nineteenth Century Studies*, London.

Williams, Raymond. 1987. *Culture and Society Coleridge to Orwell*, London.

Williamson, Jane. 1970. *Charles Kemble, Man of the Theatre*, Lincoln, Nebr.

Wills, Freeman. 1898. *W. G. Wills Dramatist and Painter*, London.

Wilson, A. E. 1934. *Christmas Pantomime*, London.

1952. *The Lyceum*, London.

Wilson, Colin. 1957. *Religion and the Rebel*, London.

Wilson, J. Dover, ed. 1963. *Matthew Arnold Culture and Anarchy*, Cambridge.

Woodfield, James. 1984. *English Theatre in Transition 1881–1914*, London.

Wordsworth, Charles. 1864. *On Shakespeare's Knowledge and Use of the Bible*, London.

Wycherley William. 1676. *The Plain Dealer*, London.

Wyndham, Horace. 1951. *Chorus to Coronet*, London.

Young, Revd J. C. 1871. *Memoirs of Charles Mayne Young*, London.

1875. *Last Leaves from the Journal of Julian Charles Young*, Edinburgh.

JOURNALS

All the Year Round
Athenaeum
Church Times
Critical Quarterly
Daily News
Devonport Chronicle
Ecclesiologist
Era
Idler
Illustrated London News
Listener
Macmillan's Magazine
Manchester Evening News
Manchester Weekly Times
Marlburian
Mechanics' Magazine
Monthly Review
New Review
Nineteenth Century
Nineteenth Century Theatre Research
Oxford Chronicle and Berks and Bucks Gazette
Punch
Quarterly Review
Queen's College Magazine
Saturday Review
Sheffield Iris
Sketch
Spectator
Star
Thanet Guardian
Theatre
Theatre Notebook
The Times

Index

acting profession
 numbers, 46, 145–6
 salaries, 47–8, 145
Actors' Association, 182
Actors' Benevolent Fund, 171
Actors' Church Union, 180–5
Actresses' Franchise League, 145
Aeschylus, 7, 51, 140, 155
Ainger, Revd, 80, 106
Albert, Prince Consort, 41, 43, 60, 62, 80, 240
Alleyn, Edward, 42, 232
Anderson, Mary, 164, 172
Archer, Frank, 138
Archer, William, 177, 203, 206–7, 220
Aria, Mrs, 221, 230, 236
Aristotle, 19, 53, 64
Arnold, Matthew, xiv, 63, 111, 136, 179, 199,
 200, 210, 231, 241
 as HM Inspector of Schools, 189
 model for Mr Luke, 136
 on drama and theatre, 4, 188–9, 190
 on religion, 68, 121
Arnold, Dr Thomas, 14, 109, 133
Atheista Fulminato, 16, 179
Athenaeum Club, 37, 94, 136, 188

Baird, Dorothea (Mrs H. I. Irving), 158, 163,
 230
Baird, Mrs J. B., 150, 158
ballet, 64, 121, 162, 167, 173–4
Bancroft, Mrs (Marie Wilton), 147–8, 151, 163,
 164, 240
Bancroft, Squire, 102, 139, 147–8, 163
Barham, Revd R. H., 38–9, 50
 Ingoldsby Legends, The, 38, 135, 229
Barnes, J. H., 81
Barnes, Kenneth, 115
Barnes, Revd Reginald, 157
Barrett, Wilson (William Henry), 181, 186–7,
 204–10, 239
 as Wilfred Denver in *Silver King, The*, 187–8
 play, *Sign of the Cross, The*, 186, 206–10

Bateman, Isabel, 164
Bath, 22–4
Baylis, Lilian, 172
Beale, Dorothea, 154–7
Bell, George, Bishop of Chichester, 178
Bellew, Revd J. C. M., 37, 81–2, 100, 147, 225
Bellew, Kyrle, 82
Benham, Revd William, 66–7, 153, 177
Bennett, William Sterndale, 153
Benson, Constance (*née* Fetherstonhaugh), 157,
 196
Benson, E. F., 228, 229
Benson, Edward White, Archbishop of
 Canterbury, 228, 234
Benson, Frank, 140, 141, 156, 159, 183
Bentham, Jeremy, xiv, 1–3, 4, 13, 76, 99, 193,
 200, 237
Best, Revd Thomas, 22–4, 60, 73, 92
Betterton, Thomas, 138
Bible, The, 101, 102, 135, 137, 166, 196–7, 200,
 204, 211, 239
 readings, 40–1, 83
 texts, 22, 24, 25, 49, 58, 101, 103, 132, 137,
 169, 233, 241
Birch, Revd William, 35, 36
Birkbeck, George, 69
Blanchard, E. L., 88
Blomfield, Charles, Bishop of London, 6–7, 29,
 33, 50, 59, 86, 167
Boucicault, Dion, the Younger, 163
Bourchier, Arthur, 115, 139, 140, 141, 142, 163
Bowdler, Dr Thomas, and Henrietta, 95
Boyd-Carpenter, Dr William, Bishop of Ripon,
 102, 139, 147, 194
Bradford, 234–5, 236
Bradley, Revd G. G., 228
Britannia Theatre, 33–4, 120, 123–4, 179, 207
 pantomime, *Will O'The Wisp*, 123
British Museum, 94, 95
Broad Church, The, xiv, 50, 63, 68, 109
Brooke, Revd Augustus Stopford, 119, 178
Brookfield, Charles, 129

Brougham, Henry Peter, Baron, 69, 70, 75, 83
Brown, Ford Madox
  Work, 75
Browning, Robert, 37, 105
Bulwer Lytton, Edward George, 1st Baron
  Lytton, 3–5, 17, 37, 95, 99, 130, 216
  plays, *Duchess de la Vallière, The*, 30, *Money*, 5,
    14, *Richelieu*, 158, 213
Bunn, Alfred, 29, 32, 38, 48
Burbage, Richard, 138
Burdett-Coutts, Angela, Baroness, 64–5, 235
Burnand, F. C., 49, 83, 126, 174, 215, 225
Buss, Frances, 154
Butler, Samuel, 36, 63
Byron, George Gordon, 6th Baron, 15, 179, 215
  plays, 26, 86, *Werner*, 220

Caine, Thomas Henry Hall, 204–6
Calvert, Charles, 27, 63, 65–6, 105, 119, 214
  pantomimes, 121–2
Calvert, Mrs Charles, 214
Calvert, F. B., 24–5
Cambridge, University of, 47, 125–9, 232
  Amateur Dramatic Club (ADC), 49, 126–8
  Cambridge *Conversazione* Society (Apostles),
    10, 14, 31, 225
  Downing College, 159
  Girton College, 151, 159
  Trinity College, 7, 78, 126, 129, 158, 167, 225
Cambridge Garrick Club, 126
Campbell, Mrs Patrick, 201
Canterbury Cathedral, 178, 224
Carew, James, 150
Carlyle, George William Frederick Howard,
  7th Earl of, 94, 100, 117
Carlyle, Jane Welsh, 37, 212
Carlyle, Thomas, xiv, 11, 38, 70, 75, 93–4, 107,
  129
  model for Donald Gordon, 136
Carroll, Lewis, *see* Dodgson, Revd Charles
census, 46, 145–6, 163
Charterhouse School, 201
Chartism, 60, 70, 76, 96
Chaucer, Geoffrey, 74, 153, 155
Cheltenham Ladies' College, The, 154–7
Christian Socialism, xiv, 50, 60–1, 63, 68, 75,
  168, 176, 204, 206, 238
Church and Stage Guild, 170, 172–5, 178, 180,
  183
Church of England, xiii, 7–8, 15, 22, 71, 103,
  148, 173, 204, 224, 234, 237, 240
  number of clergy and their income, 46–7
Clough, Arthur, 63
Colenso, John William, Bishop of Natal, 67, 128
Coleridge, Samuel Taylor, xiv, 14–17, 54, 101,

103, 121, 179, 205, 208, 215, 220, 225, 226,
  233, 238, 241
  Cain, 27, 203
  clerisy, 14, 75, 79
  Remorse, 15, 28–9, 203
  Shakespeare, 92–3
Collier, Jeremy, 21
Collier, John Payne, 9, 42, 93
Collins, Wilkie, 95, 203
Colman, George, the Younger, 29–30, 220
Congreve, William, 16, 22
Cons, Emma, 89–90
Cook, Thomas, and Sons, 111, 112
Cooke, T. P., 216
Cookesley, Revd Gifford, 49, 126
Cooper, Thomas, 96
Cory, William Johnston, 166
Courthope-Todd, Revd and Mrs, 171
Courtney, W. L., 112, 140, 141, 142, 229
Covent Garden Theatre, 4–7, 8, 9, 12, 29, 76, 92
Craig, Edward Gordon, 150
Craig, Edy, 150, 151, 224
Craven, Hawes, 222
Creswick, William, 100–1, 212
Cuddesdon Theological College, 49, 174
culture (cultivation), 15, 75, 168, 190, 234–5,
  239, 240

Dale, Revd Thomas, 73
Dante, Alighieri, 226
Darwinism, 67, 201
Davidson, Randall, Archbishop of Canterbury,
  67, 177
Dickens, Charles, 37, 42, 67, 79, 82, 87, 94, 95,
  129, 130
Disraeli, Benjamin, 33, 233
Dodgson, Revd Charles (Carroll, Lewis), 122,
  133–6, 140, 143, 150, 157–8, 173, 175
Don Juan, 16–17, 179–80
Donne, William, 10, 125
  as Examiner of Plays, 31–2, 125, 126
Dramatic, Equestrian and Musical Sick Fund,
  42
Drury Lane Theatre, 4–7, 15, 16, 29, 86, 123,
  172, 234
  pantomimes, *Aladdin*, 123, *Babes in the Wood,
    The*, 123
Dublin, 35, 70, 100, 178, 216
Dulwich College, 42, 232
Duncombe, T., 32–3

East, Revd John, 22–4, 60
education, 4, 78, 99, 189–90
  Commissions, 47, 63, 78
  Forster's Act (1870), 63, 239

Egg, Augustus, 94, 95
Elgar, Sir Edward, 56
Eliot, T. S., 178
  play, *Murder in the Cathedral*, 178
Elliott, Gertrude (Mrs Forbes-Robertson), 183
elocution, 77, 79, 154, 192, 197, 212, 239
Engadine
  English church, 147
English Literature, study of, 73–4, 153–5, 190
Etheridge, George, 22
Eton College, 8, 39, 40, 41, 43, 45, 49, 50, 56,
    80, 84, 98, 100, 126, 141, 149, 161, 166, 174,
    201, 224, 240
Evangelicalism, 73, 81, 118, 133, 160, 166, 169,
    170, 179, 238
Everyman, 118–19, 124, 172

Fabian Society, The, 176, 178
Farr, Florence, 145, 154
Farrar, F. W., Revd, 73, 110, 112–15, 175, 180
  as a preacher, 175, 224–8
  education and teaching career, 74, 224–8
  Eternal Hope, 175, 214, 218, 225–7
Faucit, Helen (Lady Martin), 56–7, 62, 80–1,
    100, 105, 109, 138, 147, 151, 164, 191, 240
Fechter, Charles, 81, 100
Fitzball, Edward, 216
Fitzgerald, Percy, 216
Flower, Charles, 101, 105
Flower, Edward Fordham, 98–100
Flower, Sarah Adams, 99
Fontane, Theodor, 88
Forbes-Robertson, Johnston, 89, 115, 160, 172,
    201–2
Forster, Edward William, *see* education
Forster, John, 37, 39, 94, 95
Fox, W. J., 99
Fraser, James, Bishop of Manchester, 47, 48, 62,
    63–6, 78–9, 81, 105, 120–1, 136, 138, 144,
    170, 238
Furnival, F. J., 93, 118

Gaiety Theatre, 34
Galsworthy, John, 130
Garibaldi, General Giuseppe, 97–8
Garrick, David, 15, 98, 138, 233
Garrick Club, 38–9, 50, 94, 129, 130, 158
Gilbert, Sir William Schwenck, 135
Gladstone, Rt Hon. William Ewart, 39–40, 44,
    59, 63, 163, 173, 193, 228, 232–3, 235, 240
Godwin, E. W., 134, 150
Godwin, George, 193
Goethe, Johann Wolfgang von, 217
Goldsmith, Oliver
  Vicar of Wakefield, The, 220

Gounod, Charles François, 179, 217
Granville, Revd G., 100
Greek drama and theatre, 109–10, 120, 154,
    163
Greet, Philip Ben, 159, 172–3, 177, 183, 184, 230
Guild of St Matthew, 168, 178, 203

Hallam, Arthur, 10, 39, 125
Halliday, Andrew, 101
Handel, George Frideric, 29, 104
Hare, Julius, 13, 14, 74
Harker, Joseph, 220, 222
Harris, Augustus, 123, 172
Harris, Frank, 112
Harrow School, 74, 109, 126, 141
Harvey, John Martin, 184
Haweis, Revd R. H., 66, 194
Hawthorne, Nathaniel, 202
Hawtrey, Charles
  play, *Private Secretary, The*, 84–5
Headlam, Revd Stewart, 151, 166–71, 180, 203,
    238
  model for Revd Morell, 178
Heine, Heinrich, 216
hell, 23, 34, 58–60, 117, 122, 135, 138, 169, 176,
    179, 180, 201, 217, 226, 238
Herman, Henry, 187, 189, 206
Hill, Octavia, 89–90
Hole, Revd Donald, 180–5
Hollingshead, John, 34, 89, 99, 112
Holman Hunt, William, 119
Hood, Revd Paxton, 65–6
Hood, Thomas, 216
  Dream of Eugene Aram, The, 229
Hook, Revd Walter Farquhar, 117–18
Horne, R. H., 26, 88, 95, 99, 118
Houghton, Baron, *see* Milnes, Richard
    Monckton
House of Commons, 5, 32, 98
House of Lords, 5–6, 7, 34, 67
Housman, Laurence, 119
Howley, William, Archbishop of Canterbury,
    37
Hughes, Tom, 63, 78, 90
  Tom Brown's Schooldays, 141
Hullah, John Pyke, 76, 153
hymns, 16, 56, 64, 96, 99, 186, 206–7, 234

Irving, Edward, 40, 212–13
Irving, Henry (John Henry Brodribb), 63, 80,
    106, 107, 125, 134, 135, 142, 143, 150, 151,
    158, 159, 163, 166, 172, 175, 180, 181, 183,
    184, 193, 201, 210, 211–36, 238, 239, 241
  commemoration lecture at Oxford, 138–9
  death and funeral, 234–6, 241

Irving, Henry (John Henry Brodribb) (*cont.*)
    knighthood (1895) and leadership of
        profession, 233
    plays, *Becket*, 214, 221–4, 234, *Bells, The*, 213,
        214, 215, 227, *Corsican Brothers, The*, 220,
        Eugene Aram, 215–16, *Faust*, 135, 159, 180,
        215, 217–20, *Hamlet*, 205, *Henry VIII*, 221,
        Iron Chest, The, 220, *Lyons Mail, The*, 220,
        Macbeth, 220, *Olivia*, 220, *Vanderdecken*, 215,
        217, *Werner*, 220
    religious upbringing, 211–12, 214, 218
    views on the moral value of the theatre,
        231–3
    wife, 213–14
Irving, Henry (Harry) Brodribb, 214, 227,
    228–9, 230
Irving, Laurence Sidney, 177, 214, 227

Jackson, John, Bishop of London, 169, 173,
    177
James, Henry, 203, 217–18
Jerome, Jerome K., 112–14, 181
Jerrold, Douglas, 89, 95, 126
Jones, Henry Arthur, 134, 179, 186, 210, 224,
    231, 232, 233, 239
    plays, 'Coleridge', 200, *Judah*, 200–1, *Michael
        and his Lost Angel*, 186, 196, 201–4, 206,
        Saints and Sinners, 200, *Silver King, The*, 187
    religious upbringing, 193–4
    views on the theatre, 194–200
Jones-Evans, Revd John Llewelyn, 215
Jonson, Ben, 16, 39, 82, 90
Jowett, Dr Benjamin, 143, 238, 239
    model for Dr Jenkinson, 18, 136–8
    'On the interpretation of Scripture', 67
    Vice-Chancellor of Oxford University, 136,
        139

Kean, Charles, 27, 39, 41, 42, 43–5, 49, 62, 100,
    129, 133, 150, 240
Kean, Mrs Charles (Ellen Tree), 43, 62
Kean, Edmund, 15, 24, 138
Keate, Revd John, 40–1, 50
Keble, John, xiv, 40, 50–3, 103, 176
    Christian Year, The, 51–3, 103, 107, 176
Kelly, Charles (Wardell), 129, 134, 150–1
Kemble, Charles, 5–7, 9, 22, 38, 47, 126, 199
    as actor, 25, 39
    as Examiner of Plays, 30
    manager of Covent Garden, 5–6, 13
    readings, 80
Kemble, Fanny (Frances), 6–11, 25, 33, 50, 80,
    83, 147, 151, 162, 164, 240
    as Juliet, 6, 12–13
    in *Fazio*, 8

John Mitchell Kemble's Cambridge friends,
    11–12, 25, 57, 125
    on religion, 8, 60
    play, *Francis the First*, 9–10
Kemble, Henry, 129
Kemble, John Mitchell, 7, 82, 83, 126
    as Examiner of Plays, 30–1, 125
    at Cambridge University, 10–12, 47, 51, 125
Kemble, John Philip, 5, 7, 15
Kendal, Mrs (Madge Robertson), 66, 148–9,
    151, 163, 164, 172, 194, 240
Kendal, William H., 149, 163, 172, 194
Kingsley, Charles, 14, 73, 74, 79, 90, 92, 119, 122,
    153, 161, 166, 205
    Alton Locke, 62, 89, *Water Babies, The*, 122
    Plays and Puritans, 61–2
    play, *Saint's Tragedy, The*, 58, 60–1, 200
Knight, Charles, 94–5
Knowles, James Sheridan, 25–6, 38, 99, 126, 132

Lacy, T. H., 24
Lang, Alexander Matheson, 142, 159, 205
Lang, Cosmo Gordon, Archbishop of
    Canterbury, 141, 142, 172, 178
Langtry, Lillie, 161
Latitudinarianism, xiv, 50, 67, 68, 109, 238
Lee, Henry Prince, Bishop of Manchester, 47,
    63
Leicester, 96
Lemon, Mark, 94
Leno, Dan, 123
Lent (closure of theatres), 32–3, 34
Lewes, G. H., 32, 94, 111
    play, *Noble Heart, The*, 32
Lewis, M. G.
    play, *Castle Spectre, The*, 36
Liddon, Canon Henry Parry, 49, 133, 174–5
Lind, Jenny, 31, 109
London, University of
    King's College, 59, 71–3, 88, 125, 129, 160,
        225
    University College, 59, 71–3, 78
Lord Chamberlain, 5, 17, 29, 31, 32, 34, 85, 102,
    125, 205
Ludlow, J. M., 60, 166
Lyceum Theatre, 166, 175, 180, 186, 205, 232,
    234

MacColl, Canon Malcolm, 111
Macready, William Charles, 11, 24, 27, 38, 49,
    62, 76, 91, 92, 99, 109, 126, 138, 139, 161,
    188, 240
    at Rugby School, 35–7
    evening school in Sherborne, 62, 78–9
    profession, 37, 48

Macready House, 171
Mallock, W. H., 18, 136, 226
Manchester, 41, 47, 75, 214, 238
Manning, Revd Henry Edward (later
    Cardinal), 48–9, 56, 119, 221, 233
Marlborough College, 74, 142, 160, 225, 227–9
Marlowe, Christopher, 91, 217
    play, *Dr Faustus*, 120
Marston, Westland, 26, 88, 95, 99, 162
Martin, John, 26–7, 29, 179
Martin, Lady, *see* Faucit, Helen
Martin, Sir Theodore, 57, 62, 106
Martineau, James, 14
Mathews, Charles, 15
Matthison, Edith Wynne, 234
Maturin, Revd Charles, 50, 179
    play, *Bertram, or The Castle of Aldobrand*, 15–17,
        54, 93, 208
Maurice, Revd John Frederick Denison, xiv, 50,
    90, 91, 92, 125, 126, 143, 152, 167, 175, 178,
    180, 200, 205, 221, 225, 226, 238
    at Cambridge University, 10–14
    at King's College, London, 59, 73–4
    attitude to the theatre, 57–8, 76
    Fanny Kemble, 57
    hell, 23, 58–60, 138
    Professor of Moral Philosophy, 166
    Queen's College, Harley Street, 74, 152
    Working Men's Colleges, 74–5, 125, 205
Mayhew, Charles, 89
Mayor, Flora, 159
McCarthy, Lillah, 181
Mechanics' Institutes, 69, 75, 76
Melbourne, William Lamb, 2nd Viscount, 92
Methodism, 22, 211, 212
Mill, John Stuart, 3, 13, 159
Millais, Sir John Everett, 151
Milman, Henry Hart, Dean of St Paul's, 8–10,
    11, 17, 37, 40, 50, 59, 94, 109, 110, 117, 120,
    130, 160, 199
    play, *Fazio*, 8–9, 87
Milnes, Richard Monckton, 1st Baron
    Houghton, 10, 11, 100, 112, 125, 126
Milton, John, 82, 110, 111, 153, 156, 213, 217, 226
Molière, 40, 155, 179
Moore, George, 161, 232
Morley, Henry, 79, 88, 118, 153
Morley, Samuel, 90
Moultrie, Revd John, 56–7, 62
Mozart, Wolfgang Amadeus, 179
Mystery plays, 24, 117–18, 120, 123, 163, 179

National Association for the Promotion of
    Social Science, 66, 149, 193
National Theatre, 99, 193, 237

Neale, John Mason, 164
Neilson, Adelaide, 48, 162–3, 166
New Shakespeare Society, 93
Newman, Revd John Henry (later Cardinal),
    xiv, 14, 40, 63, 91, 92, 103, 173, 199, 200,
    234
    as preacher, 55–6
    Dream of Gerontius, The, 56
    on education, 70, 74
    on poetry, 53–5

Oberammergau Passion Play, 64, 108–17, 124,
    224
Old Vic Theatre (Royal Victoria Coffee Hall),
    62, 89–90, 119, 172, 226
Olivier, Laurence, 160
oratory, 36, 40–1, 239
Otway, Thomas, 16, 39
Owen, Robert, 99
Oxford, University of, 47, 80, 126, 129, 232
    Balliol College, 136, 140
    Brasenose College, 8, 140, 162
    Christ Church, 71–2, 83, 116, 131, 140, 141
    Keble College, 175, 182
    Lincoln College, 63
    Magdalen College, 129, 133
    New College, 140, 141, 229
    Newdigate Prize, 8, 109
    Oriel College, 40, 63
    Oxford University Dramatic Society
        (OUDS), 138, 139, 140, 142
    Professor of Poetry, 8, 50
    St John's College, 147, 230
    University College, 119
    Worcester College, 22, 83
Oxford Movement, The, xiv, 50, 63, 68, 176,
    182, 238

pantomimes, 66, 120–4, 206
Passion Week (closure of theatres), 33–4
Patent Theatres Monopoly, 5–6, 86, 99, 117,
    192, 237
Pater, Walter
    model for Mr Rose, 136
Paxton, Sydney, 66
Peel, Sir Robert, 70, 83
Penley, W. S., 84–5
Phelps, Revd Robert, 89, 128
Phelps, Samuel, 86, 91, 98, 100, 101, 128, 212, 240
    as Hamlet, 212
Piggott, E. F. S., 32, 115
Pinero, Arthur Wing, 201, 207, 233
Planché, J. R., 120, 193
Plato, xiii, 18–19, 51, 58, 67, 137, 139, 143
Poel, William, 90–1, 118–19, 172

Powell, Baden, 121
Princess's Theatre, 41, 42, 122, 130, 131, 133, 188
Pugin, A.W. N., 60, 71, 81
Puritanism, xiii, 21, 61–2, 70, 82, 124, 138, 139, 161, 176–7, 183, 191, 193, 210, 235, 239
Pusey, Dr Edward Bouverie, 55, 133, 164, 202

Queen's College, Harley Street, 74, 125, 152

Rachel, Elisa Félix, 109, 190
Reade, Charles, 129–33, 139, 143, 172
    play, *It Is Never Too Late To Mend*, 130–1
Reading Gaol, 130, 177
readings, 80–4, 166, 228
Redford, William, 118
Reform Bill, The (1832), 3, 7, 69
Religious Drama Society, 178
Restoration stage, xiii, 21, 163
Robertson, Tom, 148
Robertson, W. Graham, 151
Robins, Elizabeth, 112–14
Roman Catholic Emancipation, 7, 14, 22, 27
Rossetti, Dante Gabriel, 205
Royal Academy of Dramatic Art, 151
Royal Dramatic College, 42–3
Royal General Theatrical Fund, 87, 171
Rugby School, 35–7, 49, 50, 67, 109, 133, 141, 158, 162, 174
Ruskin, John, xiv, 73, 90, 105, 155, 204
    model for Mr Herbert, 136
Russell, Lord John, 33

Sadler's Wells Theatre, 86, 101, 212
Sargent, John Singer, 151
Saxe-Meiningen, Duke of, 105
Scott, Clement, 1, 115, 134, 160–1, 207, 216, 221, 225
Scott, Sir Walter, 15, 83
Select Committee appointed to Inquire into the Laws affecting Dramatic Literature, The (1832), 1, 3, 5, 9, 22, 29, 96, 199, 237
Select Committee appointed to Inquire into the Workings of the Acts of Parliament for Licensing and Regulating Theatres and Places of Public Entertainment, The (1866), 31
sermons, 40, 55, 63–6, 79, 81, 84, 99, 101–3, 106, 118, 119, 175, 194, 225, 229
Seymour, Mrs Laura, 131
Shakespeare, 15, 16, 24, 39, 40, 77, 80, 87, 92–107, 226
    morality of plays, 25, 62, 75, 92, 103
    plays, *As You Like It*, 154, *Coriolanus*, 158, *Hamlet*, 24, 54, 64, 81, 93, 126, 143, 167, 198, 205, 212, 213, 228, *1 Henry IV*, 141,

Henry VIII, 221, *Julius Caesar*, 88, 157, *King John*, 74, *King Lear*, 92, 138, 155, *Macbeth*, 154, 157, 158, 220, *Measure for Measure*, 162, *Merchant of Venice, The*, 125, 140, 157, 190, *Merry Wives of Windsor, The*, 138, *Much Ado About Nothing*, 11, 102, 125, 126, 135, 154, *Othello*, 64, 142, *Richard II*, 41, *Twelfth Night*, 141, *Winter's Tale, The*, 150
    tercentenary (1864), 77, 96, 100, 101, 102, 104, 105, 112, 125
Shaw, George Bernard, 112–14, 177, 196, 202, 233
    as drama critic, 123, 209
    plays, *Androcles and the Lion*, 209, *Candida*, 178, *Man and Superman*, 179–80
    religious subjects, 178–9
Sheffield, 22–3, 24
Sheridan, Richard Brinsley, 15, 40
    play, *Rivals, The*, 167
Shrewsbury School, 36, 63
Siddons, Sarah, 5, 11
Smiles, Samuel, 69, 95–6, 238
Smith, Adam, 2–3
Society for the Diffusion of Useful Knowledge, 69, 95
Solly, Henry
    drama and plays, 79, 85
    Working Men's Clubs, 76
Sothern, E. A., 128
Spooner, Dr William, 229
St Augustine, xiii, 24
    Confessions, 20–1
St Mary's Church, Oxford, 50, 136
St Paul's Cathedral, 8, 94, 175
St Paul's Church, Covent Garden, 184
Stanfield, Clarkson, 95
Stanford, Villiers, 222
Stanley, Revd Arthur Penrhyn, 48, 109, 153
    Dean of Westminster, 62, 64, 90, 109, 136
Stanley, Edward, Bishop of Norwich, 37, 109
Stead, W. T., 112–14
Sterling, John, 10–13, 50, 125
Stoker, Bram, 221
Stratford-upon-Avon, 82, 98
    Holy Trinity Church, 98, 104, 105, 106
Surrey Theatre, 9, 101
Swanwick, Miss Anna, 79, 105

Tait, Archibald Campbell, 67, 133, 177, 228, 234, 240
    Archbishop of Canterbury, 67
    Bishop of London, 48, 67, 86, 166
Talbot, Edward Stuart, Bishop, 182–3
Talfourd, Sir Thomas Noon, 99, 140
Tatian, 20

Taylor, Tom, 73, 74, 78, 88, 105, 130, 134, 153
  plays, *Ticket-of-Leave Man, The*, 78, *Our American Cousin*, 86, 128
Telbin, W., 222
temperance, 89, 122, 131, 187, 189, 194, 204, 211, 231–2
Tempest, Marie (Mary Susan Etherington), 163–4
Temple, Dr Frederick, 23
  Archbishop of Canterbury, 48–9
  Bishop of London, 173–4
  Headmaster of Rugby School, 67
Tenniel, John, 95
Tennyson, Lord Alfred, 10, 37, 58, 126, 129, 138, 214, 218, 221, 222, 235, 240
  plays, *Becket*, 125, 138, 221–4, *Cup, The*, 125, *Queen Mary*, 125
  poems, 10, 59, 235
  Princess, The, 153, 155
Ternan, Nelly, 66
Terriss, William, 222
Terry, Ellen, 48, 129, 134, 143, 147, 152, 158, 159, 183, 201, 222, 224, 236, 240
  personal life, 132, 134, 150, 162
Terry, Marion, 201
Tertullian, xiii, 20, 24
Thackeray, William Makepeace, 10, 37, 122, 129, 160
theatres
  used for religious services, 67, 226
Theatrical Mission, 171
Thomas, Brandon, 143
  play, *Charley's Aunt*, 143
Thorndike, Russell, 159, 183
Thorndike, Sybil, 159–60, 177, 183
Thorne, Sarah, 157, 159, 173
Tractarianism, 50, 54–5, 167, 168
Tree, Herbert Beerbohm, 151
Tree, Mrs Herbert Beerbohm (Maud Holt), 154, 163
Trench, Maria, 115
Trench, Revd Richard Chenevix, 11, 50, 74, 100–1, 103, 115, 125, 126, 153, 233
Tupper, Martin F., 131
Tweedie, Mrs Alec, 112–14, 115, 154

Unitarianism, 76, 88, 98, 99, 169
urbanisation, 47, 237, 239
Utilitarianism, 3, 5, 13, 14, 70, 75

Vanbrugh, Irene (*née* Barnes), 157–8, 163, 183
Vanbrugh, Violet (*née* Barnes), 157–8, 163
Vaughan, Revd C. J., 109, 167, 225
Vezin, Hermann, 66
Victoria, Queen, 41, 44, 80, 92, 95, 97, 106, 204, 224, 240

Wagner, Leopold, 120, 123, 163
Wagner, Richard, 216
Wales, Prince of, 90, 111, 127, 128, 140, 161, 224, 232
Wales, Princess of, 90, 111, 155, 232
Ward, Dr A. W., 119
Ward, Genevieve, 172, 222
Wardell, Charles, *see* Kelly, Charles
Watts, G. F., 134, 151
Webb, Sidney, 113
Webster, Benjamin, 43, 151
Westminster Abbey, 41, 90, 94, 105, 175, 222, 225, 226, 235, 241
Whateley, Richard, Archbishop of Dublin, 40, 95, 101, 118
White, Revd James, 37, 87, 94
Wilberforce, Samuel, Bishop of Oxford, 133–4, 136, 147, 174
Wilde, Oscar, 151, 177, 202, 233
  play, *Salomé*, 32
Williams, Raymond, 14, 75, 190
Wills, W. G., 206, 216, 217, 220
Wilton, Frederick, 33–4
Winchester College, 142
Windsor, Dean of, 42, 224
Wiseman, Cardinal Nicholas, 56
Wooll, Revd John, 36–7, 50
Wordsworth, Charles, Bishop of St Andrew's, 102–3
Wordsworth, John, Bishop of Salisbury, 228
Wordsworth, William, 27, 215
Working Men's Club and Institute Union, 76, 78, 80
Working Men's Colleges, 74–5, 91, 125
Wycherley, William, 16, 22
  play, *Plain Dealer, The*, 237
Wyndham, Charles, 183

Young, Charles Mayne, 82–5
Young, Revd Julian Charles, 82, 91, 100, 111, 212